LIBRARY OF NEW TESTAMENT STUDIES

656

Formerly the Journal for the Study of the New Testament Supplement Series

Editor
Chris Keith

Editorial Board
Dale C. Allison, John M. G. Barclay, Lynn H. Cohick, R. Alan Culpepper, Craig A. Evans, Jennifer Eyl, Robert Fowler, Simon J. Gathercole, Juan Hernández Jr., John S. Kloppenborg, Michael Labahn, Matthew V. Novenson, Love L. Sechrest, Robert Wall, Catrin H. Williams, Brittany E. Wilson

Divine Christology in the Epistle to the Hebrews

The Son as God

Nick Brennan

LONDON • NEW YORK • OXFORD • NEW DELHI • SYDNEY

T&T CLARK

Bloomsbury Publishing Plc

50 Bedford Square, London, WC1B 3DP, UK
1385 Broadway, New York, NY 10018, USA
29 Earlsfort Terrace, Dublin 2, Ireland

BLOOMSBURY, T&T CLARK and the T&T Clark logo are
trademarks of Bloomsbury Publishing Plc

First published in Great Britain 2022
This paperback edition published 2023

Copyright © Nick Brennan, 2022

Nick Brennan has asserted his right under the Copyright, Designs and Patents Act, 1988, to be identified as Author of this work.

For legal purposes the Acknowledgements on p. ix constitute an extension of this copyright page.

Cover design: Charlotte James

All rights reserved. No part of this publication may be reproduced or transmitted in any form or by any means, electronic or mechanical, including photocopying, recording, or any information storage or retrieval system, without prior permission in writing from the publishers.

Bloomsbury Publishing Plc does not have any control over, or responsibility for, any third-party websites referred to or in this book. All internet addresses given in this book were correct at the time of going to press. The author and publisher regret any inconvenience caused if addresses have changed or sites have ceased to exist, but can accept no responsibility for any such changes.

A catalogue record for this book is available from the British Library.

Library of Congress Cataloging-in-Publication Data
Names: Brennan, Nick, author.
Title: Divine Christology in the epistle to the Hebrews : the son as God / Nick Brennan.
Description: London ; New York : T&T Clark, 2021. | Series: Library of New Testament studies, 2513-8790 ; 656 | Includes bibliographical references and index. | Summary: "This book explores the depiction of the Son as divine in the Epistle to the Hebrews, and how this concept is particularly present in, and theologically necessary to, the Epistle's argument"– Provided by publisher.
Identifiers: LCCN 2021013798 (print) | LCCN 2021013799 (ebook) | ISBN 9780567700964 (hb) | ISBN 9780567700995 (epub) | ISBN 9780567700971 (epdf)
Subjects: LCSH: Bible. Hebrews–Criticism, interpretation, etc. | Jesus Christ–Divinity–Biblical teaching.
Classification: LCC BS2775.52 .B74 2021 (print) |
LCC BS2775.52 (ebook) | DDC 232/.8–dc23
LC record available at https://lccn.loc.gov/2021013798
LC ebook record available at https://lccn.loc.gov/2021013799

ISBN: HB: 978-0-5677-0096-4
PB: 978-0-5677-0100-8
ePDF: 978-0-5677-0097-1
ePUB: 978-0-5677-0099-5

Series: Library of New Testament Studies, volume 656
ISSN 2513–8790

Typeset by Newgen KnowledgeWorks Pvt. Ltd., Chennai, India

To find out more about our authors and books visit www.bloomsbury.com
and sign up for our newsletters.

To my wife
Inge

And our children
Elijah, Micah and Aya

My fellow runners
δι' ὑπομονῆς τρέχωμεν τὸν προκείμενον ἡμῖν ἀγῶνα
ἀφορῶντες εἰς ... Ἰησοῦν (Heb 12:1, 2)

Contents

Acknowledgements		ix
List of Abbreviations		xi

1	Introduction		1
	1.0	Introduction	1
	1.1	State of the question	5
	1.2	On predicating divinity	20
	1.3	Outline of the work	25

2	The Son as divine eschatological saviour (1:6, 10–12)		29
	2.0	Introduction	29
	2.1	Accounting for the role of Ps 102 and Deut 32 in the catena	31
	2.2	Considering the OT sources	41
	2.3	Reading the quotations in common	67
	2.4	Conclusion	70

3	The Son as divine eschatological builder (Heb 3:3, 4)		73
	3.0	Introduction	73
	3.1	Situating the flow of thought in Heb 3:1–6	73
	3.2	Evaluating the logic of the syncrisis	75
	3.3	Combining the trajectories	82
	3.4	The role of the Nathan Oracle and agency in Heb 3:3, 4	87
	3.5	The connection of eschatological building to divine prerogative in Hebrews	93
	3.6	The Son's properly divine work of redemptive building	109
	3.7	Conclusion	112

4	The Son as bearer of the divine life		115
	4.0	Introduction	115
	4.1	Christ's person in relation to priesthood	122
	4.2	Supra-human and divine notes in relation to the Son in Heb 7	128
	4.3	Conclusion	142
		Excursus	144

5	The Son as divine surety		147
	5.0	Introduction	147
	5.1	The character of God and the oath to Abraham in 6:13–20	149
	5.2	The NC as the full flowering of the AP	154
	5.3	The Son's faithful response to the Father as the linchpin of the NC	158
	5.4	Faith in God, trust in Christ and the Son as the surety of God's promises	163
	5.5	Conclusion	169
6	Polyvalent sonship and the divine Son		171
	6.0	Introduction	171
	6.1	Evaluation	176
	6.2	The eternal image in the Son	179
	6.3	The analogical image in the many created sons	183
	6.4	The Son's work as fulfilling the sonship of the many	189
	6.5	The dual sonship foreshadowed in the Davidic son	193
	6.6	Conclusion	197
7	Conclusion		199
	7.1	Summary	199
	7.2	Reflections	201

Bibliography	205
Index of References	223
Index of Authors	233

Acknowledgements

This book, and the original thesis on which it is based, represents a project in which I have received much support, encouragement and prayer from others, to whom I am greatly indebted.

The thesis was begun in Dunedin, New Zealand, and the Department of Theology at the University of Otago provided a truly congenial atmosphere for research. Particularly significant were my supervisors, Paul Trebilco and Chris Holmes, whose kindness, efficiency and acumen helped the project greatly. At a personal level, the friendship of fellow doctoral students in the department, particularly my office-mate Jono Ryan, provided much solace and support through the process. The closing stages of thesis writing saw the family and I move to Australia, and the staff and students at Queensland Theological College showed their kindness, through both interest in the work and the support of colleagues. The final stages of revision of the book for publication happened during a further move to teach at Westminster Seminary California, and it seems a fitting locale in which to complete it, among a faculty who have had a formative influence on my own thinking.

I am greatly thankful to my mother and father who, along with my parents-in-law, have been greatly supportive of my studies, and us as a family, during the rather peripatetic last decade. Inge, my wife, deserves the greatest thanks of all. Her constant help, encouragement and selfless hard work are the stays of daily life; without her I would be a much poorer man.

And last of all, thanks and praise are due to God, Father, Son and Spirit, whose presence enables all my work—*may the words of my mouth, and the meditation of my heart, be pleasing in your sight, O Lord, my Rock and my Redeemer.*

Abbreviations

Unless otherwise noted, all abbreviations below follow those set out in Ed. Alexander, Patrick H. et al. *The SBL Handbook of Style: For Ancient Near Eastern, Biblical, and Early Christian Studies* (Peabody, MA: Hendrickson, 1999).

Further abbreviations used are:

DSI	*De Septuaginta Investigationes*
JGRChJ	Journal of Greco-Roman Christianity and Judaism
JSJSup	Supplements to the Journal for the Study of Judaism
NSBT	New Studies in Biblical Theology

1

Introduction

1.0 Introduction

Within the classic taxonomy of NT Christology as either high or low, in the history of scholarship the Epistle to the Hebrews has largely been seen as a signal example of the former. This perception has frequently seen Hebrews ranked alongside the Fourth Gospel as the clearest portrayal of Christ as the divine Son of God in the NT.[1] In line with this, one frequently finds statements portraying the Christology of Hebrews as a clear precursor to the two natures Christology of Chalcedon.[2]

---

[1] "Commentaries extol the first chapter of Hebrews as an example of one of the 'highest Christologies' in the New Testament" (Amy L. B. Peeler, *You Are My Son: The Family of God in the Epistle to the Hebrews*, LNTS 486 (London: Bloomsbury, 2014), 24). See also Richard Bauckham, "Monotheism and Christology in Hebrews 1," in *Early Jewish and Christian Monotheism*, ed. Loren T. Stuckenbruck and Wendy E. S. North (London: T&T Clark, 2004), 168; William L. Lane, *Hebrews 1–8*, WBC 47a (Nashville, TN: Thomas Nelson, 1991), cxxvii; C. K. Barrett, "The Christology of Hebrews," in *Who Do You Say That I Am?: Essays on Christology*, ed. Mark Allan Powell, David R. Bauer, and Jack Dean Kingsbury (Louisville, KY: W/JKP, 1999), 114; Luke Timothy Johnson, *Hebrews: A Commentary*, NTL (Louisville, KY: W/JKP, 2006), 39; and the list of citations in Peeler, *My Son*, 24n39. This concurs with the role Hebrews played in the early church regarding the divinity of the Son: Athanasius, *Decr.* 3.6; *Ep. Serap.* 1.16, 19; 2.1, 2; 3.2; *C. Ar.* 4.12; Chrysostom, *Hom. Jo.* IV.2, a role which was revived in the rise of anti-Trinitarianism and Unitarianism in the seventeenth and eighteenth centuries, e.g. Robert Robinson, *A Plea for the Divinity of Our Lord Jesus Christ* (Cambridge: Fletcher & Hodson, 1776), 43; John Owen, *An Exposition of the Epistle to the Hebrews*, ed. W. H. Goold (Grand Rapids, MI: Baker Book House, 1980).

[2] Gareth Lee Cockerill, *The Epistle to the Hebrews*, NICNT (Grand Rapids, MI: Eerdmans, 2012), 129; D. Stephen Long, *Hebrews, Belief: A Theological Commentary on the Bible* (Louisville, KY: W/JKP, 2011), 28–30; Johnson, *Hebrews*, 50; Bauckham, "Monotheism," 185; "The Divinity of Jesus Christ in the Epistle to the Hebrews," in *The Epistle to the Hebrews and Christian Theology*, ed. Richard Bauckham, Daniel Driver and Trevor Hart (Grand Rapids, MI: Eerdmans, 2009), 32; C. Kavin Rowe, "The Trinity in the Letters of St. Paul and Hebrews," in *The Oxford Handbook of the Trinity*, ed. Gilles Emery and Matthew Levering (Oxford: Oxford University Press, 2011), 52; Oscar Cullmann, *The Christology of the New Testament* (Philadelphia, PA: Westminster Press, 1959), 97. For an example of the role of Chalcedonian thought in the exegesis of Hebrews in an earlier interpreter, see Daniel Keating, "Thomas Aquinas and the Epistle to the Hebrews: 'The Excellence of Christ,'" in *Christology, Hermeneutics, and Hebrews: Profiles from the History of Interpretation*, ed. Jon C. Laansma and Daniel J. Treier, LNTS 423 (London: Bloomsbury, 2012), 85–6. On the role in earlier patristic commentary, see Rowan A. Greer, "The Jesus of Hebrews and the Christ of Chalcedon," in *Reading the Epistle to the Hebrews: A Resource for Students*, ed. Eric Farrel Mason and Kevin B. McCruden (Atlanta, GA: SBL Press, 2011), 231–50. For the sense in which I am meaning divine here see in particular the discussion under Section 1.4.

Perhaps because of the effect of these truisms, the status of the Son's divinity within Hebrews has received little specific attention in the last century. This is surprising both against the backdrop of a burgeoning revival in Hebrews studies[3] and of a rising interest in divine Christology more broadly.[4] Some of this neglect may well arise not only because of the majority status of high Christology in Hebrews but also because analysis of its Christology has been dominated by concepts other than divinity, Christ as Son and High Priest, which are materially central.[5] The result has been that explicit works on the divinity of Christ in Hebrews have been few, and monograph-level treatment entirely absent.[6]

Where the topic is explicitly discussed, explorations raise as many questions as they answer. One may take, for example, the discussion of Hebrews' contribution to

---

[3] Mason speaks of "an explosion of interest in the book in recent decades" (Eric Farrel Mason and Kevin B. McCruden, *Reading the Epistle to the Hebrews: A Resource for Students*, SBLRBS (Atlanta, GA: SBL Press, 2011), 1). Similarly George H. Guthrie, "Hebrews in Its First Century Contexts: Recent Research," in *The Face of New Testament Studies: A Survey of Recent Research*, ed. Scot McKnight and Grant R. Osborne (Grand Rapids, MI: Baker Academic, 2004), 414. On the current state of Hebrews studies, see Bryan R. Dyer, "The Epistle to the Hebrews in Recent Research: Studies on the Author's Identity, His Use of the Old Testament, and Theology," *JGRChJ* 9 (2013): 104–31.

[4] The literature relating to those supporting Early High Christology is voluminous but see, in particular, Richard Bauckham, "The Throne of God and the Worship of Jesus," in *The Jewish Roots of Christological Monotheism: Papers from the St. Andrews Conference on the Historical Origins of the Worship of Jesus*, ed. Carey C. Newman, James R. Davila and Gladys S. Lewis, JSJSup 63 (Leiden: Brill, 1999); *God Crucified: Monotheism and Christology in the New Testament*, Didsbury Lectures (Grand Rapids, MI: Eerdmans, 1999); *Jesus and the God of Israel: God Crucified and Other Studies on the New Testament's Christology of Divine Identity* (Grand Rapids, MI: Eerdmans, 2009); Larry W. Hurtado, *Lord Jesus Christ: Devotion to Jesus in Earliest Christianity* (Grand Rapids, MI: Eerdmans, 2003); *One God, One Lord: Early Christian Devotion and Ancient Jewish* (London: T&T Clark, 1988); Chris Tilling, *Paul's Divine Christology*, WUNT 2/323 (Tübingen: Mohr Siebeck, 2012); Martin Hengel, *Studies in Early Christology* (London: T&T Clark, 2004); David B. Capes, *Old Testament Yahweh Texts in Paul's Christology*, WUNT 2/47 (Tübingen: J.C.B. Mohr, 1992); Loren T. Stuckenbruck and Wendy E. S. North, *Early Jewish and Christian Monotheism*, JSNTSup 263 (London: T&T Clark, 2004); Crispin H. T. Fletcher-Louis, *Jesus Monotheism: Volume 1: Christological Origins: The Emerging Consensus and Beyond* (Eugene, OR: Wipf & Stock, 2015); Simon J. Gathercole, *The Preexistent Son: Recovering the Christologies of Matthew, Mark, and Luke* (Grand Rapids, MI: Eerdmans, 2006), to which one might add the qualification of these approaches in the more methodologically Trinitarian counterparts of Matthew W. Bates, *The Birth of the Trinity: Jesus, God, and Spirit in New Testament and Early Christian Interpretations of the Old Testament* (Oxford: Oxford University Press, 2015); Wesley Hill, *Paul and the Trinity: Persons, Relations, and the Pauline Letters* (Grand Rapids, MI: Eerdmans, 2015).

[5] William R. G. Loader, *Sohn und Hoherpriester: eine traditionsgeschichtliche Untersuchung zur Christologie des Hebräerbriefes*, WMANT 53 (Neukirchen-Vluyn: Neukirchener Verlag, 1981), 1–6; Cf. also Peeler, *My Son* on the former and Eric Farrel Mason, *"You Are a Priest Forever": Second Temple Jewish Messianism and the Priestly Christology of the Epistle to the Hebrews*, STDJ 74 (Leiden: Brill, 2008) on the latter. I have chosen to speak of the Author of Hebrews as "the Pastor," predominantly influenced at this point by the commentary of Cockerill who employs this title (Cockerill, *Epistle*).

[6] One might fruitfully compare this state of affairs with the way Trinitarian concerns, and especially issues around the divinity of Christ, form a major aspect of Owen's magisterial commentary on Hebrews, occasioned by the anti-Trinitarian convictions of his Socinian interlocutors. On the nature of anti-Trinitarianism in Owen's Britain, see chapter 8 of Stephen R. Holmes, *The Quest for the Trinity: The Doctrine of God in Scripture, History and Modernity* (Downers Grove, IL: IVP, 2012); Robert Dan and Antal Pirnat, eds., *Antitrinitarianism in the Second Half of the Sixteenth Century* (Budapest: Akadémiái Kiadó, 1982).

Trinitarian theology in the 2011 *Oxford Handbook of the Trinity*. There, C. Kavin Rowe writes that

> Hebrews employs a highly complex theological grammar ... simultaneously maintain[ing] and extend[ing] the [God] discourse of the Old Testament. "God" is ... the God of the Old Testament, and yet this God is described also in relation to a human Son that is internal to his eternal identity – Jesus the Christ.[7]

However when Rowe turns to the data of Hebrews the discussion of Jesus' deity scarcely reaches beyond Heb 1. Certainly this chapter of Heb 1 has played a dominant role in the history of interpretation;[8] however, it leaves the reader with the question whether Hebrews' contribution to divine Christology is limited to a small number of statements in its first chapter. Perhaps the witness of Hebrews on this point is, then, significant without being extensive.

For others, however, the portrayal of Christ as divine in Hebrews is less straightforward. For example, Attridge notes the obviously high Christology of Hebrews' Exordium.[9] At the same time he notes that, as a whole, the Epistle's Christology exhibits various "tensions" within the portrayal of Christ's sonship, the product of various incorporated traditions.[10] For Attridge, though divine Christology might describe a strand within Hebrews,[11] the reconciliation of these strands is able to be "integrated into a coherent theoretical framework only with difficulty."[12]

Alongside these two positions, the most extensive body of literature engaging with Christ's divinity in Hebrews has developed a minority report which challenges those who assume a high Christology. The view was initially articulated by George

---

[7] Rowe, "Trinity in Hebrews," 48.
[8] Understandably Rowe is constrained by space and holds that his attention to Hebr 1 is due to its "importan[ce] rhetorically for the whole Letter" (ibid., 45).
[9] Harold W. Attridge, *The Epistle to the Hebrews: A Commentary on the Epistle to the Hebrews*, Hermeneia (Philadelphia, PA: Fortress Press, 1989), 39–43.
[10] Moffitt similarly characterizes the result of Attridge's understanding of the Pastor's Christology as a "fissure fraught" one (David M. Moffitt, *Atonement and the Logic of Resurrection in the Epistle to the Hebrews*, NovTSup 141 (Leiden: Brill, 2011), 34, 35). As will be seen, tensions around the portrayal of Christ as Son and deliberation over the Son's divinity are, though not identical, parallel issues which are often played out along similar lines, tending to revolve around the relationship of eschatological or metaphysical discourse in the Letter. On this see Chapter 6.
[11] Attridge does note that the high Christology of the Exordium does not disappear subsequently, but represents "a basic constituent of Hebrews' portrait of Christ," which seems to appear at other points throughout the Epistle (*Hebrews*, 55).
[12] Ibid. For a slightly sharper judgement of irreconcilability, see John Knox, *The Humanity and Divinity of Christ: A Study of Pattern in Christology* (Cambridge: Cambridge University Press, 1967), 35–7. Further reservations come not only in handling the internal consistency of Hebrews' own thought but also the assumed compatibility of the later metaphysics of the council and the worldview of Hebrews. On this, see particularly D. Friedrich Büchsel, *Die Christologie des Hebräerbriefs* (Gütersloh: C. Berterlsmann, 1922), 177–213; Silviu N. Bunta, "The Convergence of Adamic and Merkabah Traditions in the Christology of Hebrews," in *Searching the Scriptures: Studies in Context and Intertextuality*, ed. Craig A. Evans and Jeremiah J. Johnston, LSNT 543 (London: Bloomsbury, 2015), 285. And with more reserve Paul Ellingworth, *The Epistle to the Hebrews: A Commentary on the Greek Text*, NIGTC (Grand Rapids, MI: Eerdmans, 1993), 66, 67.

Caird[13] and then subsequently developed in the work of L. D. Hurst, J. D. G. Dunn and Kenneth Schenck.[14] The overall strategy of their argument has been to problematize the relation of Hebrews' Christology to the later creeds, arguing that Son's portrayal in Hebrews falls well short of the personal pre-existence envisioned in them and does not comport with later Trinitarian statements on the Father and Son's eternal relations as God.[15] Though this body of scholarship would seem rather damning to the concept of the Son's divinity in Hebrews, it would be fair to say that it has not received wide reception within scholarship, mainly being regarded as an interesting but unconvincing thesis.[16] It at least, though, raises the question whether Christ's divinity in Hebrews is as unassailable as has sometimes been assumed.

Most striking, alongside these three views above, is a fourth strand of scholarship, in which key concepts and texts in Hebrews, which in the past were read as connecting to Christ's divinity, are re-read in a way that seems to remove the salience of the Son's divinity from the Epistle.[17] One might argue that the lack of articulation of Christ's divinity in such studies is simply a product of the focused nature of biblical studies, particularly monographs and articles. However, at times, the Son's divinity seems striking in its absence; when the standard texts are re-read to exclude the Son's divinity one is left to ask where else in Hebrews it might be found, or if it may be found at all.[18]

In this way contemporary scholarship on the divinity of Christ in Hebrews could be largely described along the lines of a threefold taxonomy of views: assumption of the divinity of Christ in the Epistle as quite secure; challenge to the former; and a striking silence about the concept. This book attempts, against the backdrop of these views, to argue that the concept of Christ's divinity within Hebrews is both more secure and more important than the above taxonomy suggests, but before moving on to how I address this topic, it will be helpful to more extensively survey the nature of these strands of modern Hebrews scholarship on the divinity of the Son.

---

[13] George Bradford Caird, "Son by Appointment," in *The New Testament Age*, ed. William C. Weinrich (Macon, GA: Mercer University Press, 1984), 18–24.

[14] L. D. Hurst, "The Christology of Hebrews 1 and 2," in *The Glory of Christ in the New Testament: In Memory of George Bradford Caird*, ed. L. D. Hurst and N. T. Wright (Oxford: Oxford University Press, 1987), 151–64; James D. G. Dunn, *Christology in the Making: A New Testament Inquiry into the Origins of the Doctrine of the Incarnation*, 2nd ed. (Philadelphia, PA: Westminster Press, 1989), 54, 208, 209, 252; Kenneth L. Schenck, "A Celebration of the Enthroned Son: The Catena of Hebrews 1," *JBL* 120 (2001): 469–85; "Keeping His Appointment: Creation and Enthronement in Hebrews," *JSNT* 66 (1997): 91–117.

[15] For an outline of the views of Dunn and Schenck in relation to the pre-existence of the Son in Hebrews, see Section 1.1.2.

[16] See, e.g. Peeler, *My Son*, 23–9; Bauckham, "Divinity of Jesus," 22n13; John Webster, "One Who Is Son: Theological Reflections on the Exordium to the Epistle to the Hebrews," in *The Epistle to the Hebrews and Christian Theology*, ed. Richard Bauckham, Daniel Driver and Trevor Hart (Grand Rapids, MI: Eerdmans, 2009), 80, 81.

[17] Below I discuss the monographs of Compton and Moffitt, but one might also consider the discussion of Christ's priesthood in Mason, *Priest Forever*.

[18] This comparative absence of the divinity of Christ in much discussion of the Christology of Hebrews mirrors Sonderegger's observation that "the Godhead of our Lord Jesus Christ has received far too little attention, praise and adoration in modern Christological dogmatics." Her comments at least raise the questions whether this is, at least in part, itself due to the "Christological turn" in much twentieth-century Western theology, which has often lent much more weight to the "human story" of Jesus (*Systematic Theology*, vol. 1 (Minneapolis, MN: Fortress Press, 2015), xvii, xviii).

1.1 State of the question

As suggested above, many writers have adopted positive views of the Son's divinity in Hebrews; however, these treatments are often limited to the exegesis of select verses. They frequently do not interact at much length with the principal questions that have been raised in challenging an understanding of the Son's divinity in Hebrews, and they rarely do much to integrate the concept into the reading of the whole Epistle.[19] Some have made more positive cases for the Son's divinity in Hebrews, and with an awareness of its detractors, but, with the exception of Bauckham's work, these normally are made in pursuit of other aspects of Hebrews' thought.

It is helpful then to survey Hebrews' literature under the three groupings mentioned above: first, those that make a strong, positive case for the Son's divinity in Hebrews; second, those who oppose or strongly modify it; and third, works in which divinity is conspicuously absent. I have chosen in this taxonomy to focus on monographs, essays and articles, rather than commentaries, as the former tend to deal with issues of divinity more systematically and in more detail than the latter.

1.1.1 Positive assessments of the divinity of the Son in Hebrews

1.1.1.1 Richard Bauckham

Two essays written by Bauckham in the 2000s represent the most focused work on the divinity of Christ in Hebrews in recent scholarship.[20] They form part of a wider programme in NT Christology, often identified with the Early High Christology movement, which Bauckham himself has termed "a Christology of divine identity."[21] Central to this programme is that later patristic articulation of the divinity of Christ is a faithful reception of the NT's witness, however transposed into a different, more metaphysical, idiom.[22] Though the later fathers spoke about the equality of God and Christ in terms of "quiddity," what God is, in contrast, Second Temple Jewish literature predominantly conceived of God's identity via various proper divine functions.[23] God was distinguished from all other reality via narrative explication of "who" this God was, is and will be. This "quissity" revolved around central convictions about God as: sole creator of all; sovereign over all; eschatologically to be recognized as God by all; possessing the unique divine Name; properly worshiped alone as God.[24] In Jewish

---

[19] Though certainly several modern commentaries on Hebrews adopt positions which might be characterized as positive on the Son's divinity (e.g. Craig R. Koester, *Hebrews: A New Translation with Introduction and Commentary*, AB 36 (New York: Doubleday, 2001); F. F. Bruce, *The Epistle to the Hebrews*, rev. ed., NICNT (Grand Rapids, MI: Eerdmans, 1990); Johnson, *Hebrews*) the genre of commentary does not always demonstrate to what extent the author sees the concept as a pervasive or theologically productive concept for Hebrews. An exception to this would be that of Cockerill, where Christ's divinity functions as a theological lodestone for much of his reading of the Epistle (*Epistle*, 109–11, 164–7, 300–7, 323, 324).
[20] Bauckham, "Monotheism," 167–85; "Divinity of Jesus," 15–36.
[21] Bauckham, *Jesus and the God of Israel*, 233; "Monotheism," 167; "Divinity of Jesus," 15.
[22] Bauckham, "Monotheism," 185.
[23] Bauckham, *Jesus and the God of Israel*, x.
[24] Bauckham, "Monotheism," 167.

thought these actions exclusively identified the One God of Israel, over and against all other created things.

In Bauckham's view, the NT authors' belief in Jesus' divinity is clearly seen in the way in which they apply to Christ these distinct divine categories, in describing his person and work. This move to understand Jesus as one with Israel's God developed because of Christ's exaltation to the divine throne itself, which conceptually drove the NT authors to insist on Christ's eschatological supremacy, his eternality and creational agency. In this way Christ "was included in the divine identity"[25] by the earliest Christian writers, and the resultant NT writings demonstrate that "the earliest Christology was *in nuce* the highest Christology."[26]

Bauckham's 2009 article in essence applies his programme to the shape of Hebrews' Christology,[27] demonstrating how Hebrews articulates such a divine identity Christology. His argument focuses on the three titles of Son, Lord and High Priest, each of which for Bauckham clearly portrays the Son as fully divine.[28] This appears as early as the Exordium, in which the Son's "narrative identity"[29] is described in terms uniquely proper to God: the Son is the creator of all (1:2); sovereign over all; and sits on the divine throne (1:3). The following catena explicates "the full divinity of Jesus" through the medium of scriptural interpretation.[30] He is spoken of as the unique Son who is superior to the angels, themselves markers of "ontological status,"[31] above whom alone is God. He is the eternal Creator, while they are mere changeable, created servants.[32] This eternal divinity is at the heart of what it is for the Son to be Son, an identity he did not attain.[33] For Bauckham the begetting of Ps 2 is as an eternal one,[34] and the name received in 1:3, not that of Son, but of God's own Name itself, YHWH.[35] The catena as the narrative of the Son's messianic enthronement is, in effect, his cosmic enthronement in which he assumes the sovereignty that is alone proper to God.[36]

For Bauckham this divine lordship of the Son is entwined with his office as High Priest, one which relates to his divinity.[37] As the great High Priest, Jesus alone sat down enthroned as Lord and Priest on God's own throne, thus making it "the throne of grace (4:16), where [believers] find the mercy of God."[38] That the Son's High priesthood is dependent on his divinity is made clear in his comparison to the figure of Melchizedek (7:3). There Melchizedek is described in terms which, though applicable only at the textual level to Melchizedek himself, truly apply to the Son.[39] His description as ἀπάτωρ

---

[25] Ibid., 168.
[26] Ibid.
[27] Bauckham, "Divinity of Jesus," 15–36.
[28] Ibid., 18.
[29] Ibid., 19.
[30] Ibid., 24.
[31] Ibid., 22, 23.
[32] This involves reading the phrase ὁ ποιῶν τοὺς ἀγγέλους αὐτοῦ in Ps 103:4 LXX as a reference to the Son as "maker." Bauckham, "Divinity of Jesus," 25.
[33] Ibid., 18, 19.
[34] Ibid., 33.
[35] Bauckham, "Monotheism," 175; "Divinity of Jesus," 25.
[36] Bauckham, "Monotheism," 177, 183; "Divinity of Jesus," 18, 19.
[37] Bauckham, "Divinity of Jesus," 27.
[38] Ibid., 32.
[39] Ibid.

ἀμήτωρ ἀγενεαλόγητος (7:3) is a reflection of both Hellenistic "true-god" language and Jewish language about God as unbegotten.⁴⁰ Thus the eternal divine life of the Son is that "indestructible life" (ζωή ἀκατάλυτος 7:16) which qualifies him for his work as enduring high priest.⁴¹ This indestructible life is fully consonant with the eternality of the Son frequently on display in Hebrews, a further divine trope in both Jewish and Hellenistic sources.⁴²

For Bauckham, then, Hebrews evidences a Christology of divine identity. The Son as Lord and High Priest is necessarily human, but also clearly and necessarily divine—included in the one identity of the true God—witnessed to both by Hebrews' theology and particularly its deployment of OT texts. Its Christology is absolutely consonant with that of the later fathers, though its mode of expression is not one of natures but the narrative idiom of Hebrews' milieu, that of Jewish theological discourse about the one, true God.⁴³

1.1.1.2 Amy L. Peeler

A second significant work with regard to the Son's divinity in Hebrews can be found in Peeler's 2014 monograph.⁴⁴ Unlike Bauckham, Peeler's focus is not Son's divinity, but rather the concept of God's family within Hebrews' thought. Her thesis is that a familial concept strongly underlies the nature of the relationships and characters of God, Christ and the people of God in the Epistle.⁴⁵ Within this framework Peeler argues that the identity of Christ as Son has a reflex of portraying God as Father,⁴⁶ and, in this vein, that the "exalted Christology" of Hebrews is a strongly "relational Christology" in which the mutual, defining relationship of the Father and Son is unfolded both by word and action.⁴⁷

Important to Peeler's thesis is that this Father-Son relation is not additive to God, but rather constitutive of the divine identity; the Father has always been such because he has always been the Father of the Son.⁴⁸ As such then, discussion of the way in which the Son shares in the Father's divinity becomes a significant aspect of the first chapter of Peeler's monograph.⁴⁹ Here she explores both the Exordium and the catena of 1:5–14 and observes how Hebrews portrays the Son as sharing in the divine identity of his Father via two principal categories. First, the Son shares in certain actions which are seen to be properly God's:⁵⁰ creation (1:2),⁵¹ rule (1:3) and reception of worship

---

⁴⁰ Ibid., 29 relying on Jerome H. Neyrey, "'Without Beginning of Days or End of Life' (Hebrews 7:3): Topos for a True Deity," *CBQ* 53 (1991): 439–55.
⁴¹ Bauckham, "Divinity of Jesus," 29.
⁴² Ibid.
⁴³ Ibid.
⁴⁴ Peeler, *My Son*.
⁴⁵ Ibid., 3, 5, 6.
⁴⁶ Ibid., 29.
⁴⁷ Ibid., 61.
⁴⁸ Ibid., 11n12, 12, 12n14, 14.
⁴⁹ Ibid., 10–63.
⁵⁰ Ibid., 58, 59.
⁵¹ Ibid., 21–4.

(1:6).⁵² Second, the Son is granted the Father's name as part of his inheritance (1:4).⁵³ Peeler sees this name explicated in the two vocatives of catena; the Son is Lord (1:10) and God (1:8). This combined title of "Lord God" is the name of the Father, shared by the eternal Son.⁵⁴

Thus Peeler believes it is entirely proper to speak of the Son's sharing in that which properly belongs to God. As the eternal Son he is the true image of his Father (1:3).⁵⁵ In Peeler's view then, though it appears the Father has a certain primacy with respect to the Son, both are essential to God's identity, each mutually defined by their eternal relationship to the other. The Son, as relational sine qua non of God's identity, is thus divine.⁵⁶

1.1.1.3 Angela Rascher

Like Peeler's monograph, that of Angela Rascher is not strictly concerned with the divinity of the Son in Hebrews.⁵⁷ Rather her work focuses on the interrelationship of Christology and OT interpretation in Hebrews.⁵⁸ This is investigated under a twin set of hypotheses which, Rascher argues, are central to the Epistle: that the OT acts as a lens for the explication of the Christ-event; and that the nature of the Christ-event leads to the re-interpretation of Scripture.⁵⁹ The consequent exploration of these hypotheses results in a substantial exposition of the Christology of Hebrews, one which heavily features the Son's divinity.

For Rascher the depiction of Christ in the Epistle is focused on the use of scriptural citation and its framing and development. Hebrews' usage of scripture focuses not on written documents but rather the OT "in the mouth" of God and the Son.⁶⁰ The Son's identity is thus constituted by divine speech: the Son is who he is, because of what God says to him. This immediate divine speaking of scripture removes quotations from their contexts, placing them beyond logico-temporal relationships, beyond time.⁶¹

This central conviction in Rascher's analysis of the role of Scripture in Hebrews as divine dialogue is integrally related to her depiction of the Son in several key ways. First, the Son's identity as immediately dependent on God's address, coupled with supratemporal nature of these speech acts, means that not only is the Son "Son" because God addresses him as such, but equally, because this speech is untimed, he is eternally Son.⁶² This is related to a further argument around the personal continuity of

---

⁵² Ibid., 54.
⁵³ Ibid., 15, 19, 20.
⁵⁴ Ibid., 59.
⁵⁵ Ibid., 16, 17, 56, 57.
⁵⁶ Ibid., 21, 61.
⁵⁷ Angela Rascher, *Schriftauslegung und Christologie im Hebräerbrief*, BZNW 153 (Berlin: Walter de Gruyter, 2007).
⁵⁸ Ibid., 1.
⁵⁹ Ibid.
⁶⁰ "In den Zitateinleitungen werden … deutlich, … die vielfältige Beziehung[en] von Gott und Jesus Christ" (Rascher, Schriftauslegung, 37).
⁶¹ Ibid., 40, 45.
⁶² Ibid., 58, 58n61, 76.

the Son's identity in the phases of his career. The Son is the united subject of his pre-existence, humiliation and exaltation, and these stages are not heavily demarcated, but rather mutually interpenetrating and dependent on the continuity of his person.[63] In this way the glory of the Son is not consequent, in Rascher's reading, on the Son's temporal career, but rather the presupposition of it. It is the eternal Son that pre-exists, is incarnate and is exalted. His eternal, divine person is the presupposition of his work.[64]

Second, this stress on the personal continuity of the Son, especially in his pre-existence, is furthered by other elements of the Son's portrayal as divine. This divine portrait predominantly is resourced from Hebrews 1 and revolves around God's address of the Son in the catena (1:5–14).[65] This address includes (a) the Son's personal pre-existence, evident in his participation in the work of creation and his description as eternal, (b) the attribution to the Son of the divine name and attributes and (c) the Son's own speaking of Scripture in parallel to God's divine speech of Scripture.[66] Thus, for Rascher, the depiction of the Son as "Son" can be theologically encapsulated in the language approximating the pro-Nicene theologians,[67] that "Die Beziehung von Gott und Sohn kann in Hebr als die der zwei gleichberechtigten göttlichen Personen beschrieben werden."[68]

In Rascher's analysis, thus Hebrews unveils as Son who is personally pre-existent and divine, his character explicated in the dialogue of Scriptural texts between the Son and God.

1.1.1.4 C. Kavin Rowe

A final positive attitude towards the divinity of Christ in Hebrews appears in C. Kavin Rowe's discussion of the nature of its Trinitarian thought. Rowe aims to demonstrate this underlying Trinitarian grammar of the Epistle, though with some caution as to what a Trinitarian reading involves.[69] Though, according to Rowe, predications of divinity, and their derivation from prooftexts, may play a part in making a case for Trinitarian concepts, a more fundamental method is to demonstrate how a set of "Trinitarian judgements" are presupposed, without which the theological fabric of the Epistle makes little sense.[70] This, for Rowe, coheres with what he perceives as a faithful trajectory between the NT's discourse about God, the Son and the Spirit, and later

---

[63] Ibid., 73, 74.
[64] Ibid., 60–3.
[65] Ibid., 51.
[66] Ibid., 51, 75–85.
[67] On the language of pro-Nicene theologies see Lewis Ayres, *Nicaea and Its Legacy: An Approach to Fourth-Century Trinitarian Theology* (Oxford: Oxford University Press, 2004), 6.
[68] Rascher, *Schriftauslegung*, 85.
[69] Rowe, "Trinity in Hebrews," 42. This happens in a joint discussion of Hebrews alongside the Pauline corpus with some helpful closing comparison of the two.
[70] Ibid., 43–5. This, in essence, is the application to the Pauline corpus and Hebrews of his views on how biblical texts exert "Trinitarian pressure" outlined in "Biblical Pressure and Trinitarian Hermeneutics," *Pro Ecclesia* 11 (2002): 295–312.

creedal formulation, in which a canonical, Trinitarian sub-structure was explored in a more discursive fashion.[71]

In demonstrating this Trinitarian structure of Hebrews, Rowe particularly comments on the relationship of the Son to God in Heb 1, 2.[72] For Rowe, though Hebrews assumes OT discourse on the One God's identity, it extends that language to the Son.[73] He is addressed with God, and by God, as himself God. The language of "Lord" seems to straddle both the God who spoke in the past (10:8–11, 16) but may also be equated with the Son (7:14).[74] Though discourse about the Son's role in creation is indebted to the OT figure of Wisdom, its application to the Son is not as figurative intermediary, but as a real human being, the exalted Jesus. In fact, the catena of Heb 1 paints a coherent picture of the exalted human being, Jesus Christ, who is, at the same time, eternal God: a Son commanded, by God himself, to be worshipped (1:6), an act, in the Jewish mindset, due only to God.[75]

This pattern of statements in Heb 1 thus shows a twofold emphasis at work: on the one hand, a continuity with the identity of OT God language and, on the other hand, a reworking and expansion of divine language proper. Thus Hebrews exhibits a set of theological judgements parallel to the Pauline corpus, in which the interrelation of the Father, the Son and the Spirit in the economy of salvations reveals a tripersonal God: three distinct persons included in the identity of the one God.[76] Hebrews does not really argue for such a theological development, but rather assumes it, developing a kind of discourse, in which the Son clearly shares in the identity of the One God and in which God cannot be truly spoken of without also speaking of the man, Jesus Christ.

For Bauckham, Peeler, Rascher and Rowe, then, Hebrews portrays the Son as clearly divine. Within their views, one may also note certain commonalities. First, Bauckham has played a formative role in analysing Christ's divinity, evident in his language of "identity" which is echoed by many.[77] There is a sense, however, that reliance on Bauckham's strengths may likely bring with it common weaknesses.[78] Second, the concept of "relation" is seen as a productive avenue for positive development of the Son's divinity.[79] However, the weaknesses of "relation" in exploring the divinity

---

[71] Rowe, "Trinity in Hebrews," 52. See further the discussion of this kind of Trinitarian grammar in Scott R. Swain, "The Bible and the Trinity in Recent Thought: Review, Analysis and Constructive Proposal," *JETS* 60 (2017): 40.

[72] Rowe, "Trinity in Hebrews," 45. Issues of space constrain his reading to the first two chapters of Hebrews, but it does leave one wondering where he would go later in the Epistle to demonstrate the same kind of issues he raises in discussion.

[73] Ibid., 45, 48.

[74] Ibid., 46.

[75] Ibid., 45, 46, 48.

[76] Ibid., 48, 52.

[77] J. R. Daniel Kirk, *A Man Attested by God: The Human Jesus of the Synoptic Gospels* (Grand Rapids, MI: Eerdmans, 2016), 17. Peeler affirms Bauckham's approach (*My Son*, 11n12) and appeals to Bauckham and "identity" at Peeler, *My Son*, 5n11, 14n11. Similarly, Rowe, "Biblical Pressure," 44 and in particular his summary of the Christology of Heb 1 "That the Son is internal to the identity of God" (Rowe, "Biblical Pressure," 46).

[78] On which see my discussion of Bauckham in Section 1.2. For challenge to Bauckham's approach see the varying degrees of pushback from Tilling, *Paul's Divine Christology*, 61, 62; Kirk, *A Man Attested by God*, 17–21; Fletcher-Louis, *Jesus Monotheism*, 68–101.

[79] See Peeler, *My Son*, 3, 41, 61; Rascher, *Schriftauslegung*, 40, 45. This is parallel to similar developments in Pauline Christology, e.g. Hill, *Paul and the Trinity*, esp. 30–48; Tilling, *Paul's Divine Christology*,

of the Son are rarely considered. Though the concept gained currency through the Social Trinitarianism important to late-twentieth-century Trinitarian revival, its reliance on the concept of "persons in relation" does not seem to furnish readers of the NT with the kind of conceptual tools necessary to a fully orbed articulation of the Son's divinity.[80] To speak of the Son as God with God, one must be able to articulate some kind of sharing in divinity, however conceived. In more classical Trinitarianism this role was played by the concept of consubstantiality, and it is not entirely clear that appeal to language of "persons in relation" is able to do the kind of heavy lifting that the more classical concepts were.[81] Third, expectedly Heb 1 exerts a strong gravitational pull on discussions about the divinity of the Son in Hebrews. Rowe's piece draws most evidence from there, as do Peeler and Rascher, and this adds to a sense that divinity is limited in its influence. If Heb 1 is as "important rhetorically" to the scope of the whole Epistle,[82] why is the supposed focus on the Son's divinity not reflected substantially elsewhere? Fourth, though Bauckham's work represents the most formidable of the positions discussed above, it is limited in certain ways, not least that it canvases evidence in a wide but brief manner. This brevity means that certain pieces of the evidence are entirely missed,[83] and others are not defended against objections that have been raised. This is coupled, at times, with what seems like a one-sided focus on divinity, where integration with other aspects of Hebrews is lacking.[84]

The overall result is that while the above authors do much to advance the divinity of the Son, their arguments raise questions around issues of methodology in articulating the Son's divinity, how pervasive the concept is and how well-integrated into the Epistle as a whole. These questions are only heightened by those whose interaction with the Son's divinity is much less conclusive.

---

and also in general Bates, *The Birth of the Trinity*. Frequently the line of influence here is traced back to the seminal article by Dahl, Nils A. Dahl, "The Neglected Factor in New Testament Theology," *Reflections* 73 (1975): 5–8. I am not suggesting that concept of "relation" may not make a significant contribution to the overall picture of Christology and theology proper, nor that relation played no role within patristic explication of Trinitarian doctrine; however, apart from some ability to speak of the "one-ness" of God, I cannot see how the equal divinity of the Persons of the Godhead can be really maintained, and I think this has been too little reflected upon in the adoption of the language of relations by those renewing Trinitarian discussion in NT studies.

[80] On the revival of Trinitarian doctrine in the twentieth century see Christoph Schwöbel, "The Renaissance of Trinitarian Theology: Reasons, Problems and Tasks," in *Trinitarian Theology Today: Essays on Divine Being and Act*, ed. Christoph Schwöbel (Edinburgh: T&T Clark, 1995), 1–31; and on the relation between Trinitarian revival and classical Trinitarianism see chapters 1 and 9 of Holmes, *The Quest for the Trinity*.

[81] Notwithstanding the employment of the concept of perichoresis, for criticism of which see Karen Kilby, "Perichoresis and Projection: Problems with Social Doctrines of the Trinity," *New Blackfriars* 81 (2000): 432–55.

[82] Rowe, "Biblical Pressure," 45.

[83] See the list of texts in discussing high Christology in Hebrews in Dunn's discussion (Dunn, *Christology*, 53, 54), which is ironically more extensive than Bauckham's.

[84] I have in mind here particularly the discussion of Christ's "indestructible life" in 7:16 and Bauckham's handling of the concept of sonship (Bauckham, "Divinity of Jesus," 20, 21, 27–32), though again the brevity of the essay and the way in which it seeks to canvas a broad range of evidence perhaps explains these weaknesses.

1.1.2 Negative or revisionist assessments of the divinity of the Son in Hebrews

1.1.2.1 James D. G. Dunn

J. D. G. Dunn's monograph, Christology in the Making,[85] has acted as something of a lightning rod for contemporary discussion of Hebrews' Christology, especially with regard to pre-existence and divinity. The work attempts to trace the development of the doctrine of incarnation through the writings of the NT as a whole. Dunn begins with the conviction that in the latest writings of the NT, in particular John's Gospel, we find represented a clear incarnational theology, in which Jesus is clearly the embodiment of a pre-existent and eternal divine person.[86]

Dunn's predominant interest in this development of incarnational thought is whether John's Gospel represents the fullest expression of NT incarnational thought, or, in contrast, a late and "alien intrusion."[87] To pursue this question Dunn analyses various key figures and concepts within the Hellenistic/Jewish worlds of the NT, and questions to what extent they influence NT Christological development, especially pre-existence.[88]

Dunn's conclusions are twofold (a) that the equating of Jesus with the Jewish concept of Wisdom represents the most significant driving force in the development of incarnational thought in the NT and (b) that the NT documents can be loosely schematized along a spectrum of views from weakest to strongest: Jesus is equated with wisdom without connotations of pre-existence; equated with Wisdom in ways which imply an idealized kind of pre-existence; and finally, only in John, as a personally pre-existent figure.[89]

Dunn analyses the Christology of Hebrews at several junctures and locates it in the penultimate category of idealized pre-existence.[90] This follows, for Dunn, two lines of thought centred on Heb 1, which stand in considerable tension.[91] First, Dunn evaluates Hebrews' use of Son of God language in reference to Jesus. He notes that the Epistle makes certain "high" statements about Jesus as the Son: as the radiance of the divine nature (1:3); the agent of creation (1:2); the builder of God's house (3:3, 4); addressed as God (1:8); like the eternal Melchizedek (7:3); sent by the Father into the world (10:5). At the same time, certain things are predicated of the Son, especially his appointment, which sit rather ill with these prior descriptions. The Son is appointed heir and hence Son (1:2); he is appointed to a task as Moses was (3:2); becomes like Melchizedek through resurrection (7:16); and is appointed by God as Saviour.

For Dunn this tension, between what the Son supposedly eternally is and yet also what he becomes in time, is encountered even in the Exordium.[92] Dunn understands

---

[85] Dunn, Christology.
[86] Ibid., ix, xiii.
[87] Ibid., xiv, 3, 6.
[88] Ibid., xx, 65–81, 129–62, 163–75, 213–29.
[89] By the time of the second edition it seems as if Dunn's views have developed, resulting in less certainty around whether the Fourth Gospel really does present a clear incarnational concept, rather than an apersonal incarnation of divine Wisdom. See Dunn, Christology, xxvi–xxxii.
[90] Ibid., 54.
[91] Ibid., 53, 54.
[92] Ibid., 164.

Heb 1:1–3a as a hymn, which applies terminology to the Son related to Wisdom.[93] Jesus is equated with God's eternal attributes, parallel to Jesus' identification with Wisdom elsewhere in the NT, revealing the early Christian belief that it was in, and through, Jesus that God was acting to fulfil his final purposes.[94] At the same time, however, lest we straightforwardly carry over eternal qualities to the Son, one must note that the exalted predications speak of the Son in his exalted state—the Son in time who has been resurrected.[95]

In both cases then, of Jesus as Son of God and divine Wisdom, there are elements of eternal and divine predication, alongside stress on his eschatological inheriting of certain features. For Dunn, the reason for this tension is the mixed worldview of the Epistle. Hebrews has combined elements of both Platonism and Hebraic thought, melding Platonic cosmology with Hebrew eschatology.[96] For the Pastor, Jesus Christ as Son and Wisdom represents the fulfilment of God's eternal purposes. The way in which Jesus is seemingly equated with divine predicates does not signal real personal preexistence or divinity. Rather it represents an idealized pre-existence, dependent on the Platonic concept of the Ideal.[97] Jesus Christ is the eschatological realization of purposes which have existed in the mind of God, as God's wisdom, since before the ages began.

Thus for Dunn, though he would place Hebrews far along the scale of NT thought, the Son of Hebrews is not a personal and pre-existent divine being.[98] In fact this makes Hebrews more squarely orthodox in maintaining a clear monotheistic conception so central to Jewish and Christian identity, something that John's Gospel stretches to near breaking point.[99] For Dunn then, Hebrews would not be able to be corralled in support of the Son's divinity, if one has in mind the positions of the first group above or of the Christology of later pro-Nicenes.[100]

1.1.2.2 Kenneth Schenck

Schenck's exposition of the Christology of Hebrews appears predominantly in two articles,[101] both of which extend the work of Caird and Hurst, and overlap substantially with Dunn's position.[102] The insights of Caird and Hurst, according to Schenck, involve recognizing the controlling pattern that humiliation/exaltation plays in the use of Ps 8 in 2:5–9, and how this informs a proper reading of the catena (1:5–14).[103] Grasping

---

[93] Ibid., 207, 208.
[94] Ibid., 209, 252.
[95] Ibid., 54, 208.
[96] Ibid., 257, 258. Dunn particularly appeals to the language of the earthly tabernacle as a ὑποδείγμα καὶ σκία (8:5) of the true and heavenly one, as an example of this blending of the Platonic and the Judaic.
[97] Ibid., 258.
[98] On the obvious entanglement of concepts of pre-existence and divinity, see Dunn, *Christology*, 13.
[99] Ibid., 262–5.
[100] For Dunn, indeed, Nicene theology can be rehabilitated if it can be read to mean no more than a kind of Logos Christology, in which the incarnation is of an apersonal divine trait; otherwise Nicene Christology breaks Jewish monotheism, which for Dunn is unacceptable (ibid., xxxii).
[101] Schenck, "Keeping His Appointment"; "Enthroned Son."
[102] Caird, "Son by Appointment"; Hurst, "Christology."
[103] Schenck, "Keeping His Appointment," 92, 94n99; "Enthroned Son," 471.

this, for Schenck, necessitates reading the Christological focus of Hebrews through the twin lenses of eschatology and exaltation.[104] This results in a reworking of the nature of assertions about pre-existence in Hebrews, especially with respect to Christ's role in creation, and a re-investigation of what divine attributes, functions and titles mean when attached to the Son in the Epistle.

The first of these articles[105] focuses on two sets of tensions in the depiction of Christ in Hebrews. These involve tensions in the sonship language and in the portrayal of Christ's involvement in creation.[106] This first surrounds whether Christ became Son at some point in his career or always was Son.[107] Schenck surveys various options for reconciling Hebrews' diverse statements and advocates a solution in which both sets of propositions are held through a conceptual distinction of person and office.[108] Christ always was the Son in regard to his person, but became the Son in fulfilment of his royal office, being enthroned at God's right hand.[109] This proposed solution of Schenck may, at first blush, suggest a reading which depicts the Son as a personally pre-existent figure. However, his exploration of the second tension mirrors significant features of Dunn's position, which problematizes such an understanding. For Schenck, that Hebrews can speak, on the one hand, of the Son's instrumentality in the creation of the ages (1:2) and, on the other hand, of creation as the immediate work of God (2:10; 3:5; 11:3) demonstrates that Hebrews' Christology is indebted to Jewish concepts of Wisdom and Word.[110] The result is that Hebrews does not portray Christ as personally pre-existent, but rather the eschatological effector of God's will. Christ is pre-existent in the sense that he operates in continuity with the God's will, which was from eternity.[111]

These two solutions proposed in Schenck's article may seem to conflict with each other. However, it seems that for Schenck, the absence of any concept in Hebrews that the Son "became" Son is a statement not about his pre-eternity but about the Son in his historical mission.[112] The Son was Son throughout his earthly career, but for Schenck this does not imply an eternal, pre-creational, personal existence of the Son.

If Schenck's first article challenges a significant element of Christ's divinity in Hebrews, his personal pre-existence, the second article[113] speaks more broadly to predication of divine attributes, which have often been taken as supporting Christ's divinity in the Epistle. The aim of this second article is to extend Schenck's focus on the Son's eschatological work to a reading of the whole catena.[114] Here, for Schenck,

---

[104] Schenck, "Keeping His Appointment," 93.
[105] Ibid.
[106] Ibid., 91, 92.
[107] Ibid., 94, 95.
[108] Ibid., 99.
[109] This act of becoming is particularly supported in Schenck's reading by his focus on an eschatological reading of the catena, laid out in the second article, "Enthroned Son."
[110] Schenck, "Keeping His Appointment," 92, 104–5.
[111] Ibid., 105–12.
[112] He is willing, e.g. to see the description of the Son as Son at 5:8 as more than merely proleptic, pace Ernst Käsemann, *The Wandering People of God: An Investigation of the Letter to the Hebrews* (Minneapolis, MN: Augsburg Pub. House, 1984), 98, but this is in reference to the Son's incarnate career. Schenck, "Keeping His Appointment," 95.
[113] Schenck, "Enthroned Son."
[114] Ibid., 469–71.

the catena's horizon is exclusively on what the Son has accomplished and what applies to him in his exalted state.[115] Predications in which the Son is addressed in divine terms are coupled to a specific temporal horizon:[116] that of "today," the incepted New Creation order, the age to come.[117] To construe these as meaning that the Son has an eternal nature, or shares in the God's nature, represents a misreading of Hebrews. The catena represents what the Son has come to be called as cosmic enthroned King, a king whose authority is subservient to God's own.[118] Applications of texts concerning eternity to the Son are simply predications about the permanence of his reign, into which he has entered; the Son's address as God is his ruling on God's behalf as final intermediary, not unlike the destiny of mankind generally, outlined in Ps 8.[119]

The result of Schenck's analysis is, in effect, a position similar to Dunn's and yet one more wide-ranging in handling Hebrews and its Christology. For Schenck the focus of Hebrews' Christology is on the Son's career in time, in particular, what he becomes as royal Son and ministering High Priest. The Epistle does not deny impersonal pre-existence but neither does it evidence particular interest in such a concept. The eternity which matters for Christ and his brothers is that "from now on" (Heb 1:1, 4; 3:13). Similarly, the Son's address as eternal God and Lord is a function of his assumed office.[120] They do not compete with the unique sovereignty of the One God because they do not rise to the same level. In Hebrews, God is alone sovereign and alone worshiped; the Son is venerated and rules, but in a lesser way.[121] Thus, though Schenck sees the depiction of Christ in Hebrews as a step along the way to later patristic Christology, the two are rather different, even standing in disagreement. For Schenck, the Son of Hebrews is neither personally pre-existent nor properly addressed as God with God, if that is intended to attribute a common divinity, equality of sovereignty or common worship.

For both Dunn and Schenck then, to understand Hebrews' association of the Son with the God's attributes or titles as meaning that he is of like divine status with the Father is to mistake the shape of Hebrews' Christology for later Trinitarian thought with which it cannot be legitimately equated.

1.1.3 The seeming theological irrelevance of the divinity of the Son in Hebrews

1.1.3.1 David M. Moffitt

David Moffitt's 2011 monograph[122] seeks to engage, and overturn, a widely held understanding that resurrection is largely absent from Hebrews, being either

---

[115] Ibid., 471, 472.
[116] Ibid., 475–84.
[117] Ibid., 475, 476.
[118] Ibid., 478–80.
[119] Ibid., 484.
[120] Ibid., 473.
[121] Ibid., 484n452.
[122] Moffitt, *Atonement*.

subsumed or replaced by the emphasis on Christ's heavenly exaltation and session at God's right hand.[123] In response, Moffitt argues that resurrection is a fundamental concept within the Epistle and is, in fact, axiomatic for various key elements of the Epistle's thought.[124] His predominant modus operandi is to demonstrate the career of the Son as enfleshed, and that the ascension represents the entrance of an enfleshed person into the heavenly world as a representative human being. For Moffitt the key Christological themes of Christ and High Priest necessitate a focus on the humanity of Christ: the Son's enthronement as the fulfilment of human destiny to rule the cosmos, and the Son's enfleshed ascension as the representative entrance of humanity into the heavenly tabernacle.[125] Within this methodology, focus on the humanity of Christ is understandable; Moffitt must establish the key relationship of enfleshment as a presupposition to exaltation, in order to sustain his argument for the necessity of resurrection to the logic of atonement.[126] However, within the overall portrait the divinity of the Son receives short shrift. When it briefly appears in discussion of aspects of Hebrews, it is handled in such a way that it seems essentially sidestepped. Divinity is mentioned, then problematized, and resolution is sought in a way that returns Moffitt to Christ's enfleshment as the key idea.

This is particularly evident in Moffitt's handling of the flow of Heb 1 and 2. In discussing the Exordium, Moffitt admits that the exalted description of the Son seems to suggest that he "is some kind of highly exalted heavenly being."[127] The catena similarly seems to represent the Author "portray[ing] the Son in Heb 1 as acting and being addressed as though he were on par with God himself."[128] However, Moffitt immediately turns to evidence that "complicate[s] a simple equation between God and the Son."[129] For Moffit, that the exalted identity of the Son is consequent on some prior action, for example, the act of purification in 1:3, and is connected to language of appointment "imply a sequence of events in which the Son's status relative to that of angels and his peers actually changed."[130]

As Moffitt's argument progresses on this point we find that its resolution lies not in a holding together of natures, or discussion of divinity and humanity as somehow co-involved, but rather a straightforward appeal to the Son as human. The exalted nature of the Son is actually the consequence of his possession of flesh and blood, in contrast to angelic beings who are disqualified from eternal rule as spirits.[131]

At the same time as he sustains this argument, he discusses the work of Bauckham, especially with reference to the latter's 2009 article.[132] He notes that Bauckham's reading of the Epistle makes Christ's sonship and priesthood both turn on the issue of

---

[123] Ibid., 1, 3.
[124] Ibid., 2.
[125] Ibid., 43.
[126] Ibid., 2.
[127] Ibid., 47.
[128] Ibid.
[129] Ibid., 48. Moffitt does not seem to have in mind here the issue of the confusion of the persons or collapsing of the Father and Son together.
[130] Ibid., 48, 49.
[131] Ibid., 49–53, 141, 148.
[132] Bauckham, "Divinity of Jesus," 15–36.

Christ's divinity. Moffitt roundly rejects this as "fail[ing] to do justice to the texture of the argument" in Heb 1, arguing that "Hebrews puts the spotlight in both cases on the humanity of the Son."[133]

One might say at this point that the direction of Moffitt's argument is simply a matter of focus: Moffitt is pursuing an argument, which is itself dependent on the thoroughgoing humanity of the Son. Further, because of the mysterious nature of asserting a united person who is in possession of two complete natures, Christological discourse is not a zero-sum game—more talk about humanity is not, by necessity, less talk about divinity. Indeed, Moffitt, at several points, makes positive statements about the divinity of the Son, for example, when asserting that Bauckham's work is essentially right in "discern[ing] the need for the Son to be both divine and human in his sonship"[134] and in agreeing that "The Son's elevation to the throne and high priestly ministry may not be exclusive of his divine identity."[135]

However, Moffitt's own assertions to the contrary, his project as a whole seems more problematic to Christ's divinity in Hebrews than his comments admit. For in handling the flow of the argument in Hebrews, Moffitt frequently exegetes verses which have been usually seen as supporting Christ's divinity in a way that suggests that Christ's humanity supplies a sufficient and full explanation of such. Christ's exaltation as Son is his exaltation as human Messiah, assuming the throne intended for humanity.[136] His establishment as priest is the resurrected ascension of an enfleshed human into the heavenly tabernacle, itself a proleptic entrance of humanity in the one Man.[137]

The sheer scope of Moffitt's discussion of Hebrews' thought, and the way in which Christ's humanity relates to it, though it may not strictly result in a kind of theological zero-sum game, seem to operate as such at the level of exegesis and structure. A monograph which canvasses so much of Christ's identity as Son and High Priest, with little discussion of the "how"s and "why"s of the supposed necessity of the Son's divinity, and with the level of profundity involved in Moffitt's analysis, surely begs the question: is the divinity of Christ really necessary for a broad and deep reading of the Epistle? Moffitt's argument in effect adduces nothing that is theologically opposed to the Son's divinity, but in terms of its ability to explain central concepts in Hebrews it seems to question the necessity of such a hypothesis.[138]

---

[133] To be fair to Moffitt he does mention that he thinks Hebrews does exert "Trinitarian pressure" (Moffitt, *Atonement*, 47n42) but in a way quite different to Bauckham's arguments, and one would imagine such "pressure" would have to include the Son's deity; it is hard though to gather from Moffitt's argument quite from where this pressure would come, especially when many of the key issues have been rerouted towards concepts of exalted and glorious humanity.

[134] Ibid.

[135] Ibid., see also ibid., 207.

[136] Ibid., 42, 137.

[137] Ibid., 43, 45, 193–4, 218, esp. 193n130.

[138] This is particularly reflected in the way that Moffitt can appeal approvingly to Socinus' understanding of Heb 7, which via "emphasis on the humanity of Jesus appears to have enabled him to trace the logic of the argument in Hebrews 7 with particular clarity" (ibid., 193n130). But if a reading which has no need of the divinity of Jesus in such an important chapter as Heb 7 "trace[s] the logic of the argument ... with particular clarity" does this not suggest the divinity of the Son is an unnecessary aspect of Hebrews' theological landscape?

1.1.3.2 Jared Compton

Though the purpose of Compton's monograph,[139] which focuses on the structuring function of Ps 110 in Hebrews, is rather different to Moffitt's, Compton's argument leads to some interestingly similar results in handling the Son's divinity. What is more, his reading in particular of Heb 1 represents a refinement of some of Moffitt's comments who, though he raises the attribution of divine titles to Christ in 1:8, 10–12, having problematized them as demonstrations of the Son's equality with God, never returns to discuss them.

Like Moffitt, Compton's reading of Heb 1, 2 focuses on the enthronement of Jesus as Israel's Messiah and the salvific consequences of his enthronement as Son (Heb 1) for the many sons (Heb 2).[140] Again, like Moffitt, Compton's focus on the catena as the account of the Son as the exalted descendant of David might be thought to stumble when encountering the "God" texts of the catena. Compton, to his credit, recognizes this fact, particularly in relation to the Pastor's use of Deut 32:43 in 1:6 and Ps 102:25–7 in 1:10–12, as the application of divine titles, actions and worship to Jesus.[141] As Compton notes, these verses seem to "complicate" his reading of the catena as "the resurrection of the Son, … receiv[ing] the status that was reserved for David's true heir, Israel's long awaited Messiah."[142] To see the catena as basing the exaltation of the Son on his divinity, for Compton, both removes the catena from the established orbit of Davidic Messianism and further introduces "Christian presuppositions" which would defeat an argument from Scripture. Compton, however, demonstrates that these texts, which in their original context were addressed to God, may be understood otherwise and that introducing divinity at this point "is not as inevitable as it may first appear."[143]

Fundamental to this re-reading is Compton's conviction that ultimately Christ's divinity cannot ground the Son's exaltation—the catena is concerned with what the Son has "become," not what he is:

> It would be slightly odd, therefore, for the author to suggest that one quality that makes the son superior is that he is now divine. One does not become divine, at least in any authentically Judeo-Christian sense—which is precisely what those arguing for this position intend (i.e., uncreated, unchanging, et al.).[144]

Furthermore, to bring in the divinity of Christ here is to rely on Christian presuppositions in the context of a chain of citations intended to prove the validity of the Pastor's claims about Christ to the unconvinced, a method which would involve a kind of vicious circularity. Rather, the catena presupposes the Jewish concept of intermediaries who seemingly participated in certain divine properties. Compton principally has in mind

---

[139] Jared Compton, *Psalm 110 and the Logic of Hebrews*, LNTS 537 (New York: Bloomsbury T&T Clark, 2015).
[140] Ibid., 20–3, 39–40.
[141] Ibid., 23, 24.
[142] Ibid., 19.
[143] Ibid., 24.
[144] Ibid.

the figures of Wisdom and Word, the descriptions of which in Judaism approach the Pastor's description of the Son.¹⁴⁵ In addition, the figure of the Israelite King could himself share these same features, demonstrating considerable "overlap" between his own person and that of YHWH. As Compton notes, "The king was, after all, God's son (Ps. 2.7; 2 Sam. 7.14/1 Chron. 13.17; Ps. 88.28 LXX; cf. 109.1). His rule was the visible expression of YHWH's rule."¹⁴⁶

By these two steps Compton thus shifts these addresses to Christ as to God, back into the orbit of kingship and Davidic Messianism.¹⁴⁷ He proceeds to solidify this connection by demonstrating that, in fact,

> both texts [Deut 32:43 and Ps 101:26–28 LXX] are open to messianic interpretation, especially when one realises the extent to which the rule of Israel's king and Yhwh overlapped (see, e.g., 1 Chron. 28.5; 29.23; 2 Chron. 9.8; 13.8).¹⁴⁸

In essence then, what Hebrews predicates of the Son is really nothing other than what was predicated of monarchs in the ANE, and to the Israelite king described in Ps 44 LXX. The exalted king is addressed as God, though clearly he is a Davidide, however exalted.¹⁴⁹ At least for Compton's reading of the catena it is no more necessary to predicate divinity of the Great Davidic Son, Jesus, than it would be to do so of his ancestor David or the one addressed in Ps 44 LXX; the final exalted human Davidide is a sufficient referent on whom the citations terminate, and a royal Messiah the sufficient goal of the Pastor's scriptural proofs.¹⁵⁰

1.1.4 Results of the survey

These various positions on Hebrews' Christology raise a question about the portrayal of the Son's status. Is the Son considered to be divine in the Epistle, as the first group argue, and, if so, in what sense? Is this assessment of the Son's divinity merely an issue of pre-existence or not?¹⁵¹ Is the divinity of the Son, if established, limited to Heb 1, or is it a more pervasive feature of the Epistle? Even if the theme is pervasive, is the concept of the Son's divinity significant for the Epistle's theology? That is, while there has been some pushback from the second group outlined above, a broad selection of Hebrews scholarship seems to suggest by its nature that, even if the Son's divinity is sustained in the Epistle, it is theologically irrelevant to its central arguments or theological foundations.¹⁵²

---

¹⁴⁵ Ibid., 27–30.
¹⁴⁶ Ibid., 27.
¹⁴⁷ Ibid., 31.
¹⁴⁸ Ibid.
¹⁴⁹ Ibid., 32, 33.
¹⁵⁰ Ibid., 31–6.
¹⁵¹ Even Koester's rather positive discussion almost exclusively seems to focus concepts of high Christology in Hebrews as connected to issues of "Pre-existence and constancy" which dominate the summary in his section on Christology in Hebrews (*Hebrews*, 104, 105).
¹⁵² Sometimes this point is made explicitly. See, e.g. though Schenck holds that Hebrews teaches pre-existence at some level, the concept is "not determinative for the author's subsequent argument" (Schenck, "Keeping His Appointment," 114).

This understanding of the state of research on Jesus' divinity in Hebrews poses three central questions which have guided this work. First, is the Son in Hebrews portrayed as divine and in what sense? Second, is this concept a fairly limited one or a pervasive element of the Epistle? Third, and finally, is the divinity of the Son in Hebrews a necessary aspect of its Christology, and theologically salient to the Epistle, intersecting with other central concepts; or is it, on the other hand, a "subsidiary crater,"[153] debate over which arises not from Hebrews but from unnecessary and anachronistic creedal interests?

Before moving on to outline the chapters that follow, one prolegomenal issue first requires clarification: the concept of divinity in relation to the Son.

1.2 On predicating divinity

In evaluating whether the Son is portrayed as divine, one must first have some sense of what one means by "divinity" in this context and what it might mean to predicate divinity of the Son in Hebrews. The question as to what constitutes the markers of divinity in NT Christology in relation to its cultural and religious milieu has been variously proposed and contended within modern debates, reaching a fever pitch in proposal of, and reaction to, the Early High Christology movement.[154] However, at root, the assumption is shared that predicating divinity of the Son is essentially to see an NT author assigning various elements of what is properly God's alone to the Son.[155]

The way in which this argument has been pursued is varied, and especially what constitutes these "properly divine" elements has been much contended. To fully survey the proposals is beyond the scope of this work and has been well done by others in the field.[156] However, in establishing my own approach it is helpful to note two false moves which I believe have hindered discussion of divine Christology in the literature, the effect of both of which is to truncate the NT evidence which ought to be considered. Both of these elements may be demonstrated from the work of Richard Bauckham within his project of a Christology of divine identity.[157]

---

[153] That is, in Schweitzer's well-known turn of phrase, a concept which, though present, is essentially dwarfed by other theological concerns which are more central to the overall system of thought (Albert Schweitzer, *Paul and His Interpreters: A Critical History* (London: A. and C. Black, 1912), 225).

[154] See footnote 4.

[155] Bauckham, *Jesus and the God of Israel*, 19; Hurtado, *Lord Jesus Christ*, 53; *Jewish Monotheism?*, SBLSP 32 (Atlanta, GA: SBL Press, 1993); Tilling, *Paul's Divine Christology*, 72, 73.

[156] The most perceptive survey is that of Tilling in *Paul's Divine Christology*, 11–62.

[157] I choose Bauckham here not because of the weakness of his position but because it is to my mind the strongest and most wide-ranging of the positions of those propounding an early high Christology. The sheer impact of Bauckham's work in the field can be seen in the reception of "identity" in articulation of high Christology, e.g. Nina Henrichs-Tarasenkova, *Luke's Christology of Divine Identity*, LNTS 542 (London: Bloomsbury, 2015). However, though the nature of Bauckham's thesis in effect admits a wide range of NT Christological data, say in comparison to Hurtado, I believe it can be widened further and that some of his opening moves vis-à-vis the nature of divine identity are not without problem.

The first arises when one constructs a standard for divinity through appeal to the world surrounding a NT author(s). This method implicitly suggests that if we construct a portrayal of who God is, in what is properly predicated of God alone in the world of Second Temple Jewish literature, we may then use this standard as one against which the portrayal of Christ in the NT literature can be measured.[158] To the extent that the Son's portrait overlaps with this Second Temple Jewish portrait of God, to that extent he is portrayed as divine. The shortcomings of this approach are not principally that it contributes nothing to the evaluation of NT Christology, but that it potentially represents a theological incongruence. In coming to the conception of who the Son is, it is clear that, for NT authors, their Christology does not represent a tacked-on understanding of the Son to an otherwise unmodified Jewish system of thought, and, in particular, to an unreconstructed doctrine of God. Rather, the concept of divinity and the doctrine of God proper become themselves re-configured through the understanding of who Jesus Christ is.[159]

Because of this, the attempt to merely match predication will always prove inadequate. It cannot account for the way in which similar predications may function differently within different systems of thought.[160] For this reason, the primary ruler for establishing divine criteria in assessing the Christology of Hebrews must first and foremost be the theology of Hebrews itself.[161] This may be further extended to the

---

[158] Bauckham, "Monotheism," 168.

[159] See Francis Watson, "The Triune Divine Identity: Reflections on Pauline God-Language, in Disagreement with JDG Dunn," *JSNT* 23 (2001): 105–6; N. T. Wright, *The New Testament and the People of God*, vol. 1, Christian Origins and the Question of God (Minneapolis, MN: Fortress Press, 1992), xv.

[160] My point here is not that the comparing of predications is illegitimate but that this must be done with a sense of the operation of these predications within an overall system of thought. An example of how this can fail to function is the way in which Bauckham excludes the concept of covenant from his discussion of divine Christology "because it does not so clearly distinguish [God] from all other reality, …, and so was not prominent in Jewish statements of God's uniqueness from this period" (Bauckham, "Monotheism," 167n163). Whether or not this is a correct understanding of the Jewish literature, it is certainly not a correct understanding of Hebrews where covenantal concepts, God's character and Christ are significantly related in ways which connect to divinity. On this see Chapter 5 of the present work. The central point here, though, is that such connections and their signalling of divinity are dependent on what Hebrews does with various elements of Jewish thought, but the connections themselves are not "measurable" as divine predication by comparison with literature outside of Hebrews. One might equally consult Bauckham's remarks that the address of the Son with the title "God" via scriptural quotation in Hebrews "should not be given too much significance" because of the parallel phenomenon of the application of Ps 82:1 to the figure in 11QMelch col ii 1.10 (Bauckham, "Monotheism," 182). The assumption being that only what is unique can signal divinity with respect to Christ. But again this assumes ability to compare predications without recourse to their overall significance in comparison to other features.

[161] What I have in mind here is at least analogous to the kind of application of Wittgenstein's view of language by Lindbeck under the name of a "cultural-linguistic" view of doctrine (George A. Lindbeck, *The Nature of Doctrine: Religion and Theology in a Postliberal Age*, 25th anniversary ed. (Louisville, KY: WJKP, 2009). His position I think can be applied to NT Christology in a way that sees its statements as predominantly deriving meaning in relation to the whole symbolic grammatical system, without necessarily rejecting "cognitive-propositional" accounts in the way Lindbeck holds. Thus, the grammar of NT Christology may speak with universal claim, but its primary roots lie within itself, rather than in adducing external rules from without. For a not dissimilar application of such "linguistic grammar" to the topic of Messianism see Matthew V. Novenson, *The Grammar of Messianism: An Ancient Jewish Political Idiom and Its Users* (New York: Oxford University Press, 2016), 11–21, who is partly reliant on Dahl's broader Christological agenda in

function of Old Testament texts and concepts, and the portrait of God which they bring with them via their obvious significance for the Epistle.

A second truncation of data occurs when one attempts to delimit what kinds of predication can be seen as proper to God. Bauckham's evaluation of data is comparatively broad in this regard.[162] However, in relation to a doctrine of God in Second Temple Judaism, he predominantly relies on the predication of proper divine action. For Bauckham, God is identified through his action in history. He is the God "who" has acted, or will act in some way, in Israel's history.[163] The power of Bauckham's project is that this focus on action enfranchises a broad set of data both in Second Temple Jewish literature and the NT. Important to this conviction is that this focus on who God is (his "quissity"), in the NT and its contemporary world, is rather different to the focus on what God is (his quiddity), which dominated later articulations of Christ's deity at Nicea and Chalcedon.[164] However, it is fascinating in this regard to note that, though certainly the articulations of Christ's divinity in later patristic material make use of a philosophical language of natures,[165] the methodology of predicating divinity actually allows for a broader assessment of predication about God and the Son in reading biblical literature than many contemporary scholars do.[166] One may take as a helpful example here the articulation of Christ's deity in the work of Gregory of

---

Nils A. Dahl, "Sources of Christological Language," in *Jesus the Christ: The Historical Origins of Christological Doctrine*, ed. Donald Juel (Minneapolis, MN: Fortress Press, 1991). Also particularly instructive is Watson's demonstration of the way in which Christology reshapes theology proper in Paul's writings (Watson, "The Triune Divine Identity," 99–124). In this he critiques Dunn, who by contrast, advocates carrying over various "axiomatic beliefs … [which] were never challenged" with respect to the role of monotheism in Paul's thought (ibid., 103, 104).

[162] On the other side of the spectrum one might compare Hurtado's focus on the single criterion of worship, Hurtado, *Lord Jesus Christ*, 53; *Jewish Monotheism?*, 348–68.

[163] Bauckham, *Jesus and the God of Israel*, ix; "Monotheism," 167.

[164] Bauckham's opposition of quissity and quiddity (*Jesus and the God of Israel*, 7; sim. Watson, "The Triune Divine Identity," 105–6) is less marked than, e.g. J. Daniel Kirk's, for criticism of which see Matthew Levering, "God and Greek Philosophy in Contemporary Biblical Scholarship," *JTI* 4 (2010): 173–4. On the preference for language around God's identity rather than his nature in modern theological method, and the necessity of integrating both, see the programmatic comments of Sonderegger, *Systematic Theology*, vol. 1, xi–xxi.

[165] The extent to which this language of natures, as significant as it is in creedal formulations, is actually the principal theologically generative element in, e.g. the theology of the Cappadocian fathers is generally over-assumed. Other concepts which are, at the surface level, much closer to the idiom of NT Christological discourse play in fact a significant role in accounts of the equality of the Father and the Son. See, cf., the description of the divine persons as of "one goodness, and one power, and one deity" in *Ad Eust.* 3a in Anna M. Silvas, *Gregory of Nyssa: The Letters: Introduction, Translation and Commentary* (Leiden: Brill, 2006), 237, and the discussion of the role of "power" in the unity of the Father and Son in Michel R. Barnes, *The Power of God: Dunamis in Gregory of Nyssa's Trinitarian Theology* (Washington, DC: CUA Press, 2001), esp.1–11, 291–2. One might equally compare the Nyssen's account here with that of Augustine in his reflections on the language of 1 Cor 1:24 in which Christ is described as God's Wisdom and Power in *De Trinitate* VI.1 and the discussion of Maarten Wisse, *Trinitarian Theology Beyond Participation: Augustine's De Trinitate and Contemporary Theology*, T&T Clark Studies in Systematic Theology 11 (London: T&T Clark, 2011), 63–70.

[166] Bauckham does note that attribute language plays a role in Second Temple Judaism (*Jesus and the God of Israel*, 9), but because he sees it as less a distinctive mark of God's identity in the contemporary Jewish literature it receives very little development in his work, and is certainly not axiomatic.

Nyssa.¹⁶⁷ Though in speaking of the divine persons he can refer to the divine nature, the apophatic shape of his thought means that he believes it is impossible to say what that divine nature is.¹⁶⁸ This does not mean we know nothing about God. On the contrary, for Gregory, because God has revealed himself in history, we may, on the basis of divine revelation, make predications about the divine nature.¹⁶⁹

Gregory's view has remarkable strengths as a resource for thinking about divinity in the NT.¹⁷⁰ It both rejects metaphysical speculation that is, at times, unduly attached to the fathers, because we cannot define the divine nature the Trinitarian Persons share;¹⁷¹ at the same time, it does not prima facie restrict what sorts of predications might be made about that nature. What is proper to God may thus, where predicated of the Son, be seen as signalling divinity and spans the whole range of personal attributes, actions and character.¹⁷² For Gregory this more sensitive approach to divine Christology has an

---

[167] For an overview of Nyssen's Christology, see Lucas F. Mateo Seco and Giulio Maspero, *The Brill Dictionary of Gregory of Nyssa*, Supplements to Vigiliae Christianae 99 (Leiden: Brill, 2010), 139–40.

[168] God's nature is, for Gregory, ὑπὲρ αἴσθησίν τε καὶ γνῶσιν ἀνθρωπίνην ἐστίν (*De Beat* GNO VII/2, 141, 27). Similarly *Ad Eust*. 8b in Silvas, *The Letters*, 243; *Ad Petr*. 3e in Silvas, *The Letters*, 252; *Ad Ablabium* Edward Rochie Hardy, *Christology of the Later Fathers* (Louisville, KY: WJKP, 1954), 259. See further the comments of Giulio Maspero, *Trinity and Man: Gregory of Nyssa's Ad Ablabium* (Leiden: Brill, 2007), 31; Lewis Ayres, "On Not Three People: The Fundamental Themes of Gregory of Nyssa's Trinitarian Theology as Seen In: To Ablabius: On Not Three Gods," in *Re-Thinking Gregory of Nyssa: Introduction—Gender, Trinitarian Analogies, and the Pedagogy of the Song*, ed. Sarah Coakley (London: Wiley-Blackwell, 2002), 34, 35.

[169] *Ad Ablabium* in Hardy, *Christology of the Later Fathers*, 259; e.g. central to Nyssen's thought is that the divine nature may be predicated as both indivisible and inseparable (*Ad Ablabium* in Hardy, *Christology of the Later Fathers*, 261).

[170] For the application of divine "names" to Christ see *Contr. Eunom*. II.293b–304 in Lenka Karfíková et al., eds., *Gregory of Nyssa, Contra Eunomium II: An English Version with Supporting Studies: Proceedings of the 10th International Colloquium on Gregory of Nyssa*, Supplements to Vigiliae Christianae (Leiden: Brill, 2007), 125, 126 and the discussion of Mateo Seco and Maspero, *The Brill Dictionary of Gregory of Nyssa*, 144, 145. In Book III of *Contra Eunomium*, Gregory notes this in regard to the Father and Son's sharing of the same goodness, strength and eternity, and in this regard cites Heb 1:3 and 7:3 (Johan Leemans, ed. *Gregory of Nyssa: Contra Eunomium III: An English Translation with Commentary and Supporting Studies: Proceedings of the 12th International Colloquium on Gregory of Nyssa (Leuven, 14–17 September 2010)*, Supplements to Vigiliae Christianae 124 (Leiden: Brill, 2014), 154, 155).

[171] Gregory is further aware where, and at which points, his own terminology is different in meaning from scriptural language, for which see his comments in Heb 11:3 in *Ad Petr*. Silvas, *The Letters*, 257, 258. On the tendency to neglect the possibility of appropriate metaphysics in the handling of the New Testament see Swain, "Bible and Trinity," 45, who remarks that "the metaphysical pattern of divine naming is the most understudied pattern of divine naming among recent work on the Bible and the Trinity," though he notes the work of Jenson, Levering and White as engaging this tendency (Robert W. Jenson, *Systematic Theology* (New York: Oxford University Press, 1997); Matthew Levering, *Scripture and Metaphysics: Aquinas and the Renewal of Trinitarian Theology*, Challenges in Contemporary Theology (Malden, MA: Blackwell, 2004); Thomas Joseph White, *The Incarnate Lord: A Thomistic Study in Christology*, Thomistic Ressourcement Series (Washington, DC: Catholic University of America Press, 2015).

[172] To contrast Gregory's position absolutely with Bauckham's concept of divine identity is a slight oversimplification, especially when one notes that, for the former, all proper naming of God arises out of the divine *energeia* through which the divine nature becomes able to be spoken of, so *Ad Eust*. 6d, e, 7h in Silvas, *The Letters*, 241, 243. To be able to say, e.g. that "God is powerful" or "God is good" comes about via God's activity *ad extra*, which reveals himself to creatures. However, for Gregory, this means the *energeia* reveals, but does not constitute, God's nature. As Maspero summarizes, "The *ad extra* manifestation of God renders eternity present in history, without

ear to the full range of data, including not only Bauckham's proper divine functions[173] but also recognizing that Scripture portrays God in other ways: as the sole possessor of certain incommunicable attributes; as the possessor *par excellence* of communicable attributes; in the attribution of actions that are part of the divine prerogative and rely on divine power; in the possession of character which is proper to God; in the covenantal involvement of God with his creation and with his peculiar people.[174]

Thus a narrative construction of God's identity and more philosophical language about divine qualities and attributes ought not be seen as incompatible, either with each other or with biblical revelation;[175] God's quissity and quiddity are interrelated, because God's incomprehensibility extends to both, and yet both form the partially and truly revealed substance of God-talk in the biblical witness.[176] As Levering writes,

> In the Bible, [the divine] attributes are never separated from God's acts in history. The Psalms bear witness to this unity of the divine attributes and God's creative and salvific actions. Consider Ps 146, where the psalmist describes God as Redeemer and Creator and then proceeds to apply the attributes of power and understanding to God. ... Similarly, Ps 145 proclaims God's goodness and righteousness in light of God's creative and redemptive actions. ... On this view, "universal" attributes of God need not be opposed to faithful description of "the God of particulars, the God whose [attributes are] tied to a particular story in which God has promised to act in a way, to bless a particular people."[177]

While then, as with many, I am indebted to the discussion of Bauckham in what follows, I have sought to approach Hebrews with these two caveats in mind: first, an attempt to let Hebrews itself be the primary standard for divine nature or identity; and second, a desire to not omit certain aspects of predication about the Son which form part of the Epistle's witness to his deity. In this vein, I have sought to concentrate on exegeting particular texts from within Hebrews, evaluating their significance for the portrayal of the Son as divine within the theology of the Epistle, and in light of significant OT texts and their contexts where they feature in the argument. This I would argue is to attempt a sympathetic and self-consistent Christological reading

---

introducing any change in God" (Maspero, *Trinity and Man*, 34). The result of his position is thus a much wider consideration of divine "names" than is often allowed by some proponents of EHC. On proposing a wider taxis of "names" in the construction of Trinitarian theology see also Swain, "Bible and Trinity," 45–7.

[173] Bauckham, *Jesus and the God of Israel*, x.

[174] On the obvious presence of attribute language in describing God in the NT see Levering, "Greek Philosophy," 174.

[175] On the preference for narrative mode in modern methodology of theology proper and its perceived opposition to metaphysics see Francesca Aran Murphy, *God Is Not a Story: Realism Revisited* (Oxford: Oxford University Press, 2007), 13–22.

[176] As Ayres notes, the pro-Nicene theologians of the late fourth century saw "the importation of philosophical themes and technical language ... not as a necessary *transposition* of ideas, but as an *elucidation* of the text of Scripture. Thus, it seems fair to suppose a fairly close connection between the narrative and symbolic" (Ayres, *Nicaea*, 277).

[177] Levering, "Greek Philosophy," 175 citing J. R. Daniel Kirk, *Unlocking Romans: Resurrection and the Justification of God* (Grand Rapids, MI: Eerdmans, 2008), 8.

of the Pastor, whose thought is profoundly marked by his conviction that God has revealed himself, his quiddity and quissity, truly in the prophets in the OT writings and finally and uniquely in his Son. Further, I have attempted in my investigation to engage the full range of predications about the Son's divinity, arguing that where it is predicated of him what is properly predicated of God, whether in respect to character, attributes or actions, that there the Pastor is predicating divinity of the Son.

1.3 Outline of the work

The focus of the argument that follows will be to address the questions raised above, regarding the presence, pervasiveness and theological salience of the divinity of the Son in Hebrews. I have not attempted an entire overview of the Christology of the Epistle, nor a systematic survey of all the ways in which the Pastor may or may not signal the divinity of Christ. This is predominantly due to the state of contemporary scholarship on Hebrews outlined above. The first method would simply have resulted in something far too large; the second, I believe, would not have spoken to the kinds of objections that have been raised over the evidence which has often been used in support of the Son's divinity in Hebrews, or to the issue of theological salience, and consequently the integrity of Christ's divinity to the Epistle, that I believe has often been left to one side.

The approach I have chosen is rather to canvas different sorts of arguments, ranging from tight exegetical points, often those controverted or less explored, to more thematic aspects which relate to the Epistle's central concepts.[178] The aim in this methodology has been threefold: first, to deal specifically with objections to texts or themes to which standard appeal has been made in support of the Son's divinity;[179] second, to re-appropriate neglected aspects of pre-critical exegesis where it detected the divinity of Christ in the Epistle, and to bring it as a theological resource into fruitful dialogue with modern exegesis;[180] third, in attempting the first two, to draw out how

---

[178] Because of this, certain texts which have often been appealed to in discussion of the Son's divinity in Hebrews, rather than receiving separate discussion, are integrated into the discussion of other texts or related thematic investigations. See, e.g. the relation of Christ's work of creation in 1:2 is predominantly handled in relation to the role of Ps 101 LXX in Chapter 2, and the language of Christ as the divine image in 1:3 under the discussion of Sonship in Chapter 6. This is due to the fact that, abstracted from other aspects of the Epistle's thought it can be difficult to discern whether these statements can be properly handled through the kinds of Wisdom concepts of Dunn and Schenck, the Adamic connections of Moffitt, or are signals of divinity.

[179] In this case awareness of how Hebrews has been used in the history of interpretation, and in relation to Christ's divinity, has informed the selection of texts and arguments.

[180] This *desideratum*, of engaging with the patterns of judgement of older exegetes, is neither straightforwardly either "history of interpretation" (*Auslegungsgeschichte*) nor "history of effects" (*Wirkungsgeschichte*). The former tends to simply outline how the text has been read by past interpreters. The latter, through its roots in the work of Gadamer, especially *Truth and Method* (1st Eng. ed.; London: Sheed & Ward, 1975), tends to locate the text's predominant existence and meaning in the present experience of readers. In essence neither approach seems to undertake the work with a view to the helpful role of past teachers in the life of the Church and in connection to the ongoing reception of the Bible by the people of God. Though the approaches do not themselves encode this feature, it nonetheless often appears in various ways in the work of some involved in using a *Wirkungsgeschichtliche* approach. So, e.g. one may note at a larger scale Ulrich

broader aspects of the Pastor's argument intersect with the divinity of the Son in the Epistle. The chapters that follow tend to evidence at least one, or several of these aims at once, and progress as follows.

The first three chapters focus on detailed exegesis. In Chapter 2, I concentrate on the often-noted application of OT God texts which in Hebrews feature as addresses by God to the Son (1:6; 10–12). These texts have often been adduced as evidence of the Son's divinity in Hebrews. However, alongside this hermeneutical move has often been seen as arbitrary or perhaps even pointing away from conclusions about deity. I attempt to demonstrate that the logic of the Pastor's use of the OT at these points not only affirms the divinity of the Son but speaks to the soteriological significance of the exaltation of the Son of God, as God.

In Chapter 3, I outline how Heb 3:3, 4 often functioned in earlier writers as a prooftext for Christ's divinity, but has tended to be dismantled or disregarded as such in modern scholarship.[181] I argue that the text does form part of the witness to the divinity of the Son in Hebrews, by identifying Jesus as the God who builds the final house of his people, exercising a final creative power that alone belongs to the Creator God.

Chapter 4 continues the focus on exegetical detail, but with an eye to broader sections of Hebrews. I briefly survey debate over how the "indestructible life" of Jesus in 7:16 is to be handled in relation to the divinity or humanity of Christ. I argue that both aspects must be kept in mind in order to form a correct understanding of the text, and that often false choices between the two have led to unstable readings. Further, that within this dual focus on Christ's humanity and divinity, the divine nature of the Son plays a foundational role in "the indestructible life" which qualifies the Son for his High Priestly ministry.

Chapters 5 and 6 move towards more synthetic treatment of two ideas in Hebrews, both of which, I argue, reinforce Christ's divinity. Chapter 5 explores the largely neglected connection of the Son's divinity to the covenants in Hebrews. I argue that Hebrews' understanding of the oath-bound character of God's promises clarifies the Son's central role in establishing the New Covenant as a divine one, in that the Son's action as covenant surety is the properly divine fulfilment of God's self-binding oath

---

Luz's commentaries on Matthew (Ulrich Luz, *Das Evangelium Nach Matthäus*, EKK 1 (4 vols.; Neukirchen-Vluyn: Neukirchner Verlag., 1985–2002) and see, in particular, his comments on his own methodology in Ulrich Luz, *Matthew 1–7*, Hermeneia (Minneapolis, MN: Fortress Press, 2007), 60–7), and at a smaller scale, Anthony Thiselton's essay on the Spirit, "Reception History or *Wirkungsgeschichte*? 'The Holy Spirit in 1 Corinthians: Exegesis and Reception-History in the Patristic Era,'" in Anthony Thiselton, *Thiselton on Hermeneutics: Collected Works with New Essays* (Grand Rapids, MI: Eerdmans, 2006), 288–304. In particular, the methodology of the latter, though articulated in terms of *Wirkungsgeschichte*, approaches more an act of theological retrieval, in which past modes of theological exegesis are brought to bear on contemporary exegetical debate as a generative resource. On the contemporary role of reception history and *Wirkungsgeschichte* in biblical studies, see Robert Evans, *Reception History, Tradition and Biblical Interpretation*, LNTS 510 (London: Bloomsbury, 2014); Emma England and William John Lyons, eds., *Reception History and Biblical Studies: Theory and Practice*, OTS 615 (London: Bloomsbury T&T Clark, 2015). On theologies of retrieval see John Webster, "Theologies of Retrieval," in *The Oxford Handbook of Systematic Theology*, ed. John Webster, Kathryn Tanner and Iain R. Torrance (Oxford: Oxford University Press, 2009), 583–99.

[181] With some notable exceptions for which see Chapter 3.

in the promises to Abraham. Chapter 6 seeks to resolve issues around the central concept of Christ as Son, which have often been controverted in supporting or denying the Son's divinity in Hebrews. I argue that the Sonship which is basic to the Christ's identity is one with pretemporal origins that depict him as divine, and yet this must be understood alongside two other sonships, human and Davidic, through which it is displayed. I suggest it is within this framework that appeal to classic prooftexts to the Son as God's radiance (1:3), or the Son as himself the enthroned "God" (1:8), make most sense, and that, though the descriptions may involve humanity in a secondary way, they ultimately portray a Son who is far more than only human.

In these chapters, then, I hope to demonstrate that much earlier scholarship, along with the bulk of readers from earlier centuries, has been correct to see Hebrews as a rich witness to the identity of the Son as God. But, moreover I hope to suggest that this witness is not limited only to the earliest verses of the Letter, but is a pervasive aspect of its thought, and indeed theologically salient to the reading of the Epistle to the Hebrews as a whole and its theological thought.

2

The Son as divine eschatological saviour (1:6, 10–12)

2.0 Introduction

The opening verses of Hebrews begin with the fact of God's latter-day speech: "having spoken in the past … God has spoken at the end of these days in a Son" (1:1).[1] This revelation of the Son then becomes the principal doctrinal aspect of what the Pastor wishes to convey to his hearers, one aimed at supporting the repeated calls to renewed and enduring faith and faithfulness in response to his last days' speech.[2] The ensuing description of the Son in 1:1–4 consists in some of the New Testament's most exalted prose, portraying him and his role as one spanning the whole work of God, protological to eschatological, binding the Son to God's action in history and identifying him with the very effulgence of his own glory and substance.[3]

Just as the climax of God's speech is eschatological, so the description of the Son here is similarly focused on end-time achievement, in his making purification for sin and consequent heavenly session.[4] The immediate movement to the catena of 1:5 relies on the continuity of God's speech, first in the prophets, now in latter days, that was already established in 1:1.[5] Thus it is widely agreed that the catena expounds, by way of

---

[1] Cf. on the significance for God's speech in Hebrews Jonathan I. Griffiths, *Hebrews and Divine Speech*, LNTS 507 (London: Bloomsbury, 2015); David Wider, *Theozentrik und Bekenntnis: Untersuchungen zur Theologie des Redens Gottes im Hebräerbrief*, BZNW 87 (Berlin: Walter de Gruyter, 1997).
[2] On the integrations of expositional and hortatory sections of Hebrews, see Andrew T. Lincoln, *Hebrews: A Guide* (London: T&T Clark, 2006), 52–4; Barnabas Lindars, *The Theology of the Letter to the Hebrews* (Cambridge: Cambridge University Press, 1991), 27–9.
[3] "The rhetorical artistry of this exordium surpasses that of any other portion of the New Testament" (Attridge, *Hebrews*, 36). For discussion of the especially important language of 1:3 and its relation to the sonship concept in the Epistle, see Chapter 6 of the present work.
[4] Ibid., 39.
[5] Knut Backhaus, *Der Hebräerbrief: Übersetzt und erklärt von Knut Backhaus*, RNT 38 (Regensburg: Friedrich Pustet, 2009), 92; Albert Vanhoye, *Situation du Christ: Hébreux 1–2* (Paris: Cerf, 1969), 119. On the nature of continuity and discontinuity in Heb 1:1, 2 with a stress on the continuity of revelation, see Gene R. Smillie, "Contrast or Continuity in Hebrews 1.1–2?," *NTS* 51 (2005): 543–60. See also Attridge, *Hebrews*, 38.

Scriptural citation, the Son described in vv. 1–4 especially against the backdrop of his excellence above the angels.[6]

Considering the degree of agreement in modern scholarship on the matter thus far, it is rather surprising that the question of what catena contributes to the portrayal of Christ, and to the argument at hand, has been rather controverted.[7] At least some of this difficulty arises from the Pastor's succinct method of argument. Rather than expansively unpacking a single text, as he does later in the Epistle, at 1:5–6 he progresses through a chain of texts as if they were sufficient to make his argument for him, accompanied by little in the way of explanation.[8] Quite then how this chain of texts makes his point, and quite what point he is making, have occasioned some debate, within which two texts have proved especially difficult: 1:6 and 1:10–12. Both of these texts share a common trope, that of assigning to the Son OT texts which, in their original contexts, refer to God. Thus the debate surrounding them is significant to my investigation for several reasons.[9]

First, many interpreters have seen the assigning of these OT God texts to the Son as a significant part of the picture of the Son's divinity in the Epistle.[10] Some serious difficulties, though, have attended this view, both in discerning to which OT texts the Pastor is appealing and of understanding what has motivated the Pastor's OT selection of these texts.[11] This uncertainty concerning sources, along with a sense of the seeming arbitrariness of his selection, has left something of a question mark over whether we have rightly understood the Pastor at this point.[12]

Second, a consequence of the relative uncertainty surrounding this first position has led some to reread the significance of these texts in a way that removes their perceived support for the divinity of the Son in Hebrews. This alternative argument sees the catena as almost purely associated with the humanity of the Son in his exaltation,

---

[6] "The catena clearly performs the function of establishing, on scriptural grounds, the most significant elements of that schema as they are stated in the exordium" (Attridge, *Hebrews*, 53). See also Johnson, *Hebrews*, 74; Hans-Friedrich Weiss, *Der Brief an die Hebräer*, KEK (Gottingen: Vandenhoeck & Ruprecht, 1991), 159; Stephen Motyer, "The Psalm Quotations of Hebrews 1: A Hermeneutic-Free Zone?," *TynBul* 50 (1999): 6.

[7] See most recently Joshua W. Jipp, "The Son's Entrance into the Heavenly World: The Soteriological Necessity of the Scriptural Catena in Hebrews 1.5–14," *NTS* 56 (2010) Also Schenck, "Enthroned Son," 469, 470.

[8] "Il faut avouer que l'absence d'explications comporte aussi ses inconvénients, surtout pour le lecteur moderne!" (Vanhoye, *Situation*, 123).

[9] A natural corollary of the assigning of God texts to the Son in the catena is the giving of the divine name to the Son in the words of Ps 45:6, 7 in 1:8, 9. Because of the way in which the original Psalm is seemingly addressed to a human figure, the Israelite King, the issue is better handled within the discussion of the nature of sonship language in the Epistle, on which see Chapter 6 of the present work and especially Section 6.5. See also similar comments of C. F. D. Moule, *The Birth of the New Testament*, 2nd ed., BNTC (Companion Volume) (London: Black, 1966), 78.

[10] Gareth Lee Cockerill, "Hebrews 1:6: Source and Significance," *BBR* 9 (1999): 61; ibid., 112; Johnson, *Hebrews*, 78; Brooke Foss Westcott, *The Epistle to the Hebrews: The Greek Text with Notes and Essays*, 3rd ed. (London: Macmillan, 1906), 28; Ceslas Spicq, *L'Épitre aux Hébreux*, vol. 2 (Gabalda, 1953), 18, 20.

[11] E.g. Motyer, "Psalm Quotations," 6 terms the usage of OT in 1:6, 10–12 "the hardest cases" in analysing the Pastor's OT hermeneutic in the catena.

[12] See, in particular, the very similar challenges over the argumentative force of the quotations in relation to divinity by Compton, *Psalm 110*, 24 and Moule, *The Birth of the New Testament*, 78.

whether as representative human ruler[13] or as enthroned Davidic Messiah,[14] and sees appeal to divinity at this point as mistaken.

Third, in light of this debate, I believe a more robust handling of the texts can be offered which both demonstrates something of the underlying logic of the Pastor's OT hermeneutic, and not only supports the role of 1:6, 10–12 in portraying the Son as divine but also makes apparent certain key assumptions of the Pastor about the nature of the Son's advent. That is, his assigning of his particular OT texts to the Son not only suggests belief that the Son is divine but, in part, demonstrates why he sees this to be the case: in the Son the end-time work of God to save his people has become apparent, in such a way as to identify the Son as God.

With this in mind, the current chapter sets out to investigate the role of 1:6 and 1:10–12 in the catena of Heb 1, not simply because of the way in which they call the Son God but because of the way in which they hint at wider hermeneutical presuppositions at work in the Pastor's thinking, namely, that the Pastor identifies the Son with the God of the Old Testament on the basis of his personally accomplishing the promised end-time work of God in redeeming the people of God.[15] The chapter will pursue this argument through three sections. First, by considering explanations of why the Pastor has selected these texts to function within the catena. Second, by considering the two OT citations, in their original contexts and in their appropriation in Hebrews. Third, and finally, a comparison of the two texts together, seeking to identify common threads in them in relation to the identity of God and his end-time action in the Son.

2.1 Accounting for the role of Ps 102 and Deut 32 in the catena

In surveying how previous interpreters have sought to explain the use of these two citations in the catena, we must first recognize that the significance given to these verses has varied in connection with an overall reading of Heb 1 and 2 and its flow of argument. Those who have argued that the theme of human exaltation binds the two chapters together have tended to downplay reference to the deity of Christ in Heb 1 and these verses have been relatively neglected in such readings.[16]

---

[13] Moffitt, *Atonement*, 49–53, 141, 148.

[14] Compton, *Psalm 110*, 19, 24.

[15] For the similar view of Wright in regard to NT Christology generally, see N. T. Wright, *Paul and the Faithfulness of God*, vol. 4. Parts III & IV, Christian Origins and the Question of God (Minneapolis, MN: Fortress Press, 2016), 655, 688; *Jesus and the Victory of God*, vol. 2, Christian Origins and the Question of God (London: SPCK, 2012), 615–24.

[16] Moffitt, *Atonement*, 45; Hurst, "Christology," 152–7; George Bradford Caird, "The Exegetical Method of the Epistle to the Hebrews," *CJT* 5 (1959): 49; "Son by Appointment," 75–7; Schenck, "Keeping His Appointment"; "Enthroned Son," 115–21. Though, as Hurst demonstrates, the strategy explored below of identifying the one worshipped in Deut 32:43 as corporate Israel lends itself well to arguments of human exaltation (Hurst, "Christology," 159). Those following this line of reasoning have not necessarily denied that the Son is both human and divine (cf. Moffitt, *Atonement*, 47n42) but rather that the freight of the catena is to be subsumed under the theme of human exaltation, mainly argued for because this is a status into which Christ enters (ibid., 48, 49). Indeed, certain aspects of the catena fit very well with such a reading, especially those that can be related to themes

In contrast, those who have seen the flow of thought of Heb 1 and 2 as a pattern of "exaltation/humiliation" tend to see a portrayal of the exalted Christ in divine terms and have investigated our two citations more thoroughly, identifying them as a means by which the Pastor signals the deity of Christ.[17] The Pastor has taken texts which seem originally to speak of God and given them to Christ.[18] However, exactly why these texts have been chosen has proved difficult to discern. Various proposals have been made to explain the function of these divine texts in the catena, which may be subsumed under the three main approaches.[19]

2.1.1 The citations as expressions of the Pastor's prior convictions

One way of handling the Pastor's selection of these two texts, and application to Christ, has been to argue that he is already convinced of Christ's divinity and that these citations are merely an expression of such a conviction without any argumentative

---

of a Davidic Kingship or elements that resonate with the description of human design and its telos in Christ, as outlined in the exposition of Ps 8 in 2:5–9. There is, undoubtedly, a definite and necessary human element to the Son of the catena. He is clearly a Davidic Son (1:1–4) and thus one with human, familiar origins, factors to which the Pastor is sensitive in his later argument (7:14). However, to limit the function of the catena solely to a portrayal of Christ as an exalted human figure seems to find its very weakness in how little attention its advocates give to the two citations which address Christ as God. Schenck, building on Caird's article ("Son by Appointment," 18–24), has perhaps developed the most consistent and sophisticated reading within this view in respect to the texts that seem to push beyond humanity in Christ's identity especially in regard to creation (Schenck, "Keeping His Appointment," 106). He argues that the language of the Son's involvement in creation (1:2, 3, 10–12) may be seen as testimony rather to the Son as the agent and locus of creation's fulfilment. However, the allusions to Wisdom in Heb 1 are scarcer than his argument seems to make them (Cockerill, *Hebrews*, 99) and to require that we see Hebrews straightforward statements about the Son as a person as, in fact, statements about a principal which come to fruition in him is simply too subtle. Cf., on this Bauckham, "Hebrews 1," 184, 185. Peeler also points out that the role of speech between God and the Son makes such a view (similarly represented by Dunn) altogether unlikely: "the dialogue captured in the citations … call into question Dunn's charges of the 'impersonal tone' of this passage, and decrease the likelihood that God is conversing with an aspect of himself" (Peeler, *My Son*, 49 citing Dunn, *Christology*, 55). The foregoing views share in common a tendency that having identified human elements in the catena, and in particular human trajectories in the Davidic texts cited in support of Christ's ascendancy above angels, they seem to unduly limit the fulfilment of such texts to the shape of the types themselves, rather than entertaining the possibility that the fulfilment of a type may move beyond the horizon of the initial text; the human element of the catena is a sine qua non of its fulfilling figure, but not necessarily an exhaustive description of him.

[17] Attridge, *Hebrews*, 54; on patterns of reading the relation of Heb 1 and 2 especially in regard to the Son's humanity see Moffitt, *Atonement*, 52n59, 59n29.

[18] Herbert W. Bateman, *Early Jewish Hermeneutics and Hebrews 1:5–13: The Impact of Early Jewish Exegesis on the Interpretation of a Significant New Testament Passage*, American University Studies, 7. Theology and Religion (New York: Peter Lang, 1997), 222; David Arthur DeSilva, *Perseverance in Gratitude: A Socio-Rhetorical Commentary on the Epistle "to the Hebrews"* (Grand Rapids, MI: Eerdmans, 2000), 97. For a better manner of articulating this appropriation of the text to the Son see the comments below.

[19] A good number of the hermeneutical options broadly proposed for Hebrew's use of the OT as a whole can be seen to have come into play in 1:6 alone. See the helpful taxonomy of views put forward by Guthrie ("Hebrews' Use of the Old Testament: Recent Trends in Research," *CurBS* 1 (2003): 284–90) and that of Motyer, "Psalm Quotations," 7–22.

reason for their selection.[20] Hermeneutically, this may be evaluated as a removal from,[21] or relegation, of context,[22] or a perception of a deeper meaning revealed by the advent of Christ, one not bound by the original context.[23] The broadest version of this position is that held by Ellingworth who writes,

> The author's approach to the OT may be summarized as follows: Christ, by whom God has now spoken his final word (1:1f.), was alive and active in creation (1:2) and throughout Israel's history. Any part of the OT may thus in principle be understood as speaking about Christ, or as spoken to or by him.[24]

This line of interpretation may be thought of as narrowly circular: the Pastor is convinced that Christ is God; these texts cited speak of God's actions, and so may be straightforwardly given to Christ in citation.[25]

2.1.2 Citation of texts on the basis of "multiple persons" perceived in the original

Another trajectory of reading, shaped by a sense that the Pastor's use of Scriptural citation is normally argumentative, has searched for some feature of the texts which might explain the Pastor's use in relation to the Son. It is noted that such texts were not, as far as we are aware, read messianically in the first century, but that the Pastor has discerned something in them which points to Christ's supremacy above the angels, especially his divinity.[26] The main motivation proposed for the use of these two texts has interestingly centred around the same feature: the possibility of finding referents in the original OT texts, which seem to distantiate God from another figure and ascribe to this second figure either the worship of God or address as God. I will now turn to

---

[20] Cockerill, "Source," 61, 112. See also the statements marshalled by Caird which represent a very low view of the Pastor's exegetical methods (Caird, "Exegetical Method," 44). Similar is the reasoning of Hofmann, noted by Delitzsch, that the Pastor's use of Ps 102 "is not cited to prove from Scripture what Scripture says of Jesus; but it only serves … to express in Scripture's language … the author's own faith concerning the Lord Jesus, and assumed by him as existing in the minds of his readers" (Johann C. K. Hofmann, *Der Schriftbeweis: ein theologischer Versuch*, vol. 2 (CH Beck, 1860) cited in Franz Delitzsch, *Commentary on the Epistle to the Hebrews*, vol. 1 (T&T Clark, 1874), 82, 83). Cf. also John Owen's interaction with Socinian objections in *An Exposition of the Epistle to the Hebrews*, ed. W. H. Goold, vol. 2 (Grand Rapids, MI: Baker Book House, 1980), 198–9.
[21] Attridge, *Hebrews*, 57; Hugh Montefiore, *A Commentary on the Epistle to the Hebrews*, HNTC (New York: Harper & Row, 1964), 43.
[22] Rascher, *Schriftauslegung*, 33, 52.
[23] Spicq, *Hébreux*, 2. Such a position is often associated with those holding a *sensus plenior* position and tends to be represented by Catholic scholars (Guthrie, "Hebrews' Use," 284).
[24] Ellingworth, *Hebrews*, 41, 42. Such a view is remarkably similar to that of Vaihinger, relayed by Delitzsch, who argues that the Pastor "may have regarded all Old Testament passages in which Jehovah (the Lord) is spoken of as requiring or admitting immediate application to Christ" (Delitzsch, *Hebrews*, 1, 71). Cf. Ellingworth, *Hebrews*, 119.
[25] Perhaps the predominant argument against such a view would be that it could only result in an absolute confusion of God and the Son, something which clearly did not come about among early Christians, so Vanhoye, *Situation*, 166.
[26] Attridge, *Hebrews*, 50; Spicq, *Hébreux*, 2, 14.

outlining how this has been worked out for each of our two texts and a discussion of the weaknesses of such a proposal.

2.1.2.1 *The possibility of multiple persons in Deut 32:43*

The issue of what is motivating the Pastor to cite his Old Testament source in Heb 1:6 is of course inextricably linked to which text he is citing. However, the majority of commentators have taken Deut 32:43 as a more likely source for the citation and so we explore here only those commenting on Deut 32:43.[27]

Within the context of Hebrews, it seems that the Pastor intends the αὐτῷ of the citation to be taken as a reference to Christ, and thus worship is ascribed to him at the command of God. Consequently, interpreters have sought a basis for this reading and have seen the Pastor as pursuing the following argument: Deuteronomy speaks of God commanding angels to worship another figure, one unidentified in the original citation, but identified as Christ by the Pastor. Such a position then seeks to demonstrate that there is a basis for the Pastor's reading, though different methods have been employed to make this move. Glasson, for example, has argued that the syntax of Deut 32:43 demands a distantiation between God who gives the command and the one referred to by the pronoun, the syntax opening up a "theological space" for multiple agents.[28]

A more common approach has been to align the worship with an embodiment of Israel, thus seeking to align this corporate firstborn with the quotative frame employed by Hebrews.[29] The most convincing exposition of this latter view is, in my opinion, Andriessen's, who relates this idea of the bringing of the firstborn into the world and his worship to the entrance of Israel into Canaan envisioned in Deuteronomy.[30] He draws on a pattern of promised reverence to Israel as Jacob's sons to argue that the Song in Deut 32 is claiming that this worship will be given by the nations and angelic beings to Israel at their entrance into the promised land.[31] He thus argues that the Pastor has drawn on a typological line of firstborn worship which finds its fulfilment in Christ as one going into a new and heavenly οἰκουμένη.[32]

---

[27] For a defence of Deut 32:43 as the source of the quotation, see Section 2.2.1.1.
[28] T. F. Glasson, "'Plurality of Divine Persons' and the Quotations in Hebrews I. 6ff," *NTS* 12 (1966): 271. Glasson suggests that this is the way that Justin is reading Deut 32:43 and adducing it as part of his argument for a plurality of persons in the godhead. However, at this point in the *Dialogue* (Justin, *Dial.*, 130), Justin is actually returning to his prior line of argument concerning the OT's promise of the inclusion of the Gentiles, having, to his mind, settled the issue of Christ's deity (Justin Martyr, *The Fathers of the Church*, trans. Thomas B. Falls, vol. 6 (Christian Heritage, 1949), 340). Thus it is not clear that Glasson's argument, that there is post-apostolic evidence for a tradition of reading multiple persons in Deut 32:43, remains valid.
[29] With regard to the use of πρωτότοκος in 1:6, Andriessen states, "c'est l'entrée triomphale dans la terre promise, qui a suggéré ce titre … à l'auteur" ("La Teneur Judéo-Chrétienne de He 1:6 et 2:14b–3:2," *NovT* 18 (1976): 298).
[30] Ibid., 295–8, 300–2. Cf. also Moffitt's comments on Andriessen's views and the similar view of Schierse (*Atonement*, 65–8).
[31] Andriessen, "Teneur," 302, 303.
[32] This line of argument is essentially that of Bruce, though with further dependence on *The Life of Adam and Eve*, 13–14 (Bruce, *Hebrews*, 57).

However, it seems to me that none of these arguments can fully sustain the necessary multiple referents to God and another figure in Deut 32, for the following reasons.

First, because of the issue of syntax. Though the pronoun in Deut 32:43 precedes the proper noun, it seems unlikely that this would have led the Pastor to view the pronoun as referring to another figure. The most natural referent of the pronoun is either anaphorically to the principal subject of the preceding verses, namely God, or kataphorically to God in the following phrase πάντες ἄγγελοι θεοῦ. Glasson seems to simply assume that a pronoun cannot function kataphorically, or that the Pastor could not have seen it as such, without much argument in support.[33] Further, the inversion of what might be the expected arguments in Greek is the result of the calquing of the poetic Hebrew syntax of Deuteronomy and its defamiliarizing word order.[34] The Pastor would have been very familiar with this aspect of Septuagintal Greek, widespread as it is in the Greek Psalter, and it seems unlikely he would attribute such significance to a device.[35]

Second, for Andriessen's interpretation to hold, we must see a reference to corporate Israel in the third person pronoun. However, the wider context tells against separating the pronoun from a reference to God in the Song. Though references to the people of God in the Song move between plural and single,[36] when a pronoun is used for the people without a clear antecedent noun the pronoun is consistently plural;[37] it would seem rather jarring and unexpected to refer to the people via a singular pronoun at this point. Further, and most damaging to an idea of multiple persons, the command for worship in the text arises from YHWH's actions to overturn the faithlessness of Israel, forging the connection that he, as the one who has acted rather than any other god, ought to be worshipped.[38] The attempt to see Israel as a fitting object of worship seems without foundation in the narrative of the Song.[39]

Third, though the typological trajectory seems initially attractive it contains elements, as Delitzsch notes, that seem "too farfetched."[40] That is, that neither the tone of the Song nor the natural affinity of the πρωτότοκος language fit with the proposed typological

---

[33] Glasson, "Plurality," 271.
[34] Lim describes it as "a style of translation that is a virtual tracing of the original source text." Timothy H. Lim, "Deuteronomy in the Judaism of the Second Temple Period," in *Deuteronomy in the New Testament: The New Testament and the Scriptures of Israel* (London: T&T Clark, 2007), 19. On defamiliarization in Hebrew poetic syntax see Michael Patrick O'Connor, *Hebrew Verse Structure* (Winona Lake, IN: Eisenbrauns, 1997) and Nicholas P. Lunn, *Word-Order Variation in Biblical Hebrew Poetry: Differentiating Pragmatics and Poetics* (Carlisle: Paternoster Press, 2006).
[35] On literalism in OG Psalms, see Staffan Olofsson, *As a Deer Longs for Flowing Streams: A Study of the Septuagint Version of Psalm 42-43 in Its Relation to the Hebrew Text*, DSI 1 (Göttingen: Vandenhoeck & Ruprecht, 2011), 18-20. On the preservation of Hebrew word order in the Greek Psalter see Staffan Olofsson, "Studying the Word Order of the Septuagint. Questions and Possibilities," *SJOT* 10 (1996): 217-37.
[36] 32:5a (pl.), 5b (sg.), 6a (pl.), 6b (sg.), 7a (pl.), 7c (sg.) etc.
[37] 32:11, 12, 17, 20, 21, 23-26, 28, 30, 31, 37, 38.
[38] Vanhoye, *Situation*, 164.
[39] This may well have been the "larger context" mentioned by Hurst when, in reference to reading Deut 32:43 as directing worship to corporate Israel, he writes, "This is the way I read the text until George Caird pointed out the difficulty of such an interpretation in the light of the larger context of Deut 32" ("Christology," 159n128).
[40] Delitzsch, *Hebrews*, 1, 70.

trajectory argued. For this typological argument to work the timing of worship in the Song ought to be rendered at the time of entrance into Canaan. In contrast, the Song's view of coming action "takes its stand in the far future,"[41] beyond the initial entrance. It also requires that the primary resonance of the πρωτότοκος language of the citational frame be that of Israel as a corporate firstborn. However, following the quotations of Ps 2:7 and 2 Sam 7:14 in 1:5 the scriptural environment would lead to much greater affinity with David as firstborn and an allusion to Ps 89(88):28.[42]

Fourth, Andriessen, in arguing his view, concedes that it does not cohere well with the Septuagintal text of Deuteronomy as it stands.[43] He must posit, with van der Floeg,[44] a textual tradition of the Song, available to the Pastor, in which Israel was clearly worshipped, but "dont les scruples juifs ont plus tard détourné le sens pour référer la *proskunèse* à Dieu."[45] Not only does this represent an argument unsupported by any textual witness, it is contraindicated by Hebrew texts we possess.[46] The argument is, moreover, difficult to resolve with the logic of Andriessen's own support for it: he argues, convincingly, that prostration to Israel is an established theme in the Pentateuch, which is alluded to at this point in the Song of Moses;[47] why then, if found unsavoury by later readers, has it only been expunged at this point in the Septuagintal text?

These interpreters, who pursue a logic of multiple personalities at work in Deut 32:43, have rightly sought to find the kind of Scriptural method evident elsewhere in the Epistle and extend it to the Pastor's use of this verse, assuming that he saw something in Deut 32 that led him to connect its angelic worship to the Son. But the idea of multiple persons is difficult to defend from the text of Deut 32, and thus fails in explaining the Pastor's argumentative selection of that text.

2.1.2.2 *The possibility of multiple agents in Ps 102*

If the Deuteronomy citation has provided little for interpreters to work with in finding motivation for the Pastor's ascription of that text to Christ, the citation of Ps 102:26–28 in Heb 1:10–12 has perhaps provided even less. The Psalm seems clearly to be about YHWH as Creator, such that it is difficult to see how a second figure might be found in the text.

However, one feature of the LXX text has seemed to provide a possibility: a difference in reading of the consonantal text between the MT and the LXX. Both seem to follow the same consonantal Vorlage. However where the MT has at 102:24 "He

---

[41] Ibid.
[42] Lane, *Hebrews 1–8*, 26. The psalm has normally formed the first point of call for sourcing the πρωτότοκοςlanguage (Attridge, *Hebrews*, 56). On the affinity of 1:6a with the preceding quotations, see Weiss, *Hebräer*, 163 and Motyer, "Psalm Quotations," 16n45. *Pace* Andriessen, "Teneur," 298.
[43] Andriessen, "Teneur," 301, 302.
[44] J. S. van der Ploeg, "L'Exégèse de l'Ancien Testament dans l'Epitre aux Hébreux," *RB* 54 (1947): 201–3 cited in Andriessen, "Teneur," 302.
[45] Cf. Bruce, *Hebrews*, 57.
[46] 4QDeut^q. The LXX at this point might be spoken of as Qumranic with respect to its Vorlage and neither the LXX nor the Qumran MSS demonstrate any evidence for expunging a call to worship Israel in the text.
[47] Andriessen, "Teneur," 302, 303.

has oppressed in the way of his strength," the LXX has read ענה not as the Piel of ענה II, but as the Qal 3ms of ענה I "to answer," and thus, "he has answered in the way of his strength."[48] So Bacon argues the text opens up the idea of God answering another figure who is neither the psalmist nor YHWH. The Pastor has seen this "answering" as extending to vv. 26–28 (27–29) and as the address of God to another as the Creator Lord who founded the heavens and earth.[49] This would then furnish an argument for the Pastor's use of the quotation. As Bruce reasons:

> But to whom (a Christian reader of the Septuagint might well ask) could God … address as "Lord," as the maker of earth and heaven? Our author knows of one person only to whom such terms could be appropriate, and that is the Son of God.[50]

However, this suggestion seems to suffer from similar weaknesses to the reading of Deut 32:43 above. Bacon implicitly recognizes that the αὐτῷ opens up three characters within the Psalm but several factors suggest this need not result in Bacon's conclusion.[51] First, though the presence of a third referent alongside God and the psalmist seems to be required by the LXX rendering of v. 26 (27) it does not straightforwardly assign these three referents. It is more likely to see this line as spoken by a speaker external to the psalmist's perspective commenting on God's answer to the psalmist himself. After all, the entire Psalm is one of dialogue between the psalmist and God, in which the former, in his weakness and transience, cries out to the latter for aid. A response from God would most naturally be aimed at answering the prayer of the psalmist himself. Further, for someone as familiar with the Psalter and its style as the Pastor obviously is, such a shift of pronominal perspective would not seem unusual.[52]

More damaging to Bacon's suggestion is the distance of this "answering" from the citation itself. It is separated by a return to the psalmist's prayer to YHWH, marked by his ongoing contrast of his temporal frailty with YHWH's unassailable eternity (24b, 25), and even more damagingly would require YHWH to utter the plea of 24b (Τὴν ὀλιγότητα τῶν ἡμερῶν μου ἀνάγγειλόν μοι).[53] To attempt to dislocate the statement of vv. 26–28 from referring to the Lord to whom the psalmist is speaking destroys the flow and principal thought of the Psalm.[54]

---

[48] For a detailed comparison of the LXX and MT on Pss 102 (101), see Radu Gheorghita, *The Role of the Septuagint in Hebrews: An Investigation of Its Influence with Special Consideration to the Use of Hab 2:3–4 in Heb 10:37–38*, WUNT 2/160 (Tübingen: Mohr Siebeck, 2003), 60–1.
[49] Benjamin Wisner Bacon, "Heb I, 10—12 and the Septuagint Rendering of Ps 102, 23," *ZNW* 3 (1902): 282; similarly Bruce (*Hebrews*, 62) who is reliant on Bacon at this point. Others who cite this argument (whether reliant on Bacon or Glasson) are Gheorghita, *Role of the Septuagint*, 43; Lane, *Hebrews 1–8*, 30 and, with some reluctance it seems, Moule, *The Birth of the New Testament*, 77, 78. Atttridge demurs (*Hebrews*, 60n122).
[50] Bruce, *Hebrews*, 62, 63.
[51] This multiplicity of persons is, again, brought out more clearly by Glasson, "Plurality," 272.
[52] On pronoun shifts in Hebrew poetry and that of surrounding Semitic cultures, see G. Lloyd Carr, *The Song of Solomon: An Introduction and Commentary*, TOTC (Leicester: Inter-Varsity Press, 1984), 72.
[53] Motyer's comment that such an interpretation would be "far-fetched" is generous, though it is not clear how he surmounts it in his own reading (Motyer, "Psalm Quotations," 20n54).
[54] See the similar criticism of Schenck, "Keeping His Appointment," 104n133.

2.1.3 The Son as the fulfilment of YHWH's promised advent

The third proposed strategy for handling the role of the catena, evident in the commentaries of Westcott and Delitzsch, has tended to find the least support of the three in recent Hebrews scholarship.[55] This strategy proposes a broad concept of eschatological action as the motivating factor in the Pastor's quoting of our two verses. Westcott, in commenting on the Pastor's appeal to his citation, writes,

> The [use of the OT quotation] is to be explained by the general character of Deut xxxii. which gives a prophetic history of the Course of Israel, issuing in the final and decisive revelation of Jehovah in judgement. When this revelation is made all powers shall recognise His dominion, exercised, as the writer of the Epistle explains, through Christ. The coming of Christ is thus identified with the coming of Jehovah.[56]

Such a view is essentially also that of Delitzsch, which he articulates in handling the quotation of Ps 102. He considers other options but rejects them in favour of seeing the Pastor's connection as based on a "general" principle:

> that wherever the Old Testament speaks of a final and decisive advent and manifestation of Jehovah in the power and glory of the final judgement and salvation; wherever it speaks of a revelation of Jehovah which shall be the antitype and fulfilment of that typical one in the Mosaic time, of a self-presentation of Jehovah as manifested King over his own Kingdom, there Jehovah=Jesus Christ. … This principle … constitutes the innermost bond between the Two Testaments.[57]

Both Westcott and Delitzsch see the Pastor's application of YHWH texts to Christ on the basis of the fulfilment in Christ's own advent and work, of the eschatological promise of YHWH's coming and action to achieve his purposes in salvation and judgement.[58] However, such a position faces the obstacle, presented by Moule, that its method of connection is not sufficiently argumentative. As Moule objects,

---

[55] Westcott, *Hebrews*, 56; Franz Delitzsch, *Commentary on the Epistle to the Hebrews*, vol. 2 (T&T Clark, 1874), 72. Cockerill writes,

> Deuteronomy 32:43 calls on the angels to worship God because he has brought the salvation of his people to its conclusion. The pastor, however, is convinced that the exalted Son and "heir of all" (1:2) is the one through whom God has accomplished this salvation. Thus the angels are invited to worship him. Angelic homage betokens his identification with God (Cockerill, *Hebrews*, 108).

This seems to be a development from his 1999 article where such a concept is missing in his section on the "significance" of the citation's role.

[56] Westcott, *Hebrews*, 20.

[57] Delitzsch, *Hebrews*, 2, 72. For a more expanded explanation of his position see "Must We Follow the New Testament Interpretation of Old Testament Texts?," *Old Testament Student* 6 (1886): 77.

[58] At certain points Vanhoye's explanation of the application of Deut 32:43 to Christ strikes a similar note to Westcott and Delitzsch, identifying the assigning of this text to Christ on the basis of "l'accomplissement chrétien," but his main focus seems to be on the revelatory and hermeneutical role of the Spirit in bringing early Christians to the conviction that such texts were about Christ (Vanhoye, *Situation*, 164, 165). However, he comes a good deal closer to Westcott and Delitzsch in

[such a position] goes no way towards explaining how in an argument from scripture for the divinity of Christ a passage which an opponent would presumably have assumed to belong not to Messiah but to God could be used as proof of qualities claimed by the Christian apologist to belong to Christ.[59]

Whether because of Moule's comments or not, Delitzsch and Westcott's position has seemed to receive the least attention in recent handling of these more challenging aspects of the catena. It is, however, this third option which I will explore further below.

2.1.4 Seeking an argumentative logic for the "divine" citations

Before moving to explore this third option more fully, it is worth facing a methodological question raised by the preceding survey. If most proposals for a logic to the citations have been found wanting, should we not question our expectations about finding a discernible logic in the Pastor's deployment of these two citations.[60] Perhaps we are searching for a logic that is simply not there. This would essentially be to fall back to the first position, that of bare assertion. However, when discussing the Pastor's use of Old Testament texts we must bear in mind that the catena is not the sole example of his scriptural technique. It is on display elsewhere in the letter and we ought to allow his preoccupations and methods there to inform our investigation of the catena. Such a method is effectively that proposed by Caird, of beginning with what is clear in Hebrews and then moving to these less clear passages.[61] In doing so, it seems the following patterns emerge.

First, the Pastor is clearly aware of the prior speech of God, not as an assorted collection of proof texts but as a grand narrative.[62] Thus he is aware of the storyline in which biblical events exist and ordering of the texts he deploys within that storyline.[63]

Second, that far from using texts to simply express or assert his own position, he normally operates in an argumentative fashion.[64] He sees the very structure of God's

---

handling the quotation of Ps 102 in 1:8–10 where he ties the Pastor's attribution to Christ to his role in final judgement (ibid., 201, 202).

[59] Moule commenting on Westcott's views as cited above (Moule, *The Birth of the New Testament*, 78).
[60] Spicq, *Hébreux*, 2, 13.
[61] Caird, "Son by Appointment," 74 as noted by Hurst ("Christology," 151-4). Though Caird's movement is predominantly with regard to the nature of the Son the same movement is reflected in the backward direction of his argument with regard to handling the function of the OT quotations in Hebrews (Caird, "Exegetical Method," 47, 48). Perhaps the one caveat in this is that the catena does constitute a different form to the other "expositions" which represent argumentative developments of a single text (R. T. France, "The Writer of Hebrews as a Biblical Expositor," *TynBul* 47 (1996): 255; Rascher, *Schriftauslegung*, 53).
[62] Allen writes of the citations in Hebrews, that they "corporately reconstruct a familiar OT narrative that serves the author's hortatory purpose" (David M. Allen, *Deuteronomy and Exhortation in Hebrews: A Study in Narrative Re-Presentation*, WUNT 2/238 (Tübingen: Mohr Siebeck, 2008), 4).
[63] The issue of timing is often key to his arguments (2:8; 4:7, 8; 7:10). Cf. chapter 1 of Benjamin Sargent, *David Being a Prophet: The Contingency of Scripture Upon History in the New Testament*, BZNW 207 (Berlin: Walter de Gruyter 207, 2014). Also Cockerill, *Hebrews*, 56. On his clear knowledge of the surrounding storyline of his OT texts, particularly evident in his ability to cite and paraphrase, see Rascher, *Schriftauslegung*, 34, 35.
[64] France, "Hebrews as Expositor," 255, 272. Motyer points out that the Pastor's method here of simply "reporting" Scripture as his means of moving forward demonstrates that his "style of argument

revelation in the prophets as demonstrating and proving the points he is seeking to make to his audience. This is not surprising when we keep in mind his conviction that Scripture is the living and enduring Word of God that continues to speak beyond its original horizon and finds its fulfilment in Son-speech.[65]

Third, that with the above in mind, his narratively sensitive and argumentative use of Scripture tends to follow a certain pattern in its structure, one he believes emerges from Scripture itself. Namely, that prior revelation was inherently partial in manner and its fulfilment in Israel's history fell short of the self-binding promise of God. This fact for him suggests a necessary fuller horizon of fulfilment beyond that experienced by the people of God prior to the coming of Christ. So, for example, though God had designed humankind as those to whom the whole created order ought to be in submission (2:6–8a), that in fact "we do not now see all things in submission to him" (2:8b); that though God had instituted the Mosaic covenant and its necessary ally the Levitical priesthood (7:12), such an arrangement had proved unable to bring the required perfection (7:11, 19), the Mosaic covenant had been broken and another promised; that though God had held out the promise of rest ever since Creation (4:4–6), Joshua, in leading the people into the Land of promise, had not taken the people into that rest and there still remained a danger of falling short of it (4:8–11).[66] This repeated pattern, in which the OT matters are characterized by partiality, is not merely the Pastor's judgement on them, but one drawn from Scripture's own witness to these failures and partialities:[67] that Rest has not been fully entered is, according to the Pastor, simply evident in David's speaking in Ps 95 "a good deal of time later" (4:7), demonstrating that the Rest had not been entered; that the insufficiency of the Mosaic and Levitical systems is evident from God's speaking of a priesthood unconnected to Levi (7:13) and a new covenant, which immediately "ages" the Mosaic (8:13).

The result of the above is to suggest that the Pastor adduces Scripture in his argument both because it is the living Word of God, continuing to speak to his hearers (4:12–14), but also because the very structure of Scripture makes his argument for him. This is not surprising when one considers the Pastor's view of the relation of this Word to the Holy Spirit and his intention in demonstrating certain things through the words and institutions of God's prior speech.[68] To claim then, that in the catena the Pastor is simply expressing his opinions through the citation of Scripture selected in arbitrary fashion, runs against the grain of his use elsewhere in his sermon. Indeed interpreters usually avoid such a conclusion when explaining other texts in the catena,[69] and tending only to stumble over the two texts under

---

is not revelatory, but argumentative, appealing to evidence and reason" ("Psalm Quotations," 5). On the nature and necessity of argument in early Christianity over the OT as an interpreted document, see *The Birth of the New Testament*, 71–5, and Michael P. Knowles, "Scripture, History, Messiah: Scriptural Fulfilment and the Fullness of Time in Matthew's Gospel," in *Hearing the Old Testament in the New Testament*, ed. Stanley E. Porter (Grand Rapids, MI: Eerdmans, 2006), 59–82.

[65] Vanhoye, *Situation*, 123.
[66] Caird speaks of the stylistic feature of "an unfulfilled condition" which marks his arguments ("Exegetical Method," 48).
[67] Ibid., 47; Cockerill, *Hebrews*, 58.
[68] See, cf. 3:7; 9:8. France, "Hebrews as Expositor," 272.
[69] Guthrie, "Hebrews' Use," 288–9.

consideration.⁷⁰ It seems reasonable then to proceed with the assumption that the Pastor has indeed seen something which connects these OT texts to Christ, but to look for perhaps a slightly different kind of argumentative logic at work in them.

I will argue in the remainder of the chapter that indeed such a logic is at work in these two citations, argued in the position of Westcott and Delitzsch, notwithstanding the objections of Moule. This logic differs slightly from the Pastor's tendency elsewhere, pertaining not to a typology of human figures and earthly institutions, but rather what might be termed with Caird, the "unfulfilled condition"⁷¹ of God's own action. The work of Christ in salvation is being identified, via OT texts and their contexts, as a work that can only be properly spoken of as God's unique prerogative. The motivating argument is similarly circular in comparison to those who argue for mere assertion. It is, though, a wide circle rather than a narrow one, drawing in recognizable points of contact in the career of Christ. The Pastor's use of the two texts under question betrays a broad syllogism in the Pastor's thinking: the texts and contexts of Deut 32:43 and Ps 102(101): 25–27 evidence a certain work of God and a character to that work that is uniquely God's, in distinction to other parties; Christ has performed such a work; therefore Christ may be spoken of as the God in whom these texts find their fulfilment.

2.2 Considering the OT sources

I will now consider each of the original citations in their contexts and their appropriation by the Pastor to demonstrate that such a connection makes sense of his use of them and their function in his argument. In doing so I draw on the wider context of the citations, in their original OT contexts. Though one might well question in dealing with other NT authors,⁷² to what extent the writer draws on a quoted verse with a sense of the surrounding context, in the case of the Pastor this seems a relatively safe assumption for at least two reasons, one broad and one more narrow. Broadly, as we have already pointed out, the Pastor's OT hermeneutic operates not merely at the level of discrete texts, but frequently with a sense of the wider context of a text, and its place in a canonical storyline. More narrowly, in the case of Deuteronomy the Pastor demonstrates a wide knowledge of the book which has shaped his thought.⁷³ In the case of the Psalter, one may consider the way in which his reading of Ps 110 as whole, in particular the interaction of 110:1 with 110:4, has been of such significance for his view of the priesthood of Christ and the shape of the Epistle.⁷⁴

---

⁷⁰ Motyer, "Psalm Quotations," 18–19; France, "Hebrews as Expositor," 273, 274.
⁷¹ Caird, "Exegetical Method," 48.
⁷² See the representative debate between Hays and Porter over the role of metalepsis in NT citations of OT texts: Richard B. Hays, *Echoes of Scripture in the Letters of Paul* (New Haven, CT: Yale University Press, 1989); Stanley E. Porter, "The Use of the Old Testament in the New Testament: a Brief Comment on Method and Terminology," in *Early Christian Interpretation of the Scriptures of Israel: Investigations and Proposals*, ed. Craig A. Evans and James A. Sanders, JSNTSup 148 (Sheffield: Sheffield Academic Press, 1997), 79–97.
⁷³ On the pervasive role of citation and thematic correspondence between Hebrews and Deuteronomy see Allen, *Exhortation*, 44–154.
⁷⁴ On this consistent shaping of the Pastor's sermon through these key verses of Ps 110 see Compton, *Psalm 110*.

2.2.1 The Pastor's use of Deut 32:43

In moving to consider the Pastor's use of the Old Testament in 1:6 there are two important issues that must initially be addressed: first, that of the source of the Scripture quoted in 1:6b and, second, the meaning of the citational frame through which it is introduced.[75]

2.2.1.1 The source of the quotation

The question of the source of the scriptural quotation in 1:6 is perhaps the most fraught within studies of the Pastor's appropriation of OT texts.[76] In comparing the Pastor's text in 1:6b with potential OT sources there are three texts which have been noted as bearing a striking resemblance to it (Deut 32:43; Ps 96:7; Odes 2:43) which are displayed in the table that follows:[77]

Deut 32:43 Göttingen LXX	Ps 96:7 Göttingen LXX[78]	Odes 2:43 Göttingen LXX[79]
εὐφράνθητε, οὐρανοί, ἅμα αὐτῷ, **καὶ προσκυνησάτωσαν αὐτῷ πάντες υἱοὶ θεοῦ·** εὐφράνθητε, ἔθνη, μετὰ τοῦ λαοῦ αὐτοῦ, καὶ ἐνισχυσάτωσαν αὐτῷ πάντες ἄγγελοι θεοῦ· ὅτι τὸ αἷμα τῶν υἱῶν αὐτοῦ ἐκδικᾶται, καὶ ἐκδικήσει καὶ ἀνταποδώσει δίκην τοῖς ἐχθροῖς καὶ τοῖς μισοῦσιν ἀνταποδώσει, καὶ ἐκκαθαριεῖ κύριος τὴν γῆν τοῦ λαοῦ αὐτοῦ.	αἰσχυνθήτωσαν πάντες οἱ προσκυνοῦντες τοῖς γλυπτοῖς οἱ ἐγκαυχώμενοι ἐν τοῖς εἰδώλοις αὐτῶν· **προσκυνήσατε αὐτῷ, πάντες οἱ ἄγγελοι αὐτοῦ.**	εὐφράνθητε, οὐρανοί, ἅμα αὐτῷ, **καὶ προσκυνησάτωσαν αὐτῷ πάντες οἱ ἄγγελλοι θεοῦ·** εὐφράνθητε, ἔθνη, μετὰ τοῦ λαοῦ αὐτοῦ, καὶ ἐνισχυσάτωσαν αὐτῷ πάντες υἱοὶ θεοῦ· ὅτι τὸ αἷμα τῶν υἱῶν αὐτοῦ ἐκδικᾶται, καὶ ἐκδικήσει καὶ ἀνταποδώσει δίκην τοῖς ἐχθροῖς καὶ τοῖς μισοῦσιν ἀνταποδώσει, καὶ ἐκκαθαριεῖ κύριος τὴν γῆν τοῦ λαοῦ αὐτοῦ.

---

[75] The language of "source" and "significance" is Cockerill's ("Source," 51).

[76] Allen speaks of it as "the most contested in the whole letter" (Allen, *Exhortation*, 44).

[77] In making this kind of comparison we must bear in mind the presence of a "multiplicity of textual traditions" (Susan E. Docherty, *The Use of the Old Testament in Hebrews: A Case Study in Early Jewish Bible Interpretation*, WUNT 2/260 (Tübingen: Mohr Siebeck, 2009), 124) at play in the NT era, to which the NT itself serves as witness (Jennifer M. Dines and Michael A. Knibb, *The Septuagint* (London: T&T Clark, 2004), 142).

[78] A. Rahlfs, ed. *Psalmi Cum Odis*, vol. X, Septuagina: Societatis Scientiarum Gottingensis (Göttingen: Vanderhoeck and Ruprecht, 1931), 249. Rahlfs's critical apparatus notes a Lucianic reading for Ps 96:7 LXX which supports the final word in the stych as θεοῦ rather than αὐτοῦ, in essence closer in this respect to the wording of the Odes text.

[79] Ibid., 347, 348.

However, to the consternation of interpreters, none of these three provides an exact match.[80] In the past some favour was given to Ps 96 as the source, perhaps implicitly because of the absence of this stych from the Song of Moses in the MT.[81] However the discovery of the DSS has removed such an objection, as among them there is a fragment of the Song which preserves a Hebrew text itself containing several stychs missing from the MT and represented in the LXX.[82] In comparing the LXX, the MT and the Qumranic Hebrew text, 4QDeut^q, the LXX can be seen to be a conflation of two different Greek versions of *Vorlagen* which are broadly similar to that represented by the MT and 4QDeut^q. Perhaps under the influence of the discovery, recent Hebrews research has tended to favour Deut 32:43 as the quotation's source, with few exceptions.[83] There are, without doubt, certain strong arguments that can be made for Ps 96 as a potential source;[84] however, I here side with the majority of recent commentators in seeing Deut 32:43 as the source of the Pastor's quotation for the following reasons:

First, the Pastor's own quotation begins with καί, which serves no discernible rhetorical function, and is only included because of its presence in his source text. Such a καί is present in Deut 32:43/Odes 2:43 LXX but absent from Ps 96:7 LXX.[85]

Second, that though the Pastor demonstrates a strong familiarity with the Psalms generally, his evident interest in the Song of Moses as a source of both quotation and allusion is also clear in the rest of the Epistle.[86]

Third, it seems difficult to understand why, if Ps 96:7 is the Pastor's source, he would alter the second person imperative of that text to a third person imperative as it is

---

[80] This perhaps ought to be less surprising than it has tended to be as current research is highlighting the pluriformity of Greek versions in the NT era. On the state of this question see Docherty, *Use of the Old Testament*, 122–32.

[81] Cockerill, *Hebrews*, 107n137; Gert J. Steyn, *A Quest for the Assumed LXX Vorlage of the Explicit Quotations in Hebrews*, FRLANT 235 (Göttingen: Vandenhoeck & Ruprecht, 2011), 62. Steyn raises the possibility of the scribal error of *homoteleuton* having removed the lines from the MT but this only makes sense if the MS originally resembled the LXX text which might explain the absence of the stych quoted by the Pastor but not that of the following stych (καὶ ἐνισχυσάτωσαν αὐτῷ πάντες ἄγγελοι θεοῦ) which is absent from both the MT and the Qumran text ("A Quest for the Vorlage of the 'Song of Moses' (Deut 32) Quotations in Hebrews," *Neotestamentica* 34 (2000): 165). On the assumption that the quotation is taken from Ps 97 (96):7 cf. Jean Calvin, *Commentaries on the Epistle of Paul the Apostle to the Hebrews* (Edinburgh: Calvin Translation Society, 1853), 43, also John Owen, *An Exposition of the Epistle to the Hebrews*, vol. 3 (Grand Rapids, MI: Baker Books, 1980), 156 and Aquinas.

[82] For the transcribed text see Eugene Ulrich, ed. *Qumran Cave 4: Genesis to Numbers*, vol. VII, DJD (Oxford: Clarendon Press, 1994), 135–42.

[83] Gheorghita, *Role of the Septuagint*, 40; Lane, *Hebrews 1–8*, 28; Bruce, *Hebrews*, 51; Peter Thomas O'Brien, *The Letter to the Hebrews*, Pillar New Testament Commentary (Grand Rapids, MI: Eerdmans, 2010), 70, 71. Though this is sometimes articulated as a preference for the parallel of Odes 2:43. Among those who still favour Ps 96 as the source are Motyer, "Psalm Quotations," 18, 19 and George H. Guthrie, *Hebrews*, NIVAC (Grand Rapids, MI: Zondervan, 1998), 67. There are some who argue for the quotation as a "Mischzitat" (Weiss, *Hebräer*, 161; also Moffitt, *Atonement*, 72n65). However, as Allen notes, the closeness of 4QDeut^q to the Pastor's quotation makes this hypothesis unnecessary (*Exhortation*, 47).

[84] Cf. Allen, *Exhortation*, 45 and Ellingworth, *Hebrews*, 119.

[85] Allen, *Exhortation*, 45. Allen also raises the objection that the καί might be subsumed under the quotative frame rather than be part of the quotation proper but this is not reflected in the Pastor's use of λέγει elsewhere in the Epistle (ibid.).

[86] On which see ibid., 44–91. Steyn lists quotations and allusions to the Song outside Hebrews in Steyn, *Quest for the Assumed LXX Vorlage*, 61.

found in Heb 1:6b, especially considering his conservative tendencies in representing his source texts.[87]

Fourth, that considering the importance of the key word ἄγγελος for the Pastor's argument, it is important that his source text be one in which this language is present. It seems difficult to imagine him quoting a text that did not contain it, thus weakening the role of the angels which is central to his purpose in the catena.[88] This recognition would seem to make Deut 32:43 LXX, which contains the phrase ἄγγελοι θεοῦ in a later stych but lacks it in the stych under consideration, a dubious choice for the source of the quotation.[89] However, Cockerill has demonstrated the plausibility that the text available to the Pastor is a Greek text that would provide exactly the wording of Deut 32:43 but with the necessary phrase (ἄγγελοι θεοῦ) present.[90] If Deut 32:43 LXX represents a conflation of a text type like that of the MT, and a Qumran text type *Vorlage*, whether conflated in Hebrew or in Greek,[91] we can infer what a Greek version of 4QDeut[q] would look like. Removing, with Cockerill,[92] the lines of the LXX that seem to be sourced from an MT-like text type, would leave:

εὐφράνθητε, οὐρανοί, ἅμα αὐτῷ,
καὶ προσκυνησάτωσαν αὐτῷ πάντες υἱοὶ θεοῦ·
ὅτι τὸ αἷμα τῶν υἱῶν αὐτοῦ ἐκδικᾶται,

Such proximity of the two uses of υἱός with clearly different referents would be rather confusing and suggests that the text would more likely read:[93]

εὐφράνθητε, οὐρανοί, ἅμα αὐτῷ,
καὶ προσκυνησάτωσαν αὐτῷ πάντες ἄγγελοι θεοῦ·
ὅτι τὸ αἷμα τῶν υἱῶν αὐτοῦ ἐκδικᾶται

This proposal demonstrates a good number of strengths: it matches the text which the Pastor is using and also contains a closeness of angel and son language that is very similar to the Pastor's thinking in 1:14. Its translational choice of taking the אלהים of 4QDeut[q] as ἄγγελοι is also the same as the probable translational technique of the

---

[87] *Pace* Gheorghita, *Role of the Septuagint*, 41 and Allen, *Exhortation*, 45. Docherty concludes her research on the Pastor's use of his sources with the conclusion that it "reverses the burden of proof, placing it on those who would argue *against* a variant reading and *for* a definite theologically-motivated alteration of a biblical source-text by the author of Hebrews" (*Use of the Old Testament*, 140).
[88] *Pace* Steyn's suggestion that the Pastor has "shifted" the language of sons to that of angels because of a desire to rebuke some kind of aberrant angelomorphic Christology (Steyn, "A Quest for the Vorlage of the 'Song of Moses' (Deut 32) Quotations in Hebrews," 270, 271). Koester similarly argues for the insertion of angel language as attributable to the Pastor rather than his text (*Hebrews*, 193).
[89] Allen, *Exhortation*, 47–51; Ellingworth, *Hebrews*, 119.
[90] Cockerill, *Hebrews*, 106.
[91] Skehan and Ulrich suggest this conflation occurred from Hebrew Vorlagen (Ulrich, *Qumran Cave 4: Genesis to Numbers*, 141); Cockerill suggests there are reasons for holding this occurred in conflating Greek versions (Cockerill, "Source," 57).
[92] Cockerill, *Hebrews*, 107, 108.
[93] That the LXX's referent to "sons" speaks of their blood makes it very unlikely, *pace* Allen, that these sons would be taken to refer to the angels of the previous stych, ibid., 107n140.

LXX Psalter when compared with the MT.⁹⁴ Though the book of Odes is regarded with some suspicion as a potential source for the Pastor's quotation,⁹⁵ its similarity to the reconstructed text proposed by Cockerill suggests it may well represent a later witness to just the kind of text type which constituted the Pastor's source of Deut 32:43.

2.2.1.2 The meaning of the frame

Having established the source of the citation in 1:6b it is important to discern the value of the Pastor's introduction to his OT text, though this has engendered an even larger field of debate. The principal question lies in ascertaining which event the Pastor is referring to as the Son's introduction into the οἰκουμένη.⁹⁶ The major options presented by interpreters, ancient and modern, have been Christ's baptism,⁹⁷ his incarnation,⁹⁸ his ascension and session,⁹⁹ or his Parousia.¹⁰⁰ The majority of recent interpreters have tended towards the penultimate option, and this position will be assumed in the discussion which follows for the following reasons:¹⁰¹

First, the construal of πάλιν does not prove determinative against any view. If construed as adverbial it is only damaging to the incarnation view. However, there are

---

⁹⁴ Ibid., 108n141; Cockerill, "Source," 55.
⁹⁵ Gheorghita advises caution in appealing to Odes as a witness to a potential source text because of "consideration[s] of origins, availability and probable Christian editing" (Gheorghita, *Role of the Septuagint*, 42).
⁹⁶ Ardel B. Caneday, "The Eschatological World Already Subjected to the Son: The Oikumenh of Hebrews 1.6 and the Son's Enthronement," in *A Cloud of Witnesses: The Theology of Hebrews in Its Ancient Contexts*, ed. Richard Bauckham et al., LNTS 387 (London: T&T Clark, 2008), 28. What Stolz has described as an "äusserst umstrittenes Rätsel" (Lukas Stolz, "Das Einführen des Erstgeborenen in die Oikumene (Hebr 1,6a)," *Bib* 95 (2014): 405). Debate includes the function of the πάλιν, whether the grammar of ὅταν + aorist subjunctive requires a certain temporal reference, what the predominant background to the term πρωτότοκος is and the reference of the term οἰκουμένη (Caneday, "Eschatological World," 29; Stolz, "Das Einführen," 405–14). As Moffit rightly notes, the final issue of the reference of οἰκουμένη is the most determinative for one's exegesis (*Atonement*, 57), especially when it is perceived that it cannot refer to anything other than the inhabited world of the earth. Cf. Attridge's comments (*Hebrews*, 56).
⁹⁷ Bateman, *Jewish Hermeneutics*, 222.
⁹⁸ Attridge, *Hebrews*, 56; Spicq, *Hébreux*, 2, 17; also Chrysostom, Alcuin, Athanasius, Aquinas, Luther.
⁹⁹ Ellingworth, *Hebrews*, 117, 118; Bruce, *Hebrews*, 58; Backhaus, *Hebräerbrief*, 96, 97; Erich Gräßer, *An die Hebräer*, vol. 1 (Zürich: Neukirchener Verlag, 1990), 78, 79; Weiss, *Hebräer*, 163; Albert Vanhoye, "L'oikoumene dans l'Épître aux Hébreux," *Bib* 45 (1964): 249; Andriessen, "Teneur," 299, 300; Jipp, "Son's Entrance," 558; Koester, *Hebrews*, 192, 193; Cockerill, *Hebrews*, 104, 105.
¹⁰⁰ Westcott, *Hebrews*, 22, 23; Delitzsch, *Hebrews*, 2, 67; also Jerome and Gregory of Nyssa. Stolz's article represents the most recent and significant defence of the Parousia view, Stolz, "Das Einführen," 414–22. However, his arguments, though well marshalled, are not as strong as he suggests. The grammar of ὅταν + aorist does not necessarily demand a future interpretation, as he suggests, but is, rather, dependent on the principle finite verb that follows to determine the tense reference (Cockerill, *Hebrews*, 104n123). That the usual meaning of οἰκουμένη is that of the cultivated world is beyond question, but that it must have that meaning here, and has not been theologically reoriented by the Pastor, is not established, and his related argument that Christ inherits in fulfilment of Adam's role in creation must mean an inheritance of this earth is effectively to beg the question. Discerning quite what is being inherited is in fact the very question of the relationship of the οἰκουμένη of 2:5 to that of 1:6. His failure to interact with Moffitt's substantial defence of the Ascension view further weakens his case.
¹⁰¹ For perhaps the most extensive and well-argued defence of the ascension view, see Moffitt, *Atonement*, 53–144.

good reasons for seeing the πάλιν as functioning as a quotative modifier,[102] as it does elsewhere in Hebrews.[103] The syntax of the verse certainly allows such a view[104] and finds a direct syntactical parallel in the opening phrase of Wis 14:1.[105] Thus, because the πάλιν is serving to introduce the quotation it plays little role in determining the sense of the citational frame.

Second, the context of the catena strongly suggests the ascension as the horizon of 1:6. The whole catena clearly moves within the orbit.[106] This is made particularly clear through connection to Ps 110:1 at either end of the catena, in 1:3 and 1:13, coherιvγ with the concept of enthronement, and is suggested by the quotations of Ps 2:7 and 2 Sam 7:14 in the preceding verse.[107] This thread of heavenly enthronement does not exhaust every aspect of the catena, but it seems to place the burden of proof on other views of the timing of 1:6.[108]

Third, though the incarnation view has received a good deal of support, particularly in ancient commentators but also in some modern,[109] it is difficult to see how the incarnation, pictured in 2:9 as debasement below angels, can be seen as the occasion at which angels are commanded to reverence the Son.[110] On the contrary, his assumption of a Name superior to theirs in his enthronement is far more coherent with the call for angelic worship reported in 1:6.

Fourth, the usual meaning of οἰκουμένη as "inhabited world" is not a hindrance to the interpretation of 1:6 as a reference to the ascension but part of the Pastor's theological interpretation of place. For him a fundamental shift has occurred in assigning the focus and weight of what constitutes "the inhabited world" to the heavenly sphere. As Backhaus notes,

> Die Himmelswelt, die Hebr auch sonst gern mit soziomorpher (der Gesellschaftswelt entlehnter) Begrifflichkeit umschreibt (vgl. bes. 2, 5), stellt also jene Oikumene, den einzig wirklich und dauerhaft bewohnbaren Weltkreis, dar, in die Christus nach seiner Heilstat als Weltenherrscher zurückkehrt.[111]

---

[102] On quotative frames see Steven E. Runge, *Discourse Grammar of the Greek New Testament: A Practical Introduction for Teaching and Exegesis*, Lexham Bible Reference Series (Peabody, MA: Hendrickson, 2010), 145–6; Cynthia L. Miller, *The Representation of Speech in Biblical Hebrew Narrative: A Linguistic Analysis*, Harvard Semitic Museum Publications (Atlanta, GA: Scholars Press, 1996), 2, 3.
[103] 2:13 (x2); 4:5; 10:30.
[104] Pace Westcott, *Hebrews*, 22.
[105] As Bruce (*Hebrews*, 56n71) notes against Westcott (Westcott, *Hebrews*, 22).
[106] The connotations of the language of πρωτότοκος "une désignation courante du Christ ressuscité" in the NT (Rom 8:29; Col 1:18; Rev 1:5) does much to integrate the frame with the orientation of the catena, though Spicq's comment on the former does not seem to lead him to the natural conclusion that the frame raises expectations of resurrection and ascension (*Hébreux*, 2, 18).
[107] Cf. Bauckham, "Hebrews 1," 169 and Kenneth L. Schenck, "The Worship of Jesus among Early Christians: The Evidence of Hebrews," in *Jesus and Paul*, ed. B.J. Oropeza, C. K. Robertson and Douglas C. Mohrmann, LNTS 514 (London: T&T Clark, 2009), 115–18.
[108] Docherty, *Use of the Old Testament*, 158; Koester, *Hebrews*, 192.
[109] Attridge, *Hebrews*, 56; Spicq, *Hébreux*, 2, 17. Among earlier commentators also Chrysostom, Alcuin, Athanasius, Aquinas, Luther.
[110] Stolz, "Das Einführen," 407; Gräßer, *Hebräer*, 1, 77; Ellingworth, *Hebrews*, 117.
[111] Backhaus, *Hebräerbrief*, 97.

This explains the Pastor's constant refrain to move towards or look to that place where Christ is enthroned as King and Priest.[112] Though the use of οἰκουμένη for the heavenly world might appear initially confusing to his hearers, what is hinted at through it is clarified in the more expansive reference of 2:5 and the development of the heavenly world of God's rest in 3:7–4:11.[113] This representation of the heavenly world as true οἰκουμένη also connects with the role of Christ as πρόδρομος and the consequent train of thought that where the Son as ultimate πρωτότοκος has first gone, so also will the many sons be led in due time.[114]

Fifth, that 1:14, the Pastor's movement from a comparison of the Son to the angels to that of the subservience of angels to believers as a whole, raises the question as to how their status as inheritors relates to the enthronement of Christ in the catena. The resumption of the train of thought in 2:5 glosses this as τὴν οἰκουμένην τὴν μέλλουσαν, thus suggesting the hearer is to consider how Christ's entrance into the οἰκουμένη in 1:6 enables the inheritance of many in 1:14. In drawing these threads together it makes most sense to see these as equivalent realities rather than two entirely different entities, disjoined by the qualification τὴν μέλλουσαν.[115] This issue has often been articulated as whether the οἰκουμένη of 1:6 and the οἰκουμένη of 2:5 have the same or different referents,[116] but it would be better to say that the two referents are equivalent, though also distinguishable. The phrase ἡ οἰκουμένη ἡ μέλλουσα makes clear that the state into which Christ has entered now is, *in nuce*, that final eschatological state to which his hearers ought to aspire; but, at the same time the participle reminds us that the relationship of the world to come to the present heavenly sphere includes one of progression and change, the shaking of the earth and heavens (12:26, 27).

With these points in mind, the view that the horizon of 1:6 is the event of Christ's entry into the heavenly world seems by far the most preferable, being consonant with the immediate context and wider perspective of the Epistle.

Having settled these questions of the source of the citation of 1:6b and the significance of the citational frame, we now may return to the question of the Pastor's motivation for appealing to Deut 32:43 and do so, first, by considering the broad context of Deuteronomy and the function of the verse in the Song of Moses in which it is located.[117]

---

[112] 3:1; 4:16; 10:22; 12:2.
[113] In this way the Pastor's use of οἰκουμένη is to be seen as equivalent "für ihn mit dem himmlischen Vaterland (11, 14–16), der zukünftigen Stadt (13, 14) und dem himmlischen Jerusalem (12, 22)" (Gräßer, *Hebräer*, 1, 79). Sim Adams, "The Cosmology of Hebrews," in *A Cloud of Witnesses: The Theology of Hebrews in Its Ancient Contexts*, ed. Richard Bauckham, Daniel Driver, Trevor Hart and Nathan MacDonald, LNTS 387 (London: T&T Clark, 2008), 134.
[114] 1:6; 2:10; 4:11; 12:23. See Gräßer's comments on the "Schicksalsverbundenheit" of the Son with the sons (Gräßer, *Hebräer*, 1, 78).
[115] *Pace* Attridge, *Hebrews*, 56. Attridge's criticisms of Vanhoye's desire to affirm οἰκουμένη as a *terminus technicus* are legitimate but they do not remove the potential eschatological freight of the unshakeability of the οἰκουμένη in several of the Psalms in the LXX and thus of providing a rationale for its use here as a term for the heavenly world (ibid., 56n66).
[116] Cf. Caneday, "Eschatological World," 29, 30; Moffitt's section heading "Hebrews 1:6 and 2:5: One Οἰκουμένη or Two?" represents this way of framing the question well (*Atonement*, 53).
[117] On the peculiar attraction of NT authors, not least Hebrews, to the Song of Moses see Gert J. Steyn, "Deuteronomy in Hebrews," in *Deuteronomy in the New Testament: The New Testament*

2.2.1.3 *The wider context of the Deuteronomy citation in Heb 1:6*

Deuteronomy finds the people of Israel standing on the doorstep of the promised Land, about to enter, and addressed by Moses in a précis and restatement of the Law.[118] This restatement of the Law is substantially similar to that given at Sinai, but it has been reshaped by the history of Israel during the wilderness years.[119] Central to the restatement is the necessity of Israel's obedience both to gain life and blessing in the Land and to avoid the curses that threaten their land tenure. This is developed against the background of Israel's demonstrable unfaithfulness both at Sinai and subsequently.[120] The verse cited by Hebrews comes from a well-defined part of the final section of Deuteronomy, the Song of Moses, which follows the historical setting (Heb 1–4), a narrative of the covenant at Horeb (Heb 5–11), a restatement of the Law (Heb 12–26) and a pronouncement of blessings and curses held over Israel subject to their conduct in the Land (Heb 27, 28).[121] The Song following these sections introduces a rather strange note in contrast to what has preceded. Moses has repeatedly warned the people of two possible paths which may define Israel's future: of obedience leading to life or of disobedience to death.[122] Yet the Song goes on to remove all doubt as to which path Israel will choose. The pattern of Israel's unfaithfulness, frequently contrasted with the YHWH's faithfulness to his people, will continue to work itself out in the Land with disastrous consequences. Though the Law as a code sets before Israel two ways of existence, the Song makes clear that the path ahead is a foregone conclusion. This may appear somewhat difficult to reconcile with the strong exhortation to choose a particular way in the preceding chapters, but which future Israel will choose has already been hinted at earlier in the book, both through the recounting of Israel's history of prior unfaithfulness (Deut 1:26–46; 4:21–24; 6:16; esp. 9:6–29) and because the cause of this unfaithfulness has not yet been removed: YHWH has not given Israel "a heart to know, eyes to see and ears to hear" (29:3 LXX).[123]

The Song thus will act as witness against Israel as it lives in the Land. In particular it will testify that the blame for failure lies with the people. However, though the Song exonerates YHWH against the people, and predicts certain judgement, it also moves beyond it to a hope founded on YHWH's own character, one of restoration. The verse cited by the Pastor in Hebrews is taken from this latter section of the Song in which divine compassion acts on the far side of Israel's disobedience and judgement.

---

and the Scriptures of Israel, LNTS (London: T&T Clark, 2007), 152. On interest in the Song in contemporary Judaism, see Lim, "Deuteronomy," 20 and especially David Lincicum, *Paul and the Early Jewish Encounter with Deuteronomy*, WUNT 284 (Tübingen: Mohr Siebeck, 2010), 61–116.

[118] Moshe Weinfeld, *Deuteronomy 1–11: A New Translation with Introduction and Commentary*, AB 5 (New York: Doubleday, 1991), 4.
[119] Gerhard von Rad, *Deuteronomy: A Commentary*, OTL (Philadelphia, PA: Westminster Press, 1966), 15–16.
[120] Jack R. Lundbom, *Deuteronomy: A Commentary* (Grand Rapids, MI: Eerdmans, 2013), 52–3.
[121] See the fuller outline of ibid., 74–5.
[122] Ibid., 53, 54.
[123] Thus the fulfilment of promise held out in the Song itself rests on the overturning of such barriers, so ibid., 818, 819.

2.2.1.4 The shape of the song

The Song consists of a testimony against Israel (32:1–4) which is at the same time a witness to the character and work of YHWH. This "Name" has been demonstrated in Israel's history to this point (32:3), marked by faithfulness and perfection in everything (32:4), in contrast to the people who have been faithless up to the point of entry.[124] YHWH has cared for Israel as a father (32:5, 6), taking them as his peculiar possession and providing for them kindly in the wilderness (32:10–14). This language of care and provision straddles both life before and within the Land and shares in common with the rest of the Song a tendency to make little distinction between life prior to the Land and life in it.[125] In this way the Song relativizes the idea of an imminent change of attitude for Israel. Israel's unfaithfulness is of one piece, straddling life on both sides of the Jordan. So, despite YHWH's fatherly care, Israel has not been bound to YHWH but has forsaken Him (32:15), turning aside to idols (32:15–18).[126] This has served as provocation to YHWH to destroy Israel in return (32:19–22), heaping judgements on them which are described in language reminiscent of the curses of preceding chapters (32:23–25; 28:20–57).[127] This judgement particularly employs the use of foreign nations as agents, even though they constitute YHWH's enemies (32:21, 27). Israel in its foolishness will fail to understand the significance of these judgements, not grasping that they are YHWH's own just judgements against Israel (32:28–32), rather than the ascendency of foreign gods over YHWH.[128] However, this judgement will not be unmitigated. YHWH will be restrained by his concern for his own Name and the competing concern that foreign nations boast in their own strength as the cause of Israel's downfall (32:26, 27).[129] This concern for his Name becomes realized through judgement and salvation so that he will be recognized as the only God. In contrast, the failure of Israel's idols to deliver them from their predicament will testify against their reality as gods (32:34–42).[130] YHWH will turn and rescue Israel (32:40–42), and in this

---

[124] On the faithlessness of Israel in the Song see von Rad, *Deuteronomy: A Commentary*, 197 and J. G. McConville, *Deuteronomy*, Apollos Old Testament Commentary 5 (Leicester: Apollos; InterVarsity Press, 2002), 453.

[125] This is reflected in the book as a whole in the ambiguity of its location. As Lim writes, "the 'final form' of Deuteronomy does not only reflect the perspective of one standing at the threshold of the Promised Land, but also the view of one who is already there" (Lim, "Deuteronomy," 9). Cf. the comments of Weinfeld on Deut 8:7–9 and 11:10–12 (*Deuteronomy 1–11*, 59).

[126] This theme is particularly strengthened in the Song by the themes of election and YHWH as Israel's "alone" God (Patrick W. Skehan, "The Structure of the Song of Moses in Deuteronomy (32:1–43)," in *A Song of Power and the Power of Song: Essays on the Book of Deuteronomy*, ed. Duane L. Christensen (Winona Lake, IN: Eisenbrauns, 1993), 158, 159; von Rad, *Deuteronomy: A Commentary*, 196, 197; Weinfeld, *Deuteronomy 1–11*, 8).

[127] McConville, *Deuteronomy*, 457.

[128] Thus the fault is with those who are "not his sons (anymore)" not YHWH (v. 5). Though both the MT and LXX are difficult at this point this seems to be the sense. Cf. Lundbom, *Deuteronomy: A Commentary* 874.

[129] This concern is brought about by the striking "deliberation in the heart of God" (von Rad, *Deuteronomy: A Commentary*, 198).

[130] Thus he vindicates his people and saves Israel, though a certain ambiguity has been introduced over quite who constitutes YHWH's people and his enemies in the Song (McConville, *Deuteronomy*, 459; Allen, *Exhortation*, 34).

way be seen as the "alone" God,[131] recognized as such by both friends and enemies. This recognition is taken up in the final verses of the Song—a call to rejoice in and praise YHWH for his judging and saving activity. The verse cited by the Pastor in Heb 1:6b is drawn from this section, a verse in which the exalted heavenly world is called upon to worship YHWH for his mighty acts as the only God and Saviour (32:43).

2.2.1.5 *The use of Deut 32:43 in Heb 1:6*

In exploring the way the Pastor appropriates Deut 32:43 there are four aspects of the quotation that need to be borne in mind: first, the narrow context of the Song in which the citation originally is found; second, the broader context of Deuteronomy, called to mind by the narrow citation;[132] third, the original sense of Deut 32:43 and its appropriated sense in Heb 1; and fourth, the added value of the citational frame in the catena of Heb 1.[133] A full consideration of the role of the citation in Heb 1:6 requires evaluation of each of these four aspects, and it is fair to say that those interpretations which have been proposed tend to give greater weight to one or more of these aspects in explaining the use of the citation.[134]

For most interpretations the citational frame is determinative for understanding the Pastor's use of Deuteronomy.[135] Christ is portrayed as the true firstborn, whether in relation to Israel or Davidic kingship, and the joining of the frame to the citation has the effect of requiring angelic worship at the moment of the firstborn's ascension. Under such a view the reason for appealing to the Deuteronomy citation is that it speaks of worship by angels and fits well with the idea of the land entrance of the firstborn, dependent on the wider storyline of Deuteronomy.[136] Other interpretations focus on the result of bringing the quotation into league with the citational frame and thus particularly on the worship of YHWH being given syntactically to Christ.[137]

These observations, in relation to the role of the citational frame, are helpful and go some way to explaining the use of Deut 32:43 here in Hebrews, but their weakness is that they do not give full weight to all four aspects outlined above nor, in particular, do they make good sense of the citation's location and function within the Song of Moses. Certainly there are issues of the broader resonances of Deuteronomy to be considered but the narrow citation does call to mind not only Deuteronomy in general but also this particular part.

It is helpful in pursuing an interpretation that brings all four aspects together to begin first with the narrow context of the Song of Moses. In Deut 32:43 praise is

---

[131] Κύριος μόνος (Deut 32:11).
[132] On the availability of Deuteronomy as a whole to the Pastor see Allen, *Exhortation*, 9 and Lim, "Deuteronomy," 6–26.
[133] See the similar outline of issues in Vanhoye, *Situation*, 124.
[134] These four aspects are often drawn together in questions like those of Bruce: "Two questions arise with regard to the use of this quotation. Since in its original setting it is Yahweh, the God of Israel, whom all angels are to worship, why is their worship here said to be paid to the Son? And why is it paid to him when God brings him into the world?" (Bruce, *Hebrews*, 57).
[135] Allen, *Exhortation*, 53.
[136] Andriessen, "Teneur," 295–300; Bruce, *Hebrews*, 57; Moffitt, *Atonement*, 65–8.
[137] E.g. Bateman, *Jewish Hermeneutics*, 222, 223.

being commanded of YHWH by angels on the basis of his work in redemption and judgement. In assigning this verse to the Son the Pastor is giving to him the praise of God for redemption achieved, praise assigned, via the frame, at the moment of his ascension into the heavenly οἰκουμένη.[138] To thus ascribe this verse as a reference to Christ is to pull with it the relationships between praise and action inherent in the Song: into the midst of Israel's unfaithfulness Jesus has come judging, saving and consequently receiving heavenly praise. This portrayal of the Son, against the backdrop of the Son of Moses, as One stepping into the unfaithfulness of Israel and overcoming it, places him squarely on God's side. He is the faithful covenant of God who alone can act to overturn Israel's faltering history and attachment to idols.[139] The citational frame aligns the moment of this resultant praise, and with it salvific action, to the moment of Christ's heavenly entrance and session.[140] Thus within the catena he is indeed supreme to angels as the One who has achieved Israel's salvation and restoration and thus been revealed as Israel's God. The Pastor in citing this text has carried through the narrow context of the Song of Moses into his argument, one characterized by the revelation of God in his works and the proper response of worship both from earth and heaven.[141]

Indeed, there are aspects of the Song that comport very well with this reading and suggest the Pastor has it in mind. The Song itself contains an element of comparison of YHWH both with angels and other powers (32:31).[142] YHWH is distinct within the Song from angels, not only as their Creator and the one who grants their authority, but in particular as the peculiar covenant God of Israel (32:8, 9).[143] Other nations were

---

[138] Cockerill, *Hebrews*, 108.
[139] Cf. Deut 32:34–6, 39.
[140] Rascher, *Schriftauslegung*, 52.
[141] It has been suggested that this act of reverence directed towards Jesus does not suggest his full divinity or equality with God or place him on the level with the one God (Schenck, "Worship of Jesus," 121) as the act of προσκύνησις may denote simply the honour due of one socially lower to one socially higher, without equating such action with cultic devotion or worship (Cf. Larry W. Hurtado, "The Binitarian Shape of Early Christian Worship," in *The Jewish Roots of Christological Monotheism: Papers from the St. Andrews Conference on the Historical Origins of the Worship of Jesus*, ed. Carey C. Newman, James R. Davila and Gladys S. Lewis, JSJSup 63 (Leiden: Brill, 1999), 189, 190 and *Lord Jesus Christ*, 38). Schenck seeks to strengthen such an objection by appealing to the identity of the Son as a royal figure in the catena, as expressed by the quotations of Ps 2:7 and 2 Sam 7:14. To read the προσκύνησις language in this light is to see "angels bow[ing] as servants before their king as God seats him on his new heavenly throne" (Schenck, "Worship of Jesus," 119, 121). Certainly, as has been noted, the language of προσκύνησις may signify a "range of reverential gestures" (Hurtado, *Lord Jesus Christ*, 38), but the import of the language, derived as it is from Deut 32, ought not to be missed. The worship being given to Jesus is that due to the One God at the climactic moment of his recognition against the false claims to divinity and cultic devotion engendered by Israel's idolatry. Allen raises this potential significance of the *Vorlage* of the quotation of 1:6 for the προσκύνησις language but in seeking to understand its significance is immediately led back into a discussion of motivation for assigning the text to Christ, and so misses the opportunity to explore ways in which the predominant themes of the Song of Moses connect to the work of Christ (David M. Allen, "Who, What and Why? The Worship of the Firstborn in Hebrews 1:6," in *Mark, Manuscripts, and Monotheism: Essays in Honor of Larry Hurtado*, ed. Chris Keith and Dieter T. Roth, LNTS 528 (London: T&T Clark, 2015), 172).
[142] Steyn notes the presence of angels in the Song of Moses as a point of similarity with Heb 1 but fails to note that the act of comparison is also shared between the two contexts, "Deuteronomy in Hebrews," 157.
[143] In connecting to this comparison with angels, Hebrews is connecting with a central vein in Deuteronomy which contrasts the nations as worshippers of powers and Israel's commanded

assigned angels as their overlords, but Israel's Lord was YHWH. Thus to compare Jesus with angels is to place him in YHWH's place.

In seeing this worship of Jesus as connected to the achievement of salvation, it might be argued that what the Pastor is asserting is merely a kind of functionally divine Christology, but one that falls short of making full identification of God with Jesus. However, if the Song is providing the Pastor with the framework in which he is ascribing worship to Jesus and assigning to him this angelic praise, it ought to shape our expectations of how salvific function and divinity work for the Pastor.[144] Jesus cannot be seen here merely as an agent of the divine, for the context of the Song itself both recognizes the inherent danger of agency and speaks of YHWH's action in a way that removes doubt as to who is at work.[145] In the context of the Song, YHWH's action to manifest himself is, in part, aimed at the removal of other agencies at work, whether false gods, Israel or their enemies, in order to quash boasting in their own achievements. YHWH in the Song acts apart from other players to be seen and known as Israel's "alone God." Indeed the recognition of YHWH as the "alone God" is contextually very strong—he must claim his own action not only without intermediaries but also against the false pretensions of other claimants to godhood.[146] This all contributes to the thrust of the broader Song which is brought into play by the Pastor's citation. What the citational frame adds is that this promised action of YHWH is accomplished through the enthronement of the firstborn Son in the heavenly world. Thus it aligns the timing and nature of the accomplishment of this promised redemption of Israel with the work of Christ, in his ascension into the heavenly world.

With the implications of the narrow context of the Song in mind one may also introduce the broader Deuteronomic context of Land entrance. Christ has indeed inaugurated a new Land entrance by entering into the heavenly οἰκουμένη, signalling in advance aspects of Heb 3 and 4. This is nascent in the Song of Moses itself. Mere entrance into Canaan will not change the state of Israel and thus is not the ultimate fulfilment of the promises to the patriarchs.[147] However, in suggesting that Christ's entrance into the heavenly οἰκουμένη "makes old" the previous entrance, the use of the concept relies typologically on the shape of the entrance into Canaan and suggests

---

allegiance to incomparable YHWH. On this see Skehan, "The Structure of the Song of Moses in Deuteronomy (32:1–43)," 158 and Weinfeld, *Deuteronomy 1–11*, 206 and their respective discussions of the connections between Deut 4:19, 20; 29:24, 25 and 32:8, 9. On the identification of YHWH with the "most high" of Deut 32:8, 9, see Richard Bauckham, "The "Most High God" and the Nature of Early Jewish Monotheism," in *Israel's God and Rebecca's Children: Christology and Community in Early Judaism and Christianity: Essays in Honor of Larry W. Hurtado and Alan F. Segal*, ed. David B. Capes, Larry W. Hurtado and Alan F. Segal (Waco, TX: Baylor University Press, 2007), 42–3, especially the appeal to Sir 17:17 ("He appointed a ruler for every nation, But Israel is the Lord's own portion").

[144] Bauckham, "Divinity of Jesus," 17, 18, and Section 1.2.

[145] The stress on "absolute monotheism" is seen as "characteristic of Deuteronomy" by many, e.g. Weinfeld, *Deuteronomy 1–11*, 8, 212 and von Rad, *Deuteronomy: A Commentary*, 198.

[146] Westcott writes that "both [possible sources of the quotation of 1:6] look forward to the time when the subordinate spiritual powers, idolized by the nations, shall recognize the absolute sovereignty of Jehovah" (Westcott, *Hebrews*, 20).

[147] This is thoroughly consonant with the Pastor's use of the Land imagery in his argument in 4:1–11. See Cockerill, *Hebrews*, 197.

we may understand the New in terms of the shape of the Old. This is particularly interesting when one considers the role of God vis-à-vis the land in Deuteronomy, a role in which God himself opened up the Land by going before the people into it.[148] The entrance under Joshua was foremost an entrance through the πρόδρομος YHWH. Thus the wider context of Deuteronomy also introduces the category of the Land opener as God himself, strengthening the resonance between the wider context of Deuteronomy and the citational frame of Heb 1:6.[149]

This proposal for the motivation of the Pastor in drawing Deut 32:43 into his argument seeks to bring the four aspects of the quotation together.[150] It also seeks to avoid two principal assumptions that are often made in handling the Pastor's quotation:

First, that the movement of associating Christ with Deut 32:43 is not an act of mere syntax, simply replacing one referent, God, with another, Christ.[151] It seems very unlikely to me that the Pastor would agree with such a way of framing his hermeneutics. Rather the career of Christ has unpacked a granularity to the end-time work of God spoken of in the Song,[152] revealing that words originally spoken by Moses are, in fact, the speech of God to His Son.[153] To speak of the attribution of the citation to Christ as an act of the Pastor is, again, to miss the point. The attribution is an act of God unveiling the inner relationship of God and the Son. This is the thrust of the whole catena, relaying not simply the Son's status but the unveiling of Scriptural texts as in fact the speech of God to the Son which describes their foundational relationship.[154] The Son's identity is uncovered in the Father's speech to him. So the revelation of reference to the Son in Deut 32:43 is not merely the Pastor's giving of praise to the Son, but God, speaking in the Song, assigning properly divine praise to the Son.[155] Though within the context of first-century Judaism the attributing of such praise to a

---

[148] κύριος ὁ θεὸς ὑμῶν ὁ προπορευόμενος πρὸ προσώπου ὑμῶν (Deut 1:30 LXX) also Deut 9:3; 20:4; 31:3, 6. Particularly interesting among them are two verses which are closely connected to other texts which the Pastor uses. So in Deut 9:3 LXX we read, ὁ θεός σου, οὗτος προπορεύεται πρὸ προσώπου σου· πῦρ καταναλίσκον ἐστίν· where the imagery and lexical choice are identical to 12:29 and 31:6. There the description of God as going before is connected to the promise οὐ μή σε ἀνῇ οὔτε μή σε ἐγκαταλίπῃ (Deut 31:6 LXX // Heb 13:5).

[149] See Cockerill, "Source," 63, who also raises the potential resonance between YHWH's action in cleansing the Land in Deut 32:43 and "the purifying work of the Son (1:3; 9:22, 23)" (ibid.).

[150] These aspects being: the narrow context of the Song in which the citation originally is found; the broader context of Deuteronomy which may be called to mind by the narrow citation; the original sense of Deut 32:43 and its appropriated sense in Heb 1; the added value of the citational frame which anchors the quotation within the catena of Heb 1. All of these have been touched on above in preparation for the move to synthesize them in explaining the Pastor's argument.

[151] O'Brien, *Hebrews*, 71n160; Attridge, *Hebrews*, 57.

[152] By granularity, I mean that what may be represented in a homogeneous and indistinguished way in the Song of Moses develops an internal structure to it in its achievement in the Son.

[153] On the predominance of speaking words in relation to the Pastor's use of Scripture, see Vanhoye, *Situation*, 159; Rascher, *Schriftauslegung*, 31–3.

[154] In other words it is not the Son's status *simpliciter* but the Son's status in relation to God and in distinction from angels. See especially Peeler, *My Son*, 28, 29 and Harold W. Attridge, "God in Hebrews," in *The Epistle to the Hebrews and Christian Theology*, ed. Richard Bauckham, Daniel Driver and Trevor Hart (Grand Rapids, MI: Eerdmans, 2009), 103–4, also Rascher, *Schriftauslegung*, 40, 75; Vanhoye, *Situation*, 121, 151; Kenneth L. Schenck, "'God Has Spoken': Hebrews' Theology of the Scriptures," in *The Epistle to the Hebrews and Christian Theology*, ed. Richard Bauckham, Daniel Driver and Trevor Hart (Grand Rapids, MI: Eerdmans, 2009), 325–6.

[155] Steyn, "Deuteronomy in Hebrews," 157.

figure other than God might raise the spectre of idolatry, it must be conceived by the Pastor as something else. For he has deliberately called on a text which has in view the exposure of false claimants to deity and the winning of Israel's singular devotion to the One God (Deut 32:38, 39).

The second tendency among interpreters is that of assuming that the citational frame and the quotation must basically bear the same meaning.[156] Thus the principal question becomes: how can Deut 32:43 be read as a statement about the entrance of a firstborn into the οἰκουμένη? As I have tried to demonstrate above the author is doing something more theologically generative.[157] He is bringing together the eschatological and redemptive work of YHWH prophesied in the Song, for which he is praised, with the achievement and exaltation of Christ to the right hand of God. In this way he is arguing that they are not equivalent in a barely semantic way but in an equivalence of eschatology and action.[158]

In suggesting this as the best understanding of the Pastor's use of Deut 32:43, I have developed a reading similar to Westcott and Delitzsch; it might be argued, then, that such a reading is still open to the dismissal of Moule cited before.[159] However, this is not the Achilles heel he suggests. Moule seems to find argumentatively convincing a use of Scripture in Hebrews that is often referred to as typological.[160] But the reading proposed above, of the fulfilment of divine action, may be stated in just such a typological fashion. Just as OT figures and institutions fell short of promise and required future fulfilment, so also YHWH's own action in the OT fell short of what had been promised. This falling short opens up a future in which YHWH acts to fill up what was expected. This, as elsewhere in the Epistle, does not arise from the Pastor's judgement on the OT, but from the promise of God's future work which is at the heart of a text like the Song of Moses. In such a text promised eschatological action marks out YHWH and yet, the Pastor is arguing by citation, such action has been performed by the Son through his induction into the heavenly οἰκουμένη.[161] Moule's objection

---

[156] See the quotation from Allen above.
[157] *Pace* Rascher, *Schriftauslegung*, 33. Cf. Steve Moyise, "Intertextuality and Historical Approaches to the Use of Scripture in the New Testament," in *Reading the Bible Intertextually*, ed. Richard B. Hays, Stefan Alkier and Leroy Andrew Huizenga (Waco, TX: Baylor University Press, 2009), 23–32. That there is a push and pull between the OT context and text and its appropriation in Hebrews is recognized by Gheorghita: "The Scriptures were not only read in light of the Christ-event, but the Christ event was read in light of the Scriptures. Although the Scriptures were clearly interpreted through the lens of the Christ-event, they also supplied the informative and theologically formative perspective from which the Christ-event had to be interpreted" (Gheorghita, *Role of the Septuagint*, 231).
[158] Cf. F. F. Bruce, *This Is That* (Carlisle: Paternoster, 1968).
[159] Moule, *The Birth of the New Testament*, 78. For the quotation, see Section 2.1.2. Thus Moule, aware of a position similar to what I am advocating, still points to "Bacon [as] … the only scholar who has attempted a thoroughgoing explanation" (ibid.).
[160] Ibid., 68, 70.
[161] Moule's position seems to suggest that the typological argument is not open to criticism, whereas an assertion that Christ has performed the works of YHWH is. However, each requires a movement at some point of saying, in Bruce's words, "this is that" (Bruce, *This Is That*, 1). To open up the necessity of a later Davidic King, or a further priestly order, is not the same as arguing that a particular figure fills that need. Thus to proclaim Christ as the one who fills up such categories always necessitates appeal to the ministry and actions of Christ as connecting with them and is indeed demonstrated in the shape of Christian preaching elsewhere in the New Testament.

does highlight that there is an implied premise at work in this argumentative use of Deut 32:43: that Christ has achieved that end-time work of redemption that properly belongs to YHWH. We will return to this premise below.

Having proposed a way of handling the Deut 32:43 reference in 1:6b in connection with the concept of promised divine action, we will now move to evaluate the Pastor's use of Ps 101:26, 27 to see whether a similar concept may be at work.

2.2.2 The wider context of Ps 101 LXX

Ps 101 LXX is superscripted as "the prayer of a poor one, when he is exhausted and pouring out this prayer before the Lord" and intertwines two horizons that reflect one another: the psalmist's own poor condition and need of salvation, the parallel state of Zion, and the concern of God's people for her necessary restoration.[162] In the face of both of these horizons, the Psalm is marked by a movement back and forth between the Lord as a transcendent and unchanging God, whose nature and resources stand in stark contrast to the impoverished state of the psalmist in his own condition, and that of the corporate posture of Israel.[163]

The structure of the Psalm reflects both the comparability of the psalmist and Israel's condition,[164] and the contrast between the psalmist/Israel's resources and the Lord's. This pattern can be seen in the grammatical persons of the Psalm, so that the movement of the structure from the psalmist (vv. 1–12), to Israel corporately (vv. 13–24a), and back to the psalmist (vv. 24b–29) is paralleled in the movement between the psalmist ("I") and the Lord ("You"), and is perhaps the main structuring device of the Psalm.

The first section marks out the psalmist's prayer beginning with his intense desire to be heard by the Lord and that he respond quickly (vv. 1–3).[165] The phrasing of this appeal already begins to reveal the desperate situation of the psalmist: his prayer is ἡ κραυγή μου (v. 2) and his day, one ἐν ᾗ ἂν ἡμέρᾳ θλίβωμαι (v. 3). The verses that follow expand on the straits in which the psalmist finds himself: his failing strength; his weakness both physical and emotional, and his sense of isolation. Important for our discussion is that the language of "day" used already in v. 3 as the time of the psalmist's difficulty and request to God becomes a major theme in describing the psalmist's own weakness, acting as an inclusio that binds vv. 1–12 together. His days are like smoke (v. 4) and like a shadow (v. 12).[166] Each of these comparisons is accompanied by another common psalmic image of grass which dries up or withers, as a metaphor of failing vigour.[167]

---

[162] James Luther Mays, *Psalms*, Interpretation, a Bible Commentary for Teaching and Preaching (Louisville, KY: John Knox Press, 1994), 323; Hans-Joachim Kraus, *Psalms 60–150: A Commentary* (Minneapolis, MN: Fortress Press, 1993), 284.
[163] Leslie C. Allen, *Psalms 101–150*, WBC 21 (Waco, TX: Word Books, 1983), 14; Mays, *Psalms*, 323.
[164] Kraus, *Psalms*, 286.
[165] Allen, *Psalms 101–150*, 14.
[166] Mays, *Psalms*, 324. Mays notes the significant parallels in this theme to Ps 90 (ibid.).
[167] Ps 37 (36):2; 103 (102):15.

Verse 13 acts as a transition from the psalmist's situation to the Lord. In contrast, He is one who "endures" and is eternal and unchanging.[168] This enduring nature is connected to the hopes of Zion, embodied in the affections of Israel for the city.[169] In vv. 14–24a this hope comes to fruition in the Lord's acting for Zion and its people to redeem them,[170] resulting in both the release of the "sons" of Zion, who are "bound" and "destined to die" (or even dead),[171] the gathering of the peoples and the universal subjections of all powers to YHWH. The timing of this divine action in the Psalm is mixed, spoken of as both future and past; this seems to be the result of a view, parallel to the prophets, that the hope of the Lord's action is so certain that it can be spoken of as already accomplished.[172] Within this context v. 24a, noted above as a point of difference with the MT,[173] would best be read as the answer of the Lord to the hopes of the people detailed in the action of God in the preceding verses.[174] The Lord has answered in his strength in coming to restore the hopeless fortune of his people and his chosen seat, Zion.

Verses 24b–29 repeat much of the foregoing contrast of the previous two sections, but this time returning to the psalmist's own individual perspective and repeating the movement from his nature and resources to the Lord's in briefer compass.[175] The psalmist, in his desperation, is still marked by "days" that are few and threaten to be cut off (vv. 24b, 25a). In contrast, the Lord endures, here denoted by reference to the Lord's "years."[176] The verses that immediately follow are those appropriated by the Pastor in his quotation, though there exists two frequently recognized differences from LXX texts, in which the Lord's enduring nature is brought out by comparison with his

---

[168] The use of temporal phrases is a strong aspect of the Lord's description in the Psalm: εἰς τὸν αἰῶνα (v. 12); εἰς γενεὰν καὶ γενεάν (v. 12); κατ' ἀρχὰς (v. 26); διαμενεῖς (v. 27); τὰ ἔτη σου οὐκ ἐκλείψουσιν (v. 28). The interesting exception to this is the description of the Lord as ὁ αὐτός (v. 28), which is contrasted with the preceding imagery of the garment-like world which ages and changes. Thus the sense here is of the Lord as unchanging and remaining "the same" or as he is, and demonstrates that categories of eternity, via a time reference, and unchangeability, via a state reference, are equivalent in the Lord's description. Because the Lord is eternal, he is always what and who he is.

[169] As Mays notes the psalmist assumes the strong connection between the affections of God's people as afflicted ones and that the "affliction of the lowly will be relieved in the renewal of Zion" (Mays, *Psalms*, 325).

[170] "A theology of Zion as the chosen 'city of God' is assumed" (ibid.).

[171] The perfect middle/passive participle of θανατόω is employed.

[172] S. R. Driver, *A Treatise on the Use of the Tenses in Hebrew and Some Other Syntactical Questions*, The Biblical Resource Series (Grand Rapids, MI: Eerdmans, 1998), §14. Whether or not this is a sufficient explanation of the *qatal* is another matter. See chapter 3 of M. F. Rogland, *Alleged Non-Past Uses of Qatal in Classical Hebrew* (Leiden: Van Gorcum, 2001), and also in particular Jan Joosten, *The Verbal System of Biblical Hebrew: A New Synthesis Elaborated on the Basis of Classical Prose* (Jerusalem: Simor, 2012) and John A. Cook, *Time and the Biblical Hebrew Verb: The Expression of Tense, Aspect, and Modality in Biblical Hebrew*, Linguistic Studies in Ancient West Semitic (Winona Lake, IN: Eisenbrauns, 2012).

[173] See Section 2.1.2.2.

[174] That the pronominal reference is singular may be part of the underlying thread of the Psalm noted above in which the horizon of the psalmist's distress and the salvation of Israel corporately are interwoven.

[175] "The underlying relevance of the second strophe to the psalmist's personal suffering is shown by his sudden return to it at the outset of the third." Allen, *Psalms 101–150*, 15.

[176] Mays, *Psalms*, 323.

creation.¹⁷⁷ The Lord was there "at the beginning" and thus stands distinct from the creation he founded. It is marked by its ability to fade and fail, described like a piece of clothes that wears out; but the Lord is the same and does not fail. In fact, this wearing out is not merely the function of the creation in itself, but also in its relation to the sovereignty of the Lord; it ages not only by its nature but also because of the action of the Lord towards it as one who changes it (v. 27).¹⁷⁸ Verse 29 concludes the Psalm, not with, as we might expect, the psalmist's conclusion of his own hope, but the hope of God's servants generally that the nature of YHWH as enduring will give the people an enduring hope that spans their generations.¹⁷⁹

Before moving to consider the Pastor's appropriation of Ps 101:27, 28 LXX it is worth drawing together several threads from the Psalm developed above which will prove especially pertinent to the Pastor's use of it.

First, that central to the Psalm is the contrast between the psalmist and the Lord marked by issues of time and change, or put slightly differently, time and the ability to fail. Certain key words cement this contrast: the oscillation of pronouns, the distinct set of "time words" that mark out the psalmist from the Lord and even the verbs which are associated with the psalmist but negated in respect to YHWH.¹⁸⁰ The psalmist has "days," the Lord, "years" (v. 28) and "generations" (v. 13). For the psalmist these days ἐξέλιπον (v. 4) and ἐκλίθησαν (v. 12); by contrast, the Lord's years οὐκ ἐκλείψουσιν (v. 28).

Second, this comparison turns not merely on the difference of time, but also on the consequent issue of power.¹⁸¹ The psalmist is faced by a situation and enemies that are beyond his strength. The way he portrays himself extends not only to time but also bodily weakness and his dependence on food (vv. 4, 5). This portrayal parallels the people of God more broadly, who are "bound" (v. 21) and in need of release, those who are "dead" (v. 21b) and thus entirely destitute of power. God's immutability in the Psalm is conversely connected to his unfailing quality of action: his response to Israel's impotence is "the way of his strength" (v. 24a). This significance is further highlighted by God's transcendence above the situation of the psalmist and Israel, a transcendence in which he stands beyond the restraints of the situation but still can bring his power to bear in it. The Lord is not "bound" by Israel's (or the psalmist's) circumstances or troubles. He stands without creation and is sovereign over it (v. 27c). Thus he hears and regards from a point of distance, as κύριος ἐξ οὐρανοῦ, stepping into Israel's situation from without, unhindered by what weakens and oppresses creatures.

Third, and parallel to the above point, this connection between God's enduring nature, which issues in and founds his action and strength, may be related to God's

---

[177] On textual differences between LXX texts and the Pastor's quotation of Ps 101:26, 27, see Docherty, *Use of the Old Testament*, 136, 137 and Gheorghita, *Role of the Septuagint*, 43, 44.

[178] Note the passives of both παλαιωθήσονται and ἀλλαγήσονται.

[179] This enduring quality is not only explicit in the language of eternity (v. 29b) but is also implicitly present in the reference to the people in generational terms, as "the sons of your servants" (v. 29a) and "their seed" (v. 29b).

[180] Allen, *Psalms 101–150*, 15.

[181] Allen notes this as an issue of God's kingship in the psalm: "this kingship … is necessarily manifested in the time and space of their historical experience" (ibid., 14).

covenantal relationship to Israel and the psalmist. The contrast of the psalmist/Israel's finitude and weakness with YHWH's eternity and transcendence is not speculative or abstract, but rather called upon and remembered in prayer because the Lord is the God of Israel.[182] He can be confidently expected to act on Israel's behalf, because of his covenantal relationship to them as Κύριος ὁ θεὸς οἰκτίρμων καὶ ἐλεήμων (Exod 34:6; Ps 101:14). Thus, though the Lord's nature stands in contrast to the psalmist/Israel, the result of his enduring eternity and transcendence is brought to bear on the side of God's covenant people for their benefit.[183] That is, the very distinctiveness of the Lord over and against his people becomes the ground of their appeal and confidence in the action of God for them.

Fourthly, one may note the eschatological character of the Psalm which would well suit the Pastor's appropriation of the text. A time (v. 14b) of God's action is expected which is future, and yet also immanently at hand (v. 14c). This time is associated with the appearance of YHWH's glory in a way that fills up Old Covenant promises: establishing Israel's place securely, liberating the people, drawing in the nations, subjecting all powers to the Lord and rebuilding Zion.[184]

2.2.2.1 Appropriation of Ps 101:27, 28 LXX

Before moving to discuss the reason why the Pastor may have appropriated this text as a reference to Christ as God, and his consequent superiority to angels, it is first worth considering the pragmatic function of the quotation in its place in the catena in Hebrews. By evaluating the role of the quotation in the Pastor's argument it ought to highlight what his primary categories of interest are in Ps 101 LXX, and thus to assist in discerning what has motivated his Christological reading.

The quotation of Ps 101:27, 28 is placed within the second opposition of the catena, which, in a reversal of the first comparison of 1:5, 6, moves from what God says πρὸς τοὺς ἀγγέλους (v. 7) to what God says πρὸς τὸν υἱόν (v. 8).[185] The Pastor selects one text as God's speech about the angels, namely, Ps 104(3):4. The context of this Psalm strongly focuses on the character of God as creational king and the way in which all creation lies at his disposal.[186] The syntax of the argument structure of v. 4, if read in abstraction from the Psalm, would seem to concern the Lord transforming his angels into various creational phenomena: winds and fiery flames.[187] However, the context

---

[182] This is frequently noted by commentators. The poet "supports [his prayer] not by the eternity of God in itself, but by the work of rejuvenation of the world and of the restoration of Israel ... because he is the ever living One" (Franz Delitzsch, *Biblical Commentary on the Psalms*, vol. 5 (Grand Rapids, MI: Eerdmans, 2011), 644). See also Mays, *Psalms*, 324 and Allen, *Psalms 101–150*, 16.

[183] Cf. Owen's parallel statements about the nature of God's resources in Christ becoming "for" believers (Owen, *Hebrews*, 3, 211).

[184] This relates to the sense of futurity of Zion's hope (Kraus, *Psalms*, 286).

[185] Lane, *Hebrews 1–8*, 28; Backhaus, *Hebräerbrief*, 98. Cockerill notes the frequency of μέν/δέ constructions in Hebrews in 3:5, 6; 7:5, 6, 8, 18–20; 8:4, 6; 9:23; 10:11, 12.

[186] Vanhoye, *Situation*, 171, 172.

[187] There is some debate over whether the Pastor's appropriation of the language of angels as πνεύματα ought to be seen in conjunction with the language of 1:14, and thus with the sense "spirits," or as "winds" (Koester, *Hebrews*, 194). The remaining parallelism with πῦρ in the following stych, though, would suggest that the description ought to remain in the semantic domain activated in

of the Psalm in its original sense suggests that the verse ought to be understood as stating that the Lord to whom all creation is subject dispenses with his creation as his servants; he thus makes the winds and fire, his mere servants and emissaries.[188] His control over such uncontrollable and awesome elements thus betokens his own supreme power.[189] Most commentators argue that though the Hebrew syntax allows either of these interpretations, the Greek syntax reduces the two options to that of the former,[190] thus seeing the Pastor's use of the text as focused on the inherent mutability of the angels: God changes them at will into elements.[191] Support for such a reading is claimed from Rabbinic and Targumic statements about the nature of angels that demonstrate a similar concept.[192] However, the issue of the syntax of Ps 103:4 LXX is less certain than it appears.[193] It is possible that it may still be open to interpretation as God's appointing or creating of the natural elements as his messengers and servants. This is due to the semantics and syntax for the verb ποιέω. The verb can take either one direct object (transitive) or two (ditransitive), with one direct object and one indirect. In the first case, the sense of ποιέω would be equivalent to "create," with the syntax "A creates B." In the second, the sense would be "make into" or "change," with syntax "A makes B into C." Most interpreters see this latter meaning and syntax at work. Thus the verse reads "He makes his angels (into) winds." This reading is then defended by appeal to the syntax of ditransitive constructions and that, in such cases, the direct object can be distinguished from the indirect as the more definite of the two. In this case the noun phrase, τοὺς ἀγγέλους αὐτοῦ as the more definite, is seen as the direct object, and thus what God is changing into something else.[194] However, because the verb ποιέω does not require two objects, it may be that the two noun phrases represent not two objects, one direct and one indirect, but one object and one oblique. Normally an oblique noun phrase would be marked by the dative or by using a preposition. So, for example, we might imagine the reconstructed sentence ὁ ποιῶν πνεύματα ὡς τοὺς ἀγγέλους αὐτοῦ

---

the Psalm, rather than being interpreted with reference to 1:14. See Cockerill, *Hebrews*, 108n148 and Westcott, *Hebrews*, 25. Pace Moffitt, *Atonement*, 47–53.

[188] On potential theophanic and Sinaitic overtones see Lane, *Hebrews 1–8*, 29; Cockerill, *Hebrews*, 109.
[189] Philip Edgcumbe Hughes, *A Commentary on the Epistle to the Hebrews* (Grand Rapids, MI: Eerdmans, 1977), 61; Bruce, *Hebrews*, 58.
[190] Spicq, *Hébreux*, 2, 18, 19; Gräßer, *Hebräer*, 1, 81.
[191] Spicq, *Hébreux*, 2, 19. See also Lane, *Hebrews 1–8*, 28, 29 and Attridge, *Hebrews*, 104.
[192] Attridge (*Hebrews*, 104) notes relevant OT texts as Exod 3:2; 19:16–18; Dan 7:10. Other passages appealed to are 1QH 1:10b, 11; 4 Ezra 8:21f and TgPs 104:4. Exod Rab. 25.86a notes the appearances of angels in different forms: as a woman (Zech 5), as men (Gen 18) and as wind and fire in Ps 104. Such support need not rely on access to these documents but simply the interpretative potentiality of such a reading of the text within a Jewish milieu. However the lateness of texts like Targum Psalms makes the weight of the support given by them rather slight. On uncertainties for the dating of Targum Psalms, though with a suggestion of dating around C4–6 CE see David M. Stec, *The Targum of Psalms*, The Aramaic Bible (Collegeville, MN: Liturgical Press, 2004), 1, 2.
[193] Vanhoye does seem to leave open the possibility that the syntax might be as ambiguous as the MT's, even in Greek, though he speaks of the reading of "making winds his messengers" as "sans être absolument impossible, l'autre construction serait moins nauturelle" (Vanhoye, *Situation*, 171). Pace Ellingworth, *Hebrews*, 120.
[194] Bateman, *Jewish Hermeneutics*, 127, 128; those supporting this often cite Daniel B. Wallace, "The Semantics and Exegetical Significance of the Object-Complement Construction in the New Testament," *Grace Theological Journal* 6 (1985): 113–60.

πνεύματα or ὁ ποιῶν πνεύματα τοις ἀγγέλοις αὐτοῦ. However, it is possible to move the oblique phrase syntactically to the left in Greek, in which case the oblique becomes rendered in the accusative.[195] This would result in a sentence structure identical to what we have in Heb 1:7. Thus the Greek syntax in fact preserves the same ambiguity of the Hebrew of Ps 104:4.[196]

If this is the case, it makes less certain the meaning that most interpreters associate with the LXX reading, namely that changeability is at stake, which they see as predominantly residing in the semantic freight of ditransitive ποιέω.[197] However, if the meaning of the LXX is equivalent to the former meaning of the MT, then what the Pastor is doing reflects an adaptation of the text to his ends, not that of a re-reading of the syntax, but rather by drawing out what is essentially the reflex of the statement of Ps 103:4 LXX.[198] Because God is King, the whole creation is at his bidding to act as his emissaries and servants in the world; thus angels, in the Pastor's reading, are simply subsumed with all other agents and emissaries of God in the world. They may be awesome, fire and wind, but in the final analysis they reside squarely within the ambit of created things, things which are inherently subject to change (Ps 101:27, 28).[199]

In contrast to the description of angels stands God's speech about the Son, drawn from Ps 44:6, 7 LXX and Ps 101:27, 28 LXX. Within this structure, the functional value of the Ps 101 quotation is developed both in its commonality with the Ps 44 quotation and in opposition to the Ps 103 quotation. This is not to exclude peculiar contributions that the quotations make that are not exhausted by the contrast with angels or their role in the catena. It is to say, however, that the central focus of each quotation ought to be sought within this structural correlation in the two quotations of 1:8–12 and opposition of the two to 1:7.[200]

---

[195] Cf. Martin M. Culy, "Double Case Constructions in Koine Greek," *JGRChJ* 6 (2009): 82–106 and Richard K. Larson, "On the Double Object Construction," *Linguistic Inquiry* (1988): 335–91. Ellingworth argues that the sense of ποιέω here is most likely ditransitive because of the proximity of τίθημι in 101:3b (Ellingworth, *Hebrews*, 121). However, considering the verbs surrounding τίθημι (στεγάζω, περιπατέω) which depict God's construction of the world as his dwelling place, the meaning "place" rather than appoint in regard to the clouds as his pathway is more likely and thus does not settle the sense of ποιέω in the verse that follows.

[196] On the sense "create" here cf. John P. Meier, "Symmetry and Theology in the Old Testament Citations of Heb 1, 5–14," *Bib* 66 (1985): 512, 513.

[197] DeSilva, *Perseverance*, 98; Changeability is often seen as inherent in the reference to πνεῦμα and πῦρ (e.g. Cockerill, *Hebrews*, 109) though Ellingworth disputes it (*Hebrews*, 121).

[198] This seems to be the sense of Calvin's argument that the text is applied "by a similitude" in which the Pastor "transfers to angels what properly applies to wind" (Calvin, *Hebrews*, 44). It is made even more likely when one considers the Pastor's ability elsewhere to make similar interpretative moves, when he, for example, reads the positive availability of rest from the negative prohibition of entrance in 4:3. On which see Chapter 6 of the present work, and Section 6.3.2.

[199] This is the predominant genius of the use of Ps 101 here. As many remark, the Psalm in its original use makes no mention of "angels" per se (Vanhoye, *Situation*, 70; Gräßer, *Hebräer*, 1, 81), but the Pastor, in his appropriation of the text, has subsumed angels within the purview of Ps 101 LXX, and thus positioned them clearly within the created world. Vanhoye arrives at a similar conclusion though via a focus on divine power. Vanhoye, *Situation*, 173–5.

[200] Though structurally this is surely unobjectionable few seem to carry out this line of thinking systematically, frequently focusing on the contrast of Ps 103 LXX with Ps 44 LXX and sometimes comparing Ps 101 LXX to Ps 44 LXX, but failing to compare both with Ps 103 LXX. This is surely required by the structural use of the μεν/δε and καί.

In comparing the use of Ps 44 and Ps 101 two aspects immediately stand out: both quotations identify Jesus as God. Ps 44:6, 7 does so via the actual predication of θεός, the other via the identification of Jesus with the creating κύριος of Ps 101.[201] Similarly striking is the accent on the language of eternity. The throne of the God-King of Ps 44:7 is εἰς τὸν αἰῶνα τοῦ αἰῶνος with the throne being taken metonymically for the one who sits as King upon it.[202] This throne however is one with an inception, suggested here by the language of anointing and appointing as King, a theme that coheres well with both 1:1-4 and the two OT quotations of 1:5. However, within Ps 44, the eternal nature of the throne is correlated with the designation of the enthroned one as "God" and is similarly reflected in the quotation of Ps 101 LXX, where the eternal nature of the Creator-King is highlighted.[203]

In bringing the horizon of the three quotations together, the Pastor's main claim of the Son's supremacy over the angels can be seen. The angels are created emissaries. The Son, on the other hand, is addressed as God, and as such is to be identified as Creator of all.[204] Associated with this status as God is thus eternality and immutability: he was "from the beginning" not a part of creation, and thus stands without it. Thus he is ever the same (v. 12c), without beginning or end.[205] This contrast of Creator and creation which stands central to the image of abiding and wearing out in Ps 101 then sends us back to the angels, for as created beings, what creation is, they are: a garment which wears out and changes. In this way by bringing together these three texts in comparison and opposition the Pastor associates the reign of Christ as Messiah with

---

[201] *Pace* Westcott (*Hebrews*, 25), the majority of modern commentators recognize the ὁ θεός of Ps 44:7 as vocative, addressing the enthroned king (e.g. Lane, *Hebrews 1-8*, 29). Cockerill notes that both Theodotion and Aquila have made this explicit with the rendering as θέε (*Hebrews*, 109n153). Westcott's argument is that the syntax allows for a predicate nominative rather than a vocative, and thus, "Your throne is God forever and ever," making comparison to similar metaphoric language of YHWH as Rock in the Psalter, but though the Rock metaphor can be understood as one of protection and assistance, it is difficult to see what the sense of God as throne would be. See the similar criticisms of Westcott's suggestion in Vanhoye, *Situation*, 179, 180. For an extensive treatment of the uses of θεός language in both the original text and its function in Heb 1:8 see chapters 8 and 9 of Murray J. Harris, *Jesus as God: The New Testament Use of Theos in Reference to Jesus* (Grand Rapids, MI: Baker, 1992).

[202] One can hardly reign eternally unless one is oneself eternal.

[203] In the quotation from the language of διαμένω (v. 11a) and especially v. 12c. Indeed, alongside issues of eternality and immutability, the contrast between the angels as servants and the Son as King is often highlighted, and this coheres well with the preceding quotations in 1:5 and the controlling influence of Ps 110 on the catena as a whole. See Ellingworth, *Hebrews*, 122; Gräßer, *Hebräer*, 1, 82; Weiss, *Hebräer* 165; Spicq, *Hébreux*, 2, 18. To discern whether the second of the three ὁ θεός is vocative, along with the first, is difficult but probably it ought to be taken as the subject of ἔχρισέν with the third as an epexegetic phrase, that is, "Therefore, God, your God, has anointed you." *Pace* Attridge, *Hebrews*, 60 and, in more detail, Harris, *Jesus as God*, 218-20.

[204] Thus 1:10-12 heightens the involvement of Christ in creation in comparison to the instrumental role of 1:2 (Rascher, *Schriftauslegung*, 78). Weiss's contrary assertion that "Die Schöpfungsaussage in V.10 in der wiederum ... die Ursprungliche Gottesanrede Κύριε mit Selbstverständlichkeit auf den 'Sohn' bezogen wird hat dementsprechend in Gesamtzusammenhang kein eigenes Gewicht" seems entirely unlikely. The language of the OT Psalms has become God's word to his Son and, as such, is "performativ ... Jesus Christus ist Sohn und Hohepreister, weil er von Gott angesprochen und eingesetzt wurde" (ibid., 38). In a similar fashion, the Son is the Creator κύριος because God addresses him as such. Cf. Peeler, *My Son*, 30-3.

[205] Cf. Weiss, *Hebräer*, 167.

his identity as God in comparison with angels, suggesting three sharp ways in which he differs from the angels and is superior to them: he is God, the Creator, they are created and creatures;[206] he is eternal, they are temporal and temporary;[207] he is unchanging, they are changeable and failing.[208] Considering the interplay of these themes in the texts cited, it seems we are to consider all of them as being brought into play in the Pastor's comparison.

There are two notable objections to such a reading of the contrast and its import for the identity of Christ in the catena. The first is that of David Moffitt, who argues that because the principal stress of the catena is that of the Son as superior to angels on account of his exalted status as an embodied human, the primary function of the texts here is consequently to stress the embodiment of the Son and his exaltation as incarnate, in contrast to the merely spiritual constitution of the angels,[209] as part of a wider narrative of the exaltation of humanity generally over the angelic sphere.[210] The central arguments he proposes are twofold. First, that the Son is exalted in relation to his μετόχοι (1:9), viewed as other humans,[211] such that the contrast of the Son to angels must be that of a human to angels, rather than because he is "the one Creator God."[212] Second, that the juxtaposition of 1:13 and 1:14 involves the opposition of the Son with the angels, as spirits. This opposition, Moffit proposes, finds its root in a contrasting of the enfleshed nature of the Son, who is enthroned as exalted man, and the purely spiritual nature of angels.[213]

However, though Moffitt is correct to see human exaltation at work in the catena, it neither exhausts the catena's significance, nor does it turn in 1:7–12 on a contrast based on physicality versus spirituality. That the Son has "companions" certainly necessitates that he is human, but the fact of his humanity at this point does not mean it is the principal contrast at play. As I have noted above, that contrast ought to be sought principally in the commonality of the Ps 44:6, 7 quotation with that of Ps 101:27, 28, which are meant to be read together in contrast to the quotation of Ps 103:4. Nor is it necessary to read the juxtaposition of 1:13 and 1:14 in quite the way that Moffitt does. Rather it seems that the movement is one of a coup de grâce with respect to the angels: because the Son's exaltation is one in which he is exalted in his humanity, angels are not merely subjected to the Son but also to the "sons" as servants.[214] This is certainly the salvific import of the Son's incarnate elevation to the throne of God and is of direct relevance to the Pastor's audience, but the significance of it for the people of God does

---

[206] Lane, *Hebrews 1–8*, 29.
[207] Meier, "Symmetry and Theology in the Old Testament Citations of Heb 1, 5–14," 514, 515.
[208] Gräßer, *Hebräer*, 1, 81, 82; Lane, *Hebrews 1–8*, 28. Among these contrasts is sometimes articulated a dichotomy between status and nature involved in the oppositions. See, e.g. Hughes.
[209] Moffitt, *Atonement*, 49–52.
[210] Ibid., 118–19.
[211] This identification is the more likely of the choice normally posed between angels and "sons" as Christ's companions (Westcott, *Hebrews*, 27; Koester, *Hebrews*, 195; Cockerill, *Hebrews*, 111), though Vanhoye makes an interesting case for excluding neither, due to the presence of both in the heavenly world to which Christ is ascending (Vanhoye, *Situation*, 193, 194).
[212] Moffitt, *Atonement*, 51.
[213] Ibid., 51, 52.
[214] Bauckham, "Hebrews 1," 172, 173.

not mean that this exhausts the grounds or significance of it for the Son himself.[215] To put it otherwise, the exaltation of the Son is not exhausted by its reference to the sons.

In this reading, Moffitt seems to inherit the shared weakness of Caird's article,[216] that having identified the thread of human exaltation between the catena and 2:5–9, to then attempt to subsume everything under this thread, even though certain aspects of it, in particular the worship rendered to the Son as God (1:6b) and his being addressed by God as God (1:8, 10) fit ill with it. Human exaltation is important in the catena but it figures within a larger reference to the person of Christ, who is more than human.[217] To put it differently, Christ here is not merely a cypher for humanity, conceived via a kind of ideal corporate solidarity; the Son is a person, Jesus Christ. The inadequacy of Moffitt's line of reasoning at this point in handling the divine aspects of 1:6, 8–12 is revealed by the way he raises such issues, problematizes them and then leaves them to one side in his later exegesis. His argument seems to assume that the fact that the Son "becomes" something within the catena must mean that divinity cannot be involved at all.[218] He does so without discussing the numerous solutions to this quandary in Heb 1 that have been proposed in the literature.[219]

Another principal objection to seeing the Pastor's quotation in 1:10–12 as supporting the divinity of the Son is that of Kenneth Schenck, developed at most length in his 1997 article.[220] Schenck cautions against taking the creational language of both 1:2 and 1:10–12 as signalling a full identification of Jesus with God, or a personal

---

[215] He is, after all, described as one over the house of God, rather than simply a member of it (Heb 3:1–6).
[216] Caird, "Son by Appointment," 18–24.
[217] At the very least the protological language of 1:2 already opens the hearers' ears to the fact that the Son cannot be reasonably described or comprehended by appeal to his earthly career alone, even if amplified by his subsequent heavenly exaltation. This is not unrelated to the eschatological thrust of the verses, so Koester, *Hebrews*, 186.
[218] Moffitt, *Atonement*, 47–9.
[219] For an articulation of the issue and some proposed solutions see Attridge, *Hebrews*, 54, 55 and Schenck, "Keeping His Appointment," 92–100. Some of these would be: that the Son's sonship is revealed in his exaltation, rather than given to him de novo (e.g. Peeler, *My Son*, 19–21); that a difference of identity and role obtains in regard to the Sonship (e.g. Schenck, "Keeping His Appointment," 99); or the traditional ascription of change to that of the Person of Christ in the union of the two natures, rather than to his divinity (e.g. Aquinas). Owen replying to the question of whether the exaltation relates to Christ's divinity or humanity responds that

> Christ is said to be made above and more excellent than angels, neither absolutely as God, nor absolutely as man, but as he was God-man, the mediator between God and man; in which respect, as mediator, for the discharge of one part of his office, he was a little while made lower than they and so the creation of heaven and earth does demonstrate the dignity of his person, and the equity of his being made more excellent than the angels in his office. And this fully removes [the] following exception, that the remembering of his deity could be no argument to prove that the humanity was exalted above the angels; for it is not an argument of the exaltation of his humanity, but the demonstration of the excellency of his person, that the apostle has in hand. (Owen, *Hebrews*, 3, 204)

For further discussion of how both eternity and development work themselves out with respect to sonship in Hebrews, see Chapter 6 of the present work.
[220] Schenck, "Keeping His Appointment," 92, 106–7. Some of this material is reworked in briefer compass in "Worship of Jesus," 118–21. Schenck notes his indebtedness to Caird's seminal article (Caird, "Son by Appointment," 18–24), though it may be said he develops a more fully articulated version of Caird's thesis.

pre-existence of Christ, but rather that the language is one of the coming to fruition of purposeful divine wisdom which finds its goal in the work of Christ.[221] This, he claims, is to take seriously the thrust of the catena, conditioned by the central role of Ps 110 and the sense of what Christ has become in these last days.[222] Thus in citing Ps 101:27, 28 LXX in 1:10–12:

> Christ's role as creator is … not the main point. … Given this context [of Christ's ascension to his eternal throne], the author may have read these verses in this way: while the role of the angels is transitory like the created realm which is their charge, Christ is the very wisdom of God which founded the heavens and earth, the one in whom they reach their ultimate destiny. He will continue forever.[223]

But the use of Ps 101 LXX will not allow this. Though there is certainly an interest in the eschatological tone of Ps 101 LXX, and its connection to Christ's role in winding up the present creation, the unchangeable character of the Lord of the quotation is grounded in his protological standing. He does not wear out like the world, because he was there before it. This suggests that in attributing the quotation to Christ it cannot be made to terminate only on eschatological categories, it must also involve the protological.[224] In this regard Schenck's equivocation on pre-existence is unhelpful, sometimes seeming to claim that the Son was son at all points of existence,[225] but at other times seeming to reconfigure this as the "pre-existence" of a principal or plan in the mind of God which reaches its goal in Christ.[226] In the context of Hebrews, such a thesis proves far too much, for the exaltation of Christ is not the only fulfilment of this divine plan. Though Christ may play a singular role, as Schenck notes, the accomplishment of human destiny in toto is at work here.[227] Does this then mean that, because the glorification of the many sons was foreordained in the mind of God, the audience ought also to draw from the catena a sense of their own "pre-existence" in the divine wisdom? Or that, on such grounds, they might see the address as Creator Lord of Ps 101 as somehow being applicable to the hearers themselves? Such questions demonstrate that to deny a personal and protological existence to Christ as necessitated by the quotation of Ps 101:27, 28 is to loosen the connection to him from its moorings and make it too far-ranging.[228]

---

[221] Schenck, "Keeping His Appointment," 111–17.
[222] This is particularly clearly articulated in "Worship of Jesus," 115–18.
[223] Schenck, "Keeping His Appointment," 99.
[224] Though it is certainly the fact that the former play a key role in unveiling the latter in the Epistle. See Koester, *Hebrews*, 186. Interesting in this regard is also the way in which comparison of God to angels seems to have played a role in the construal of God's Creator status in Second Temple Judaism Cf. *Jos. Ant.* 1.155–156, *Philo Decal.* 64 and the discussion in Bauckham, "The Throne of God and the Worship of Jesus," 45–52.
[225] Schenck, "Keeping His Appointment," 99.
[226] The "pre-existence" Schenck has in mind often seems to work out as equivalent to "the eternality of God's purposes, his *logos* for his humanity and the world" (ibid.).
[227] As Schenck recognizes, even connecting it to the same *logos* of the divine plan, "In his wisdom and reason (*logos*), he created the world with the intention that all things would be in submission to humanity" (ibid., 116).
[228] For similar criticisms of Schenck's argument cf. Cockerill, *Hebrews*, 99n64, 100 and Peeler, *My Son*, 25–9.

Thus, in spite of the objections of Moffit and Schenck, it seems that the Pastor's use of Ps 101 is designed to draw in exactly the kind of divine predication which is suggested by the original horizon of the Psalm itself. This however still leaves the question of how he can assign such a text to the Son, without the accusation of a merely arbitrary and indefensible exegetical move.

2.2.2.2 The Pastor's motivation in using Ps 101 LXX

Though the pragmatic force of the Pastor's appropriation of Ps 101 LXX has found a good level of agreement among interpreters, his motivation for selecting Ps 101 as a text to demonstrate the Son's superiority has proved more difficult. As was noted above, such motivation has been thought either entirely lacking or made to turn on, in my judgement, a rather unlikely reading of Ps 101:26, 27.[229] I noted above the weaknesses of such views and the possibility of expanding on the suggestion of Delitzsch and Westcott that the category of YHWH's advent finding its fulfilment in Christ's own person and work as the means of forging a connection between Christ and the God of both Deut 32:43 and Ps 101:27, 28.[230]

Indeed, this theme of YHWH's appearing to act on behalf of his people is equally as strong in Ps 101 as it is in Deut 32. As we saw above the psalmist is expecting a time of the Lord's action, even that such a time had drawn near (v. 14). Moreover, this action seems to involve the manifestation of YHWH's glory and presence.[231] He will appear and be recognized as God beyond the borders of Israel, drawing the nations. In this way, one can see the commonalities of eschatological promise, fulfilled in the decisive salvific action of God and his revelation as God, commonalities to which we will return in more detail below.

This is all simply to recognize the plausibility of Delitzsch and Westcott's suggestion that such a promised divine appearance, fulfilled in Christ, might well stand behind the Pastor's use of this passage. However, though it constitutes such a connection between the Psalm and Christ, it is difficult to see how it would form a connection to this text, Ps 101 LXX, in particular. Standing on its own, it would become merely a slightly more focused version of the view of Ellingworth stated above;[232] that, because the Pastor sees Christ as fulfilling this promised action of YHWH, thereby any text about God's promised action may be straightforwardly seen as referring to Christ. I suggest though that without further development of the connection, such a connection fails to provide the argumentative function that has been sought and indeed falls under the criticism

---

[229] See Section 2.1.2.2. Bacon, "Heb I, 10–12," 280–5 is frequently appealed to, to explain the move (Lane, *Hebrews 1–8*, 30; Spicq, *Hébreux*, 2, 20; Bruce, *Hebrews*, 62.
[230] Delitzsch, *Hebrews*, 1, 72; Westcott, *Hebrews*, 20.
[231] Verses 16 and 17 both speak of the "glory of the Lord." In v. 17 YHWH appears in glory. In v. 16 his glory is described in parallel to "the Lord's name," a phrase which is frequently found in conjunction with God's presence (1 Kgs 3:2; 5:3, 5; 8:17, 20).
[232] See the comments of Ellingworth, *Hebrews*, 41, 42. The suggestion that the language of κύριος, in its application to Jesus, formed a bridge by which to identify him with the κύριος of OT texts like Ps 101 (e.g. Docherty, *Use of the Old Testament*, 166, 167; Ceslas Spicq, *L'Épître aux Hébreux*, vol. 1 (Gabalda, 1953), 20; Backhaus, *Hebräerbrief*, 99), though they may be helpful, only push the question back one step further. Early Christians knew there were many κύριοι (1 Cor 8:5), but why identify κύριος Jesus as one with the κύριος of these OT texts?

of Moule mentioned above. If, though, the Pastor perceived certain aspects of the work of Christ as actually demonstrating the very qualities of YHWH's person and characteristic action, to which he appeals in quoting the Psalm, such would be sufficient to forge an argumentative link: the God spoken of in his promised coming in such and such a way, has appeared, demonstrating just such identifying work and characteristics in Jesus Christ.[233] With Ps 101 in mind then, the question of connection might be more precisely reframed: on what basis would the Pastor see the coming and work of Christ as itself embodying the divine action and/or divine posture which characterizes the God of Ps 101? This question then ought to be pursued with both a broad sense of the structure of Ps 101, as we have outlined it above, and also an awareness of the principal qualities of God which the Pastor seems to want to appropriate in drawing Ps 101:27, 28 into the catena (eternity, immutability, unfailingness). In line with the Pastor's tendency elsewhere towards raising an issue, only then to defer its discussion to a later point in the Epistle, we might also expect some of these connections raised in a terse fashion in the catena to emerge elsewhere later in the Epistle.

In proposing the question of the connection of Christ to Ps 101 in this way, there seems to me two predominant connections by which he might well be relating the person and work of Christ to the God of Ps 101. First, via the issue of the eternality of God. This concept is clearly central to the Psalm, being one of the main themes highlighted in commentaries on Ps 101, and demonstrably forms a key aspect of the contrast he sets up between the Son and angels in 1:7–12. This issue of eternality, and the adjunct property of immutability, is frequently raised in Hebrews as both integral to the nature of Christ's work and also comes into play in his abiding relation to believers.[234] He is eternal King (1:5) and eternal Priest (1:7, 8). He is unchangeably the same (13:8) in the face of the changeableness of other leaders (13:7), because he lives forever as the possessor of an indestructible life (8:16).[235] The principal objection to such a connection would be that these roles of King, and especially Priest, are roles into which Christ entered. Thus the eternity of which they speak is one with an inception but no end; these roles endure, but no more, say, than believers endure in the resurrection (6:2).[236] Note, however, that if this objection were mitigated, that the

---

[233] Thus the concept of fulfilment, so central to the Pastor's use of the OT elsewhere in the Epistle, is still the principal motivating force here. *Pace* Rascher, *Schriftauslegung*, 79. Vanhoye's discussion follows a somewhat similar direction to Westcott and Delitzsch, but peculiarly linking the sense of eschatological fulfilment to that of final judgement. Vanhoye, *Situation*, 202, 203. He thus suggests the move of identification of Christ with the eschatological role of Judge in Ps 101 and thereby a movement backward towards identification with God as Creator (ibid., 206). Though the direction of Vanhoye's argument is similar to my own here, its slight weakness is in seeking a connection through the issue of judgement to the use of Ps 101, a concept that does not seem to play a role in the contrast between Christ and angels in 1:8–12.

[234] As De Silva notes the issue of change and stability has an "axiological" function in Hebrews in that the "addressees will therefore be urged to invest only in the eternal possessions (10:34; 11:13–16; 12:26–28:13:13–14) and to consider worldly goods and security ultimately to be a bad … investment (11:24–26; 12:16, 17)" (DeSilva, *Perseverance*, 100).

[235] In exegeting 1:10–12 and its Christological import interpreters frequently move to these passages as discussions of the similar theme of Christ's stability and eternity elsewhere in the Epistle. See Hughes, *Hebrews*, 68; Koester, *Hebrews*, 104, 105; O'Brien, *Hebrews*, 76.

[236] See especially Schenck, "Keeping His Appointment," 113, 114.

conviction of eternal divine life as integral to the work of Christ would furnish the kind of argumentative logic for the use of Ps 101:27, 28: Christ has appeared at the end of the age, demonstrating by his eternal work his own eternality for his people and thus identity as the God who was "from the beginning" and whose years know no end (1:10, 12).[237] Such logic would not be foreign to Ps 101, when we consider, as was noted above, the covenantal force of God's eternality and immutability in the Psalm;[238] it is not merely what God is in abstracto that is of chief interest to the psalmist, but who God is for his people in the work of final restoration and redemption in answer to both the psalmist's and Israel's problematic temporality and mortality.[239]

Second, one might consider the possible connection via the relation of God's eternality as Creator to his transcendence and the resulting issues of power highlighted in the comments above on Ps 101. The psalmist portrays the Lord as able to act from outside Israel's situation, unbound by what constrains her, even able to help the bound and dead (101:21). Christ himself is portrayed in these terms in the Epistle to the Hebrews. He is one entering this world from without (10:5), in such a way as to be able to achieve the Lord's salvific plan (10:10). He is the one who destroys the devil, who held humanity in his thrall, through the power of death (2:14). Key to this ability is that, though he has taken on every aspect of human nature including its frailties and suffering, he has not taken on that factor that is the prime example of human inability: sin (4:15). Thus, he enters into the human situation and works redemption in a fashion which marks him out as beyond human origins. Where humanity was unable, even dead, in exact parallel to the psalmist, so Christ has appeared doing what God alone can do with resources that clearly do not stem from his humanity; rather, they are the salvific resources of the transcendent Creator who is unbound by what binds the human sons. Again, this would explain the Pastor's appropriation of the Psalm: that in Christ he recognizes the presence of the salvific ability which, in the face of human sin-weakness, belongs properly to the transcendent Creator of Ps 101 and is brought to bear in the arena of his people's desperate need.

2.3 Reading the quotations in common

Having considered the two problem texts of Deut 32:43 and Ps 101:27, 28 LXX in some detail, I suggest one final step is fruitful: that of observing the rapprochement between these two source texts themselves. Discussions of these two OT citations have often led to comparison or grouping together, as was noted above, through a recognition of the similar problems, questions of motivation and methods of resolution that have been proposed in handling the Pastor's appropriation of these texts.[240] However, though some have considered solutions to the Pastor's use of the texts which straddle both

---

[237] See also the argument with regard to this relation of eternal divine life to the work of Christ as Priest in Chapter 4 of the present work.
[238] Westcott, *Hebrews*, 28.
[239] Mays, *Psalms*, 324.
[240] E.g. Glasson, "Plurality," 271, 272.

of them, rarely have the texts themselves been compared with each other directly. This kind of comparison ought to be undertaken not simply because of the similar hermeneutical questions they raise, but equally through their mutual inclusion in the catena itself.

In constructing the scriptural catena the Pastor has brought many OT texts into relation with each other in a kind of microcosm, in which texts that are canonically distant from one another, and perhaps seem unrelated, are brought into explicit relation and dialogue with each other. Helpful in evaluating this effect of the texts on each other is the concept of intertextuality that has achieved some currency in biblical studies in recent years.[241] Though the term may represent a process that has long gone on in the reading of ancient texts,[242] the adoption of the concept has sharpened the perception of the way in which texts can have an effect when read in relation to each other.[243] In discussing various forms of intertextuality, Steve Moyise has employed an approach which he terms "dialogical" in which the horizons of both an original OT source and its NT appropriation are found to exert a kind of mutual pressure on each other.[244] This may be extended to the catena of 1:5–14 and applied to the question of the effect, not only of OT citations brought into the Pastor's own text but also of the effect of OT citations brought into such proximity to one another. Though Deut 32:43 and Ps 101:27, 28 LXX may not belong to the same pair of oppositions between the Son and angels, they both share in common a function in the Pastor's argument of describing the superior nature

---

[241] For an overview of the reception of intertextuality in biblical studies see Steve Moyise, "Intertextuality and the Study of the Old Testament in the New Testament," in *The Old Testament in the New Testament: Essays in Honour of J. L. North*, ed. Steve Moyise and J. L. North, JSNTSup 189 (Sheffield: Sheffield Academic Press, 2000), 14–41; Thomas R. Hatina, "Intertextuality and Historical Criticism in New Testament Studies: Is There a Relationship?," *BibInt* 7 (1999): 28–43 and John Barton, "*Déjà Lu*: Intertextuality, Method or Theory?," in *Reading Job Intertextually*, ed. Katharine J. Dell and William L. Kynes (New York: Bloomsbury, 2013), 1–16.

[242] Barton, "*Déjà Lu*: Intertextuality, Method or Theory?," 1, 2.

[243] For those who see intertextuality as a less than helpful concept in biblical studies, see Porter, "The Use of the Old Testament in the New Testament," 79–97 and Hatina, "Intertextuality and Historical Criticism in New Testament Studies," 28–43. Criticisms are often directed at the indeterminate way in which the term "intertextuality" is deployed or in the incompatible assumptions of "intertextuality" as a theory and biblical studies. The latter is the predominant criticism of Hatena who questions whether appropriation of the concept has really "add[ed] new insight," especially when it is found alongside concepts that are inimical to the original development of intertextuality: "the historical-critical method, ... the centrality of the author, ... an interpretation or meaning that find its boundaries within the written text and its historical context." However, Hatina seems to pose too sharp a dichotomy: either intertextuality is appropriated wholesale or the appropriation is shallow and suspect. Conversely, intertextuality has sharpened thinking on how the appropriation of texts may bring with them all sorts of resonances and effects; that it has not shifted the conception of what a text is in biblical studies does not make it any less an appropriation of the theory. Cf. on this Moyise's outlining of five "types" of intertextuality ("Intertextuality and Biblical Studies: A Review," *Verbum et Ecclesia* 23 (2002): 419) and Barton's discussion of distinctions between diachronic/synchronic and "hard"/"soft" intertextualities (Barton, "*Déjà Lu*: Intertextuality, Method or Theory?," 3, 9, 12). Where Hatina is helpful is in the reminder that what has been adopted as intertextuality in biblical studies is, for the most part, shriven of many of the concepts central to the idea as it was originally forged among structuralists. For a discussion of the work of Kristeva and Barthes in connection to intertextuality see Hatina, "Intertextuality and Historical Criticism in New Testament Studies," 29–35 and Moyise, "Intertextuality and Biblical Studies: a Review," 418–31.

[244] Moyise, "Intertextuality and the Study of the Old Testament in the New Testament," 17, 18.

of the Son as God. Thus the Pastor's appropriation of them encourages us to read these texts alongside each other, detecting common categories in which the God of these texts is described, and which may then prove significant for understanding what motivated the Pastor's Christological reading of them.[245]

2.3.1 A brief comparison

In reading Deut 32:43 and Ps 101:27, 28 LXX alongside each other certain strong similarities may be discerned. First, both texts bear a strong conception of the way in which God is distinguished from other realities. In the context of Deut 32 this theme is strongly developed against the background of idolatry. YHWH is to be distinguished as God from what are "not gods" (32:17). He is Israel's covenant God and Father who made them (32:6). But this is not to limit his role simply to Israel, rather he stands as peculiar God to them but also as the God who made all and assigns the nations their boundaries (32:8, 9). The comparison with idols raises the category of time in a way consonant with Ps 101. YHWH is the true God, as one who is ancient; the false idols with which Israel has become ensnared are newcomers, ones not formerly known (32:17). Though Ps 101 does not pursue the nature of God through a contrast with idolatry, it nevertheless uses the underlying categories of Creator and creation. The Lord is distinct from the world he made; he is eternal, the created world is passing away (Ps 101:12, 27, 28). This difference is also pursued by the Psalm as God's transcending the time of creation, being there at its beginning and also at its end, without himself being bound by them (101:26–28). Thus in these comparisons, whether more neutrally between God and the created world, or more pejoratively between God and idols, God is identified as the true and living God in distinction from other realities.

Alongside this distinction another connection lies between the two texts: that the identification of the true God in each has a strongly salvific connotation. God's transcendence and power are brought out for the sake of divine action for his people.[246] Put otherwise, who God is and who God is for Israel are closely related. This power and action of God may be brought to bear in judgement in both texts, but the hope and expectation is that YHWH will act to vindicate his people and save them with a power that he alone possesses (Deut 32:29), one which is neither accessible to idols (32:37, 38) or to themselves (32:26). His power will turn after judgement to vindicate in a way that places his sons on the opposite side of his justice to his enemies (32:43). This note of God's sole ability to rescue is pursued similarly in Ps 101. The comparison of days and years, the respective time frames of the psalmist and God, are pursued with a strongly soteriological focus. The God who is forever (v. 12), in distinction from the psalmist in his brevity, will arise (v. 13). This difference of God and his power is the

---

[245] Thus the catena illustrates Barton's argument against a neat distinction between diachronically and synchronically oriented intertextualities (Barton, "*Déjà Lu*: Intertextuality, Method or Theory?," 3). The OT texts bear a clearly diachronic relationship to the Epistle as well as to each other but in the catena the Pastor encourages his readers/hearers to associate his OT quotations in a synchronic fashion.

[246] See, e.g. in Ps 101 LXX the transition of vv. 28–29.

ground of the psalmist's confidence; God has resources as much beyond the psalmist and his situation as God himself is transcendent over the created world.

This issue of God's salvific power and action also brings to light the state of the people who are its objects, and the description of them forms another similarity between the two source texts. The psalmist is one who is lacking in power and worn out (106:1). He lacks resources and feels his aloneness in his desperate situation; there is no one to help (vv. 6, 7). The people of God in the Psalm reflect a similar condition, being bound and dead (v. 21). Similarly the Israel of Deut 32 is also weak. Its moral failings (32:5) have led to an inability to face the judgements of God; they are thus "weakened," "failing" and "slackened" (32:36).[247] The problem that is faced in both texts is the lack of resources of both Israel and the psalmist in the face of divine judgement that is detailed in the Song of Moses and hinted at in the Psalm.[248]

In comparing the two texts, then, one can discern an assumed narrative that is common to both: that of a people of God under judgement, weakened both physically and spiritually, who are exhausted of their own resources and can find no help in gods or other sources of power. The singular hope presented is in God, the Creator and Saviour, who is then looked to restore the psalmist's/Israel's fortunes. This God is identified with respect to his nature as Creator, before all and outlasting all, but is peculiarly recognized as God by his salvific ability and action which is both prophesied and hoped for. Such action will mark both a turning point in Israel's fortunes and the fortunes of YHWH in relation to his world and people. He will appear, be seen and recognized in his glory as God. In such a context the identity and action of God is praised, whether in anticipation (with the psalmist) or in the realization of his works (in the Song of Moses). By drawing these texts together into the catena the Pastor is, in effect, identifying Jesus with the climax of this narrative. He is the God who has stepped into Israel's fortunes, marked by slavery and inability, to act on his people's behalf with resources and salvific achievements that can only be associated with the appearance and identifying work of the One God. Due to him then is the ascription of praise and worship, whether that of the Song or the Psalm, as the God to whom such praise for saving works peculiarly belongs.

2.4 Conclusion

In this chapter, we have considered two problematic texts in the catena which both seem to ascribe deity to the Son by transferring to him texts that originally referred to God. In canvassing different options for the Pastor's motivation in ascribing such texts to the Son, I have argued that Westcott and Delitzsch's position is to be preferred, in which the idea of the fulfilment of God's promised action in the Son's advent and work is seen as the connective thread.

---

[247] Note Hebrews later draws on these very words in exhorting the hearers on in their faith (Heb 12:12).
[248] See Ps 101:10.

This underlying conviction at work in the catena clarifies the role of these 'divine' citations, not only in terms of the Pastor's motivation for their use but also in regard to what the Pastor is asserting through them. Not only is the catena about the exaltation of Christ, and related to the salvation of his people,[249] it is one in which that salvation is related to his divinity. The presence of the citations attests to his exaltation as one in which his divinity is revealed, confirmed and put on display. His introduction into the heavenly world by the Father, because it represents the salvation of his people, is also his open establishment as the saving God who came to rescue his people, in fulfilment of the promises of Deut 32. As the fulfilment of this divine personal coming, the Son thus rightly receives the worship due to that saving God (1:6). In the same way in 1:10–12, his ascension displays him to be the eternal God, in contrast to mutable and finite creatures, the angels (1:7), for the unchangeable and eternal salvation which he has wrought (1:3; 7:24, 25) depends upon, and reveals, the proper power of the eternal God who was before, and is above, all creation and creatures (1:10–12). In both these related aspects of salvation achieved, and divinity established and revealed, the Son thus far exceeds even the highest of creatures, the angels, as the God and Saviour of God's people.

In connection then to this underlying conviction, that God's promised saving action is fulfilled in the Son's coming and ascension, it is worth again mentioning the objection of Moule to this idea: that in assigning texts about God, to the Son as God, on the basis of the conviction that he is God, is to fail to provide any argumentative function to the use of the citations. Rather than such a recognition defeating Westcott and Delitzsch's position it ought to lead to a different conclusion. That the Pastor has recognized in the work of the Son the eschatological achievement of divine salvific prerogatives, which in his source texts mark out and identify the one God of Israel as the only true and living God. Thus in recognizing such divine salvific prerogatives at work in the work of Christ, most notably within the context of the catena, connected to the saving significance of the Son's exaltation, he has, on that basis, connected the Son to such OT passages as promise this final work and connect it to the identity of the One God. Such a recognition clarifies that the Pastor's use of the OT at this point does not operate apart from theological assumptions about the nature of Christ's work which are shaped by the accomplishment of that work in history.

This concept of the work of the Son as the proper eschatological work of God, promised beforehand in the prophets, will be further traced out in the chapters that follow, and may be seen not least in relation to the building of God's eschatological house in Heb 3:3, 4, which is considered in the next chapter.

---

[249] On which see, as noted before, and most convincingly Jipp, "Son's Entrance," 557–75.

3

The Son as divine eschatological builder (Heb 3:3, 4)

3.0 Introduction

In this chapter I seek to explore the portrayal of Christ in relation to God's house in 3:1–6. The overarching argument is that these verses portray the Son as engaged in a divine eschatological prerogative: the work of building God's house or household. To this end, I first investigate two trajectories in handling the flow of thought in this section of Hebrews. The first is predominantly associated with pre-critical exegesis. The second has tended to be represented by modern exegetes.[1] I will suggest that the benefits of each may be combined in a more synthetic reading that not only maintains an assumption about Christ's divinity which pre-critical exegetes recognized but also incorporates the structure of the passage suggested by many modern commentators. This reading of 3:1–6 is then substantiated in two ways: first, by evaluating an allusion to the Nathan Oracle in these verses and, in particular, the questions it raises over who builds God's house(hold); second, by exploring references in Hebrews to eschatological construction as a divine prerogative.

3.1 Situating the flow of thought in Heb 3:1–6

Before focusing on the inner structure of 3:1–6, it is worth noting that this section has proved difficult to set within the flow of Hebrews. Syntax suggests that the section is well anchored, observable in the ὅθεν of 3:1, tying the passage to what precedes, and the διό of 3:7, to what follows.[2] Further verbal and conceptual ties to the surrounding concept are easily demonstrated.[3] The direct address of the hearers as "holy brothers"

---

[1] Though it is difficult to subsume the large degree of commentary that 3:1–6 has attracted under such a neat taxonomy there is some heuristic benefit in it, in discerning certain logical forces at play in reading this passage, despite the fact that individual commentators sometimes straddle these hermeneutical "lines."
[2] Lane, *Hebrews 1–8*, 73, 79; Ellingworth, *Hebrews*, 197.
[3] Attridge, *Hebrews*, 106; Cynthia Long Westfall, "Moses and Hebrews 3.1-6: Approach or Avoidance?," in *Christian-Jewish Relations through the Centuries*, ed. Stanley E. Porter and Brook W. Pearson (London: A&C Black, 2000), 193–7.

(3:1) picks up the clear familial language that is central to 2:10–18. The hearers' designation as "sharers in a heavenly calling" directs the reader both backward to the ascension of Christ, whence he calls the many sons heavenward, and also forward to the language of participation that is repeated in 3:14.[4] This forward connection is further strengthened by the repetition of κατέχω language in 3:6 and 3:12, along with warnings about perseverance which both verses share.

The description of the central characters of Moses and Christ also function to connect 3:1–6 to its textual environs. Moses' description as θεράπων and as one giving μαρτύριον is paralleled by the representation of the OT economy as the λαληθεὶς λόγος of 2:1–4. Christ's description as Apostle and High Priest (3:1) provides a fitting summary of key aspects of the Son's ministry and identity to this point in the Epistle, especially with the nearby introduction of Christ's priesthood in 2:17.[5]

It is then surprising, considering this easy demonstration of so many connective threads, that the place of 3:1–6 in developing the argument of the Epistle has often proved difficult to detect.[6] This tendency probably results from mistaking what is the key assertion of the section. Such false starts often centre around the act of syncrisis between Moses and Christ generally,[7] or more specifically the comparison of faithfulness.[8] However, though this syncrisis is obviously important to the flow of thought in the section, Westfall's suggestion that the key assertions of the section are at its boundaries (3:1, 6) seems to make better sense of the whole.[9] The consequence of Westfall's argument is to see the passage as primarily focused on the participation of the hearers in the house of the Son.[10] This argument can be supported in several ways: first, this accent on participation in the Son's house, and its benefits, connects to the principal themes of 2:10–18. There the focus is on the identification of the Son in his humiliation with the other sons, and his opening up of a "common destiny."[11] Second, as both Gräßer and Schierse note, one could coherently read the section skipping from 3:1 to 3:6 while preserving the coherence of thought, suggesting that vv. 2–5 serve simply as an augmentation of the theme of 3:1, 6.[12]

---

[4] On the call as heavenly in "end" and "origin," see Cockerill, *Hebrews*, 158; Spicq, *Hébreux*, 1, 64.
[5] Cockerill, *Hebrews*, 159. Cf. also Koester, *Hebrews*, 243; Lane, *Hebrews 1–8*, 75.
[6] Cynthia Long Westfall, *A Discourse Analysis of the Letter to the Hebrews: The Relationship between Form and Meaning*, LNTS 297 (London: T&T Clark, 2005), 116, and particularly the comments of Christopher A. Richardson, *Pioneer and Perfecter of Faith: Jesus' Faith as the Climax of Israel's History in the Epistle to the Hebrews*, WUNT 338 (Tübingen: Mohr Siebeck, 2012), 49.
[7] Some even making syncrisis *the* structuring device. Similar is A. Stebler, "Beweistelle für die Gottheit Jesu Christi: Zu Hebr 3.1–6," *ThPQ* 76 (1923): 462. Westfall also notes Ellingworth and Buchanan as holding an equivalent view ("Moses," 175).
[8] Luke Timothy Johnson, *Hebrews: A Commentary*, 1st ed. (Louisville, KY: Westminster John Knox Press, 2006), 105.
[9] Westfall, *Discourse Analysis*, 121.
[10] Westfall, "Moses," 190. Pace Ellingworth, *Hebrews*, 197. Koester notes the "prestige" attached to belonging to a socially noteworthy household in connection with the significance of belonging to the Son's house and his exalted glory (Koester, *Hebrews*, 253). Westfall's identification of two houses in the passage, Moses' and Christ's, seems difficult to square the passage. On the unity of God's house in the passage, cf. Backhaus, *Hebräerbrief*, 139; Cockerill, *Hebrews*, 153, 169; Bruce, *Hebrews*, 94n18.
[11] "Schicksalsverbundenheit" (Gräßer, *Hebräer*, 1, 78). On this connection more broadly see Erich Gräßer, "Mose und Jesus: Zur Auslegung von Hebr 3:1–6," *ZNW* 75 (1984): 7.
[12] Gräßer, "Mose und Jesus," 12, 13; Franz Joseph Schierse, *Verheissung und Heilsvollendung: Zur theologischen Grundfrage des Hebräerbriefes* (Munich: Karl Zink Verlag, 1955), 104.

The movement forward to 3:7, however, proves more challenging than Westfall's analysis suggests. Though household membership is central, it must be combined with the key issue of faith and faithfulness, which then forges a connection between Moses's audience and the Pastor's hearers.[13] This theme ought to be balanced by recognizing that, while there is a heightened call for faithfulness to those who participate in the Son, his supremacy over Moses provides a ground for hope, that the one "whose house [they] are" is himself supremely πιστός not merely as example, but in his office as Apostle and High Priest.[14] Thus, the Son's heavenly ministry, in its faithfulness, enables the very steadfastness to which they are being called. As Cockerill writes, "By his faithfulness this 'Jesus' has become ... the one fully sufficient to empower God's people for faithful perseverance."[15] The theme of membership in God's household is related to the greatness of the Son's person and work, who is over that house. In this way the syncrisis of Moses and Christ, and particularly their personal honour and glory, can be seen as serving the progression of the comparison.[16] With this understanding of the syncrisis in mind, one can proceed to evaluate how its logic progresses.

3.2 Evaluating the logic of the syncrisis

The comparison of Moses and Christ does not seem to have been occasioned by any kind of Moses polemic.[17] In fact the syncrisis sets out with a statement of equivalence (3:2). Christ is to be considered in his faithfulness to God, as Moses was also faithful in God's house.[18] This equivalence, however, already hints, in its expression, at the greatness of the Son: Moses is spoken of in terms of office and his relation to God's house; the Son, conversely, is spoken of in his person and in direct relation to God himself. The comparison immediately moves in 3:3 to stress that Christ is even more worthy of honour than Moses, drawing on the language of Num 12:7.

This choice of OT intertext by the Pastor, from which he seeks to demonstrate the superiority of Christ as Son, is perhaps surprising. In its original context, the Num 12:7 quotation speaks Moses' authorization in unique terms. Whereas God speaks

---

[13] Though it is sometimes suggested that the discussion of Christ's fidelity is for the sake of then appealing to the "necessity of Christian fidelity" in 3:7ff (Attridge, *Hebrews*, 114; Koester, *Hebrews*, 225; Marie Isaacs, *Sacred Space: An Approach to the Theology of the Epistle to the Hebrews* (Edinburgh: T&T Clark, 1992), 135), this seems to miss that Christ's faithfulness more than simply exemplifies perseverance, it enables it. So see Gräßer, *Hebräer*, 1, 172; Jason A. Whitlark, *Enabling Fidelity to God: Perseverance in Hebrews in Light of the Reciprocity Systems of the Ancient Mediterranean World* (Carlisle: Authentic Media, 2008), 152; Backhaus, *Hebräerbrief*, 137.
[14] Ellingworth, *Hebrews*, 202.
[15] Cockerill, *Hebrews*, 154.
[16] In one sense then, the interest of the passage is not really in Moses per se, but rather what the Pastor can do with the OT witness to Moses' exalted standing. So Gräßer, *Hebräer*, 1, 165.
[17] Attridge, *Hebrews*, 105; Spicq, *Hébreux*, 2, 6. Neither is the passage concerned to contrast Moses and Christ as heads of divergent "Heilsökonomie[n]" (Gräßer, *Hebräer*, 1, 5).
[18] Thus as Isaacs notes, the contrast *pace* Spicq, *Hébreux*, 2, 63, is not greater glory associated with a greater degree of faithfulness, but rather greater glory because of equivalent faithfulness but in a much greater role (Isaacs, *Sacred Space*). On the potential for the language as either "fedele" or "degno di fede" especially in relation to Jesus see the discussion of Franco Manzi, "La Fede Degli Uomini e la Singolare Relazione Filiale Di Gesù Con Dio nell'Epistola agli Ebrei," *Bib* 81 (2000): 38–41.

in shadowy and indirect fashion to a prophet (Num 12:6),[19] to Moses the LORD speaks directly: στόμα κατὰ στόμα (Num 12:8). These statements rebuff Aaron and Miriam's suggestion that they are Moses' equals (Num 12:2), not only lowering them in comparison to Moses but even excluding them from the prophetic office by removing them personally from the discussion.[20] Moses' status at the same time is exalted. He is no mere prophet, but a receiver of clear and unmediated revelation. His jurisdiction is commensurate: he is a servant in *all* God's house (12:7). His role as a mediator, or even *the mediator*, of revelation is connected to his unmediated access to God—to him he speaks "mouth to mouth"—even beholding God's glory.[21]

This characterization of the ministry of Moses as unmediated, direct and privileged probably alludes to the foundational events of Exod 32–34 and the revelation of God at Sinai. The Sinai gathering, and Moses' role in it, ties access and revelation together, a connection strengthened by Num 12:8, that Moses τὴν δόξαν κυρίου εἶδεν. Reflecting on this connection of Num 12 and the Sinai gathering suggests that we are meant to think of Moses, in comparison to Jesus, as himself a kind of apostle and high priest.[22] Indeed, in the Num 12 episode, in which Moses' supreme stature is affirmed, he is also called upon to act, not only as an intermediary of revelation from God to his people but also as an intermediary from the direction of the people to God: Aaron's request for Miriam's healing is directed through Moses who intercedes on their behalf to God. In every way, then, in Num 12 Moses is supreme in his mediatory status, and the testimony of God in Num 12:7 is a climatic affirmation of this standing.

However, in bringing over the quotation about Moses' supremacy above all other mediators, the Numbers text becomes a standard against which Christ's supremacy over Moses is demonstrated.[23] This comparison does not denigrate Moses[24]—bettering Christ by finding fault with Moses—but rather demonstrates that a position superior to the supreme Old Covenant Apostle and High Priest is in fact latent within the Numbers language itself. If Moses was highest in the house, might not someone be positioned outside of it, and, thereby, over it? This superior position, the Pastor asserts, is that of Christ, the Son.[25]

---

[19] This is furthered by the description of God that he does not speak to Moses δι' αἰνιγμάτων (Num 12:7), suggesting that this "riddle" like quality is to be identified with the dreams and visions of Num 12:6, and thus with the character of God's normal relation to the prophets.

[20] That is the prophet to whom Moses is compared is a "he" not a "you," suggesting that Aaron and Miriam are not even included in the former, let alone on par with Moses.

[21] Cf. the comments of Owen, *Hebrews*, 3, 516.

[22] For those tending to downplay any sort of hieratic overtone for Moses as θεράπων see Hughes, *Hebrews*, 128; Christopher A. Richardson, *Pioneer and Perfecter of Faith: Jesus' Faith as the Climax of Israel's History in the Epistle to the Hebrews*, WUNT 338 (Tübingen: Mohr Siebeck, 2012), 49, 50. For those suggesting both terms are to be borne in mind in the discussion of Moses see Bruce, *Hebrews*, 56; Koester, *Hebrews*, 249; Gert J. Steyn, "Moses as Therapwn in Heb 3: 5-6: Portrait of a Cultic Prophet-Priest in Egypt?," *JNSL* 40 (2014): 113–25. Most acknowledge that it is certainly present in Philo. For the exalted status of Moses in first-century Judaism see Isaacs, *Sacred Space*, 138–40.

[23] That is, the Pastor "macht *mit* Mose eine Aussage über den Christus" (Gräßer, "Mose und Jesus," 13, 22).

[24] And so the fading of Moses' glory which is of such importance in 2 Cor 3:12–18 is in no way called to mind by the Pastor here. Backhaus, *Hebräerbrief*, 139; Otto Michel, *Der Brief an die Hebräer*, KEK 13 (Göttingen: Vandenhoeck & Ruprecht, 1966), 97.

[25] The lack of denigration is particularly signalled by the choice of text through which Moses is represented (Gräßer, "Mose und Jesus," 21). Spicq makes a similar observation but ties this "tact"

It is within this development of the degree of greater glory which obtains to the Son, that the logic of Heb 3:3–6a functions, and which has caused such disagreement among interpreters, one author going as far as to call its logic "tortuous."[26] In order to investigate this logic I will first lay out two predominant trajectories which have held sway, and which analyse the progression of thought in vv. 3, 4 differently. These differences are of particular interest through the way in which they see a potential identification of the Son as God in these verses, and correspond to an understanding of 3:3, 4 as either a tight syllogism or a loose analogy.

3.2.1 Heb 3:3, 4 as a syllogistic statement of Christ's deity

For many pre-critical interpreters the significance of the flow of thought in Heb 3:3, 4 took on the character of a *locus probans* for the deity of Christ.[27] This determination was reached by reading 3:3, 4 an example of syllogistic reasoning. This syllogism encouraged the identification of parties in compared pairs, such that the Son was frequently seen as both the builder of 3:3b, 4a, and, at times, the God of 3:4b, observing that, as with any syllogism, certain unstated premises were at work in the Pastor's argument. In exegeting such an argument it then becomes significant to note where those assumptions lie and how they sustain the logic of the syllogism.

John Owen's exegesis of these verses may be taken as a signal example of this syllogistic approach.[28] His outline of the argument's structure closely resembles that of other earlier commentators, such as Thomas Aquinas, Ps-Oecumenius and others.[29] In handling vv. 3 and 4 within this structure Owen exegetes the flow of thought, at the same time noting the assumptions and omissions on which the syllogistic reasoning relies.[30]

For Owen, 3:3a constitutes a proposition: Christ is greater than Moses.[31] The remainder of vv. 3 and 4 then provides an argument which proves this proposition,

---

of the Pastor to the perception that his audience would resent an exploration of Moses' infidelity (Spicq, *Hébreux*, 2, 63, 64). It is better, rather than connecting this choice of the Pastor either to a lack of criticism of the Mosaic economy, with Gräßer, or a concern for the audience's sympathies, with Spicq, to recognize that Moses can be viewed under two different perspectives: as a mechanism for perfection the Mosaic economy is ἀσθενὲς καὶ ἀνωφελὲς (7:18); but as a revelatory testimony to Christ, Moses as revealer was πιστὸς ἐν ὅλῳ τῷ οἴκῳ αὐτοῦ ν (3:5). Cf. Koester, *Hebrews*, 246. On the relation of Moses' role as a μαρτύριον and the later "speaking" of God in the climactic revelation in Christ see Jon Laansma, *"I Will Give You Rest": The "Rest" Motif in the New Testament with Special Reference to Mt 11 and Heb 3-4*, WUNT 98 (Tübingen: Mohr Siebeck, 1997), 268n278.

[26] "Der etwas gewundene Gedankengang" (Backhaus, *Hebräerbrief*, 139). Also see the comments of Lane, *Hebrews 1–8*, 72; Schierse, *Verheissung und Heilsvollendung*, 110 and Johnson, *Hebrews*, 107, 108.

[27] The phrase *locus probans* is Stebler's ("Beweistelle," 461).

[28] Owen writes of the functioning of v. 3 that "plainly the apostle reasons syllogistically in this case" (Owen, *Hebrews*, 3, 533). See also his comments at ibid., 539.

[29] Cf. ibid., 487–554. For a very similar structural outline see Johannes Braun, *Commentarius in Epistolam Ad Hebraeos* (Amsterdam: H. & T. Boom, 1705), 184.

[30] For Owen the way in which 3:3, 4 draw out various assumptions or unstated premises flow from the Pastor's desire "to show that his argument had a real foundation in the things from which the parity of reason insisted on by him did arise" (Owen, *Hebrews*, 3, 554).

[31] Ibid., 539.

beginning with the statement of 3:3b, that builders exceed in honour the structures built by them. In Owen's thought, this can only function via an assumption. As he writes, "The assumption included is, 'But Christ built the house, and Moses was only of the house or a part of it; and therefore he had more glory than Moses.'"[32] He recognizes that in order for this identification to hold certain assumptions are made in 3:3 which are either stated or alluded to in the clauses that immediately follow. In this vein, 3:4a supplies one of these supposed minor premises which completes the connection of 3:3a and 3:3b. The Pastor's statement, that "every house is built by someone" (3:4a) establishes that the existence of a house in which Moses served requires that there is one who built it.[33] 3:4b is similarly taken to be a "confirmation" of one of the preceding assumptions. Owen notes that in fact in his day, three different views prevailed. One view read 3:4b as confirming that builders have greater glory than their constructions. A second saw it as confirming the tacit assumption in 3:3 that Christ is indeed the builder of God's house, as the house of God can be built "by none but him who is God."[34] A third group, who Owen identifies as Socinian, saw the clause as nothing "but a mere illustration of what was before spoke, by a comparison of Christ and his works about his house, and God and his house in the creation of all."[35] Owen's preference is for the second reading which he seeks to confirm in his exegesis.

For Owen, this mainly arises from the conviction that v. 4b must contribute to the argument of 3:3, 4. In pursuing this he begins by explaining that the house which Moses served in and Christ built is "the building of the Church in all ages," thus raising the question of who could build such a house.[36] 3:4b is then taken as an answer to this question, the explicit statement of which both buttresses the assumption that Christ built the house and suggests to Owen that this is indeed the assumption at play. Though Owen notes the debatable configuration of the predicate nominative in v. 4b, whether θεός represents the subject or predicate, in his judgement, "amount[s] unto the same."[37] What is key is that it is seen as a sentence answering the question "who is capable of building the house of God to which Moses belonged?" The clear answer is—God alone. For Owen, to assign this θεός statement either to the Father or to the work of creation generally falls short for two main reasons: it deflects the language of building to that of creation as a whole, which Owen argues, is not under discussion, and further, would, if read in this way, become an entirely extraneous statement, in no way supporting the foregoing assertions. Hence the language of the building of πάντα ought to be identified with the house of God and its diverse administration at various stages of history,[38] and the word θεός be seen as designating the

---

[32] Ibid., 533, 540, 542–6.
[33] Ibid., 554. Braun's argument from v. 4a, while resulting in a similar reading of v. 4b to Owen, is rather different, relying on an antithesis of the kinds of houses and agencies at stake in v. 4. In this he draws on Ephrem the Syrian's rendering of v. 4a = מן אנשא הו מתבנא (Braun, *Ad Hebraeos*, 194) leading Braun to read v. 4 as a contrast between human and divine production: "Omnis domus materialis ab … homine … aedifactur; sed haec domus Spiritualis, Ecclesia Dei, ab ipso Deo aedificatur." Thus he concludes "Is autem est Christus: ut vel ex hoc loco constet divinitatis Christi" (ibid., 195).
[34] Owen, *Hebrews*, 3, 534.
[35] Ibid.
[36] Ibid., 555.
[37] Ibid.
[38] So ibid., who notes that this is also Beza's view. Similar is Calvin, *Hebrews*, 80.

Son.³⁹ Thus, taking the verses as a whole, and drawing together the various predications and assumptions Owen sees at work, the following syllogism results:⁴⁰

Proof:
Every house is built by someone (3:4a)
AND Builders are worthy of more honour than their constructions (3:3b)
Jesus built the house of which Moses was only a part (assumed minor proposition)
  AND is a spiritual house alone buildable by God (assumed minor proposition)
    Such that, that one who built all (i.e. Jesus), is God (v4b)
ERGO
Proposition: Jesus is worthy of greater honour than Moses (3:3a)

Of greatest significance for Owen is that the two minor propositions which are assumed in the argument are necessary in order to make the argument work. That Jesus built the house of which Moses was only a part is both a development of the language of the Num 12:7 quotation, but also for Owen necessary in order to connect 3a and 3b.⁴¹ Similarly one must see an assumption that the house, of which Moses was a part, is a house alone buildable by God. How else, he avers, can the mention of God building all things contribute to an argument for the greatness of Christ over Moses? Such a statement makes sense only if it is extolling the necessary divine power required to build the house which Christ built.⁴²

For Owen, then, 3:3, 4 represent an example of syllogistic reasoning connecting divine power, divine building and the action of Christ in order to construct an argument for the supremacy in honour and glory of Christ over Moses, which is the Pastor's main point.⁴³

---

³⁹ Spicq, though demurring from this position himself, lists as those seeing Christ's deity in view in v. 4b: Ps-Oecumenius, Theophylact, Thomas, Cajetan, Estius, Moses Stuart, Lemmonyer, Rohr and Seisenberger (Spicq, *Hébreux*, 1, 68). Bisping's commentary also lists Theodoret and Cornelius a Lapide (Augustus Bisping, *Erklärung des Briefes an die Hebräer* (Münster: Aschendorff, 1854), 82). This view is also taken by Cockerill (*Hebrews*, 165n140, 166). Bruce states that the syntax makes this view "just possible" but it is "simpler" to view it as identifying God as Creator of all (*Hebrews*, 93n14). Owen interestingly notes a diversity of opinion on v. 4b as to whether it contains an assertion of Christ's deity but, like Cockerill, he holds it must in order to preserve something of a logical force to an argument for Christ's supremacy (*Hebrews*, 3, 555, 556).

⁴⁰ The way in which I have arranged it here is to try to bring out the reconstructed argument as I think Owen sees it, though it is, in form, different to that of Heb 3:3, 4. One cannot help but wonder if the difficulty of stating Owen's position in the form of the text of Heb 3 itself is indicative of at least some weakness or lack of conclusiveness in the argument he puts forward. Cf. Owen, *Hebrews*, 3, 554.

⁴¹ "That this assumption is included in the words is evident ... to infer the purpose of the apostle" (ibid., 533).

⁴² In reading 3:4b, Owen argues that it must be Christ who is meant, for to introduce the general creating work of God at this point, without reference to Christ, "would disturb the series of his discourse, and render it equivocal" (ibid., 555). This is, in effect, the opposite of Michel's judgement: "Dieser klare Aufbau wird dann gestört, wenn man das θεός in V.4b auf Christus bezieht" (Michel, *Hebräer*, 97).

⁴³ Owen, *Hebrews*, 3, 533, 556. This functions with two syllogisms, the second developed as Christ's superiority as owner over Moses as servant. This two-argument structure is still retained by some more modern exegetes; see, e.g. Spicq, *Hébreux*, 2, 63.

3.2.2 Heb 3:3, 4 as a loose analogy

Modern interpreters have tended to move away from this syllogistic identification of terms in 3:3, 4 which was so crucial for Owen. With this movement away from syllogism towards analogy, the portrayal of Jesus as divine in these verses has equally become much less certain, and perhaps altogether unlikely.[44]

Such an analogical reading often begins by noting the three parallel relationships that are adduced in vv. 3, 4: (a) Christ is to Moses, (b) as a builder is to a house and (c) as God is to all things. In this analogical view, the last of the comparisons is seen as signalling a cosmic scope, and with it, the concept of God as Creator of all things.[45] This recognition of three parallel analogies tends to lead to a focus on the internal relationships between the pairs (e.g. builder and building), while noting that this does not demand that each pair be identified with any other. The proverbial character especially of the middle syncrisis, of a builder whose honour exceeds that which is built, often leads interpreters to see it as an ad hoc comparison with little theological freight.[46] Within this reading, Vanhoye's comments are often noted, that to press an identification across the three comparisons leads to an absurd conclusion: to identify Christ as the builder, is to say Moses is a house, with the incommensurateness of equating an inanimate building with a person.[47] Or, as Attridge puts it,

> The argument is made unnecessarily complex by the assumption that there is a material correspondence between the terms of the analogy. Hebrews is not suggesting that Jesus is the builder of the house. And certainly not that the "house" is Moses, or any of the possible items that can be symbolized by the term, such as the people of God or the church.[48]

Objections to the identification of parties in the analogies are raised not only due to dissonant imagery but also in relation to the flow of 3:1–6 in toto. Lane argues that such identification of terms, between vv. 3, 4a leads to an "understanding of v4 [that] cannot be integrated with the development [of the verses], since there the action of building is assigned to God, and not to Jesus."[49]

---

[44] Describing the movement between the three comparisons as not "a one-to-one comparison, but a comparison from analogy" (Lala Kalyan Kumar Dey, *The Intermediary World and Patterns of Perfection in Philo and Hebrews*, SBLDS 35 (Missoula: SBL Press, 1975), 167). Cited approvingly in Gräßer, *Hebräer*, 1, 167.

[45] Lane, *Hebrews 1–8*, 77; Attridge, *Hebrews*, 110; some commentators note that the πάντα may have in and of itself a redemptive focus connecting either with the soteriology of the Letter generally (Spicq, *Hébreux*, 2, 67) or with the Rest passage which then comes into view (Koester, *Hebrews*, 245).

[46] So that the comparison is seen as "a general illustrative analogy" (Attridge, *Hebrews*, 104), as having "no theological significance" (Lane, *Hebrews 1–8*, 77) or as having "Sprichwort-Charakter … und sollte nicht theologisch gepresst werden" (Backhaus, *Hebräerbrief*, 139).

[47] Albert Vanhoye, *La Structure Littéraire de l'Épître aux Hébreux*, 2nd ed. (Paris: Desclée De Brouwer, 1976), 89.

[48] Attridge, *Hebrews*, 110 citing Moffatt, Montefiore, Teodorico. Gräßer cites Spicq, D'Angelo and Swetnam as pursuing this "falschen Identifikation" (*Hebräer*, 1, 167n177).

[49] Lane, *Hebrews 1–8*, 72. See also the similar reasoning of Ellingworth, *Hebrews*, 203.

The Son as Divine Eschatological Builder   81

In parallel with this focus on the analogical character of vv. 3, 4 follows two frequent observations. First, in contrast to Owen's reading, vv. 3–5a are read as one single argument, the climactic statement of which is in v. 5a.[50] Jesus is of greater worth of glory than Moses, ultimately because he is the Son over the house. The analogies adduced in vv. 3, 4 function within this argument, merely illustrating how one thing may exceed the glory of another. God, as the builder of all things, is the supreme illustration of one who has more glory in comparison to another. Thus, second, not only is the identification of Jesus as God via 4b syntactically unlikely, such a reading would unnecessarily truncate the flow of argument and leave the remains of 5a as a disconnected appendage.[51] It would further constitute a bizarre theological truncation: why continue to argue for the supremacy of the Son over Moses, when one has concluded, syllogistically or not, that he is God? Surely nothing more could be added.[52]

Such a reading, though perhaps chastening an overly enthusiastic desire to identify terms in 3:3, 4, is open to certain difficulties. If the pairs are seen as simply illustrative of one another, how exactly does this illustration further the Pastor's argument? Similarly, is it really the case that the ascendancy of God over his creation is only related to Christ's superiority to Moses as a kind of illustration? The Pastor's style seems to weigh against such an affirmation, as he is not normally given to mere "edifying aside[s]."[53]

A few who support an analogical reading soften these objections by including a certain degree of permeability within the three analogies. This particularly obtains to the concept of glory. That is, some relationship between the glory and the honour of the Son (3:2) and the glory of the God "who created all things" (3:4b) is seen as being necessary to the argumentative flow of 3:1–6. This raises the question of the nature of this derivation of glory from the Father to the Son, which is often developed from other aspects of the Epistle, in particular, the theme of inheritance. The Son, as God's heir, inherits what is God's, and thus may perhaps be said to share in the glory of the One who builds all things (1:2).[54] Such explorations of how the illustrative analogies serve the overall argument and make it cogent are, however, rare, and the proposals made rather tentative.[55]

---

[50] See in particular Lane's discussion of the use of conjunctions in 3:1–6 and criticism of seeing 3:2–5 as representing two arguments (*Hebrews 1–8*, 72, 73).

[51] Ibid., 72.

[52] Spicq, *Hébreux*, 2, 68.

[53] James Moffatt, *A Critical and Exegetical Commentary on the Epistle to the Hebrews* (New York: Scribners, 1924), 42.

[54] So Westfall, "Moses," 188; Johnson, *Hebrews*, 108. These attempts agree in seeing 3:1–6 as reactivating the conceptions of the Exordium particularly around Christ as God's agent in creation (Backhaus, *Hebräerbrief*, 140). Stebler effectively describes this reading as allowing "kein neuer unabhängiger Gottesbeweis zu suchen sein" (Stebler, "Beweistelle," 463).

[55] At times, one wonders whether the lack of reflection on the argument of vv. 3, 4 is occasioned by too much focus being given to deconstructing the syllogistic view, though with an attendant lack of offering a positive reading of the Pastor's argument. One of the more theologically reflective readings is that of Johnson, *Hebrews*, 108, who though noting that the argumentation is "murky in its details" seeks to draw the passage together by seeing the Pastor as affirming both that "God is the source of all things" and that "the Son … is not simply another creature … but is also *as Son* a participant in the creation of all things" (ibid., 109). Similar are the comments of Bruce:

> Christ, the Son of God, through whom the universe was made and to whom it has been given by His Father as His heritage is founder and inheritor of the household. No distinction

The result of this analogical trajectory in reading 3:3, 4 is not necessarily always coupled with a denial of some role for Christ in building God's house. Nor does it necessarily negate the possibility of identification of Christ with God as something at play in the text. However, it does make the nature of Christ's relation to God's house, and its theological freight, altogether more uncertain.[56]

3.3 Combining the trajectories

In proposing an interpretation of 3:1–6 I wish to suggest that there are certain strengths that can be maintained from each of the above trajectories and combined into a more nuanced and satisfying reading of these verses. This, I propose, maintains that Christ is being portrayed as divine in these verses, but also takes into account the concern for delicacy in treating the analogical relationships of vv. 3, 4 and the overall argumentative orientation of the verses towards v. 5a.

It is first worth noting that some of the criticism of the pre-critical *locus probans* view is overdrawn. To see Moses in v. 3a as parallel to, and in some way identifiable with the house of v. 3b, is simply to realize that the Pastor knows where his argument is going: the people of God are a house (Num 12:7; Heb 3:6). Moses was a servant within the house of the Son, but also one identified as a member of it, choosing to suffer as one of God's people in the face of his reward (11:25, 26).[57]

However, though criticisms of the syllogistic view are too blunt, the analogical view does make some positive contributions. Chief of these is the recognition that vv. 3, 4, though suggestive, do not make a clear argumentative point on their own. They rather set out three pairs of correspondences. In particular the third of these (ὁ δὲ πάντα κατασκευάσας θεός) ought to be read as a description of God's supreme glory as the Creator in relation to his cosmos.[58] Thus the point of each pair is the same: one of each character (Christ, builder, God) has supreme glory over the other (Moses, house, world). The escalating movement of the analogies towards God's work in creation highlights that God is the one who is supremely worthy of honour.[59] Recognizing this

> can be made between the Father and the Son in this regard: God the Father, the Maker of all things, is inevitably the founder of His own household, and it was through his Son that He brought into being all things in general and His own household in particular. (Bruce, *Hebrews*, 93)

> The only weakness of these proposals is the tendency to rely on the language of creational agency without asking whether this pattern is reflected in the same way in redemption, a theme which is manifestly testable within the thought of Hebrews.

[56] For rather unspecific articulation of the Son's relation to God in this passage cf. Attridge, *Hebrews*, 104; Koester, *Hebrews*, 251 and Gräßer, *Hebräer*, 1, 167n178.
[57] Cockerill, *Hebrews*, 166. *Pace* Ellingworth, *Hebrews*, 204. See similarly Bruce's connection of this one house in which both Moses and the Pastor's audience belong with the heroes of faith in 11:4–5 (*Hebrews*, 93n45).
[58] Notwithstanding the objections of Owen noted above.
[59] Attridge, *Hebrews*, 110. This is not, as might be supposed, a point about the ultimate agency of God behind all other agencies, that whenever anything is built by someone, God somehow stands behind that project as the ultimate builder enabling every building project. Rather it is a more exclusive claim about agency—God alone is the one who built the Universe, everything, and thus is worthy

makes it clear that, strictly speaking, there is not a decisive argument made in vv. 3, 4 but rather a part of a thread that is heading for 5a. That is, Christ has supreme glory as Son rather than servant.[60] These points comport with many modern readings. However it seems to open certain questions which are frequently not addressed. How does the Pastor's movement to the supreme glory of builders over houses, including God over his Universe, support the supreme glory of the Son? And how does the relation of the Son's glory relate to the glory of God as Creator over all things?[61]

To the former question, it is tempting to suggest that the analogy of houses and builders is purely an illustrative one and is not to be pressed. But the word οἶκος, both in terms of lexical frequency and its importance to the discussion at hand, problematizes such a weak view proposal.[62] Similarly, the threefold repetition of κατασκευάζω suggests that not only houses but also the fact of their construction is significant.[63] Furthermore, the issue of house is not one that floats free as a metaphor. It is grounded and connected to the theological warp and woof of the discourse. This occurs through its presence in the key Scriptural expression of Num 12:7, its critical function in locating Christ and Moses' statuses, and the inclusion of the Pastor's audience as part of this house. Thus, though the issue of houses and their construction may certainly find parallels in proverbial statements,[64] in this context it is both theologically and rhetorically well integrated into the discourse. In the thought of the Pastor, that a builder is more glorious or honoured is no mere maxim. Rather the truth of it relates to that world in which builders find themselves. The doctrine of creation here is no mere convenient illustration but the foundation of the theological relation between artificers and their constructions.[65]

Recognizing the way in which the three parallel relationships head for the supreme glory of God as Creator of all things leads to the latter question. If God is identified as supremely glorious through his creative work, how is the Son identified as supremely

---

of supreme glory, a qualitatively different kind of glory. Cf. Stebler, "Beweistelle," 466; Cockerill, *Hebrews*, 164; *pace* Richardson, *Pioneer*, 56–7.

[60] Christ's position is elevated above Moses' not only as "Son" rather than "servant," but also via the contrasting prepositional phrases of "over" rather than "in" the house. It seems altogether unlikely that Layton's survey of the language of "over the house" (Scott C. Layton, "Christ over His House (Hebrews 3.6) and Hebrew," *NTS* 37 (1991): 473-7) is at all relevant, confined as it is to the world of servants.

[61] Johnson is provocative in his phrasing of this issue: "Hebrews … quietly adds that every house has a builder … , and God is the one who has built everything. … One can scarcely argue with the assertion, particularly in light of 1:1 and 1:10. But what is the point of the assertion here?" (Johnson, *Hebrews*, 109). In a parallel fashion several commentators note that the inner verses of 3:2–5 must result in an argument for the supremacy of the Son, even though the expansion of the metaphor of builders and buildings seems to terminate on God; it is not, however, the supremacy of God which is at stake, rather the nature of Jesus' supremacy. So Ellingworth, *Hebrews*, 195; Montefiore, *Hebrews*, 72.

[62] On the "lexical cohesion" generated by the repetition of οἶκος see Westfall, "Moses," 189.

[63] The range of κατασκευάζω in relation to buildings both covers the actual aspect of construction (cf. Heb 11:7) and an act of furnishing a structure (Num 21:7; frt. Heb 9:2).

[64] See the examples derived from Menander and Philo of similar proverbs in Koester, *Hebrews*, 244, 245; Backhaus, *Hebräerbrief*, 139, 140.

[65] See the similar comments of Spicq, *Hébreux*, 2, 67.

84 Divine Christology in the Epistle to the Hebrews

worthy of glory? Often this is left unexplored. Koester's comments at this point both highlight the issue and fail to fully explore it:

> If the honor due to the builder is greater than the honor due to the house, then the glory due to God is greater than the honor due to the creation. It is fitting to respect the creation just as it is fitting to honor Moses, but this should not be confused with giving glory to the Creator and the Son, who is over all that has been made (Heb 3:6; cf. 1:10–12).[66]

This both seems to recognize the need to connect the glory of God to the glory of the Son, but then does so rather by appeal back to the catena, rather than to the immediate context of the discussion of houses and their builders.[67] Though Koester's suggestion seems weak at this point, it highlights that a connection must be sourced. Without one, as Cockerill argues, it "leave[s] [v4b] as a foreign body in the text."[68] Westfall similarly notes that a connection must be made in order to complete the line of thought and integrate vv. 3, 4 into the flow of vv. 3–5a. In order to forge this connection she makes use of the concept of inheritance.[69] The argument runs that glory is supremely God's, but as Son, the Son inherits the Father's glory (1:2). This suggestion is certainly coherent but, I would suggest, is not the most likely connection through which to relate the glory of God as Creator and the glory of Christ over Moses as Son, for the following reasons:

Though the connection of Sonship to inheritance is certainly not foreign to Hebrews, there is no suggestion of its role here. Further it is hard to see how it would connect to the internal verses of vv. 3, 4. It is one thing to say that these verses do not, by themselves, constitute an argument; it is quite another to suggest that they play almost no role in forging the argument. On the contrary, in seeking a mechanism for the ascription of glory we ought to pay attention to the clear axiological judgement suggested by the three analogies: glory comes from building. Glory is owed and bestowed because of accomplishment.[70] This is further emphasized by both the depiction of Moses and Christ in 3:1–6 and the surrounding verses. Moses has glory

---

[66] Koester, *Hebrews*, 252. A similar gap is evident in Lane's assertion that 3:1–6 comprise "an exegetical and theological demonstration of Jesus' superiority as Son to Moses, the servant," though his outlining of the flow of thought makes it appear much more to be simply an assertion of the fact (Lane, *Hebrews 1–8*, 79).

[67] Koester's reference back to 1:10–12 (*Hebrews*, 252), it seems to me, is absolutely appropriate but I suggest that 3:1–6 has its own contribution to make here.

[68] Cockerill, *Hebrews*, 167. Cockerill's contention is that in order to avoid this result, v. 4b must be construed as a predication of the deity of Christ. This seems to me an unnecessary conclusion—rather a connection must be forged in reading the text between the supreme glory of God and the glory of the Son over Moses.

[69] Westfall, "Moses," 188.

[70] *Pace* Attridge who, in raising the question of whether this glory is to be associated with the Son's pre-existence (1:3) or with the exaltation (2:9), suggests that "to specify the source of Christ's glory is unnecessary" (Attridge, *Hebrews*, 110). This is, however, to leave Christ's position unsubstantiated from Scripture and less defined that the glory of Moses is contextually, a move too weak to bear the weight of the argument. Attridge's comment that God's "counting worthy" of Christ in context suggests that "the exaltation context is operative here" seems nearer to the point (ibid.).

as one authorized in God's house. Thus he has a glory which is commensurate with the role he fulfils in God's economy. Similarly the Son is one faithful and glorious in relationship to his appointment by God. The wider context of Hebrews supports such a connection between glory and achievement.[71] Glory and honour are that promised to humanity, and yet unfulfilled until the coming of the Son to share in "their things," on account of which he stands now glorified and honoured in the heavenly realm (2:8–9). This is further highlighted in 5:5, 6 in speaking of the glory which Christ has not taken upon himself but is bestowed by the Father. This action is parallel to his inauguration as High Priest on the basis of his personal qualifications. Thus, in the context of Hebrews, glory is tied closely to achievement, which in 3:1–6 is played out within realm of building, whether of houses in general, God's "house" or God's world.[72]

How then, when God is identified as the supremely glorious One who constructed the cosmos, can such glory be predicated of the Son? Or, to put it otherwise, how can the language and status of Christ as Son be seen to connect with this concept? Three ideas seem to provide potential avenues for forging this connection which would include the Son as builder with God in the construction of God's house and thus in sharing the glory that belongs to the builder.

First, one may consider the associations included in the concept of sonship in the world surrounding the New Testament. We have already mentioned the disposal of goods in an inheritance, but this is only one aspect.[73] Equally significant is the presupposed resemblance of fathers and sons, not least exemplified in patterns of shared profession.[74] A son is one who is like his father, sharing the family traits and the family career. This emphasis is reflected elsewhere in NT assumptions about sonship, especially evident in ethical behaviour (Matt 5:9, 45; John 5:19; Acts 13:10; Rom 8:14; 1 Thess 5:5). With this sense of resemblance and shared trade in mind, we may see how the nature of Christ as Son over the house of God connects back to the conception of God as supremely glorious Creator. The Son has been counted worthy of glory because he shares together with his Father in the work of building God's house, a work of divine prerogative, which means he shares the glory of the one who is the supreme builder.[75]

[71] O'Brien, *Hebrews*, 132.
[72] On the issue of Christ's glory here as achievement or innate possession see the discussion in Owen, *Hebrews*, 3, 547, 548, where Owen concludes that in 3:1–6 it is primarily economic achievement and consequent glory that is in view. On connections to preceding glory language see Michel, *Hebräer*, 13.
[73] On the significance of inheritance to concepts of sonship in the Roman world see the evidence of Michael Peppard, *The Son of God in the Roman World: Divine Sonship in Its Social and Political Context* (Oxford: Oxford University Press, 2011), 51–3, 56. Peppard's argument for this centrality of inheritance may be accepted without seeing such as excluding discourse about filial origins, an antithesis which is so important for Peppard, but is handled in a more balanced fashion by Novenson. For which see chapter 3 of Novenson, *Grammar*. On inheritance in Hebrews in relation to the Son see Dana M. Harris, "The Eternal Inheritance in Hebrews: The Appropriation of the Old Testament Inheritance Motif by the Author of Hebrews" (PhD Diss., Trinity Evangelical Divinity School, 2009), 256–66.
[74] On the width of sonship language in the New Testament and the various connotations, see D. A. Carson, *Jesus the Son of God: A Christological Title Often Overlooked, Sometimes Misunderstood, and Currently Disputed* (Wheaton, IL: Crossway, 2012), 15.
[75] See also, rather allusively, both Spicq "Parlant du Christ, selon sa nature humaine, il suggère l'identification de son action divine, comme Fils avec celle du Père" (Spicq, *Hébreux*, 2, 68) and the footnoted comments of Hughes who speaks of a certain "ambivalence" between God as builder

This suggestion is possible, but it is altogether the least able to be tested, relying, as it does, purely on cultural resonances of the concept of sonship.

A second route to sourcing the connection is through allusion to the Nathan Oracle (2 Sam 7 // 1 Chr 17). Such an allusion has been suggested by numerous commentators and has been most extensively developed by Mary Rose D'Angelo.[76] D'Angelo's thesis has received significant criticism,[77] but an argument in its favour here would be its provision of a scriptural background that connects the title of Son and an exalted position over the house of God, with the parallel action of building such a house for God. Exactly how this forges a link between the Son and the glory that properly and most fully belongs to the supreme architect, God, will be explored further below.

A third route is to raise the possibility that, although Owen's reading overly presses 3:3, 4, by making everything hang on the details of a tight syllogism, his detection of assumptions about the relation of God to the building of God's house may still have merit. Owen saw at work in 3:3, 4 the assumption that the building of God's house is itself a work of divine prerogative, due to its spiritual nature. Thus, potentially, to picture Christ as involved in that work of building would provide a mechanism for the accrual of glory above that of Moses. This could function without the need for viewing 3:4b as a predication about Jesus. Indeed, when one considers some of the connections at work in 3:1–6, particularly in regard to the question of agency, there is a degree of plausibility to Owen's suggestion, which is already hinted at in Johnson's explanation noted above. God's glory is tied not only to the act of creation, and the complementary agency of Christ, but also to that of redemption (2:10). In fact the movement of 3:3, 4 makes sense if the author sees a link between agency in redemption (3:3) and agency in creation (3:4). Thankfully the concept of God's agency in redemption, and even more specifically God's agency in relation to the building of God's house, is illuminated by later statements of Hebrews, particularly in relation to the final Temple, City and Rest of God. Owen's concept of the assumption at work in 3:3, 4 may then, at the very least, be specifically tested as to whether it is reflected in later statements about God's house and its construction.

The remainder of this chapter will explore these proposed second and third connections. First, I will explore the potential allusion to the Nathan Oracle in 3:1–6 and how its function might contribute to the portrayal of the Son in these verses. Second, I will demonstrate how Hebrews develops connections between eschatological

---

and Jesus as builder with comparison to 1 Chr 17 (Hughes, *Hebrews*, 134n125). This "ambivalence," which I take to be very suggestive, will be explored further below.

[76] Mary Rose D'Angelo, *Moses in the Letter to the Hebrews*, SBLDS 42 (Missoula, MT: Scholars Press, 1979), 70–93. See also Albert Vanhoye, "L'oracle de Natan dans l'Epître aux Hébreux," in *Gesù Apostolo e Sommo Sacerdote: Studi Biblici in Memoria Di P. Teodorico Ballarini*, ed. E. Vallauri, A.-S. DiMarco, and I. Volpi (Rome: Marietti, 1984).

[77] D'Angelo draws on the article of Sverre Aalen ("'Reign' and 'House' in the Kingdom of God in the Gospels," *NTS* 8 (1962)), cited approvingly by Lane (*Hebrews 1–8*, 76, 77) and Isaacs (*Sacred Space*, 136) and referenced by Bruce (*Hebrews*, 93n45). Some have seen 1 Chr 17:7 and 1 Sam 2:35 as important for understanding 3:1–6 but without adopting D'Angelo's view of an actual citation at 3:2 (Ellingworth, *Hebrews*, 201). Other commentators have found "the alleged allusions … unconvincing" (Attridge, *Hebrews*, 190n153); similarly Cockerill, *Hebrews*, 163n127; Gräßer, "Mose und Jesus," 15n66; Richardson, *Pioneer*, 50n144.

building and divine agency in an attempt to demonstrate that Owen's assumptions around divine building in 3:3, 4 are, in fact, both well-founded and in harmony with the wider theology of Hebrews. In so doing, I hope to demonstrate that, while modern exegetes have rightly cautioned against an overly syllogistic reading, the argument of 3:3, 4 requires something like Owen's assumed premises. The result of this is to demonstrate that Heb 3:1-6 implicitly portrays Jesus, the Son, as participating in the properly divine action of redemption as builder of God's House(hold), and thus accrues a glory, honour and status which not only exceeds that of Moses but is of an altogether different degree.

3.4 The role of the Nathan Oracle and agency in Heb 3:3, 4

3.4.1 Is there an allusion to the Nathan Oracle in Heb 3:1-6?

In assessing the presence of an allusion to 2 Sam 7:14 or its parallel in 1 Chr 17:14 in 3:1-6, recent scholars have tended to interact with the discussion of Mary D'Angelo.[78] D'Angelo argues that the pattern of textual allusion in Heb 3:1-6 employs a "very complex midrashic treatment of a number of texts."[79] In contrast to the prevailing view, which sees a partial citation of Num 12:7 at Heb 3:2, she asserts that the principal citation is 1 Chr 17:14. To support this assertion, she invokes both broad semantic ties between the texts,[80] and, in particular, the semantic correspondence of "the rather unusual use of πιστώσω in 1 Chr. 17.14 and the πιστὸν ὄντα of He. 3.2."[81] Such a tie, according to D'Angelo, relies on the meaning of πιστόω as "to make πιστός."

D'Angelo's position has not gone without criticism.[82] Of those denying its plausibility, the most developed critique is that of Cockerill.[83] He raises three objections to the presence of 1 Chr 17:14 in Heb 3:2. First, that D'Angelo's assertion of semantic equivalence between πιστόω and πιστός is decidedly unlikely. Second, that D'Angelo's

---

[78] D'Angelo, *Moses in the Letter to the Hebrews*, 70-93. Debating the potential allusion to the Nathan Oracle is altogether a more manageable task than that of deciding which of the two accounts he is reliant on. Considering that the Chronicles account is seen as often having a more singular focus on a Davidic scion (William M. Schniedewind, *Society and the Promise to David: The Reception History of 2 Samuel 7:1-17* (New York: Oxford University Press, 1999), 128, 153, 154), it may suit the Pastor's purpose better. However, the likelihood is that the Pastor would have made little distinction between the giving of the promise and its ongoing reception and development in later scriptural material. On which see the comments of Pomykala on the perception of ancient readers of a "flat text" (Kenneth Pomykala, *The Davidic Dynasty Tradition in Early Judaism: Its History and Significance for Messianism*, Early Judaism and Its Literature (Atlanta, GA: Scholars Press, 1995), 11).

[79] D'Angelo, *Moses in the Letter to the Hebrews*, 69.

[80] Particularly with respect to the titular language of "Son of God" and "Christ" (ibid., 71n79 in dependence on Aalen, "'Reign', 'House,'" 236).

[81] D'Angelo, *Moses in the Letter to the Hebrews*, 72, 73. D'Angelo further appeals to Aalen's argument for the Targumic association of the Nathan Oracle with the Oracle to Eli and especially 1 Sam 2:35 (ibid., 78-83 referencing Aalen, "'Reign', 'House,'" 233-40).

[82] Attridge, *Hebrews*, 190n153; Gräßer, "Mose und Jesus," 15n66; Richardson, *Pioneer*, 50n144.

[83] Cockerill, *Hebrews*, 163n127.

argument requires seeing the phrase ἐν τῷ οἴκῳ αὐτοῦ as modifying the participial phrase describing Jesus (πιστὸν ὄντα) rather than the phrase describing Moses' faithfulness, which it immediately follows. However the latter is syntactically more likely and closely follows the phraseology of Num 12:7, suggesting that it is the text being cited rather than 1 Chronicles. In addition, that by taking the phrase in relation to Jesus, the later assertion of 3:6 that the Son is "over" rather than "in" the house of God is directly contradicted. Third, Cockerill argues that the disputed textual variant ὅλῳ in 3:2 points to Num 12:7 as the clear intertext there. For, if it is original, it is decisive in activating an appeal to Numbers, and, if not, it constitutes an early witness, via scribal harmonization, that 3:2 was recognized by early readers as arising from the same source as 3:5. This would negate D'Angelo's position that Num 12 does not enter the text until the later parts of 3:1–6.

Cockerill's criticisms are significant, but rather than leading one to dismiss the possibility of an allusion to the Nathan Oracle within 3:1–6, they ought rather to demonstrate weaknesses in the overstated nature of D'Angelo's case. D'Angelo is not mainly arguing for a broad influence or allusion but rather a direct quotation of 1 Chr 17:14 at 3:2, rather than Num 12:7.[84] Such a bold position places a burden of proof on her argument. One need not take the strong version of her position, however. Rather, in spite of Cockerill's criticism, there seems good warrant for suggesting the presence of an allusion to the Nathan Oracle in 3:1–6 which is both looser in function than D'Angelo suggests, though nonetheless significant. Its presence is established by the following:

First, 3:1–6 employs part of the range of meanings of οἶκος which is evident in the OT as a whole,[85] but the paronomastic use in Hebrews 3, moving between physical buildings and familial households, exactly parallels the play on words of buildings and dynasties employed in the Nathan oracle in relation to the Temple of God (1 Chr 17:4) and David's lineage (1 Chr 17:10).[86]

Second, the concept of Davidic dynasty, on which both these aspects of the Nathan oracle turn, is already suggested as relating to the Son by the quotations of 2 Sam 7:14//1 Chr 17:3 in the catena (1:5).[87] The Pastor is attributing to him the identity of the true and ultimate Son of David. In identifying Jesus as the Son *par excellence* it would be natural to apply to him the function most closely associated with the Davidic heir, which indeed immediately proceeds the adoption formula of 2 Sam 7:14, namely, αὐτὸς οἰκοδομήσει μοι οἶκον τῷ ὀνόματί μου (2 Sam 7:13). This is further strengthened by the use of πρωτότοκος in reference to the Son in 1:6a, almost certainly alluding to David's relationship to YHWH in Ps 88:28 LXX.[88]

---

[84] D'Angelo, *Moses in the Letter to the Hebrews*, 72; Cf. the greater nuance of Ellingworth, *Hebrews*, 201.
[85] See Michel "οἶκος," *TDNT* 5:119–31.
[86] P. Kyle McCarter, *II Samuel: A New Translation with Introduction, Notes, and Commentary*, AB 9 (Garden City, NY: Doubleday, 1984), 217; George H. Guthrie, "Hebrews," in *Commentary on the New Testament Use of the Old Testament*, ed. G. K. Beale and D. A. Carson (Grand Rapids, MI: Baker Academic, 2007), 952; Joseph A. Fitzmyer, *The One Who Is to Come* (Grand Rapids, MI: Eerdmans, 2007), 34.
[87] Ellingworth, *Hebrews*, 201; Lane, *Hebrews 1–8*, 76.
[88] Peeler, *My Son*, 52.

Third, that 3:6 constitutes the first occurrence of the term "Christ" in relation to the Son,[89] may also support a royal and Davidic element to the passage.[90]

Fourth, though Cockerill is right to challenge whether the syntax and semantics of 1 Chr 17:4 LXX are equivalent to Heb 3:2, such a tight kind of relation need not be pursued. The differences in word meaning and referent in the two passages need not exclude the possibility of allusion. In both passages there is a collocation of house language with language related to the πιστ- root and a relationship explored between them. Thus the talk of Jesus as πίστος in Heb 3:1–6 may be sufficient to call to mind the application of the unusual πιστόω of the Nathan oracle in portraying the Son of God as the great Son of David (1:5, 6).[91]

3.4.2 The function of the Nathan Oracle in relation to Heb 3:1–6

Having discussed the possibility of an allusion to the Nathan Oracle in the opening verses of Heb 3, it remains to be demonstrated how such an allusion might support the reading of Heb 3:3, 4 advanced above. To do so it is first necessary to consider the oracle given to David, which has occupied such a significant place in the development of Jewish and Christian thought.[92]

The Nathan Oracle records a dialogue between YHWH and David concerning the building of YHWH's house.[93] David having finally ascended to the throne and settled in his royal palace (2 Sam 7:1), takes the initiative to build a permanent house for God (2 Sam 7:2). Though initially he is encouraged by the prophet Nathan, YHWH sends word via his prophet to David that this is not what will happen. Rather, God will establish David and build him a house, a succession which will neither fail in its rule nor be rejected as David's predecessor, Saul, had been (2 Sam 7:4–17).[94] This promise

---

[89] Subsequent occurrences are 3:14; 5:5; 6:1; 9:11, 14, 24, 28; 10:10; 11:26; 13:8, 21.

[90] On the use of Christ as a substantive and discussion of divine begetting see 1QSa 2:12 and the discussion of William Horbury, *Jewish Messianism and the Cult of Christ* (London: SCM Press, 1998), 9–11. On the emergence of messianic conceptions see Fitzmyer, *The One Who Is to Come*; Antti Laato, *A Star Is Rising: The Historical Development of the Old Testament Royal Ideology and the Rise of the Jewish Messianic Expectations*, University of South Florida International Studies in Formative Christianity and Judaism (Atlanta, GA: Scholars Press, 1997); Michael F. Bird, *Are You the One Who Is to Come?: The Historical Jesus and the Messianic Question* (Grand Rapids, MI: Baker Academic, 2009); John J. Collins, *The Scepter and the Star: Messianism in Light of the Dead Sea Scrolls*, 2nd ed. (Grand Rapids, MI: Eerdmans, 2010) and chapters 3, 4 of Andrew Chester, *Messiah and Exaltation: Jewish Messianic and Visionary Traditions and New Testament Christology*, WUNT 207 (Tübingen: Mohr Siebeck, 2007). As Bird notes, the tendencies in discussion of this issue are to swing between a "rubber-band definition of messianism" where there are little conceptual controls, and a "linguistic straitjacket" where uses of "messiah" become overly controlling (*Messianic Question*, 35).

[91] Of sixteen occurrences of πιστόω in the LXX texts, seven are bound up with either the giving of the Davidic promise or later desire for its fulfilment.

[92] On the influence of the Nathan Oracle and its reception see Schniedewind, *Promise to David*, 140–67; Pomykala, *Davidic Dynasty*, 174.

[93] 2 Sam 7:1–29.

[94] On issues of conditionality in the Davidic promise see Jon D. Levenson, "The Davidic Covenant and Its Modern Interpreters," *CBQ* 41 (1979): 205–15; David Noel Freedman, "The Chronicler's Purpose," *CBQ* 23 (1961): 438, 439; Lyle M. Eslinger, *House of God or House of David: The Rhetoric of 2 Samuel 7*, JSOTSup 164 (Sheffield: JSOT Press, 1994), 1, 93.

includes in it a subsidiary element, that, after David's death, a son of David will arise to build the envisioned permanent house for YHWH (2 Sam 7:13). The latter part of the dialogue is taken up with David's response to this promise of YHWH (2 Sam 7:18–19), in which he is amazed at God's commitment to his dynasty, abases himself and calls on God to do what he has said.[95]

Comparison has often been drawn between the Nathan oracle and Heb 3:1–6 because of the overlapping issues of paronomasia involving house language, and the related agencies of God and David in the building of various houses, physical and metaphorical. This relevance is further enhanced by the eschatological tendencies in which later readers of the Nathan oracle focus on a figure beyond Solomon; this is reflected as early as the Chronicler,[96] but also evident in various aspects of Second Temple Judaism, and is appropriated by the Pastor in a parallel fashion in relation to the Son as true Son of David.[97] There are further elements of the Nathan Oracle, however, that have either been neglected or received only passing note in relation to Hebrews, but are nonetheless significant for understanding patterns of agency in Heb 3:3, 4 and go some way to resolving its perceived tensions.

First, though the language of physical and metaphorical houses is obviously shared between the oracle and Heb 3, some development has taken place in the concept of David's house in a manner somewhat paralleled at Qumran.[98] The language of house, rather than referring to a Davidic lineage of kings descending through time, has now become applied to a people at a single moment in time (3:6).[99] Rather than a dynasty of kings we have a community, a messianic people. This is due in part to the promise of descendants being found to terminate on a single individual, a Son *par excellence*, which, rather than collapsing the promise, transforms the promise towards that of

---

[95] On the lexicalizing of David's humility in the text see Eslinger, *House of God*, 75.
[96] Schniedewind, *Promise to David*, 128; Freedman, "The Chronicler's Purpose," 440–2; Fitzmyer, *The One Who Is to Come*, 33, 34. Though see Pomykala, *Davidic Dynasty*, 69–104.
[97] On different evaluations of how widespread Davidic expectations were in Second Temple Judaism see the discussions of Schniedewind, *Promise to David* and Pomykala, *Davidic Dynasty*. Though there is certainly a range of opinion in Early Judaism on the issue of a future Davidic King (cf. Josephus, *Ant.* 10.143 and Pss. Sol. 17, 18) and though Pomykala is right to note that "all references to [the] tradition [of the Davidic promise] need not have been oriented toward hope for a messianic figure" (ibid., 8), the minimalist position is too strong. On which see the pushback in Horbury, *Jewish Messianism*, 43 and Felix H. Cortez, "'The Anchor of the Soul That Enters within the Veil': The Ascension of the 'Son' in the Letter to the Hebrews" (PhD Diss., Andrews University, 2008), 184–7.
[98] See in particular the application of 2 Sam 7:14 to a messianic figure and Ps 2 to a plurality of "elect ones" in 4Q147 1 I, 10, 18. On the transfer of cultic house imagery to the community at Qumran see Bertil E. Gärtner, *The Temple and the Community in Qumran and the New Testament : A Comparative Study in the Temple Symbolism of the Qumran Texts and the New Testament*, SNTSMS 1 (New York: Cambridge University Press, 2005), 20–25; James D. G. Dunn, *The Partings of the Ways: Between Christianity and Judaism and Their Significance for the Character of Christianity* (London: SCM Press, 2006), 50, 80. See also the discussion of Klijn with regard to various texts in the *Manual of Discipline* (esp. 1QS XI, 3–6) in A. F. J. Klijn, "Stephen's Speech–Acts VII. 2–53," *NTS* 4 (1957): 30, 31.
[99] This is not to suggest that the household only exists in that moment, clearly the Pastor sees it as including the people of God throughout history. It is the same house to which they belong, within which Moses was a servant in his day (3:2, 5). So Cockerill, *Hebrews*, 153, 169; Gräßer, *Hebräer*, 1, 168. It is rather to stress that a succession of individuals has become a community of the faithful.

many brothers for the one Son.[100] In Hebrews the promise to David, in terminating on a single individual, does not remove house language, but rather reorients it towards the many brothers of the Son, over whom he is positioned.[101]

Second, in comparing the language of house(hold)s between the two passages, one may note that patterns of agency have undergone a shift; specifically, agents have switched places.[102] In the Nathan Oracle the Davidic scion is promised to build a physical house.[103] Conversely, YHWH will build a household, a lineage for David.[104] In Heb 3:1–6 however, these roles are reversed. God is primarily construed as the creator of physical things and is compared to that of a constructor who physically builds a house (3:4b). Christ, however, is primarily connected to the construction of a household over whom he has consequent authority and honour (3:3, 4a). Thus in the Pastor's handling of the Nathan oracle, one may say either that roles have been reversed or that patterns of distinct agency have become fused. The latter may be closer to the truth in Hebrews, as more broadly in the Epistle the Son and God are not excluded from the activities which are particularly attached to each at Heb 3:1–6; the Son is elsewhere intimately involved in the physical construction of the cosmos (1:2); the Father is equally intimately involved in the redemption of a people for the Son (2:10; 6:13–20; 12:7–11).[105]

Third, this blurring of patterns of agency may itself rely on aspects of the Nathan Oracle which are developed *in nuce* in the account of Chronicles. Though close alliance between the purposes of God and the rule of the Davidic dynasty are already developed, this becomes further strengthened through the move to speak of David's house as "my house" in 1 Chr 17:14.[106] Though the language of God's Temple house closely precedes this language, the parallelism in the verse with the Davidic scion's kingdom suggests that, rather than referring to distinct entities of God's building and David's dynasty, the house of David who will rule the kingdom is at the same time God's own house reigning with his divine rule.[107]

Fourth, I noted in the exegesis of Heb 3:3,4 that the issue of divine prerogative, as suggested by Owen, might go some way to explaining the difficult logic of those verses. Attention to the shape of the Nathan Oracle strengthens this suggestion, as the oracle itself contains some similar tensions over divine prerogative with respect to the Temple. It has been routinely noted that 2 Sam 7 contains a certain ambiguity towards the initiative of Temple building. On the one hand, David's initiative is refused

---

[100] On the familial nature of the household in these verses see the sensitive discussion of Peeler, *My Son*, 113–15.
[101] On the connection of this house concept to covenant see Schierse, *Verheissung und Heilsvollendung*, 112), a move which is itself latent in the Nathan Oracle itself (2 Sam 7:14; 24).
[102] Hughes, *Hebrews*, 134n125.
[103] 2 Sam 7:13.
[104] At this point the LXX text of 2 Sam 7 diverges from the MT in speaking of David's scion building YHWH's house. The MT and the account at 1 Chr 17:10 both speak of God building David's house at this point.
[105] That is, as noted above, the patterns of agency observed in creation in Hebrews are parallel, and reflective of, patterns of agency in redemption.
[106] Pomykala, *Davidic Dynasty*, 89.
[107] Cf. Aalen, "'Reign', 'House,'" 233, 234 and Schniedewind, *Promise to David*, 13, 131.

(2 Sam 7:5–7). The tone of YHWH's response grounds the refusal in God's initiative towards David. In suggesting that he build a Temple for YHWH, David is forgetting his place and seeking to turn the relationship on its head. YHWH's reply highlights that he, YHWH, has been the prime actor in Israel's history to this point, both in the redemption and leading of Israel, and also in the David's ascension to the throne (2 Sam 7:8, 9).[108] Thus David's role is turned from active initiator to a more passive one— he becomes the object of God's own building project. This reversal is reflected in the move from Nathan's encouragement to "do whatever is in your heart" (2 Sam 7:3) to YHWH's negation of his initiative. At the same time, and rather confusingly, YHWH, in stymying David's plan and suggesting its inappropriateness, also takes it up into his economy.[109] David will not build the Temple, but rather his son. This might be simply harmonized by seeing God's refusal as one of rejecting David as builder ("not you") or that of a rejection of timing ("not now").[110] But the Nathan oracle presents a more open tension to this question in which God's supremacy and initiative are to the fore. God's response negates David's plan, while at the same time unveiling a promised Temple which will emerge from YHWH's own act to establish a Davidic heir. This tension between rejection of Davidic initiative, divine agency and the promise of Davidic involvement proves a rather difficult tension to resolve in the OT texts. However, the shape of the Pastor's Christology, in which a single individual can be considered as both David's true scion, and as one performing the personal prerogatives of God, would provide a potential answer to these tensions over Temple construction. It would equally make plausible an appeal to both the language and ideas of the Nathan Oracle, alongside assumptions of divine prerogatives in building, as undergirding elements in Heb 3:1–6.

In noting the above, it is clear that the presence of an allusion to the Nathan Oracle in Heb 3:1–6 is much more significant than has often been noted. Certainly, such an allusion would strengthen the identification of the Son as the fulfilment of the Davidic heir and, consequently, identify him as the builder of God's latter-day house. But it also contributes a background of thought which strengthens Owen's suggestions: that assumptions about divine prerogative are at work in Heb 3. The shifts in agency between the two texts, along with the latent questions about divine initiative in the Nathan Oracle, support the thread of argument that the Son, in building God's household, is worthy of divine honour. He participates in the divine economy of building which is both general in relation to the cosmos (1:2; 10–12; 2:10; 3:4; 4:3, 4) and also comes to a focus in the plan of redeeming a family of sons alongside their messianic brother (2:11–18; 10:21; 12:23).[111] Thus the work of the Son is reflective of his Father's identity in Hebrews, where his general creational and providential power is associated with his

---

[108] Eslinger, *House of God*, 27.
[109] This tension is frequently noted, see, e.g. ibid., 11; Schniedewind, *Promise to David*, 17, 18, 37; McCarter, *II Samuel: A New Translation with Introduction, Notes, and Commentary*, 221, 222.
[110] This is closer in tone to the explanation of 1 Chronicles for the rejection of David's initiative. Cf. McCarter, *II Samuel: A New Translation with Introduction, Notes, and Commentary*, 230, 231.
[111] On these familial issues see at length Peeler, *My Son*.

salvific action.[112] The one through whom, and because of whom, are all things (2:10a) is also the one who leads many sons to glory (2:10b); the Creator of all (4:4b) is the particular Saviour of Abraham's seed (2:16).

3.5 The connection of eschatological building to divine prerogative in Hebrews

Having considered the impact of the Nathan Oracle for understanding the relationship of the Son to building the house of God in Heb 3:1–6, further understanding of the nature of divine building can be found within the wider Epistle. In doing so I will demonstrate that the Son's eschatological role in building God's redemptive house(hold) imputes to him a properly divine work due to assumptions in Hebrews about the building of eschatological states as a divine prerogative.

As was noted above, pre-critical interpreters often saw in Heb 3:3, 4 that building God's house was a divine prerogative, and so implied the divinity of the Son as one building that house. They then explored this assumption through the broader teaching of the NT on the spirituality of God's house(hold). This led to appeals to texts like 1 Pet 2:4, 5 or Eph 2:18–22. This development of house imagery in early Christianity certainly sheds light on the conception of the people of God in relation to Temple imagery, and lends plausibility to Owen's suggestion that convictions about divine building underlie the Pastor's logic in Heb 3:3, 4. However, if such assumptions could also be demonstrated to arise from within the thought of Hebrews itself, this would surely strengthen the case for the reading that has been advanced.

In fact, Hebrews itself demonstrates just such assumptions around the prerogative of divine agency in eschatological building, in texts related to three sets of imagery. First are those statements which concern the nature of the heavenly tabernacle in 8:2, 9:11 and 9:24. Second are those texts which include the concept of a city or homeland as the destination for the faithful, and which God himself has established (10:34; 11:10, 16; 12:22; 13:14). Third, and perhaps less obviously related to divine action is the concept of Rest derived from Ps 95:11 and Gen 2:2 which is deployed in 3:7–4:11. This set of images is particularly significant as they relate to themes which are central to the thought of the Pastor and the argument of the Epistle.

Before moving to interact with the first grouping of texts which relate to the description of God's heavenly tabernacle in Hebrews, it is worth noting that two of the three texts involve the use of a rather unusual adjective, χειροποίητος. Both 9:11 and 9:24 employ the term in order to negate it in relation to God's heavenly dwelling place.[113] To begin to understand the use of this lexeme in Hebrews, I first will investigate the

---

[112] Interestingly Ps 89, from which the Pastor probably draws the language of πρωτότοκος φor Christ, also intertwines reflection on YHWH's oath to David and creational themes (Ps 89:1–18) and further relates the oath to David to God's covenant with his "chosen ones" (Ps 89:3).

[113] The syntax is slightly different between these two uses. In 9:11 the negation is of the substantive χειροποίητος; in 9:24 the negation attaches to the verb εἰσῆλθεν, but the effect is the same. What Christ has entered into is not "made with hands."

meaning of the lexeme outside of Hebrews. This is not attempted in order to prejudge its use within Hebrews, but the results of the survey below are not insignificant. Rather they point to the fact that meaning of χειροποίητος outside of Hebrews consistently centres on an antithesis between divine and human action, and the Pastor's use of the lexeme trades on the same concepts, particularly in relation to the eschaton and its establishment.[114]

3.5.1 χειροποίητος and ἀχειροποίητος outside of Hebrews

The use of χειροποίητος and its related alpha privative ἀχειροποίητος is not limited within the NT to the two Hebrews texts cited above but rather as Bruce notes,

> The contrast between the terms 'made with human hands' and 'not made with human hands' is a prominent feature of the primitive catechesis about the new temple which runs through the NT and early Christian apologetic.[115]

The two terms appear a total of seven times, χειροποίητος occurring in Mark 14:58; Acts 7:48; 17:24; Eph 2:11 and ἀχειροποίητος in Mark 14:58; 2 Cor 5:1 and Col 2:11. The use of the term, though centred on the concept of Temple, traverses a large number of other significant themes, including resurrection and the heavenly sphere (2 Cor 5:1), the work of Christ in its application to believers (Col 2:11; Eph 2:11) and perhaps the work of Christ in its objective accomplishment (Col 2:11).[116]

One might expect, considering the pervasive character of the lexeme, that its NT use would be well rooted in a similar Septuagintal set of themes. However, though the term occurs fourteen times in the LXX,[117] the usage is limited to criticism of idolatry. Idols are "hand made things," objects fashioned by human agency; in contrast YHWH is eternal and unmade. Despite the relative narrowness of the LXX usage of the term, those commenting on the NT use of (ἀ)χειροποίητος have often used this LXX usage to determine its NT sense.

This is particularly evident in dealing with its use in Stephen's speech in Acts 7. This section of Stephen's speech focuses on God's presence with Israel in relation to tabernacle and Temple, answering the objection of Stephen's accusers that he speaks

---

[114] In terms of lexical semantics, the use of a lexeme across a corpus establishes the semantic range but does not determine the location of a particular instance of that lexeme within that semantic range. This only occurs through the pragmatics of a particular context.

[115] F. F. Bruce, *The Book of the Acts*, Rev. ed., NICNT (Grand Rapids, MI: Eerdmans, 1988), 150. See the similar comments of "Sanctuary and Sacrifice in the Church of the New Testament," *JTS* 1 (1950): 29 and Lloyd Gaston, *No Stone on Another: Studies in the Significance of the Fall of Jerusalem in the Synoptic Gospels*, NovTSup 23 (Leiden: Brill, 1970), 69.

[116] Moule broadly subsumes these diverse uses under "the theme of new sanctuary and sacrifice" (C. F. D. Moule, "Sanctuary and Sacrifice in the Church of the New Testament," *JTS* 1 (1950): 29). The associations of the "circumcision without hands" of Col 2:11 are partly problematized by the various options in handling the phrase ἐν τῇ περιτομῇ τοῦ Χριστοῦ (Murray J. Harris, *Colossians & Philemon*, Exegetical Guide to the Greek New Testament (Grand Rapids, MI: Eerdmans, 1991), 91, 92).

[117] Lev 26:1; 26:30; Jdt 8:18; Wis 14:8; Isa 2:18; 10:11; 16:12. The alpha privative equivalent does not occur at all in the LXX.

κατὰ τοῦ τόπου τοῦ ἁγίου (Acts 6:13). In defending his stance towards the temple, Stephen includes in his history of Israel references to both the Mosaic tabernacle and the οἶκος which Solomon built for YHWH. At the same time he seems to reject the latter by describing it in apposition to the term χειροποίητος (Acts 7:48), as something unbefitting YHWH. This is buttressed by an appeal to Isa 66:1, 2 in which YHWH contrasts his incommensurate nature as Creator with the concept of a physical house. Commentators have often thereby concluded that Stephen's point is not merely to portray a misunderstanding of the Temple by his opponents, but that it was essentially illegitimate, idolatrous from the moment of its inception.[118] Certain arguments are adduced to support this thesis. First, that whereas Moses' tabernacle is spoken of by Stephen as commanded by God (Acts 7:44), such a description is absent with regard to the Temple. This omission is seen as forming a tacit contrast: the former was divinely sanctioned; the latter was not.[119] Second, that the juxtaposition of Solomon's building a house and Stephen's assertion that YHWH does not dwell in such seems a direct dismissal of the Temple as essentially futile. Third, that the usage of χειροποίητος in the LXX, with its purely negative associations of idolatry, suggests that the speech portrays the Temple as contrary to the true worship of YHWH.[120] In essence, Stephen's characterization of the Temple as χειροποίητος is an intrinsically moral description of the Temple. It is an object manufactured against the will of God, fundamentally mistaking YHWH's nature, and Stephen's speech is aimed at its essential idolatry.

Despite the appeal of this position it displays certain weaknesses.[121] These are demonstrated in the otherwise helpfully theological discussion of Trevor Hart on the role of χειροποίητος in Stephen's speech in his work *Making Good*.[122] Inherent in Hart's discussion is a certain tension over whether the Temple is essentially an offense, or only has become so through eschatological advent of Christ. So, on the one hand, Hart writes that

> Stephen's point, of course, is not to correct a mistaken notion of 'containment' … but to insist that the presumed focus of God's 'dwelling' … was no longer apposite.[123]

---

[118] Klijn, "Stephen's Speech–Acts VII. 2–53," 29; Craig R. Koester, *The Dwelling of God: The Tabernacle in the Old Testament, Intertestamental Jewish Literature, and the Old Testament*, CBQMS 22 (Washington, DC: Catholic Biblical Association of America, 1989), 80); and perhaps Dunn, *Partings*, 87 and Marcel Simon, "Saint Stephen and the Jerusalem Temple," *JEH* 2 (1951): 127.

[119] Koester sees this attitude as also demonstrated by the discontinuity of David's request to build God a σκήνωμα and Solomon's building God an οἶκος (Koester, *Dwelling of God*, 80). The impact of the textual issue makes this a somewhat more difficult argument to sustain. Whereas some MSS (e.g. ²ℵ, A, C) contain the reading σκήνωμα τῷ θεῷ Ἰακώβ, the stronger witnesses (e.g. P74, ℵ*, B, D) read σκήνωμα τῷ οἴκῳ Ἰακώβ, thus at least raising the question as to whether the Temple is meant. On the variant in Acts 7:46, see Simon, "Saint Stephen and the Jerusalem Temple," 128, 129.

[120] Dunn, *Partings*, 89.

[121] For others who take a less essentialist critique of the Temple, see John J. Kilgallen, "The Function of Stephen's Speech (Acts 7, 2–53)," *Bib* 70 (1989): 173–93; Ju-Won Kim, "Old Testament Quotations within the Context of Stephen's Speech in Acts" (PhD Diss., Pretoria University, 2007), 193; Bo Reicke, *Glaube und Leben der Urgemeinde: Bemerkungen zu Apg. 1-7* (Zürich: Zwingli-Verlag, 1957), 134 cited in Gaston, *No Stone on Another*, 157.

[122] Trevor A. Hart, *Making Good: Creation, Creativity, and Artistry* (Waco, TX: Baylor University Press, 2014).

[123] Ibid., 51n63.

He then proceeds to cite Manson's comments that Stephen's "point is that the Temple was not intended, any more than the Tabernacle, to become a *permanent* institution, halting the advance of the divine plan for the people of God."[124] These elements of Hart's reading suggest that the Temple is not inherently problematic, but rather has become so in the aftermath of Christ's advent. If idolatry is suggested it is an undue continuing attachment to Temple even though what the Temple pointed to has arrived.

Within a matter of pages, however, Hart seems to change tack and support a view that the Solomonic Temple in Stephen's speech is inherently illegitimate:

> The temple built by Solomon, [in] contrast [to the tabernacle], while well intentioned, was from the outset primarily a venture of human initiative and action, … it has in Israel's hands, … become an obstacle to Israel's appropriation of God's promise.[125]

Though it is challenging to resolve all of Stephen's speech into a singular view of the Temple, in the final analysis, this view that the Temple is essentially against God's will, rather than simply being made obsolete through the progress of redemptive history, does not seem to make sense of Stephen's speech and the tensions in Hart's articulation of the matter suggest this failure.[126]

Several reasons support that it is the initial suggestion of Hart, that eschatological change is in view, that is correct. First, it is deeply unlikely that Stephen's Jewish audience would have seen the Temple as literally circumscribing the presence of God and can hardly be the point of the appeal to Isa 66:1, 2;[127] second, the narrative thread of divinely sanctioned and sketched tabernacle followed by Temple may just as easily be read as the legitimate succession of one by the other;[128] third, David's initiative in moving for a permanent structure is related to his "having found favour with God" (Acts 7:46) in Stephen's description, suggesting that the impetus is not viewed as essentially negative; fourth, the Solomonic Temple in its inception in Kings and Chronicles combines elements of divine authorization in both design and attitude, alongside recognition of divine incommensurability, that make it difficult to see how tabernacle and Temple could be pitted against one another in Stephen's speech;[129]

---

[124] Thomas W. Manson, *The Epistle to the Hebrews: An Historical and Theological Reconsideration; the Baird Lecture, 1949* (London: Hodder & Stoughton, 1951), 34.

[125] Hart, *Making Good*, 53.

[126] In fact, Hart keeps drawing near in his discussion to attributing complete disobedience in building the Solomonic Temple but then drawing back as it is difficult to square with OT texts. See, e.g. that the Temple is "constructed in relative independence" but "(albeit not actual contradiction)" (ibid.).

[127] Sweeney notes similar tensions in the arguments of others supporting an essentialist critique of the Temple as an institution ("Stephen's Speech (Acts 7: 2-53): Is It as 'Anti-Temple' as Is Frequently Alleged?," *TrinJ* 23 (2002): 199).

[128] Ann Conway-Jones, *Gregory of Nyssa's Tabernacle Imagery in Its Jewish and Christian Contexts*, OECS (Oxford: Oxford University Press, 2014), 86.

[129] Williamson notes the striking use of תבנית in 1 Chr 28 and sees it as "clearly intended as an echo of the 'pattern' of the tabernacle and its furnishings, shown to Moses on Mount Sinai in Exod. 25.9, 40" (H. G. M. Williamson, "The Temple in the Book of Chronicles," in *Templum Amicitiae: Essays on the Second Temple Presented to Ernst Bammel*, ed. William Horbury, LNTS 48 (Sheffield: Sheffield Academic Press, 1991), 26). On the relation of tent and temple see also Conway-Jones, *Tabernacle Imagery*, 86 and Koester, *Dwelling of God*, 34.

fifth, the juxtaposition of Isa 66:1, 2 with the tabernacle and Temple thread is equally problematic for each institution, as its force relates not to mobility or permanence but to the simple contrast of divine incommensurability and physical structures.[130]

Following these arguments, I suggest that a proper reading of Stephen's criticism cannot be first essential and moral, but rather eschatological first, and only then moral. Nothing was essentially wrong with the tradition of tabernacle and Temple in Stephen's view, given as they were by God. But now that the Righteous One has come, whom the prophets foretold (Acts 7:52), the provisionality of the Mosaic economy, both in Law and Temple, is fully revealed. The antagonism of Stephen's audience to this reveals them as idolaters, more attached to symbols than the God whose purposes they symbolize. Thus the use of χειροποίητος language in Stephen's speech certainly draws in the related LXX associations of idolatry but also appeals to a strand of eschatology which raises the question of divine and human agency in relation to the dwelling place of God.[131]

This test case in handling the use of (ἀ)χειροποίητος in Acts 7 demonstrates the way in which evaluation of this lexeme in the NT has tended to be hampered by studying LXX occurrences of the lexeme, rather than theme of agency in relation to divine dwelling places which most closely matches the horizon of NT use. The principal OT text which seems to lie at the root of this language is Exod 15:17,[132] within the Song of the Sea relating Israel's journey up from Egypt (Exod 15:13–18). The Song speaks of YHWH's redemptive acts as a warrior, leading his people out of Egypt and guiding them safely to his dwelling place. This is described in Exod 15:17 as YHWH's bringing them "to the mountain of your inheritance, to your prepared dwelling, which you have prepared Lord, a sanctuary, O Lord, which your hands have established." The original reference of this "sanctuary," whether to the mountain of Sinai or that of Zion, has

---

[130] On the coherence of Isa 66:1, 2 with similar OT texts Schramm writes, "We have already met with the idea of the temple as a house of prayer in Isa. 56.7. I would argue that Isa. 66.1; Isa. 56.7 and 1 Kgs 8.23–53 all reflect a certain reinterpretation of the temple, but to regard any or all of them as 'anti-temple' would be a gross misnomer" (Brooks Schramm, *The Opponents of Third Isaiah: Reconstructing the Cultic History of the Restoration*, JSOT 193 (Sheffield: Sheffield Academic Press, 1995), 165 cited in Matthias Albani, "'Wo sollte ein Haus sein, das Ihr mir bauen könntet?' (Jes 66,1): Schöpfung als Tempel Jhwhs?," in *Gemeinde ohne Tempel = Community without Temple: zur Substituierung und Transformation des Jerusalemer Tempels und seines Kults im Alten Testament, antiken Judentum und frühen Christentum*, ed. Beate Ego, Armin Lange, Peter Pilhofer and Kathrin Ehlers (Tübingen: Mohr Siebeck, 1999), 41).

[131] See Sim. J. P. M. Sweet, "A House Not Made with Hands," in *Templum Amicitiae: Essays on the Second Temple Presented to Ernst Bammel*, ed. William Horbury, LNTS 48 (Sheffield: Sheffield Academic Press, 1991), 387.

[132]

The history of the exegesis of Exodus 15:17 shows how a tradition developed of a temple not built by human hands but by God, which was already prepared in heaven, and which would become available to human beings at the end of time. It was to this tradition that the saying in Mark probably refers: by promising to destroy the temple and build another not made with hands, Jesus was heralding the last days. (Conway-Jones, *Tabernacle Imagery*, 84)

Juel also contends that Exod 15:17 lies as an "exegetical tradition" behind Mark 14:56 (*Messiah and Temple: The Trial of Jesus in the Gospel of Mark*, SBLDS 31 (Missoula, MT: Scholars Press, 1977), 151–3).

been much debated.¹³³ But, whatever the initial referent, from the perspective of later readers, one need not choose between the two. A later reader would rather recognize the parallels between the tabernacle and Temple and the sanctuary-like mountain of Sinai.¹³⁴ The significance of this initial description is that it depicts a heavenly and divinely wrought sanctuary which descends on Sinai, and upon which the wilderness tabernacle is patterned. The identification of God's heavenly sanctuary as that established by YHWH's own hand does not, in this context, foreshadow a criticism of Moses' tabernacle; the latter is prescribed on the very assumption of the former.¹³⁵ But it forms a contrast and correlation, imbedded in the very inception of the tabernacle, which relates to both spaces and agencies: one sanctuary is heavenly and made by the hand of God; the other, though divinely prescribed, is earthly and fashioned by human hands.¹³⁶

Within intertestamental literature, and that contemporary to the NT, the use of the lexeme (ἀ)χειροποίητος seems to inhabit this conceptual world. At times the term is employed to stress human agency and its limits¹³⁷ or the nature of the Mosaic tabernacle.¹³⁸ It continues to be employed in the description of idolatry generally,¹³⁹ its places of worship¹⁴⁰ and Israel's sin with the golden calf in particular.¹⁴¹ An interesting corollary though is the connection between the concept of idolatry, the true God and his dwelling. The idea of idols as "hand made things" is at times contrasted with the fact that God himself is "not made with hands."¹⁴² And this seems related, then, to the conception that a dwelling place "made with hands" is somehow un-ideal for a God who is himself un-made.

It is difficult to relate the concept of (ἀ)χειροποίητος to Second Temple understandings of a heavenly or eschatological Temple with any kind of generalization, as contemporary views on such were far from monolithic.¹⁴³ As Sanders notes in his survey of texts related to Temple expectations, the evidence

> does not lead to the conclusion that all Jews everywhere, when thinking of the future hope of Israel, put foremost the building of a new temple. Further, when the

---

[133] David Noel Freedman, "Temple without Hands," in *Temples and High Places in Biblical Times* (Jerusalem: Hebrew Union College, 1981), 21, 22.
[134] This is hinted at in the language of Jer 31:23. Cf ibid., 24.
[135] This is certainly reflected in the way that the Pastor employs Exod 25:40 in 8:5. On connections of Exod 15:17 and 25:40, see ibid., 26; Conway-Jones, *Tabernacle Imagery*, 86, 87.
[136] For the role of the Spirit in equipping its builders, see Exod 35:30–35.
[137] Josephus, *Bel.* 1.419; *Ant.* 4.55.
[138] Philo *Mos.*, 2.88. Note that the use here is entirely without negative connotations—that the tabernacle is "made with hands" is in no way hostile to its divine prescription.
[139] Sib. Or. 3:13, 606, 618, 722; 4:28. For similarly worded critique, see 1 En. 46:7; 2 En. 10:6.
[140] Sib. Or. 14:62.
[141] Philo *Mos.* 2.165.
[142] Sib. Or. 3:13; 4:6; 2 En. 33:4; Philo *Mos.* 2.168. 1 En. 46:7 similarly contrasts the fashioning of idols by human hands with God as "Lord of the Spirits." It can also be associated metonymically with God's dwelling (Sib. Or. 4:11) and God's throne (2 En. 22:2). This may also be related to concepts of a heavenly temple evident in 1 En. 14:8–23; 90:28, 29.
[143] It seems it is always tempting to overstate the homogeneity of contemporary Judaism on this issue perhaps in light of the use of these themes in the NT. Cf. e.g. the homogenizing tendencies of the discussion in Dunn, *Partings*, 67.

temple is explicitly mentioned, it is not depicted in a uniform manner. To be more precise, sometimes it is not depicted at all (II Mac.2.7; Jub. 1.17, 27; 11QTemple 29.8–10), and sometimes it appears that the present second temple is in mind (I En. 25.5; II Macc. 2.7). Sometimes the new temple is modestly expected only to be larger and grander than the present temple (Tob. 14.5, "glorious"; I En. 90,28f, "greater and loftier"; T . Benj. 9.2, "more glorious than the first"), in which case it will be built by human hands (see Tob. 14.5); but sometimes the extravagant language of Micah 4 and Isa. 2 is recalled (Ps. Sol. 17.32; Sib.Or. 5.425). In some instances it is definitely said or clearly implied that God will build or provide a new temple (I En. 90.28f.; Jub. 1.17; 11QTemple 29.8–18), and in Sib.Or. 5.425 the builder is a "blessed man from heaven." Thus we can speak of neither a universal expectation nor of a clear and consistent one.[144]

In spite of this diversity the language of (ἀ)χειροποίητος still often features significantly, both in discussions of a heavenly tabernacle and in expectations of an eschatological dwelling place. With respect to the latter, there is significant propagation of the theme raised in Exod 15:17 of the relationship of heavenly to earthly temples. This continues to include contrast of divine action in building with human action,[145] and is occasioned by a certain key idea: the perception of discontinuity between heavenly tabernacle/temples and their earthly counterparts, through the "paradoxical imagery" employed in description of the former.[146]

The construction of such eschatological Temple structure evidences many of the tensions we have noted at work in Heb 3. At times a messianic figure seems connected to its construction (Zech 6:12, 13 LXX; 1 En. 53:6; Sib. Or. 5:423) and at other times God himself is explicitly the builder (Tob 14:5, 6; 1 En. 90:28, 29; Jub. 1.15; Pss. Sol. 17.21–34; 11QTemple 29.8–10).[147] It might be thought that this is simply to be harmonized by appeal to a conception of God's action through a messianic figure.[148] Though this may explain the patterns of agency in certain texts, in others it is too neat. In some of these contexts God is sole agent and will himself build the eschatological Temple as opposed to another (e.g. 11QTemple 29:9, 10).[149] And yet at the same time

---

[144] E. P. Sanders, *Jesus and Judaism* (Philadelphia, PA: Fortress Press, 1985), 86, 87. Cf. also Andrew Chester, "The Sibyl and the Temple," in *Templum Amicitiae: Essays on the Second Temple Presented to Ernst Bammel*, ed. William Horbury, LNTS 48 (Sheffield: Sheffield Academic Press, 1991), 48 and J. T. A. G. M. Van Ruiten, "Visions of the Temple in the Book of Jubilees," in *Gemeinde ohne Tempel = Community without Temple: zur Substituierung und Transformation des Jerusalemer Tempels und seines Kults im Alten Testament, antiken Judentum und frühen Christentum*, ed. Beate Ego et al. (Tübingen: Mohr Siebeck, 1999).

[145] See the parallelism of Wis 9:16 which associates the phrase τὰ ἐν χερσίν with τὰ ἐπὶ γῆς in contrast to τὰ ἐν οὐρανοῖς.

[146] Conway-Jones, *Tabernacle Imagery*, 94.

[147] Gaston's contention that the evidence for connections between Messiah and Temple building is perhaps slimmer than might be expected is well-made (Gaston, *No Stone on Another*, 105, 147–8), but his reading of the sources is at times overly minimalist.

[148] William Horbury, "Herod's Temple and 'Herod's Days,'" in *Templum Amicitiae: Essays on the Second Temple Presented to Ernst Bammel*, ed. William Horbury, LNTS 48 (Sheffield: Sheffield Academic Press, 1991), 112n112.

[149] Note the stressed pronouns and dative of benefit.

patterns of unique agency are sometimes placed alongside the Messiah in ways that are difficult to resolve.[150] In other passages it is simply difficult to discern quite what the structure of agency is. In Sib. Or. 5:414–433 it is unclear whether it is a messianic figure building city and temple, God building them, or even if the structures, which are being built by God and/or the "blessed man," are the same realities.[151] Central to this recognition is that a "simple" harmonization between divine and messianic building is less than simple. If the eschatological Temple is to be seen as reflecting heavenly realities, and being built without hands, how can mere statements of compatibilism between divine and human agency, between YHWH alone building and a messianic figure building, be seen as distinguishing such a structure from the compatibilism evident in that archetypal tent, the Mosaic tabernacle?[152]

In tracing the above development of concepts related to divine and human agency in building, it is significant to note that the tension evident in the texts of Second Temple Judaism is itself bound up with the reception of those OT traditions noted above. In particular, the existence and supremacy of a tabernacle of God which is "made without hands" alongside the eschatologizing expectations of a true Davidic seed who will build God's house.

The development of the use of (ἀ)χειροποίητος language in the NT, with prominent connections to themes of Temple and eschatology, seems to have been occasioned through its use within the Jesus tradition, as is evident in the synoptic gospels.[153] Both Mark and Matthew record accusation against Jesus in his trial before the high priest that he had spoken of "destroying this Temple and after three days rebuilding it" (Matt 26:61; Mark 14:48). Mark alone records this report of Jesus' teaching by his accusers in a form that utilizes a contrast involving χειροποίητος and ἀχειροποίητος.[154] According to Jesus' accusers, Jesus had spoken of destroying τὸν ναὸν τοῦτον τὸν χειροποίητον (Mark 14:58a), and in three days construct another temple, which is ἀχειροποίητον (Mark 14:58b).[155] B. F. Meyer notes that the flow of the trial as reported

---

[150] Chester, "Sibyl and Temple," 51. This is paralleled by issues of the earthly or heavenly origin of various renewed or recreated temple structures (C. C. Rowland, "The Second Temple: Focus of Ideological Struggle?," in *Templum Amicitiae: Essays on the Second Temple Presented to Ernst Bammel*, ed. William Horbury, LNTS 48 (Sheffield: Sheffield Academic Press, 1991), 186). This tension is particularly evident in 4QFlor.

[151] See the discussion of Chester, "Sibyl and Temple," 39, 47. In particular the disagreement over agencies in Sib. Or. 5:414–433 between ibid., 50 and Gaston, *No Stone on Another*, 148.

[152] I am here using the word "compatibilism" in the sense of the compatibility of divine and human action in a single event in which the former has a causal priority with regard to the latter without removing the nature of secondary causes. For an articulation of which see Aquinas, *Summa Theologica*, I 83.1.

[153] Juel notes Vincent Taylor's view that perhaps Mark actually coined the term ἀχειροποίητος (Juel, *Messiah and Temple*, 150). On its relation to Jesus tradition see Sweet, "A House Not Made with Hands," 365–6; Moule, "Sanctuary and Sacrifice," 30; Gaston, *No Stone on Another*, 65n61. On the issues of Mark's intention for readers in encountering the "false witness" see Juel, *Messiah and Temple*, 118, 119, 123, 137.

[154] Matthew's text does not include the χειροποίητος language (Matt 26:61).

[155] Sweet notes, in a way that parallels the issues discussed above surrounding Stephen's view of the Temple, that the destruction language may not constitute predominantly Temple criticism but immanent eschatological change: "The point of [Jesus'] words will then have been not necessarily a criticism or condemnation of the Second Temple but rather the imminence of the New Age, in

in Mark proceeds from this comment to the question of the High Priest whether Jesus is claiming to be the Christ (Mark 15:61), bearing witness to expectations of a relationship between eschatological Temple building and messianism in Palestinian Judaism that may well connect to the Nathan Oracle and its reception.[156] However, if, as was noted above, the temple saying reflects the development of exegetical tradition surrounding Exod 15:17, then Jesus' self-proclamation as one who would build the ναός ἀχειροποίητος may have claims beyond merely human messianism. As Juel notes in comparing the reception of Exod 15:17, "The decisive difference is the identity of the builder of the temple: in all of the traditions using Exod 15:17, it is God; in Mark, the builder is Jesus."[157]

In the remainder of the NT, the use of (ἀ)χειροποίητος language draws on these themes of Temple and eschatology but also connects to broader themes of redemption, in particular divine agency in salvation (Col 2:11; Eph 2:11) and the resurrection body (2 Cor 5:1).[158] The latter of these topics seems, at first, a novel development in the language's use, but stems from connections implicit in the synoptics, and explicit in John's gospel, between the rebuilt temple and the raised body of Jesus (John 2:21, 22).[159] This rich vein of themes is not only found across texts but can be activated summarily, as is evident in Paul's discussion in 2 Cor 5:1–10.[160] In this text Paul employs language of an οἰκίαν ἀχειροποίητον which God has created for believers (2 Cor 5:1), and which connects issues of heavenly dwelling,[161] body,[162] resurrection,[163] eternity and new creation.[164] This interplay of themes not only reflects their theological integration in the early Christian world, but the parallel associations of (ἀ)χειροποίητος language which juxtapose what is done in this age by human agency versus the eschatological and "hand-less" agency of God.

In canvassing these NT occurrences one may note that the pair ἀχειροποίητος and χειροποίητος is one of the exceptions to the rule that semantic range is not determined by etymology. The pair χειροποίητος and ἀχειροποίητος effectively creates a dichotomy between divine and human action, between what humanity is capable of doing and what God alone is capable of.[165] As Lohse writes, "Im Neuen Testament zeigt

---

which God would bring in a new Temple. The coming of the new meant the end of the old" (Sweet, "A House Not Made with Hands," 369).

[156] This connection he sees is essentially supplied by the connection of Nathan Oracle to the Messiah in 4QFlor (Ben F. Meyer, *The Aims of Jesus* (London: SCM, 1979), 179).

[157] Juel, *Messiah and Temple*, 153.

[158] Interesting in connection to the application of God's work to individuals is the use of similar phraseology at Qumran. In 1QHa VII.15, in speaking of how the community member has resolved himself to a life of consecration, he (seemingly) attributes his entrance into such a way of life as having coming about rvb dyb al.

[159] On the theme of Temple in relation to Jesus in John, see Alan Kerr, *The Temple of Jesus' Body: The Temple Theme in the Gospel of John*, LNTS 220 (London: Bloomsbury, 2002) and Nicholas Perrin, *Jesus the Temple* (London: SPCK, 2011), 55–6.

[160] Sweet, "A House Not Made with Hands," 383.

[161] ἐν τοῖς οὐρανοῖς (2 Cor 5:1); ἐξ οὐρανοῦ (2 Cor 5:2).

[162] 2 Cor 5:6. The language of clothing and unclothing is strongly related to this concept (2 Cor 5:4, 8).

[163] Particularly highlighted by the replacement of "mortality" with "life" (2 Cor 5:4).

[164] αἰώνιον (2 Cor 5:1). In contrast the language of σκῆνη (2 Cor 5:1) employed in relation to the mortal body highlights the impermanence of this age. On "newness" in relation to the term see Moule, "Sanctuary and Sacrifice," 33, 40.

[165] Sweet, "A House Not Made with Hands," 374.

χειροποίητος an allen Stellen, an denen es verwendet wird, den Gegensatz des von Menschenhänden Errichteten zum Werk Gottes an."[166]

3.5.2 Eschatology and building in Hebrews

With this understanding of (ἀ)χειροποίητος in mind, we may return to the texts concerning building in Hebrews which were mentioned above in pursuit of the question that was raised as to whether Hebrews itself supports the construction of God's house as a properly divine work, viewed through the relation of divine agency to eschatological states.

The set of texts under examination are those within Hebrews which discuss the construction of various realities in terms of God's unique and exclusive action, and do so in two instances using the language of (ἀ)χειροποίητος. This collection of texts centres around three discrete metaphors which are of key importance in the Epistle in connection to eschatological states: heavenly sanctuary, eschatological homeland and divine rest. Though these images seem to have little metaphorical overlap, their role within the theology of Hebrews demonstrates that they are different ways in which the Pastor articulates a single reality to his hearers, governed by varied pastoral needs.[167] This variation is predominantly occasioned by a desire to represent a difference of temporal perspective.[168] When discussing the present situation of Christ, and the resultant access of believers to his help, the imagery of heavenly tabernacle is employed. On the other hand, when stressing the need for perseverance and that the believer is one who still is "boasting in hope" (3:6) awaiting the future consummation, the imagery of final city, homeland or rest is employed. Each of these sets of imagery is spoken of in terms of God's action, and is either explicitly or implicitly contrasted with the products of human agency.

These metaphors of tabernacle and land, as a result of their distinct rhetorical functions, tend each to have an affinity for a spatial axis, whether horizontal or vertical, and a temporal category. The tabernacle world is one above (9:24), with its shadow below (8:4). The world of estrangement and waiting is "now" and "here" (2:8; 13:14) with the true homeland one that is to come (2:5; 13:14). At the same time, though the metaphors tend to find a weighted centre in spatiotemporal categories, their ultimate

---

[166] E. Lohse *TWNT* 9, 424–6.
[167] Attridge, *Hebrews*, 126, 128, 323. Similarly Erich Gräßer, *An die Hebräer*, vol. 3 (Zürich: Neukirchener Verlag, 1990), 69; William L. Lane, *Hebrews 9–13*, WBC 47b (Nashville, TN: Thomas Nelson, 1991), 547; Jared Calaway, *The Sabbath and the Sanctuary: Access to God in the Letter to the Hebrews and Its Priestly Context*, WUNT 349 (Tübingen, Germany: Mohr Siebeck, 2013), 60, 61, 69 and Peter Walker, "Jerusalem in Hebrews 13: 9–14 and the Dating of the Epistle," *TynBul* 45 (1994). This is all strengthened by the shared structures of promise and fulfilment in regard to each, for which see Kenneth L. Schenck, *Cosmology and Eschatology in Hebrews: The Setting of the Sacrifice*, SNTSMS 143 (Cambridge: Cambridge University Press, 2007), 60–75, and the coordinate theme of unfaithfulness which is commonly adduced, so Cockerill, *Hebrews*, 183.
[168] Cockerill, *Hebrews*, 63; Jon Laansma, "The Cosmology of Hebrews," in *Cosmology and New Testament Theology*, ed. Jonathan T. Pennington and Sean M. McDonough (London: T&T Clark, 2008), 138.

relation displays a degree of permeability.[169] Thus the heavenly tabernacle is typified in a bicameral structure (9:1–4), whose first and second compartments relate closely to first and second covenants, essentially mapping categories of space into categories of time and eschatology.[170] Its structure teaches in parabolic form the eschatological nature of the heavenly tabernacle (9:9).[171] Further the heavenly world is itself the subject of eschatological events which are realized as final through the shaking of "not only the earth but also the heavens" (12:26). That the heavenly world as tabernacle does not stand aloof from temporal events is further evident from its role as the stage on which the clearly temporal events of Christ's ascension and entrance are acted out.[172] In similar fashion, though the images of city, homeland and rest primarily operate along the horizontal (time) axis, at times they become tinged with spatial categories. Arguments surrounding God's rest relate to a time of inception (4:3, 4),[173] yet also are typified in images bound up with the land.[174] The application of the unusual σαββατισμός language to this reality draws on both holy space and holy time in describing it.[175] This blending of categories reaches its climax in the description of the goal of believers as the heavenly Zion mountain to which they have come, a location which is both land and sanctuary in one.[176]

Thus it is not surprising that we find the same oppositions of divine and human agency in connection to all these realities: sanctuary, homeland and rest. Ultimately they represent the same reality, and therefore patterns of agency which are ascribed to one must ultimately be applicable to the other. Recognizing this helps the reader see that this full set of images needs to be evaluated together, and assessed cumulatively, if the force of the theme within Hebrews on divine construction is to be given its due weight.

---

[169] Gräßer, *Hebräer*, 3. The concept is significant for Calaway's whole thesis on the intertwining of Sabbath and Sanctuary motifs, so Calaway, *Sabbath*, 1, 26, 29. On the strong, but not exclusively, local nature of the rest of 3:7–4:12 see also Laansma, "*I Will Give You Rest*," 277–83.

[170] Calaway, *Sabbath*, 110; Schenck, *Cosmology*, 98. For criticism of Hurst's view on the identity of the first and second tents as Mosaic and heavenly (L. D. Hurst, *The Epistle to the Hebrews: Its Background of Thought*, SNTSMS 65 (Cambridge: Cambridge University Press, 1990), 26, 27), see Schenck, *Cosmology*, 97 and Bruce, *Hebrews*, 147, 148.

[171] On issues of the connection of the bicameral type to the antitype see Attridge, *Hebrews*, 218; Albert Vanhoye, *The Letter to the Hebrews: A New Commentary* (New York: Paulist Press, 2015), 143, 144; Lane, *Hebrews 9–13*, 229, 238; Erich Gräßer, *An die Hebräer*, vol. 2 (Zürich: Neukirchener Verlag, 1990), 143–7; Schenck, *Cosmology*, 170; Koester, *Hebrews*, 99; Laansma, "The Cosmology of Hebrews," 142.

[172] Calaway notes the way in which Christ's movement functions as a "co-ordina[tion of] heavenly space–time" in Hebrews (Calaway, *Sabbath*, 140).

[173] As Cockerill notes this connection of Ps 95:11 to Gen 2:2 is not merely via the technique of *gezerah sheva* but by the commonality of language about God's own rest (*Hebrews*, 200).

[174] Though the true entering in is argued to have not taken place under Joshua (4:8) the very argument from it presupposes at least some degree of typology to the land of Canaan *pace* Laansma, "*I Will Give You Rest*," 275.

[175] Laanma stresses the "festal" character of σαββατισμός, rather than merely the meaning of "cessation from works" (ibid., 278). See also Attridge, *Hebrews*, 131.

[176] Cockerill, *Hebrews*, 63.

3.5.2.1 A divinely built sanctuary

The texts in view here are 8:2; 9:11 and 9:24. Each of these employs some opposition between divine and human agency in the construction of tabernacle structures. As noted above 9:11 and 9:24 achieve this by using χειροποίητος language to describe the heavenly tabernacle.[177] To similar effect, but with different lexis, 8:2 speaks of the construction of this tabernacle as an act of pitching by "the Lord, not man."

The Pastor's motivation to discuss the nature of the divine and human building is found in his aim to convince his audience of the finality and efficacy of Christ's priestly ministry.[178] He achieves this through discussion of Christ's priesthood, in parallel with exposition of the nature of the old and new covenants and their respective priesthoods (7:12). Complementary to this discussion is his development of the two very different tabernacles in which the respective priestly ministries are carried out. Thus the discussion of tabernacles is chiefly about demonstrating the supremacy of Christ's priestly ministry.[179]

This argument proceeds not primarily by denigrating the Mosaic structures, as somehow ill-founded or imperfect,[180] but rather through demonstrating that the Mosaic tabernacle and its λειτουργία were preparatory and typological. The Mosaic tabernacle was only a sketch and representation (8:5), an ἀντίτυπον of something else (9:24). Thus the Mosaic tabernacle shared with the Law as a whole, its existence as a σκιά, rather than the reality of the thing itself (10:1). The Pastor buttresses this argument through appeal to the reception of the tabernacle's design at Sinai.[181] There Moses was shown something else, of which the Mosaic structure was a copy (8:5, 6). Thus the very manner of the design's reception demonstrated its preparatory and derivative nature. Similarly the structure of the tabernacle betokens its partial status. Its bicameral nature concealed the inner glory of the holy of holies away from the

---

[177] In the discussion that follows I rely on the assumption that the language of tent in 9:11 refers to the heavenly places as a tent (Attridge, *Hebrews*, 246; Cockerill, *Hebrews*, 470; Lane, *Hebrews 9–13*, 237) rather than to the body of Christ as a "greater and more perfect tent," as some have concluded on the basis of 10:20, see, e.g. Augustine, Ambrose, Chrysostom, Ps-Oecumenius, Estius, Calvin, Beza as listed by Spicq, *Hébreux*, 2, 256. As Spicq notes, the debated nature of spaces in the discussion rather supports a local than an instrumental reading (ibid.). The significance of this local phrase in 9:1 is not, though, to represent the tent as something which Christ passes through on the way to something else, but rather to represent the barrier-like quality of a tent as considered from without. Thus, with those advocating the instrumental reading, the διά phrases of 9:11 and 10:20 are both to be taken with the same sense. However they both portray Christ's ascent as an act of passing through a barrier. Though the syntax of 10:20 might lead one to identify the καταπέτασμα with Christ's body, this is not syntactically necessary. On the interpretative options see Gräßer, *Hebräer*, 3, 17. Such a reading further avoids the rather awkward identification of Christ's body as a way through the barrier (ὁδὸν πρόσφατον καὶ ζῶσαν) and the barrier (καταπέτασμα) itself, e.g. Cockerill, *Hebrews*, 470. For a survey of the different configurations of 9:11 and 10:20 see Schenck, *Cosmology*, 155–6. and James Swetnam, "'The Greater and More Perfect Tent': A Contribution to the Discussion of Hebrews 9, 11," *Bib* 47 (1966): 92, 93.

[178] Schenck, *Cosmology*, 38, 105; Lane, *Hebrews 9–13*, 234, 251; Spicq, *Hébreux*, 2, 232.

[179] Gräßer, *Hebräer*, 2, 147. Also Cockerill, *Hebrews*, 391.

[180] Gräßer, *Hebräer*, 3, 190. Coining of the heavenly tent as ἀληθινός (8:2) rather points to the typical function of the Mosaic σκηνή, which, in essence, reinforces its God-givenness and value at a revelatory level.

[181] 8:5, 6 drawing on Exod 25:40.

people,¹⁸² separated not merely by the veil of a tent, which might be thought of as merely a vehicle for the divine presence, but by a whole tent compartment: the first tent (9:1, 2). In the thought of the Pastor the nature of this Mosaic structure thus distinguishes it as penultimate both temporally and spatially. It is linked to the current age (9:9), that is, it is firmly pre-eschatological. It is "of this creation,"¹⁸³ and thus to be identified with τὰ σαλευομένα (12:27). It is earthly, not heavenly (8:4; 9:23, 24). By contrast the true tent belongs to the "matter itself" (10:1). It is "in heaven" and "heaven itself" (8:1; 9:24), a place of unbroken and immediate access to God, rather than the punctuated and occasional presence of the Mosaic structures (9:7, 8). It is further associated with eternal things and the eschatological time of the "good things which have come about" and "reformation" (9:10, 11).

It is within the description of the latter that the Pastor deploys the language of divine agency in contrast to human hands. The heavenly and true tent, heaven itself, is a holy of holies not made with hands (9:11, 24). This is in distinction from the Mosaic, which is reflexively portrayed as the achievement of human construction. When one considers the exalted nature of the Mosaic tabernacle this is a striking move. Not only does the Pastor affirm the divinely revealed nature of the design of the Mosaic tent, but surely he would have been aware of the Pentateuchal record of the divine equipment by the Holy Spirit of Oholiab and Bezalel in its construction.¹⁸⁴ That is, the Mosaic construction was not only divinely designed, but even divinely superintended in its construction. But in spite of all this, the Pastor still sees it as essentially man-made. This reality for the Pastor places it squarely within the realm of this present creation.

There is a clear axiological judgement at work in this distinction. What is made directly by God is superior and ultimate, in comparison to what is fashioned by human hands, even where that is divinely sanctioned and superintended.¹⁸⁵ Further, these verses clarify that the language of χειροποίητος is clearly, in the Pastor's mind, one that sets in antithesis divine and human action in line with the survey of the lexeme given above, a point which is, at times, obscured in commentary on these verses.¹⁸⁶ The eschatological events and their achievements are the work of "the Lord, not man" (8:2). Thus the construction of the true tabernacle, which is the proper *locus* of the true and ultimate ministry of Christ, is necessarily divine *both in initiative and in execution*. It is final, effective and ultimate, because it is divinely built, rather than the work of human hands (9:11, 24).

---

[182] This is particularly brought out by the repeated use of the word "gold" in description of elements of the tabernacle relating to the radiance of divine glory, but all of which are confined to the inner tent and thus absent from the outer (9:4(x3)).

[183] By inference from its contrast with the heavenly tent of 9:11.

[184] Exod 35:30–35.

[185] As Koester notes, this entails two assumptions: (a) what is of divine production is greater than that of human production, and (b) what is heavenly is greater than that which is earthly (*Dwelling of God*, 413).

[186] So Attridge describes the lexeme as "contrasting mere human contrivances with what … is of divine origin" or what is "spiritual, rather than simply the cosmos" (Attridge, *Hebrews*, 147). Neither of these distinctions is quite precise enough to capture the Pastor's sense here. Neither is it, with Spicq, a contrast in respect to materiality and immateriality, or with Gräßer, a Platonic contrast of *Urbild* and *Abbild*, both of which fall short of the precise distinction of agencies which the Pastor's argument requires (Spicq, *Hébreux*, 2, 235; Gräßer, *Hebräer*, 2, 190).

3.5.2.2 A divinely founded city

Parallel to the sanctuary as the place of the believers' current access is the metaphor of city or homeland as the believers' hope. The latter is predominantly portrayed as future and unseen, and most clearly explored in connection to the nature of faith and the testimony of the faithful in chapter 11.[187] Though the metaphors of sanctuary and Land are variously deployed, with predominant connection to present and future respectively, they both share in the mutual description as heavenly rather than earthly realities.[188] This connection stresses their close relation with the underlying connections in Hebrews between eschatology and cosmology.[189] In essence the heavenly world represents, in the presence of God, the seeds of the eschaton in which the people of God are perfected in that presence.[190]

The language of city and homeland seems to be occasioned by two key issues within Hebrews. On the one hand, it is used when highlighting the suffering and loss which the Pastor relates, both to his hearers' past experience and to expectation of continuing earthly existence (10:32–39). In order for his hearers to persevere in faith they must continue in their initial confidence (10:35), which was demonstrated in an understanding that what they possessed in the gospel was something "better and abiding" (10:34), in comparison to earthly possessions. What is implicit in these statements becomes more explicitly applied in 13:10–14. The willingness of believers to experience present exclusion and reproach, parallel to the crucifixion of Jesus, in which they are to go outside the camp with him, is predicated on the truth that "here [they] have no abiding city, but ... seek one that is coming" (13:13).

On the other hand, this kind of longed for city is strongly correlated to the faith of the patriarchs, suggesting that their current social exclusion is, at the same time, an inclusion in the illustrious company of God's believing people.[191] The promises to Abraham in which they share involved a promised τόπος (11:8). The consequent life of Abraham and his descendants, lived as aliens and strangers, involved pursuit of a heavenly homeland (11:9, 10). Thus, by sharing in this common hope and common faith, the Pastor's audience will share in the future outcome of the people of God, a heavenly city.[192]

---

[187] Cockerill, *Hebrews*, 540.
[188] 4:3, 4; 12:22–3. The broken opposition of 13:14 is particularly instructive here, in which the lack of a homeland "here" is contrasted with the future city.
[189] Schenck, *Cosmology*, 23.
[190] On heaven as the realm of ultimate perfection in Hebrews, see ibid., 73. Whatever the precise denotation of the τελειόω language in Hebrews, its connotations surely are oriented around access into the presence of God. So see John Scholer, *Proleptic Priests: Priesthood in the Epistle to the Hebrews*, LNTS 49 (Sheffield: JSOT Press, 1991), 200. For a concise overview of proposals for handling the disputed perfection language of Hebrews see Kevin B. McCruden, *Solidarity Perfected: Beneficent Christology in the Epistle to the Hebrews*, BZNW 159 (Berlin: Walter de Gruyter, 2008), 4–24.
[191] Attridge, *Hebrews*, 323. This is perhaps strengthened by the sense of πατρίς as a familial place, so Cockerill, *Hebrews*, 552.
[192] Signalled both by the connection of city language in 11:10 and 12:22; 13:14 (*Hebrews*, 552) and the statement of 11:40.

Similar to the discussion of the tabernacle, divine agency language is then employed in discussing the formation, nature and superiority of this heavenly abode of the saints. So the patriarchs are characterized as those longing for τὴν τοὺς θεμελίους ἔχουσαν πόλιν ἧς τεχνίτης καὶ δημιουργὸς ὁ θεός (11:10).[193] At first the phrase related to divine agency in 11:10 (ἧς τεχνίτης καὶ δημιουργὸς ὁ θεός) seems unrelated to the nature of the city itself, rather merely a qualification of it.[194] However, as Lane notes in reliance on the work of Argyle,[195] relative pronouns at times in *Koine* Greek preserve the causal sense found in classical Greek.[196] Hence, the phrase which describes God-as-builder, rather than merely standing in unspecified relation to the city, implies a causal relation between its nature and God's activity. The city for which the patriarchs longed has foundations *because* it is built by God. Though there is not an explicit contrast lexically with human agency in this statement, the sense seems to be equivalent to phrases associated with the tabernacle. The pursuit of a city founded by God is reflected in the visible attitude of those not seeking an earthly city established by human culture but rather embracing a tented existence.[197] This assumes that those cities founded by human culture are somehow lacking in their ability to realize the permanent abode of God's promises. Cockerill, drawing out the implications of this contrast, notes the Pastor's assumption that "Earthly cities are the transient work of mortal, sinful human beings."[198] In other words, the fact that divine purposes do not terminate on a humanly constructed city is itself related to the effects of sin on human agency and its products.

That this contrast between cities founded by God and those founded by humanity is what the Pastor has in mind is further emphasized by the language of permanence attached to the heavenly city. It is a city "with foundations" (11:10), both in contrast to the impermanence of patriarchal tents and to the passing quality of this age.[199] It is consequently that which abides (13:14).[200] In this way the eschatological city possesses traits normally associated with God himself (1:11, 12).[201] Rather than participating in the impermanence associated with this creation, the future heavenly city possesses a permanence that reflects a different kind of order: a new creation, finally brought about by the living and abiding God (3:12; 9:14; 10:31; 12:22).[202]

---

[193] On the language of τεχνίτης καὶ δημιουργός in relation to God cf. Philo, *Opif.*, 17, 18, 20, 135, 146; Wis 13:1 and the discussions of Koester, *Hebrews*, 486 and Lane, *Hebrews 9–13*, 352.
[194] As reflected in the translations of both older and more modern English versions (e.g. KJV, NRSV, NIV, NLT, etc.) that translate with sense "whose architect and builder is God."
[195] Lane, *Hebrews 9–13*, 344.
[196] A. W. Argyle, "The Causal Use of the Relative Pronouns in the Greek New Testament," *BT* 6 (1955): 165–9.
[197] Koester, *Hebrews*, 496. As Spicq notes this lack of settling by the patriarchs, "ce n'est pas par goût de nomadisme" (Spicq, *Hébreux*, 2, 347).
[198] Cockerill, *Hebrews*, 541.
[199] Attridge, *Hebrews*, 323.
[200] Koester notes the potential resonance of this statement against the claims of Rome to be an eternal city (Koester, *Hebrews*, 571).
[201] See Schenck, *Cosmology*, 123, 124 and Edward Adams, *The Stars Will Fall from Heaven: Cosmic Catastrophe in the New Testament and Its World*, LNTS 347 (London: T&T Clark, 2007), 30, 31 on the transience of the created world in 1:10–12.
[202] Cockerill, *Hebrews*, 703. That the contrast is frequently drawn, not between createdness and uncreatedness, but different orders of creation and their relation to fallenness is almost certainly to be seen in the phraseology of 9:24. That the heavenly tabernacle is οὐ ταύτης τῆς κτίσεως suggests

Though this note of divine construction is more implicit and muted than in regard to the tabernacle, it nevertheless ought to be read in concert with it. The heavenly city, as the fulfilment of patriarchal promises and faith, excludes human agency through sharing in common features with the eschatological tabernacle: permanence and heavenliness. Because of the stress on the futurity of the city and land metaphors, it stands as the goal of the audience's perseverant faith.[203] It thus represents the reward for their perseverance, and not only theirs, but also those of Old Covenant believers (11:10, 40). This reward, though coming at the end of their faithfulness, is related to God's own work of preparation. Thus the language associated with the heavenly city introduces a note that is implicit elsewhere, the language of gift.[204] The city which they desire is a city which God has prepared for them, that is, on their behalf (11:16). Rather than choosing to build an earthly city themselves, their life of earthly alienation means they will inherit a city prepared for them by God.

3.5.2.3 A divinely created rest

Though the terminology of rest is limited to the argument of 3:7–4:13, it effectively acts as a foreshadowing of the themes of city and homeland which pervade the later chapters. This metaphor of rest at times takes on land-like qualities, both from its association with the state of the Promised Land in OT texts[205] and also through its associations with Ps 95. The Rest is held out as something to be "entered into" (3:11, 18, 19; 4:1, 3, 5, 6, 10, 11).[206] This is compared both to the going out from Egypt and also the entry into Canaan through Joshua.[207] This latter entry did not realize the rest promised, but still, by its typology, ties metaphor of Rest to that of place. Pertinent to my argument is the link forged by the Pastor between this Rest, that into which believers are called to enter, and the text of Gen 2:2. The Pastor notes that the rest God offered is described as τὴν κατάπαυσιν μου, God's *own* rest.[208] By appealing to Gen 2:2, the Pastor explicates that the Rest from which the wilderness generation were barred, and into which those who believe enter, is God's own seventh day rest. This God entered subsequent to his work of creation.[209] Significant for my argument is

---

another creation in which the eschaton is more suitably at home. On which see Laansma, "The Cosmology of Hebrews," 134 and Adams, *Stars Will Fall*, 197.

[203] Gräßer, *Hebräer*, 2, 313.

[204] Taking the αὐτοῖς in 11:16 as a dative of benefit. This idea of the free gift of the city prepared by another resonates with both the language of promise in Hebrews and the recurrent language of inheritance and its connection to place (1:14 with 2:5; 9:15; 11:8).

[205] Dtr 12:9; 4 Ezra 8:52. See also Attridge, *Hebrews*, 126–8.

[206] Εἰσέρχομαι is practically a leitmotiv in this section of Hebrews.

[207] 3:16; 4:8. Though in the latter verse rather than entry language the verb καταπαύω is employed.

[208] The promissory nature of this Rest is drawn out negatively from the swearing by God in Ps 95:11 that no one would enter it. The assumption being that if God could prevent some from entering it, it must be in principle a space into which humanity could enter. On the connection of the negative oath of 3:13 to the positive oath to Abraham in 6:13–14 see Cockerill, *Hebrews*, 182.

[209] Pace Laansma, "*I Will Give You Rest*," 282 who argues that there is an association of the Divine Sabbath and Rest but not an identification. This seems though to run against the grain of the argument. The hearers are to enter God's *own* rest (4:10), and thus to rest *with* God. Cf. Cockerill, *Hebrews*, 197. And see the discussion in Chapter 6 of the present work.

this link between God's work of creation and the divine Rest which becomes a shared space which believers hope to enter by faith. Though nothing is explicitly noted in the argument about divine agency per se, the link between creation and rest in Gen 2:2 implicitly introduces one. This is because the nature of divine rest is itself the reflex of the divine action of creation: in effect, it is a consequence of it.[210] The divine act of work ceased, producing a state of divine cessation.[211] Having established the world, and in consequence to it, God entered his divine rest, creating by his act of cessation the σαββατισμός into which he subsequently called his people.[212] Because then the space of divine Rest is the reflex of the creating work, it shares in the structure of agency at work in the creating act itself. Thus, just as God is clearly the author of creation in Hebrews, alongside the exclusive nature of divine agency in contemporary Judaism,[213] so he alone is the one who founded the Rest of God.

Though connection to agency perhaps seems at its most implicit in relation to God's Rest in 3:7–4:13, its status as the obverse of creation, and thereby the sole work of God, opens up significance for the relationship of the Son to exclusively divine building projects. For if the Rest is then the reflex of Creation, it shares in the God-Son pattern of agency, a pattern which is very explicit. The God who "made all things" (3:4) and "through and for whom is everything" (2:10) is at the same time the God who, through the Son, fashioned the ages (1:2).[214] Thus because of the relationship of creation to rest, and thus creation to the eschatological place of God's people, the pattern of creational agency, which is both described as uniquely God's and also as the work of God through the Son, can be seen to hold in respect to eschatological states in Hebrews: certainly divine Rest, but also presumably divinely founded city and divinely fabricated sanctuary.[215]

3.6 The Son's properly divine work of redemptive building

The above discussion has sought to outline that a strong presumption of divine agency exists in Hebrews in relation to heavenly and eschatological realities, in ways that frequently parallel and relate to the work of creation. These are predominantly embedded in the metaphors of heavenly sanctuary, abiding city/homeland and created

---

[210] The line of thought of a Rest prepared since creation is interestingly similar to the role of the heavenly tent in Pss. Sol. 17:25 which is described as a "tent … which was prepared [by God] from the beginning" and the eternal city of 2 Bar. 4:1–4.

[211] This is not quite the same as seeing the production of the divine rest as included in the act of creation. For criticism of which see Laansma, "*I Will Give You Rest*," 282n144.

[212] On the assumption of this creational rest as teleological and invitational see Cockerill, *Hebrews*, 207.

[213] See footnote 179.

[214] Cockerill, *Hebrews*, 136n153 sees this prepositional interchange as itself indicative of the Son's divinity.

[215] This may also result from the relationship of protology to eschatology in Hebrews being worked out in the tabernacle in particular as well as divine rest. This would potentially arise from similar view of the heavenly tabernacle's preparedness (Exod 15:17; Pss. Sol. 17:25) but also must be related to the Pastor's view of the shaking of both earth and heaven. Thus in Hebrews protology forms the seeds of the eschaton, and the latter is an organic development of the former but under a glorified state (2:10; 4:1–6).

Rest. Such a demonstration goes a long way to upholding Owen's suggestion that the assumption of divine prerogative in the construction of God's house lies behind the thought of Heb 3:3, 4, and by doing so sets forward the Son as the divine builder of God's eschatological house.

However, it might be argued that Owen's assumption has not been fully satisfied. This is because the texts concerning sanctuary, city and rest and their relation to divine prerogative concern questions of heavenly and eschatological place; conversely, 3:1–6 has in view an argument unconcerned with place, and rather, connected to the issue of people. Thus, it might be said, it would be a confusion of categories to extend the nature of divine agency with regard to the former in Hebrews to the latter. If on the other hand, such a gap could be bridged, we would have succeeded in demonstrating Owen's assumption in a most powerful way: that the theology of the Epistle itself portrays the act of constructing God's people, which is attributed to Christ, as the attribution of a divine prerogative and, thus, divine status. Such a closing of the gap, between the eschatological state (house) and the people of God (household), I believe, is easily achieved in consideration of two elements.

First, this may be accomplished through further dependence on the influence of the Nathan Oracle detailed above. Hebrews depicts the house of God as the home of God's people and the identity of the people as God's house(hold). The Nathan Oracle, read with Hebrews, clarifies that these two realities are deeply entwined: the building of the ultimate divine sanctuary and the establishment of a messianic people go together. Thus to detect a clearly articulated pattern of divine agency in relation to the former creates, at the very least, a degree of presumption with regard to the latter. The fact that, as we noted above, the Nathan Oracle aligns the two construction projects, people and place, with God and David's Son, respectively, only to then be reversed in Hebrews, further serves to entwine the actions of Jesus with the work of God as that "not done with hands" (9:11, 24), and thus "not [by] man" (8:2). If it were argued that this connection, though latent in the Nathan Oracle, is not really brought into the context of Hebrews, one might then appeal to 10:21. There the phraseology which the Pastor employs to speak of Jesus' position as ἱερέα μέγαν ἐπὶ τὸν οἶκον τοῦ θεοῦ seems to bring together his role of priest in God's heavenly house with his role as Son over the house(hold) of God suggesting a relationship between the two. Whether one takes the reference of οἶκος here as in relation to the household or the house matters little, for underlying the ambiguity is the compatibility of the two. This is hardly surprising. In effect the unity of the person and work of the high priestly Son implies a relationship between the objects of his ministry, both house and household.

My second argument is more broadly theological and, to my mind, even more conclusive. This second argument requires consideration of the eschatology of Hebrews in relation to the place and people of God, especially in relation to the eschatological freight of the key passage 12:26–28.[216] The full scope of this passage lies beyond our discussion but certain points will suffice. Here the Pastor speaks of the final and decisive eschatological judgement of God in which he subjects all reality, both

---

[216] Schierse, *Verheissung und Heilsvollendung*, 171.

created heavens and earth, to a divine shaking.²¹⁷ This action, brought out by appeal to Hag 2:6, achieves the removal of things that can be shaken such that what remains is only the unshakeable things.²¹⁸ This results in the establishment of an unshakeable kingdom which is the possession of the Pastor's audience and is in effect the unfolding of realities already hinted at in the σωτηρία of 1:14 and the οἰκοθμένη μέλλουσα of 2:5. This distinction of shakeable and unshakeable ought not to be identified as a distinction between things material and immaterial,²¹⁹ or physical and spiritual,²²⁰ but rather as the distinction between things in right relation to God and things separated from and opposed to him.²²¹ The Pastor, via this distinction, essentially portrays the application to all reality of the truth that "without holiness no-one will see the LORD" (12:14). In other words, only that which shares in the LORD's own character, and is set apart to and for him, is fit to enter his established presence in the eschaton. This distinction itself further clarifies the nature of the qualifications attached to the description of the eschaton as sanctuary, city and rest. These realities are the unshakeable things, not because of ethereal or immaterial qualities, but rather because they do not share in the unsubjected nature of this age (2:8).²²² That is, they are heavenly, abiding and above all the work of God not humanity. Human agency is thus relegated to the sphere of this age; only divine agency can fit things for the unshakeable kingdom.

It is at this point that the connection of place to people in regard to the eschaton becomes clear. If this place must be fitted as an unshakeable kingdom by the unique action of God, so too must those intended to receive, enter and inherit it (1:14; 12:28). In

---

[217] Contemporary texts similarly rely on this theme of shaking as divine judgement, for discussion see Koester, *Dwelling of God*, 547 and Adams, *Stars Will Fall*, 30, 31.
[218] Though it might seem the qualification that those things shaken are πεποιήμενα would lead to viewing this as the entire removal of creation and an eschaton which is somehow uncreational, this seems unlikely when compared with the implicit eschatology of Heb 1 and 2. There we find that the Son's status is one who inherits all things, where all things are most surely creational. Further, the state of unfulfilment represented by the current age is one in which the created world is not yet subjected to humanity. Thus the eschaton seems to be already foreshadowed in these opening discussions as a created world subjected to humanity as viceregents of the Son-King. On this harmonizing of Heb 1 and 2 with the eschatology of 12:26–28 see Jon Laansma, "Hidden Stories in Hebrews: Cosmology and Theology," in *A Cloud of Witnesses : The Theology of Hebrews in Its Ancient Contexts*, ed. Richard Bauckham et al., LNTS 387 (London: T&T Clark, 2008), 28–39. For similarly positive construal of the created world in Hebrews eschatology see also ibid., "The Cosmology of Hebrews," 125–43 and Adams, "Cosmology," 122–39. On reading πεποιήμενα as the scope of God's authority rather than the reason for removal see Lane, *Hebrews 9–13*, 482.
[219] Schenck, *Cosmology*, 128.
[220] A contrast which is often implicit in Attridge's handling of creation in relation to the heavenly (*Hebrews*, 247, 262).
[221] Thus the straightforward connection of τὰ σαλευόμενα with the creation and τὰ μὴ σαλευόμενα with heaven is unwarranted and unhelpful in parsing Hebrews' eschatology (Gräßer, *Hebräer*, 2, 84, 146). The superior nature of the promised shaking is that it includes not only earth but also heaven (Koester, *Hebrews*, 547). This issue is particularly clarified in light of the language of χειροποίητος and ἀχειροποίητος which is explored above and which is to be equated with the opposition of τὰ σαλευόμενα and τὰ μὴ σαλευόμενα, rather than createdness and uncreatedness (*pace* Gräßer, *Hebräer*, 2, 334). The question of eschatology in Hebrews is not one of created versus not created, but of relation to exclusive divine action and not.
[222] Because of the relationship of sonship to the viceregency of humanity with God in Hebrews, the unsubjection of the world to humanity is, at the same time and more problematically, a sign of its unsubjection to God himself (2:5, 8).

the shared metaphor of chapters 3, 8 and 9, the eschatological household must be fitted for the eschatological house. Only if the people themselves share in this unshakeable quality, itself a result of divine agency, can they be properly oriented towards God.[223] In the terms of the Zion of 12:18–19, those who gain the firstborn inheritance are those whose spirits have been perfected by God himself.[224] This suggestion then that we ought to consider not merely the nature of the unshakeable kingdom as a kingdom of things, but also as of people in relation to God, also clarifies further the interaction of creation language in 3:1–6 which has tended to be viewed as its most extraneous aspect.[225] The question of the right and proper relation of creation to its Creator is in effect the criterion of the process of removal in 12:26–28.[226] Thus the descriptions which surround and penetrate 3:1–6 in which God is described as both the one "because of whom and through whom are all" (2:10) and "the one who created all things" (3:4) are no mere pious circumlocutions. Relation to God, and what is fitting for and to him, is the line that spans creation and redemption.[227] This only serves to strengthen the case that divine agency ought to be seen at work in 3:1–6, since the patterns of agency in creation, salvation and judgement are mutually interpreting. The one who is addressed as divine Lord (1:10) bears that name not merely because he created all things (1:2) but also because he bears all things to their proper end (1:3) and has authority to change and exchange that which is perishable for that which is eternal (cf. 1:12 and 12:26–28).

3.7 Conclusion

In this chapter I have argued for a reading of 3:1–6 that depicts the Son as the eschatological builder of God's people, God's household and thus depicts him as divine and worthy of divine glory and honour. This depiction comes about via the function of 3:3, 4 which substantiates the greater glory which Jesus has over Moses (3:3a), as the glory which the builder of God's house, the Son, has over one who is in it, Moses (3:3b). This supreme glory, which comes from building God's house, can be likened to that which God has as Creator of all things (3:4b). This connection of the Son's divine honour and glory to that which befits the Creator relies on the assumption, noted by Owen, that the work of building is one in which the Son participates in a work of divine prerogative. By surveying both the influence of the Nathan Oracle and

---

[223] Note here the frequent characterization of the just in the Psalter as those who cannot be shaken, e.g. Pss 31:23; 47:6; 115:2 (Lane, *Hebrews 9–13*, 481). That believers themselves must, by implication, be classed as "unshakeable things" is often noted. See, e.g. ibid., 483; Koester, *Hebrews*, 548; Schenck, *Cosmology*, 128.

[224] Note that the perfection of believers, when stated as their qualification, is always articulated in the divine passive (11:40; 12:23). They are ones "perfected" by another.

[225] The phrase is frequently bracketed in translation and has been described variously as a "Zwischengedanke" (Hans Windisch, *Der Hebraerbrief*, HNT 14 (Tübingen: Mohr Siebeck, 1913), 29) and an "edifying aside" (Moffatt, *Hebrews*, 42).

[226] This surely supports the discriminatory nature of the shaking that Adams criticizes in Lane's reading of chapter 12 (Adams, *Stars Will Fall*, 192; Lane, *Hebrews 9–13*, 480).

[227] It further relies on the teleological nature of creation in Hebrews and thereby the nature of redemption in it as the realizing of creation's goal through the overcoming of sin. On this theme see particularly Laansma, "The Cosmology of Hebrews," 127, 136 and Cockerill, *Hebrews*, 136.

the understanding of divine action in Hebrews' eschatology, I have demonstrated that the nature of such an assumption can be sourced not merely from appeal to broader NT teaching on the spirituality of the Church, as some past interpreters have argued, but equally, and perhaps even more convincingly, from within the thought world and assumptions of Hebrews. Thus in 3:1–6 the Son is implicitly portrayed as divine, God with his Father, because he shares in the uniquely divine prerogative of redeeming a people for God who are, by their divine creation, fitted to receive an unshakeable kingdom, a household fit to enter the final house of God.

4

The Son as bearer of the divine life

4.0 Introduction

The priesthood of Jesus as described in Hebrews is frequently seen as the Epistle's most innovative contribution to the portrayal of Christ in the NT.¹ Considering that this designation is often paired with the title "Son" as representing the two central designations of Christ in the Epistle, and whereas connections of the Son's filial identity have often been tied to eternal and divine categories, discussion of the connections between priesthood and the divinity of the Son has been more mixed.² In fact, recent scholarship exhibits positions on the connection which are polar opposites of each other.³

So, for example, supporting a close connection between priesthood and divinity, Richard Bauckham argues that though priesthood does involve aspects of Christ's humanity, divinity is central to Christ's occupation and exercise of the office of High Priest.⁴

---

1. Scholer, *Proleptic Priests*, 9, 81–90; James Kurianal, *Jesus Our High Priest: Ps. 110,4 as the Substructure of Heb 5,1–7,28*, Europäische Hochschulschriften Reihe XXIII, Theologie (Frankfurt am Main: P. Lang, 2000), 11. The title of priest is only applied to Christ in Hebrews (Mason, *Priest Forever*, 13–14, 40–2) though language connected to cultic action, which might imply the former, is fairly widespread in the NT. On which see Richard B. Gaffin, "The Priesthood of Christ," in *The Perfect Saviour*, ed. Jonathan I. Griffiths (Nottingham: IVP, 2012), 51 and on intercession in particular see David M. Hay, *Glory at the Right Hand: Psalm 110 in Early Christianity*, SBLMS 18 (Nashville, TN: Abingdon Press, 1973), 130–1.
2. For the history of interest generated by Melchizedek see Bruce A. Demarest, *A History of Interpretation of Hebrews 7, 1–10 from the Reformation to the Present*, BGBE 19 (Tübingen: Mohr Siebeck, 1976) and Fred L. Horton, *The Melchizedek Tradition: A Critical Examination of the Sources to the Fifth Century A.D. and in the Epistle to the Hebrews*, SNTSMS 30 (Cambridge: Cambridge University Press, 1976).
3. For historical contention on the relation of divinity to priesthood, see Rowan A. Greer, *The Captain of Our Salvation: A Study in the Patristic Exegesis of Hebrews*, BBET 15 (Tübingen: Mohr Siebeck, 1973), 250–9, 284, 328–43.
4. Though tempting, as Bauckham notes ("Divinity of Jesus," 29), to parse divinity towards the title "Son" and humanity towards "High Priest" this is not a straightforward reflection of the thought of Hebrews. Pace Knut Backhaus, "'Licht vom Licht': Die Präexistenz Christi im Hebräerbrief," in *Der sprechende Gott: Gesammelte Studien zum Hebräerbrief*, WUNT 240 (Tübingen: Mohr Siebeck, 2009), 84.

Hebrews understands that imperishability [spoken of in Ps 110:4] in the future as grounded in the kind of divine existence that neither begins nor ends, the fully eternal being of true deity.[5]

There are however proponents of exactly the opposite position. For example, David Moffitt argues that Christ's priesthood is related straightforwardly to the Son's humanity. Not only did the Son assume humanity in order to become that priest but the sine qua non of his priesthood is his resurrected human life:

> The qualification Jesus possesses to be the High Priest that he is confessed to be is his perfection—i.e., his enduring life. More specifically, the mortality of his humanity, which did suffer death, has been transformed. After his death he arose to an indestructible life—i.e. resurrection life. Because he has been perfected, Jesus is the ἄνθρωπος whom God called to be both the royal Son (the Christ) seated on the throne at his right hand and the ἄνθρωπος who serves forever as the High Priest of the eternal, heavenly priesthood (5:5–6; 8:1–2).[6]

Christ attained this life through his resurrection, Moffit avers, and it is this resurrected life which he now offers in heaven in presentation to God and around which sacrificial efficacy is centred.[7] This life is, according to Moffitt, what constitutes him as the true Melchizedekian priest in distinction from the dying sons of Aaron.[8] It represents the experience ahead of time of a resurrected human life, which in the future will be shared by Christ's many brothers, but now is sufficient to qualify the Son for his priestly ministry.

Significant to these disagreements is the interpretation, in particular, of Heb 7. The reason for the centrality of this chapter is that Heb 7 relates Jesus' status as High Priest to the figure of Melchizedek, who may, or may not, be described in a manner suggesting divine attributes, in particular, eternity. Two verses, 7:3 and 7:16, bear special weight in this debate, the latter being of particular interest. In 7:16 the Pastor explicitly connects Christ's becoming priest to the quality of his life. Thus the broad debate about the relation (or not) between the divinity of Christ and his High Priesthood is intimately related to the exegesis of 7:16.[9] Interpreting the verse (ideally) requires comment on exactly how the indestructible life which is predicated of Christ qualifies him for Priesthood, and quite in what that indestructible life consists. In particular, whether this life ought to be identified as an eternal property of a divinely portrayed Son or the resurrected and ascended life of Christ, newly alive from the dead and consequently

---

[5] Bauckham, "Divinity of Jesus," 29. The phrase "true deity" alludes to his agreement with Neyrey's arguments in Neyrey, "'Without Beginning of Days or End of Life' (Heb 7:3)."
[6] Moffitt, *Atonement*, 208.
[7] Ibid., 148.
[8] Ibid., 197.
[9] Cf. ibid., David M. Moffitt, "'If Another Priest Arises': Jesus' Resurrection and the High Priestly Christology of Hebrews," in *A Cloud of Witnesses: The Theology of Hebrews in Its Ancient Contexts*, ed. Richard Bauckham, Daniel Driver, Trevor Hart and Nathan MacDonald, LNTS 387 (London: T&T Clark, 2008), 78; *Atonement*, 146.

eternal.[10] Thus uncertainty over the relation of Christ's priesthood to his divinity, though at times implicit in discussion, often becomes explicit in the exegesis of this connection in 7:16.[11]

This question of the relation of Christ's indestructible life to his divinity, though certainly a live issue in modern scholarship, is not a recent phenomenon. Broadly the question of Christ's priesthood and his mediation in relation to the divine or human natures has occasioned significant debate in the history of the church. An example of this is seen in the debate between Calvin and Stancaro, into which the former was drawn at the invitation of the Polish Reformed churches.[12] Stancaro advocated the view that Christ's mediation as priest was only to be seen in respect to his human nature and that the counter-proposal, that Christ's mediation involved his divinity, was a kind of crypto-Arianism. Calvin opposed Stancaro, arguing that Christ's work as mediator included his divine nature, not merely as a cause of the effectiveness of his human mediation but as a direct aspect of his mediation itself.

A similar debate can be seen in the century that followed Calvin and Stancaro's, this time more specifically focused on the interpretation of Heb 7. This debate can be seen in polemics between Reformed Scholastics and their Socinian opponents, who sharply differed over the divinity of Jesus in Scripture.[13] One aspect of this contention played out in the exegesis of Hebrews, in particular, over the relation of Christ's divinity to his priesthood.[14] With regard to Heb 7 this question was at times framed as whether the eternality of Melchizedek related only to the office of priesthood, and thus only implied Christ's eternity *a parte post*, or, conversely, that Melchizedek's eternality was to be related to Christ's person, and thus identified Christ in Heb 7 as possessing an eternal divine life.[15] In this way an exegete like John Owen saw the issue of eternal life in Heb

---

[10] For those supporting an inclusion of divine life in 7:16, see Gareth Lee Cockerill, "Melchizedek without Speculation: Hebrews 7.1–25 and Genesis 14.17–24," in *A Cloud of Witnesses: The Theology of Hebrews in Its Ancient Contexts*, ed. Richard Bauckham et al., LNTS 387 (London: T&T Clark, 2008), 131; Westcott, *Hebrews*, 185; Montefiore, *Hebrews*, 125, 126. On the identification of the life of 7:16 as the resurrected human life of Jesus, see Koester, *Hebrews*, 353; Attridge, *Hebrews*, 203; Ellingworth, *Hebrews*, 379; Gräßer, *Hebräer*, 2, 45, 46.

[11] Particularly significant is how an interpreter makes the bridge from 7:3 to 7:16 or not.

[12] Joseph Tylenda, "Christ the Mediator: Calvin versus Stancaro," *CTJ* 8 (1973); "The Controversy on Christ the Mediator: Calvin's Second Reply to Stancaro," *CTJ* 8 (1973). For an overview of the debate, see chapter 1 of Stephen Edmondson, *Calvin's Christology* (Cambridge: Cambridge University Press, 2004).

[13] For a summary of Socinus's position on Christ's priesthood see Demarest, *A History of Interpretation of Hebrews 7, 1–10*, 21–23.

[14] John Owen, *An Exposition of the Epistle to the Hebrews*, vol. 5 (Grand Rapids, MI: Baker Books, 1980), 490, 498, 500–4.

[15] This contrast of person and office can be seen repeatedly in Demarest's historical account, *A History of Interpretation of Hebrews 7, 1–10*, 9. For contemporary examples of those relating eternity to office, see M. J. Paul, "The Order of Melchizedek (Ps 110:4 and Heb 7:3)," *WTJ* 49 (1987): 207; Joseph A Fitzmyer, "'Now This Melchizedek ...' (Heb. 7:1)," in *Essays on the Semitic Background of the New Testament* (Grand Rapids, MI: Eerdmans, 1997), 236. For the contrary position see Gareth Lee Cockerill, "The Melchizedek Christology in Heb. 7: 1–28" (PhD Diss., Union Theological Seminary, 1976), 4, 82, 112, 144; Gräßer, *Hebräer*, 2, 21. At times it can be difficult to discern quite what relation interpreters see between the potential divine life and the resurrection life of Christ. E.g. Lane, *Hebrews 1–8*, 184.

7 as both that of *a parte post* and *a parte ante*, and that this divine life was essential in qualifying Christ as the true and ultimate High Priest in the likeness of Melchizedek.[16]

In this chapter I interact with these long-standing questions that continue to be of interest for interpreting Hebrews; in particular I will investigate its description of the relation of priesthood to Christ's divinity, specifically with a view to answering the question of the nature of Christ's indestructible life in 7:16. The predominant question in mind, occasioned by the debate outlined above, is whether this life ought to be predominantly identified as a human or divine category, or whether perhaps there is a better way of framing this question. In fact, I will argue that the indestructible life which qualified Christ for priesthood engages both human and divine aspects of Christ's portrayal in Heb 7 and cannot be readily restricted to only one of these categories. Further, I argue that the divine life is theologically foundational for the Pastor's argument in qualifying the Son for his High Priestly ministry. In this way I hope to demonstrate that there exists a profound connection between divinity and priesthood in the Epistle, evident especially in Heb 7, and in particular the "indestructible life" of Heb 7:16.

Before outlining the shape of the argument that follows, it will be helpful to briefly consider the plausibility of the view that relates Christ's priesthood simply to his shared human identity with his many brothers, and the qualification for priesthood via human resurrection life.

4.0.1 The plausibility of Christ's priesthood as a purely human category

In arguing for the necessity of considering divine categories in relation to Christ's priesthood, it is helpful to consider what would represent a counter-argument to this proposal, namely, the concept that Christ's priesthood can be sufficiently outlined in purely human categories. Though such a reading is rarely explicitly pursued, it represents a helpful avenue of exploration for three reasons. First, because it demonstrates certain key issues with which any reading of Heb 7 must contend. Second, because it demonstrates that the humanity of Christ is indeed important to considerations of his priesthood. Third, because, though not always pursued consistently, or with an eye to denying the Son's divinity, interpretation of Heb 7 is frequently pursued with little reference to the divine character of the Son.[17]

A reading of Heb 7 which would satisfy this purely human relation might begin with the idea in Hebrews that Christ's priesthood has a clear point of inception. That is, it is not a role or office which the Son always had, but one into which he entered

---

[16] Owen, *Hebrews*, 5, 517. The language of *a parte ante* and *a parte post* is borrowed from Demarest as a helpful way of distinguishing between, in the latter, an eternity from an incepted point and, in the former, a truly boundless eternity (*A History of Interpretation of Hebrews 7, 1–10*).

[17] Some interpreters do more to develop deity, in particular, Cockerill, "Melchizedek Christology"; *Hebrews*, 322–5 and Bauckham, "Divinity of Jesus," 15–36. The concept is present in Kurianal, *High Priest* though I think underdeveloped. Frequently the issue is either unexplored or receives the briefest of comments, see, e.g. Mason, *Priest Forever*, 191. Equally confusing are elements in which Jesus is portrayed as becoming a participant in the life of God through the resurrection, see, e.g. Johnson, *Hebrews*, 188.

at a particular point in time. Such an idea may be seen as early as 1:3,[18] but also at many subsequent points in the Epistle, in which the exercise of Christ's priestly role is consequent on some kind of action or experience which the Son achieves or undergoes in history. So in 1:3, Christ is seen as entering his session in allusion to Ps 110:4, "having made purification for sin."[19] This act of purification is later identified as that sacrifice of himself, which Christ achieved once for all in his death (7:27; 9:12, 26–28). Its historical character is further stressed by the difficult, but nonetheless significant comment that Christ "did not suffer repeatedly from the foundation of the world" (9:26). This timed nature of the Son's self-sacrificial act seems to pin down the inception of the priesthood in Hebrews. As the Epistle makes explicit, in order to be a priest one must have something to offer (5:1; 8:3). This Christ only had subsequent to his death.[20] Further, the act of offering essential to his High Priesthood must be completed within the tabernacle made without hands (9:24), which he entered only at his ascension.[21] This line of reasoning is further supported by the explicit language of Christ's "becoming" priest which is scattered throughout the Epistle (2:17; 5:5, 10; 7:28),[22] language which is often predicated on prior action undertaken "in the flesh" (5:7). So in 2:27 Christ's becoming "a merciful High Priest" can only follow his "becoming like his brothers in every way" (2:17). This act of taking on the things belonging to the many sons (τῶν αὐτῶν) relates not only to human nature but also to the particular experiences of suffering, testing and death.[23] Thus the ministry of help as High Priest, especially in his ability to deliver believers from the power of death, comes about consequent to his own suffering and death (2:14, 18).[24]

When the Pastor returns to this theme in Heb 5, he clarifies that the Priesthood which Christ inhabits is, in certain ways, understandable from the pattern of priesthood in Aaron and his sons found in the Law (5:1–10).[25] Just as they were inducted into that ministry by another (5:4), so too Christ was designated High Priest, not by himself but by the Father (5:5, 6, 10). This act of designation is associated with the address of God in Ps 110:4.[26] Because of the connection of this verse with the temporal horizon of Christ's ascension elsewhere in Hebrews this connection is significant.[27] It seems to locate the reception of this designation at the moment of Christ's ascension and not before.[28] In this way his designation as Melchizedekian High Priest may be seen

---

[18] Weiss, *Hebräer*, 228; Mason, *Priest Forever*, 14, 17.
[19] Compton, *Psalm 110*, 20; Hay, *Glory at the Right Hand*, 143.
[20] Moffitt, "Resurrection and High Priestly Christology," 74.
[21] Ibid., 76.
[22] Compton, *Psalm 110*, 81.
[23] On solidarity and suffering in relation to Christ's priesthood, see Mason, *Priest Forever*, 21–3.
[24] Moffitt, *Atonement*, 194–6.
[25] This is often related to the twin qualities of sympathy and divine vocation ("Resurrection and High Priestly Christology," 74). Though see the slightly different emphasis of Compton, *Psalm 110*, 67.
[26] Moffitt, "Resurrection and High Priestly Christology," 77; Hay, *Glory at the Right Hand*, 145.
[27] See Michel, *Hebräer*, 58; Compton, *Psalm 110*, 12, 89; Moffitt, *Atonement*, 89; chapter 2 of Hay, *Glory at the Right Hand*; Weiss, *Hebräer*, 169; Loader, *Sohn Und Hohepriester*, 15–16 and Martin Hengel, "Psalm 110 und die Erhöhung des Auferstandenen zur Rechten Gottes," in *Anfänge der Christologie: Festschrift für Ferdinand Hahn zum 65. Geburtstag*, ed. Cilliers Breytenbach and Henning Paulsen (Göttingen: Vanderhoeck & Ruprecht, 1991).
[28] Hay, *Glory at the Right Hand*, 144, 145.

in parallel to the salvific language of the Epistle. Christ only became High Priest as one who had become the "cause of an eternal salvation" (5:9). Thus the structure of priesthood and salvation is likewise dependent on the thread of perfection language and its application to Christ.[29] Because this category of perfection only comes to its consummation subsequent to, and contingent on, Christ's testing in death, and because High Priesthood is made contingent on this perfection, therefore Christ's priesthood can only truly begin after his death.

This line of reasoning, in which Christ "becomes High Priest according to Melchizedek" (6:20), then often leads to conclusions about the relation of this incepted priesthood to Christ's filial identity.[30] If priesthood is something which Christ comes into possession of, it is trivially not something which can be eternally predicated of him. In other words, priesthood is something taken to his sonship, where the latter is associated with his eternal identity. Christ's priesthood does not arise directly from his sonship, nor is it merely an aspect of it. In other words, if Christ became High Priest, whatever he was eternally (*a parte ante*) was not priestly. And thus priesthood does not pertain to his divinity but to his human career: his suffering, his death, his resurrection and ascension as man.[31]

This logic has important ramifications for reading Heb 7, in which the Pastor lays out in what way Christ may be spoken of as High Priest according to Melchizedek. A central question there is how the portrait of Melchizedek applies to Christ and his High Priestly ministry. That he is High Priest is clear, but quite what it means that his priesthood is "according to Melchizedek" is what is at issue. To sustain the reading outlined above, one must see Melchizedek's function in Heb 7, whether as a purely scriptural trope or as an eternal/heavenly figure,[32] as pertaining to the priestly office of Christ rather than strictly to his person.[33] Christ takes on the Melchizedekian priestly office, the nature of which is spelled out by the peculiarity and greatness of Melchizedek outlined in 7:1–10. The predominant force of the Melchizedekian pattern is to argue for the possibility of a priesthood other than that of Aaron's descendants and one with a different character, eternal efficacy. Melchizedek, in this view, represents such a priesthood which is genealogically unrelated to Aaron, thus allowing Jesus, a Judahite, to participate in it.[34] This explains the import of the Pastor's description of Melchizedek with the three well-known alpha privitives of 7:3. His being "without father, without mother, without genealogy" is explained by the clarifying phrase of 7:6 that Melchizedek was ὁ μὴ γενεαλογούμενος ἐξ αὐτῶν (7:6). The nature of Melchizedek's priesthood, after which Christ's is patterned, is related to its eternity. Just

---

[29] Moffitt, *Atonement*, 194–5.
[30] Moffitt, "Resurrection and High Priestly Christology," 76; Hay, *Glory at the Right Hand*, 145, 146.
[31] Moffitt is particularly clear on this argument, "Resurrection and High Priestly Christology," 74–8. This chain of ideas is central to his identification of this inception of a new eternal life as resurrection and as the qualifying factor in Jesus becoming High Priest.
[32] On this issue see the excursus below.
[33] Compton, *Psalm 110*, 79.
[34] Michel, *Hebräer*, 163. Thus for some interpreters the role of Heb 7 is simply to demonstrate the possibility of a non-Levitical High Priest and the argument results in only assertions about the perpetuity of Christ's office of High Priest. See Moffitt, "Resurrection and High Priestly Christology," 78; Horton, *The Melchizedek Tradition*, 156–60.

as Melchizedek's priesthood had no concrete end, so also Christ, risen and ascended to God's right hand, enters into a priesthood which is uninterrupted by death.[35] On this view, it is denied that the Pastor means to imply an eternity *a parte ante* to Christ's office, only one *a parte post*; this is clear both from the fact that it is incepted at a point in time, as above, and also because its character is contrasted with the mortality of the sons of Aaron (7:8). Christ did die, but now he lives and thus has begun the endless priesthood in which he will never fail.[36]

Within such a reading, the function and significance of 7:16 is clear. The indestructible life which forms the basis of Christ's priesthood, is the risen, ascended, and thus properly human life which he came to possess after death.[37] The use of Ps 110:4 in connection with Christ's priestly becoming, with its tenor of Christ's ascension, clarifies that the life on which Christ's priesthood is founded is that gained after his sacrificial death.[38]

It must be noted in relation to such a reading that nothing suggested under it strictly denies Christ's divinity, either in Heb 7 broadly or in the exegesis of 7:16; however, if viewed as a satisfactory handling of Heb 7, it represents divinity as extraneous to understanding a central Christological category, priesthood, in the argument of the Epistle.

4.0.2 Argument

In developing an argument for the connection of divinity and priesthood in Heb 7, I hope to demonstrate that there exists certain elements of the Pastor's thought about Christ's priesthood that cannot be exhausted by appeal to human categories. The point of this demonstration is not to remove the significance Christ as *vere homo* in the Pastor's description of his priesthood. To argue such would be, in essence, to fall into an equally reductive position in which all is ascribed to deity. Rather, the presence of thought in the argument of Heb 7, which does not fit a purely human or "incepted office" view, presses us to realize that both categories of humanity and divinity must be deployed in order to understand the Pastor's thought. In effect, the Pastor, in describing Christ, attributes to him elements of deity and humanity that cannot be easily parsed from one another, in part because they are both being predicated of the same person.[39] Thus with regards to the central concern it will be shown that an account of the life of the Son in relation to his High Priesthood cannot be rightly understood apart from his divinity. This will be further reinforced in the conclusion of the chapter, where I will

---

[35] Moffitt, "Resurrection and High Priestly Christology," 76.
[36] Owen notes this direction of interpretation (*Hebrews*, 5, 337).
[37] Bruce, *Hebrews*, 169.
[38] Moffitt, "Resurrection and High Priestly Christology," 76; *Atonement*, 145–8. On similar identification of the life of 7:16 as the resurrected human life of Jesus, see Koester, *Hebrews*, 353; Attridge, *Hebrews*, 203; Gräßer, *Hebräer*, 2, 45, 46. Hay seems to favour the resurrection but also notes the possibility of a wider reference to the life that Christ had before (*Glory at the Right Hand*, 146, 147).
[39] This concept of the unity of the person is an important aspect of Chalcedonian Christology which is particularly on view both in Calvin's general discussion of Christ as Mediator (*Inst.* II.14) and in Owen's comments on Heb 7 (Owen, *Hebrews*, 5, 451, 452).

deal with the question of whether more might be said of the relationship of these dual natures of the life of Christ in connection with the indestructible life of 7:16. Significant for my overall argument is that the divine life of the Son plays a foundational role in enabling the "indestructible life" which is central to the High Priesthood of the Son. As I will conclude, the "indestructible life" of 7:16 strictly denotes the eternal divine life of the Son, but one that in the argument is viewed through the lens of the resurrection from the dead, in which the office of eternal Priest *a parte post* is bestowed on a Person who is himself fittingly, and necessarily, *a parte ante* the eternal bearer of the divine life.

This important relationship, of divinity to priesthood in the Epistle, can be seen through at least the following two lines of evidence. The first pertains to continuity of Christ's identity becoming priest. Clearly Christ does in some sense become priest in Hebrews; however, the position outlined in Section 4.0.1 makes this a very "hard" kind of inception, in which priesthood is unrelated to what precedes it. In essence priesthood is an additive quality with little relation to Christ's person. In contrast I will demonstrate that there are clear lines of continuity between Christ's pre- and post-ascension identity that connect what Christ was before to his priesthood. For the Epistle it is of prime significance that the one who became priest is the one who is Son.[40] The second argument builds on the first, suggesting that a key aspect of this continuity of identity involves the divinity of the Son. This is demonstrated through noting that, though the issue of life is in part connected to resurrection/ascension concepts in Heb 7, it ought not be limited to that. Rather, the concept of life typified in Melchizedek and patterned on the Son involves a life which cannot be merely limited to concepts of an incepted office or of exercise of it *a parte post*. That life connects to the person of the Son and corresponds to a divine life that is both *a parte ante* and *a parte post*.[41] This second argument is strengthened by noting that the resultant depiction of Christ in Heb 7 contains several tensions surrounding whether or not human categories properly apply to the Son, suggesting that he is more than merely human in respect to his person and priesthood.

The conclusion of the chapter seeks to draw these arguments together in briefly commenting on how the relation of divinity to priesthood impacts reading the indestructible life of 7:16 which qualifies Christ to be priest.

4.1 Christ's person in relation to priesthood

This first thread of evidence here pertains to elements of Hebrews that bring into question the concept of a "hard" inception with regard to Christ's priesthood, as a role which stands unrelated to his prior identity in time or eternity. I will demonstrate that elements of Heb 7 and beyond cannot be easily reconciled with such a scheme and that

---

[40] Alan Kam-Yau Chan, *Melchizedek Passages in the Bible: A Case Study for Inner-Biblical and Inter-Biblical Interpretation* (Warsaw: De Gruyter Open, 2016), 183, 184; Kurianal, *High Priest*, 62; Peeler, *My Son*, 137–9.
[41] Peeler, *My Son*, 121; Cockerill, *Hebrews*, 323; Kurianal, *High Priest*, 207.

the Pastor's thought encourages a more complex picture of Christ's person and career in relation to priesthood.

4.1.1 Priesthood and inherence in Heb 7

The schematized understanding of Christ's priesthood and its inception via the act of resurrection/ascension as was outlined above sees Priesthood merely as an attribute added to Christ with little relation to his prior identity. This may be expressed in terms of the relation of Christ's priesthood as an office into which he enters subsequent to his earthly career, in distinction from his person; in this way Christ becomes clearly what he was not before.[42] In itself this seems unproblematic. Christ becomes High Priest for his people and thus is for them what he was not before. Such an understanding, one might argue, provides sufficient basis for the Pastor's pastoral appeals. Indeed, the focus of the High Priestly language in Hebrews is frequently on what Christ is doing now for his people, in his ability to intercede for them in testing, and to provide them present access and future guarantee of entrance to the heavenly sphere (2:18; 4:16; 6:20; 10:19–22). However, though this is perhaps the rhetorical focus of the High Priestly concept,[43] it does not necessitate viewing the theological foundation of it as narrowly as stated above. Indeed, certain elements of Heb 7 contraindicate it.

In particular, Christ as Melchizedekian priest is contrasted, in particular instances, with a certain kind of extrinsic character that marked the Levites in relation to their priestly office. That is, part of the surpassing nature of the Melchizedekian priesthood is that it is an order of one member in which distinctions of the person and office break down: Christ simply *is* the High Priest according to Melchizedek.[44] So note the comment of Attridge in this regard:

> The contrast with the "Law's commands" suggests that Christ's priesthood is not an accidental attribute, something that he, like the Levites, "receives" from an external source (7:5), but is rather something intimately connected with who he is.[45]

This concept of the unity of person and office in relation to Christ's priesthood is encountered twice in Heb 7, both times contrasted with the Levites in relation to Law. So in 7:5, the Levites are designated as those who "receive the priesthood and have a command to tithe the people according to the Law." The Pastor depicts this arrangement as something relatively inferior to Christ. This is demonstrated by the use of the exceptive clause at v. 5c: even though the Levites are of one people, brothers with those whom they tithe, they must receive a kind of external authorization from the Law's

---

[42] Hay, *Glory at the Right Hand*, 144, 145; Ernst Käsemann, *Das wandernde Gottesvolk: eine Untersuchung zum Hebräerbrief* (Göttingen: Vandenhoeck & Ruprecht, 1961), 59; Moffitt, "Resurrection and High Priestly Christology," 74–8.
[43] That is, the fact that Christ is High Priest forever is certainly rhetorically focused towards his ability to ongoingly intercede for believers and save them to the uttermost (7:25), unlike the Levitical priests whose ministry could not be sustained. Cf. Lane, *Hebrews 1–8*, 197.
[44] On this relation to efficacy, see Westcott, *Hebrews*, 132.
[45] Attridge, *Hebrews*, 202.

command. Contrastingly, Melchizedek tithes Abraham to whom he is genealogically unrelated. The point here does not seem to be the relative qualities of authorization involved, the Levites from the law and Melchizedek from elsewhere. Rather the Levites receive an outward command, though it might be assumed their familial connection would suffice for office. In this way their possession of the priesthood is portrayed as extrinsic to their persons. In contrast, Melchizedek's right as priest is illustrative of the supreme dignity of his person; this is surely the import of 7:4 and controlling in how we are to read the ensuing description of Melchizedek as a substantiation of quite "how great this person was."

A similar contrast occurs at 7:16. There the nature of this authorizing command is expanded in description as this time a "fleshly law" (7:16). This is in contrast to Christ's qualification for Priesthood via his indestructible life. The fleshly nature of the command here certainly seems to refer to the issue of genealogical descent that circumscribes Levitical authority.[46] But in line with 7:5, the fleshly nature of the command suggests an element of extrinsicity.[47] The Levites inherit their Priesthood because of their relationship to another, Levi. This is strengthened by the connection of law and flesh elsewhere in Hebrews (9:10, 13), which, in similar discussions of efficacy, see σάρξ as related to a decidedly outward character that does not touch the ultimate nature of things.[48] Thus Christ's qualification of Priesthood, by means of contrast with a fleshly law, not only detaches it once more from genealogical issues but further suggests that it is not extrinsic. It is not merely a contrast of qualifying factors at work in 7:16, but rather a contrasting way in which these factors relate to the persons holding office. The way in which indestructible life qualified the Son may thus not be seen in parallel to the nature of Levitical authorization.[49] It is not merely what authorization Christ and the Levites possess that differs, but how they possess this authorization, whether as extrinsic or intrinsic.[50]

The manner in which Ps 110:4 relates to authorizing Christ's priesthood is therefore significant. It cannot be that this designating word functions in the same way with respect to Christ that the outward command functions in relation to the Levites. The use of Ps 110:4 certainly implies a kind of contingency, but it cannot be the same kind of extrinsic contingency to which the Levitical priests are subject via the fleshly command. This comports with the character of the speech acts involved in those authorizations, which Hebrews notes. Both the law and the promise are the words of God's speech (1:1). But the fact that the promise of Ps 110:4 is accompanied by an oath places it in an altogether different sphere. The hierarchy of speech acts, according to the Pastor, itself reflects a qualitative difference in the way in which the Levites and Christ possess their respective priesthoods.[51]

---

[46] Compton, *Psalm 110*, 88, 89; Lane, *Hebrews 1–8*, 183.
[47] Michel, *Hebräer*, 172.
[48] Cockerill, "Melchizedek Christology," 108.
[49] The word ἀκατάλυτος is used elsewhere in 4 Macc 10:11 and seems well translated by the English "indestructible" (Lane, *Hebrews 1–8*, 184). How of course this relates to Christ's death and natures is not recoverable from pure lexical study and requires a wider theological development.
[50] Peeler, *My Son*, 123, 124.
[51] Johnson, *Hebrews*, 184. For more on this axiological commitment to oaths and their swearing in Hebrews, see Chapter 5.

This connection of personhood and priestly ministry in Hebrews is hardly surprising when one considers the nature of atonement itself. The oneness of the Melchizedekian priesthood, in unity of person and office, differs from the Levitical system not merely in the singular nature of the minister in comparison to the many Levites but also in relation to the act of oblation itself. Christ is both minister and offering (5:1; 7:27; 8:3; 9:11, 12), and thus the act of oblation is by nature a personal issue: Christ offers his person, and this offering of self establishes, in part, its superiority and efficacy (7:26–28; 9:23).[52] The priests are many (7:22), with many sacrifices (9:25; 10:1, 2, 11) which are other than the priest himself; Christ's offering of himself and the singular and supreme nature of that offering are intimately related (10:5–10, 14).

Thus the supremacy of Christ's priesthood in Hebrews is in several ways connected to the greatness of his person and portrayed as something other than merely an extrinsic office which is unrelated to his prior identity.[53]

4.1.2 Priesthood before inception

Further to this line of enquiry, at least one text, 5:7, seems to speak of Christ's ministry before his self-offering in explicitly priestly terms that call into question a hard division between Christ's career and his priestly ministry subsequent to the resurrection/ascension. There the Son is portrayed in tearful prayer to the Father, prayer aimed at his rescue from death.[54] The verb used for the act of prayer is προσφέρω, which elsewhere in Hebrews is connected generally to cultic action (e.g. 8:3, 4; 9: 7, 9, 14 and so on). The immediate context of 5:1, 3 clearly uses the verb with this sense in describing the sacrificial ministry of the Levites. Elsewhere in the NT the verb includes instances that are less clearly cultic and include a more general sense, in which objects or persons are brought to another, often with the recognition of higher social standing implied (Matt 2:11; 4:24; 17:16; Mark 10:13; Acts 8:18 and so on). Though nowhere else is this verb clearly used in relation to offering of prayer to God, it might be argued that the act of bringing prayer to God via this verb does not imply cultic activity and thus portray Christ as priest,[55] and that, in any case, it is difficult to rely so closely on the controverted connotations of a single verb. However, that a cultic action is implied, or at least that Christ's prayer ministry here is already portrayed in cultic terms, is supported by the wider unit of 5:1–10 in which it is located.[56]

It has frequently been noted that 5:1–10 may be viewed as containing a broadly chiastic structure.[57] So in 5:1–3 the Pastor outlines the nature of the Levites' relation to the people and the nature of their offering; 5:4 moves to the nature of their qualification

---

[52] Gräßer, *Hebräer*, 2, 73; Gaffin, "The Priesthood of Christ," 52. See also Compton, *Psalm 110*, 141 on 9:27.
[53] Gräßer explicitly connects this distinction of the new priesthood as one in which "Gott *selbst* daß tut" (*Hebräer*, 2, 75).
[54] On the nature of this rescue, see Moffitt, *Atonement*, 189; Attridge, *Hebrews*, 150, 151.
[55] Kurianal, *High Priest*, 69.
[56] Scholer, *Proleptic Priests*, 133.
[57] Cf. Lane, *Hebrews 1–8*, 111; Chan, *Melchizedek*, 181; Ellingworth, *Hebrews*, 271; Mason, *Priest Forever*, 23.

for ministry via their calling; 5:5, 6 essentially apply this external call of 5:4 in parallel to Christ as High Priest, thus beginning to substantiate the key statement of 4:14–16 which 5:1–10 develops;[58] 5:7–10 then represents an elaboration of the nature of Christ's priestly ministry against the backdrop of the Levitical ministry described in 5:1–3.[59] It is exactly at this point that the concept of chiasm in the verses tends to encounter problems.[60] In the main, this is because the description of Christ's prayers for rescue from death are seen as providing a poor parallel to the description of the Levitical ministry above, especially when the middle comparison of the nature of respective "calls" is so tight and obvious. If, however, the comparison of Christ's and the Levitical ministry is seen to contain both similarity and difference the chiastic reading may be sustained and the resultant reading confirms a depiction of Christ's prayers as essentially priestly in significance in the following way.[61]

These latter verses (5:7–10) as a whole focus on the superlative nature of Christ's priestly ministry in comparison to a Levitical ministry and its officiants characterized by ἀσθένεια. This weakness attended their ministry and occasioned offerings not only for the people but also themselves (5:3). In place of this ministry, characterized by sin-weakness, Christ is depicted in a kind of weakness without sin.[62] His offering relates to his depicted εὐλαβεία. In other words, where their ministry was marked by imperfection, his is marked by a piety befitting the true Son.[63] Whether or not these prayers and requests are seen to generally characterize Jesus' earthly career or are attached to a particular event, the act of priestly offering is set before the cross.[64] Thus the Pastor depicts Christ as, at least in some sense, exercising a priestly ministry before his resurrection/ascension in a way that problematizes the idea of an inception of ministry that bears little relation to the Son's prior identity.[65]

4.1.3 Priesthood in relation to sonship

Though some have sought to argue for a view of Christ's office of Priesthood as arising automatically from his sonship,[66] the fact that there is clearly an act of becoming related

---

[58] Lane, *Hebrews 1–8*, 117.
[59] The issues of both continuity and discontinuity (especially around the difference of Christ's sinlessness) suggest that the description of "every priest" in 5:1 does not include Christ. For detailed support, see Kurianal, *High Priest*, 49–60.
[60] Compton, *Psalm 110*, 67n64.
[61] Spicq, *Hébreux*, 2, 112; Lane, *Hebrews 1–8*, 119; Compton, *Psalm 110*, 67.
[62] Cf. the description of Christ's sinless ministry in 4:15 and by implication in 7:26.
[63] Scholer, *Proleptic Priests*, 108; Ellingworth, *Hebrews*, 292. On εὐλαβεία as "reverence" rather than "fear" see Kurianal, *High Priest*, 72; Koester, *Dwelling of God*, 289, pace Calvin, *Hebrews*, 122.
[64] Lane, *Hebrews 1–8*, 120.
[65] Ibid., 119; Koester, *Dwelling of God*, 108. Kurianal objects to a sacrificial reading of Christ's prayers as if it requires a denial of the sufficiency of Christ's death in atonement, a clearly central theological concept for Hebrews (Kurianal, *High Priest*, 69). However, the sufficiency of the once-for-all-death is not to be separated from other "passive" elements of Christ's work in the incarnation, of which it is the climax. Cf. Johnson, *Hebrews*, 146 and Scholer, *Proleptic Priests*, 88.
[66] George Wesley Buchanan, *To the Hebrews*, AB 36 (Garden City, NY: Doubleday, 1972), 94–7; Gräßer, *Hebräer*, 2, 292; Chan, *Melchizedek*, 200. Westcott and Calvin take a more nuanced position in which priesthood belongs to the Son but mediately via the exalted state (Westcott, *Hebrews*, 123, 124; Calvin, *Hebrews*, 117).

to it in Hebrews tends to tell against this view. The temptation then becomes to distance priesthood from sonship such that the latter becomes purely additive in respect to the former.[67] Christ *is* Son, but, in a somewhat unrelated manner, *becomes* High Priest;[68] or even that Christ's sonship is problematic for his status as priest.[69] The thought of the Pastor however is far more nuanced. The nature of Christ's priesthood is clearly predicated on his filial identity.[70] And though it does not strictly arise automatically from it, it must still be maintained that Christ is High Priest *because* he is Son. Thus to the extent that the category of sonship is informed as a divine category,[71] priesthood will correspondingly not be exhausted by only categories of human exaltation or resurrection life.

This relationship of priesthood to sonship may be seen in various ways in the Epistle, but perhaps the clearest and most convincing connection is forged by various middle terms which draw together the Son's priestly and filial identities and seem to cause the former to arise out of the latter. Notable in this regard are concepts of obedience and perfection. Quite whatever the exact denotation of the perfection language in Hebrews is, it is uncontroversial to see the lexical group in relation to Christ's qualification as High Priest. So in 5:9, 10 his designation as High Priest is consequent on his "being perfected." However the process of perfection which involves Christ's obedience and faithfulness in the face of testing may be seen in relation to his sonship and arising from it. Christ is the ultimate Son who endured the trials of the Father's discipline and persevered in it to the end (5:8; 12:2, 4, 5). The result of this process of discipline is his perfection; and he underwent this process in spite of his pre-existing filial identity (5:8, 9). In this way the Epistle represents a clear string of connections: obedient because Son; perfected through obedience; Priest because perfected. Construed in this way one can see that, in an important sense, the Son's priesthood is not automatic. It is not formally immediate—arising without mediate causes. The Son is priest because of his career of incarnate obedience; the middle term is essential to his qualification.[72] Without incarnation necessitated to take hold of the seed of Abraham, it is unclear quite what Christ's relationship to priesthood would be. However, the plan of the Father, alluded to in the Pastor's use of Ps 40:9 LXX in 10:7, entails the taking up of a body and the consequent life of human obedience that results in perfection. Considered apart from this salvific plan the Son would not be priest; but consequent on it, priesthood becomes a necessary entailment of the Son's sonship.

Thus the idea that either priesthood arises automatically from sonship or, on the other hand, is a mere additive to it, represents a false choice. Rather within the sphere of redemption and incarnate obedience, the Son's priestly ministry is predicated upon

---

[67] On the false dichotomy of automatic relation or disconnection between the Son's filial and priestly identities, see Peeler, *My Son*, 105–8.

[68] For more on whether this apportioning of being and becoming is an appropriate way to handle sonship and priesthood see the discussion of Chapter 6.

[69] Moffitt, "Resurrection and High Priestly Christology," 77, 78.

[70] Gaffin, "The Priesthood of Christ," 61; Peeler, *My Son*, 137–9; Cockerill, "Melchizedek Christology," 112.

[71] On which see Chapter 6 of the present work.

[72] Calvin, *Hebrews*, 117, 118. In many respects this is simply a theological reflex of the fact that Christ's priesthood is only necessitated by our need and not any need in God. See Athanasius, *Inc.* 1.1.

his sonship, in such a way that who the Son is eternally cannot be separated from the intermediary role he represents in the salvation of God's people.[73]

4.2 Supra-human and divine notes in relation to the Son in Heb 7

As we have outlined above, the Epistle sketches a view of the Son's person I in relation to his becoming Melchezedekian priest that assumes a continuity in his identity as Son. The second line of argument that follows demonstrates that an important part of this continuity involves the deity of the Son as a ground upon which the priestly ministry is built, and which is necessary to its operation. My argument moves forward in two main ways: first, a consideration of the key feature of life that figures so importantly in both the description of Melchizedek and the identification of the Son; second, tensions over the Son's humanity that arise in Heb 7, which bear witness that his nature cannot be subsumed purely under the rubric of humanity.

4.2.1 The life of Melchizedek and the nature of the Son's life

In Heb 7 the Pastor explains the nature of Jesus' High Priesthood in relation to the Melchizedekian order of Ps 110:4. Such a connection to Melchizedek would surely have struck his original audience as unexpected, not least because the language of order sits awkwardly with the priesthood of a single character, after whom no order of priests is developed in the OT.[74] This strangeness is only heightened by the mysterious character of Melchizedek himself. The coupling of exalted status[75] combined with his shadowy depiction makes him an obvious candidate for the kind of reception we see in Judaism and the NT.[76]

The Pastor's explanation of what this priesthood according to Melchizedek entails begins with a selective consideration of his portrait in Gen 14:18–20.[77] Considerable

---

[73] See the lucid discussion in chapter 3 of Peeler, *My Son*.
[74] Owen, *Hebrews*, 5, 298. On the scant appearances of Melchizedek and his inner biblical development see Chan, *Melchizedek*, 1–3.
[75] The issue of tithe reception is unclear in the MT but resolved in the LXX in agreement with later reception, e.g. Jos. *Bell. Iud.* 6.438; Jos. *Ant.* 1.181; Philo *Congr.* 99; 1QapGen XXII ar 24–26. For differences between the MT and LXX on Gen 14:18–20, see Joseph A. Fitzmyer, "Melchizedek in the MT, LXX, and the NT," *Bib* 81 (2000): 67, 68.
[76] Connections to Melchizedek include varied retellings of the Genesis account (Jos. *Bell. Iud.* 6.438; *Ant* 1.10.2; Philo *Leg. All.* 3.79–82; *Congr.* 99; *Abr.* 235; 1 QapGen arr XXII, 12–17) and the figure Melchizedek in 11QMelch and perhaps 4Q401 11.3 who may or may not be identified with the figure of Genesis and Ps 110 (Mason, *Priest Forever*, 164–5). On the identity of this figure in 11QMelch see the varied opinions of Franco Manzi, *Melchisedek e l'Angelologia nell'Epistola agli Ebrei e a Qumran*, AnBib 136 (Roma: Pontificio Istituto Biblico, 1997); Paul Rainbow, "Melchizedek as a Messiah at Qumran," *BBR* 7 (1997); J. T. Milik, "Milki-Sedeq et Milki-Resa dans Les Anciens Éscrits Juifs et Chrétiens," *JJS* 23 (1972). The assessment of Mason that the evidence seems to suggest a figure distinct from God and of heavenly nature is well-balanced, though as noted, the poor state of some texts makes identification of agents a difficult proposition (Mason, *Priest Forever*, 177, 183–4).
[77] Lane, *Hebrews 1–8*, 163.

discussion has been occasioned by this portrait in the history of interpretation, particularly regarding what is implied by 7:3 about the figure of Melchizedek himself.[78] I will return briefly to this discussion in the excursus at the close of the chapter, but here it suffices to say the Pastor is involved in Heb 7 in a distinctly textual argument.[79] The argument arises, in part, because of the mysterious nature of Melchizedek's description in Genesis, but more centrally from the prediction of a figure like Melchizedek in Ps 110. Ps 110:4 provides a scriptural warrant for the idea that the description of Melchizedek in Gen 14 is more than mere historical report and has a typological significance.[80]

That the prophecy of Ps 110:4 drives the argument forward can be seen through two points the Pastor draws out, both of which signal the relativization of the Levitical order. The very existence in the text of a priesthood "not spoken of according to the order of Aaron" raises the question of why another priesthood is necessary.[81] Its oath-bound nature (7:21, 23, 28) and post-dating of the provision of the Aaronic priests (7:28) similarly augurs its supremacy to, and relativization of, what preceded it.[82] The later announcement of priesthood, postdating the command to Levi, was given with an oath, suggesting that the latter did not realize the goal of priesthood: perfection (7:11). The Melchizedekian priesthood is confirmed as requiring a different kind of priest, when one in the likeness of Melchizedek actually appears on the scene of history (7:15), demonstrating that not only is there a promise of such but that this promise has actually been fulfilled in Christ.[83]

The textual nature of this argument in developing the promise of a different kind of priest from Ps 110:4 is paralleled by the similarly textual move to discuss what Melchizedekian priesthood entails from the witness of Gen 14:18–20.[84] The Pastor's initial description in 7:1, 2 brings out the unusual greatness of Melchizedek despite the partiality of the character sketched in Genesis. He bears the titles of King and Priest and was given a tithe by the patriarch, Abraham, himself. 7:3 dwells on the fact that, in spite of the seeming dignity and importance of Melchizedek, he lacks what all others of note have in Genesis: a genealogy.[85] He is both without father and mother and without wider genealogy. The third of the alpha privitives, ἀγενεαλόγητος, may simply sum up the former two, or expand more broadly on them.[86] The term without the privative ἀ- normally signals a list of ancestors describing prior descent, though here there are reasons to include the concept of progeny which are frequently included in Genesis in genealogical lists.[87] These terms encapsulate Melchizedek's strange presence in the Genesis text, unanchored either by foregoing ancestors or succeeding descendants.

---

[78] Demarest, *A History of Interpretation of Hebrews 7, 1–10*, 132.
[79] Kurianal, *High Priest*, 103, 104.
[80] Cockerill, "Melchizedek Christology," 233; Paul Ellingworth, "'Like the Son of God': Form and Content in Hebrews 7, 1–10," *Bib* 64 (1983): 258.
[81] Michel, *Hebräer*, 132.
[82] *Pace* Chan, *Melchizedek*, 43.
[83] This seems to be the sense of the movement from πρόδηλον in 7:14 to κατάδηλόν in 7:15.
[84] Cockerill, "Melchizedek Christology," 29.
[85] Hughes, *Hebrews*, 248; Johnson, *Hebrews*, 176.
[86] Spicq, *Hébreux*, 2, 184.
[87] See the discussion of this below.

From the point of view argued in Section 4.0.1, which focuses on the nature of the Melchizedekian priesthood as one of an office with only *a parte post* eternity, it might be thought that the Pastor description of Melchizedek simply raises the issue of lineage in connection to priesthood.[88] Normal priesthood is by nature genealogical, being attached to Aaron's sons and Levi's tribe. As such the recognition that Jesus is of Judahite lineage would pose an insurmountable barrier to his holding priestly office. Thus it might be thought that the threefold description of Melchizedek is only preparatory for the statement of 7:6, in which Melchizedek is further described in relation to the Levites as the one who is not descended from them.

However, though 7:6 certainly develops one aspect of 7:3's significance, it does not exhaust it.[89] It ought to be seen as an imposition to read the focused point of 7:6, that Melchizedek was not descended from the sons of Levi, back into the broader statement of 7:3.[90] Indeed, before reaching 7:6, the Pastor summarizes its unrestricted significance in 7:4. The lack of father/mother/genealogy is interpreted to mean that he is without beginning of days or end of life,[91] his point being that the lack of ancestry associated with Melchizedek in Gen 14 makes him textually a timeless figure.[92] This might be assumed as limited to preceding time, because of the language of ancestry, but in the Pastor's gloss it relates to both temporal directions.[93] The Genesis record creates an expectation in relation to significant figures, that they will be bounded at both ends of their life by their ancestry and their deaths. The latter is frequently portrayed in an equally genealogical manner; lists of progeny in Genesis are often the natural place for a record of the person's length of life and ultimate death (e.g. Gen 5:6–31). That Melchizedek lacks familial connection, both backwards and forwards, represents a kind of eternity at the textual level. He neither comes to be in birth nor ceases to be in record of his death. Thus the expansion of 7:3 in 7:4 suggests that the issue of Melchizedek's genealogy has in mind not merely his lack of narratival entrance but also exit. Though the Pastor's argument is frequently related to the principal *quod non in thora non in mundo*, it is more particularly tied to a familiarity with how Genesis handles the entrances and exits of principal characters.[94]

---

[88] A good summary of debate over the termination of the eternity language on office or person can be found in Mason, *Priest Forever*, 30–5. Discussion frequently proposes a false choice between either an eternal Melchizedek or only eternity of an office, e.g. Lane, *Hebrews 1–8*, 165, 166; Backhaus, "'Licht vom Licht,'" 88. For a way out of this dichotomy see the Excursus below.

[89] Cockerill. Cf. Chan, *Melchizedek*, 190. Some (e.g. Ellingworth, "'Like the Son of God,'" 260) seek to remove the question at this point by appealing to the traditional character of 7:1–3 and thus suggesting it does not reflect the thought of the Pastor. However, barring the titular explanation (Compton, *Psalm 110*, 77n52), each element of 7:1–3 is developed in the discussion that follows. As Gräßer notes, all elements noted as traditional are evident in the Pastor's own style ("Mose und Jesus," 18).

[90] Peeler, *My Son*, 121.

[91] Koester, *Hebrews*, 344; Gräßer, *Hebräer*, 2, 21. Understanding that this is the import of the alpha-privative language helps resolve the sense in which Christ is "without Father." Pace Kurianal, *High Priest*, 94.

[92] Again, see the excursus at the end of the current chapter.

[93] Spicq, *Hébreux*, 2, 184.

[94] Cf. Gen 5:1–32; 6:9, 10; 9:8–27; 10:1–32; 11:10–32 and the discussion of Johnson, *Hebrews*, 176. Sim. Cockerill, "Melchizedek without Speculation," 144.

The value of this observation is focused on the last phrase of 7:3, that as one with unbounded life, and because he is portrayed as a priest in Gen 14, Melchizedek is consequently a priest perpetually.[95] The sense of this statement, in the light of what precedes in 7:3, is not merely focused on unending priestly ministry begun at a certain point from which it continues, but rather a priesthood performed in relation to a life without beginning or end.[96] Equally significant is that the Pastor already signals here a movement to Jesus. If this were left to discussion subsequent to the focusing of 7:6b it might be argued that the relation to Jesus is only in relation to *a parte post* endurance of his priestly ministry. The Pastor does not do this however. Rather he already associates three elements by the close of 7:3: the unbounded life of Melchizedek in both eternity past and future, the typological nature of Melchizedek's priestly ministry which endures and a correlation to the Son of God. If this were not enough, the Pastor's description of the relation of this Melchizedekian portrait to the Son is worded in such a way in Heb 7 as to bring out the Son's character in both time and eternity. Later in 7:15 he will describe the Son's relationship to the scriptural portrait in the order of history and fulfilment: the Son is one arising as High Priest "according to the likeness of Melchizedek."[97] However, here in 7:3 the order of promise and fulfilment is transcended by language more reminiscent of the formation of the tabernacle in Heb 8:5. Melchizedek in his textual character was himself "conformed to the Son of God"; he served as a ὑπόδειγμα καὶ σκία (8:5).[98] His timeless qualities and unbounded life in Genesis were patterned after another.[99] Again, it might be thought that this expression represents an ahead-of-time patterning of Melchizedek after the shape of what Christ would become, in history, a merely proleptic type.[100] However, this argument would not do justice either to the kind of eternity patterned in Melchizedek, which we are told is only because of the Son's nature, or to the fact that the one after whom Melchizedek is patterned is clearly a person, the Son of God, rather than merely an incepted function of unending priestly ministry.[101]

This all suggests that to attempt to read the discussion of Melchizedek here as merely paving a way for a Christ whose Priesthood is without Levitical ancestry is too restrictive. The Melchizedek described in Heb 7:1–4, drawn from the Genesis account, is one not merely unrelated to Levi, but altogether above and beyond Abraham, the father of the covenant people.[102] He stands as greater than the one who received the promises, and thus has more to do with God's side in redemptive history than

---

[95] Kurianal, *High Priest*, 96.
[96] Cockerill, "Melchizedek Christology," 112. This is essentially to recognize that the description in 7:1–3 is entirely directed towards the portrayal of Christ (ibid., 59, 484).
[97] Here "likeness" is obviously the way the Pastor has read the κατὰ τὴν τάξιν of OG Ps 110:4 (Fitzmyer, "'Now This Melchizedek …'" (Heb. 7:1)," 226).
[98] Pace Ellingworth, "'Like the Son of God'," 257. Mason, *Priest Forever*, 194 notes this similarity of the heavenly/earthly axis in other typological correspondences and its relevance at this point.
[99] Lane, *Hebrews 1–8*, 166; Horton, *The Melchizedek Tradition*, 156; Kurianal, *High Priest*, 95.
[100] One finds a similar *Tendenz* reflected in Moffitt's equivocation on whether the Son of 7:3 is considered preincarnate or incarnate (Moffitt, *Atonement*, 207).
[101] See further footnote 109.
[102] Kurianal, *High Priest*, 100. Cockerill sees 7:6 as moving from the wider lack of Abrahamic genealogy to the narrower and related lack of Levitical genealogy ("Melchizedek without Speculation," 130).

the side of the people (6:13–20).[103] Neither is it sufficient to appeal to an incepted and endless endurance of priestly office as the import of Melchizedek's role. Instead the Melchizedekian portrait is of a life unbounded in both temporal directions, without beginning or end. This life is witnessed to in the narrative structure of Genesis, to which the Pastor alludes in 7:8. The subject of the participle μαρτυρούμενος is not that of Ps 110:4, which is not introduced into the discussion until 7:11;[104] rather it is the witness of Gen 14 concerning Melchizedek as one who lives and this life is that of 7:3, without beginning or end.

Thus the discussion of Melchizedek in 7:1–10 develops a foundation which is wider than that required merely to substantiate a view of the Son's priesthood related to office. Similarly the life of the Son in reference to his priesthood cannot be limited merely to a priesthood without end.[105] Rather Melchizedek's scriptural portrait sketches a Son whose life is eternal, both in the past as well as the present and future.

4.2.2 The unbounded life of Jesus elsewhere in Hebrews

The import of 7:1–10 in developing a description of the Son as possessing a fully eternal life may be strengthened by appeal to the rest of Hebrews and the description of the Son's unbounded life there. I have already discussed at some length in Chapter 2 the significance of 1:10–12 and its quotation of Ps 102:26–29 in description of the Son. There the Pastor attributes a status to the Son which includes immutability above creation, articulated not merely as an eschatological trope, but in protological terms.[106] In fact, the language of creation is not chosen as background for its own sake, but because it acts as the natural springboard from which to speak of God's otherness in relation to creation, and his standing without its limits, including time and change. So within Hebrews, the Lord, who arises from Judah, is at the same time the Lord of Ps 102 who "was in the beginning" and is described in terms not able to be predicated of the created order. This creational background of Ps 102 reflects the theme raised at 1:3 that the Son was the one through whom the ages were made, stressing the existence of the Son prior to and without the created order. These themes of timelessness, immutability and their corollary of otherness can be related to other passages in Hebrews which strengthen the manner of handling 7:3 advocated above.

Particularly striking in this regard is the language of Ps 40 cited by the Pastor in 10:5–10. The Son is here portrayed as taking up the language of the psalm, as he comes into the world (10:5a).[107] His entrance is explicitly linked to the theme of obedience to the will of God, which contextually links together the obedience of the Davidic King to the Law with the saving plan of God.[108] This relation of the Son's mission and obedient

---

[103] See further the discussion of Chapter 5.
[104] Pace Chan, *Melchizedek*, 192.
[105] Mason, *Priest Forever*, 201.
[106] On the issue of pre-existence generally in Hebrews see Koester, *Hebrews*, 104, 105; Backhaus, "'Licht vom Licht,'" 77–100 and Aquila H. I. Lee, *From Messiah to Preexistent Son*, WUNT 2/192 (Tübingen: Mohr Siebeck, 2005), 271–8.
[107] Attridge, *Hebrews*, 273; Westcott, *Hebrews*, 311; Peeler, *My Son*, 135n173.
[108] Thus the language of τὸ θέλημά σου is doing a kind of double duty. This reference to a "book" in which the speaker finds his duties is frequently seen as the Mosaic Law, e.g. Koester, *Hebrews*, 433.

response is further enhanced by the way in which the quotation of Ps 40 is truncated. By ending the quotation where he does, omitting the auxiliary verb ἐβουλήθην which is attached to the articular infinitive clause that preceded it, the Pastor encourages an identification of concepts in his quotation that is more explicit than in the original context; it is, in effect, an interpretative citational method.[109] Because of the omission of the auxiliary ἐβουλήθην the articular infinitive clause becomes connected to ἥκω in 10:7a, with the resultant Greek sentence ἥκω ... τοῦ ποιῆσαι ὁ θεὸς τὸ θέλημά σου. Thus the quotation here is an interpretation of Ps 40 in which the Pastor demonstrates that the Son's coming into the world is both for the sake of and at the same time an aspect of his obedience to the Father. The Son's assumption of a state in which he is "made like his brothers in every way" (2:17) is thus seen in 10:5-10 not merely as one of outward necessity in relation to salvation, but equally an act of obedience rendered from the Son to the Father. That this act of obedience is logically prior to Christ's human state requires a prior personal existence from which to will the fact.[110] This citational introduction strengthens this point by describing the Psalm as spoken "as [the Son] comes into the world" (10:5).

This concept in Hebrews of Christ's identity in distinction from his human existence is further strengthened by the parallel way in which Christ's humanity is at times stated in a manner contingent on the nature of humanity to be saved. Christ shares in flesh and blood because the children do (2:14). He receives what can first be described as "their things" and helps a group, distinct from himself, described as "the seed of Abraham" (2:16). Each of these three descriptions of what it is to be human is all predicable of Christ, but at the same time his possession of them is contingent, unlike those humans he rescues. Admittedly within these passages it is principally the will of the Father upon which they are contingent, but nevertheless, the contingency still creates an expectation that Christ possesses "their things" in a way which is additive, that is subsequent to prior personal identity, in comparison with ordinary humanity, where existence and possession of these properties are mutually indistinguishable.

This clear statement of the Son's logical and temporal priority to his existence as man further clarifies the sense in which the statements of 1:3 and 1:10–12 relate to the Son's protological role. His existence in these verses, in light of the use of Ps 40, may not be relegated to merely an eschatological purpose which comes to fruition in the Son, as Schenck has suggested.[111] Rather along with 10:5-10 they suggest a real and willing Person who exists in distinction from these purposes and freely wills them with the Father. In 10:5-10 this independence is circumscribed by the state of enfleshment; in 1:3, 10–12 the scope is far greater, encompassing the created order in its entirety and separating the Son's existence from the category of the created realm.

However, it may more specifically be seen as a reference to the King's duties to the Law recorded in Deut 17:18–20, which themselves imply total Law obedience, especially considering the Davidic superscription of Ps 39 LXX. Cf. Westcott, *Hebrews*, 313.

[109] Attridge, *Hebrews*, 274. On the Pastor's handling of the Ps 40 text see Karen H. Jobes, "Rhetorical Achievement in the Hebrews 10 'Misquote' of Psalm 40," *Bib* 72 (1991): 387–96.

[110] Backhaus, "'Licht vom Licht,'" 89.

[111] Schenck, "Enthroned Son," 476 and similarly "Keeping His Appointment," 56. For criticism of Schenck's view and the personality of the pre-existent Son see Peeler, *My Son*, 23–9.

A final verse which, alongside the above, explicitly discusses the temporal quality of the Son's life is Heb 13:8. Here the Pastor raises the question of the Son's nature in relation to leaders who, though significant, have passed from the scene. In contrast to their removal, whether by death or imprisonment, stands the immutability of Jesus Christ. He is one who is "the same, yesterday, today and forever."[112] The purpose of this statement is not merely metaphysical speculation, but rather to reassure the Pastor's audience that, though their leaders may be removed, Jesus' presence and help will not change.[113] Recognizing the pragmatic force of the statement, some interpreters have argued that it is not to be construed metaphysically.[114] To read this claim of immutable fidelity of Jesus for his people as a claim of metaphysical timelessness and immutability is, it is argued, a category mistake. While this may appear a strong argument, it fails to note that it would sever not merely this statement about Jesus from metaphysical purchase in Hebrews but would apply to all language about God in the Epistle.[115] The same attributes of timelessness and immutability in relation to God are frequently described as for the sake of his people. This communication of what God is *ad extra* for his people does not, by its nature, limit the description to non-metaphysical implications; rather, it demonstrates that because of God's bond with his people, what he is in transcendence over space and time becomes a covenantal resource. What God is without creation and *in se*, he freely becomes *ad nos* by his will and action.

This is itself reflected in the background to the usage of Ps 102 as was discussed above, in which God's transcendence over the creation is raised by the psalmist in a discussion of power. Because God is unlike the psalmist with respect to categories of existence, God may do for the psalmist what he himself cannot. In the same way, the Son who bears the divine eternal life is equipped to be the steadfast and immovable one in whom his people may trust.

4.2.3 God as the living God in Hebrews

The previous significance of Jesus in relation to eternal life and its relation to his people is further sharpened by reflection on the language of God as the Living God in Hebrews (3:12; 9:14; 10:31).[116] This language is frequently associated with the description of God in the face of challenge from foreign powers or idolatry in the LXX.[117] Behind this ascription of life to God is the conviction that because God is Living he may act; life and power are correlative. This is particularly brought out negatively in 3:12 and 10:31, in which the language of God as living is raised to engender due fear in the audience in

---

[112] For further argumentation seeing this as implicitly divine in connotation see Bauckham, "Divinity of Jesus," 34–6.
[113] In this sense Weiss is right that it is "nicht in erster Linie eine 'dogmatische' Ausgabe" (Weiss, *Hebräer*, 716). But perhaps in no sense is any statement in the NT if one considers "dogmatic" to imply a lack of pastoral function.
[114] See the contrasts of Weiss, *Hebräer*, 716; Koester, *Dwelling of God*, 105.
[115] This language can both be positive and negative (3:12; 6:10, 18; 10:31).
[116] Cockerill, "Melchizedek Christology," 76. One might equally compare the use of μένω in both Hebrews and elsewhere as a description of God (e.g. Dan 6:27LXX). See Lane, *Hebrews 1–8*, 189.
[117] Josh 3:26; Deut 5:10; 1 Sam 17:26, 36; 2 Kgs 19:14, 16; Isa 37:4, 17; Dan 6:20, 26 and so on.

responding to the word of the gospel.[118] The God who they may be tempted to abandon is real and living and thus powerful to act—to their detriment. In fact, this connection between God's existence and the covenantal focusing of his presence is alluded to in verses almost immediately preceding 13:8. Not only are the Pastor's audience not to be unduly shaken by the loss of leaders, they are equally not to be beholden to money and possessions for the Lord has promised to them, "I will never leave you or forsake you" (13:5). Here God's ubiquity is sharpened in relation to his people; God is present *for* his people, such that the Lord has become, through his promises, their Lord and Helper (13:6b). Thus the fact that Jesus' immutability and unboundedness in 13:8 is related to the benefit of his people in no way distinguishes this temporal relation as only a functional or salvific statement.[119] With the God of Hebrews, Jesus' function and saving relation to his people arises from a metaphysical basis. The one who may remain with them yesterday, today and forever may do so *because he is* yesterday, today and forever, above and beyond the vicissitudes of the created order as its God.

4.2.4 Life and divinity outside of Hebrews

Further support for the nature of Jesus' life in Hebrews as a divine and unbounded life has been furnished by seeking parallels between the description of Melchizedek's life and the background of contemporary language about God or the divine. This has been undertaken with respect to both divine figures in the Græco-Roman world and the description of God in Jewish literature, most notably by Neyrey and Bauckham.[120] Neyrey suggests that the choice of the three alpha privitives in 7:3 reflects Græco-Roman language suitable for describing a "true deity" and that, indeed, this is its function in Heb 7.[121] Bauckham has extended this argument noting that similar descriptions in relation to begotten-ness and ancestry may be related to divine designation in intertestamental Jewish literature. This is particularly evident in texts like Josephus, *Ag. Ap.* 2:167–9 in which Josephus summarizes the teaching of Moses about God describing him as "one, unbegotten and eternally unchangeable."[122]

However, though this may be suggestive, it does not form the natural starting point when considered from the context of Heb 7. Rather the connection of the three alpha privitives is seen as scriptural testimony to the quality of life which Melchizedek possessed in the Genesis narrative and which truly terminates on the Son of God. It may thus be better to seek parallels in contemporary literature, not first to the language of genealogy or begotten-ness, though they become entailed, but more specifically to the language of life, and particularly unending life in relation to God.[123] Indeed such

---

[118] Cockerill, *Hebrews*, 184.
[119] It is difficult in fact, on reflection, to actually know what such would look like. Because salvation relies on potent action, it presumes a certain quiddity to the agent acting that grounds their potency, and explains why they may save and not someone else.
[120] Neyrey, "'Without Beginning of Days or End of Life' (Hebrews 7:3)"; Bauckham, "Divinity of Jesus," 27–32.
[121] Neyrey's argument also features in Gräßer, *Hebräer*, 2, 22 and Koester, *Hebrews*, 343.
[122] Texts Bauckham notes include *Apoc. Ab.* 17:11; Philo *Alleg. Interp.* 3:101; *Decalogue* 60, 64; Josephus *Ag. Ap.* 2.167; *Sib. Or.* 3:11–12; frag. 1:7–17 (Bauckham, "Divinity of Jesus," 30).
[123] This includes conceptions of immortality and eternality.

language is widespread in Jewish literature. Frequently God is addressed or described with attributes of eternality, life and immortality.[124] When appealing to the God of Israel as the True God he is frequently "the Living God." As in OT texts, this language is often activated in relation to idolatry. In a similar fashion though, it also appears where a strict contrast between God and his creation is of primary interest. Thus it is deployed in contexts of praising God as Creator and, more concretely, in contrasting his transcendence with the humble estate of humanity. This latter contrast serves to further widen the role of ingenerateness in relation to God in intertestamental literature. The living God is frequently compared with mortal humanity in its begotten-ness.[125] And thus, the corollary of the eternal life of Israel's God is that, unlike creation and humanity in particular, he is not produced or begotten from another source. Rather as Creator he is the begetter of all, himself unbegotten.

It must be noted for the sake of clarity that labels of immortality and life are not uniquely predicated of God in these contexts. At times these epithets broaden to include the heavenly world as something eternal with God or, in similar fashion, are held out as the goal to which God's people are conformed, in contrast to a moral and corrupted world.[126] However, though these terms may be predicated of beings other than the God of Israel, they play a unique role in singling out the God of Israel. Among many who live, both heavenly and earthly creatures, and with the promise that some will share in immortality, still the God of Israel is distinctly and peculiarly identifiable as the Living One.[127]

Recognizing this background, of the relationship of life as a characteristic of God, suggests that we ought to see the description of the Son patterned in the Genesis portrayal of Melchizedek as one intended to portray the divinity of the Son: one who lives with unbounded life, and thus shares peculiar and distinct divine attributes of the God of Israel.[128]

4.2.5 Tensions over descent

Having addressed the import of the language of life and the description of Melchizedek in 7:1–10, we may then note that this reading itself generates certain tensions in comparison with other statements in Heb 7 as a whole. As the Pastor moves to the Son as the one who fills up Melchizedek's portrait, and is thus promised high priest of Ps 110:4, he raises certain statements which represent formal contradictions between what is typified through Melchizedek in reference to this High Priest and aspects of the fulfilment in Christ.

---

[124] On God as eternal: *Sib. Or.* 2:281; 3:15, 715; 1 En. 12:4; 15:13, 25:3, 5, 7; 27:4. On God as immortal: *2 Bar.* 21:9–11; *Sib. Or.* 1:39, 50, 120; 2:214, 160, 187; 3:10, 628. On God as Living: *Jub.* 21:4; *3 Macc.* 6:28; *4 Macc.* 4:27; *Jos. As.* 8:6–7, 11:10; *Sib. Or.* 3:762–3, *Apoc. Ab.* 8–10.
[125] E.g. *Sib. Or.* 3:17, 42, 63; *L.A.B.* 39:3.
[126] E.g. *Sib. Or.* 2:39–54.
[127] This distinction itself relies on the fact that this "life" terminates on God differently from the way it relates to the heavenly world generally and the most straightforward difference here is surely a distinction of eternities: one only *a parte post* and one also *a parte ante*.
[128] On parallels between the Son's and God's eternal attributes, see Cockerill, "Melchizedek Christology," 143.

So, for example, having established that Melchizedek's being "without genealogy" is for the sake of patterning the unbounded life of the Son, it is surprising to encounter genealogical language applied affirmatively to the Son in the second half of Heb 7. So in discussing the Son's designation as priest κατὰ τὴν τάξιν Μελχισέδεκ, it is clear he is not named after, and does not share, Aaronic or Levitical lineage. Rather Jesus shares in a different tribe, that of Judah (7:13, 14). Neither of the verbs used to signal Christ's descent are entirely usual. In 7:13 the verb μετέχω is employed to speak of Jesus' participation in a particular tribe. This usage here is surely related to that of 2:14 which speaks of the wider participation of Christ in flesh and blood with his many brothers. The second verb used in 7:14 to describe Jesus' descent is ἀνατέλλω. This verb's usual semantic domain connects to the rising of astrological bodies (Gen 32:31; Judg 9:33; 2 Sam 23:24; Ps 104:22 LXX) or to the growing up of plants (Gen 2:5; 3:18; Deut 29:23; 2 Kgs 19:29 LXX).[129] Strikingly the verb occurs connected to both semantic domains in several significant OT prophecies which are seen as potentially messianic.[130] So, for example, in Num 24:17 ἀνατέλλω is used to portray a figure as a star rising up; similarly the verb is used to describe the arising of the צמח of Zech 6:12. The connection of these texts to the arising of a figure may serve as the background to what is clearly a genealogical use here, through its modification by the phrase ἐξ Ἰούδα.[131] The sense is further clarified through the parallel verb ἀνίστημι, used in 7:15 to speak of the coming onto the scene of the promised figure of Ps 110:4. Though the arising from Judah and the connections to Num 24:17 may draw in resonances with royal promises, the predominant stress is on the compatibility of Jesus as a non-Levite with the Melchizedekian priesthood as a pattern.

The argument which seeks to connect Jesus in terms of his known genealogy, and thus a fitting fulfiller of Ps 110:4, creates a high degree of tension with the description of Melchizedek as handled above.[132] On the one hand the Son is a figure, who has been portrayed in a character purposefully shaped by God's role in the writing of prophetic Scripture (1:1). On the other hand, the Son who arises κατὰ τὴν ὁμοιότητα Μελχισέδεκ can be described in terms of his genealogical descent from Judah. It is tempting to harmonize this tension by simply narrowing the former to an issue of non-Levitical genealogy.[133] In this way the focus of both promise and fulfilment is on the un-Levitical character of Jesus.[134] However, as noted above, the point of Melchizedek's lack of genealogy, though it includes lack of Levitical genealogy, does so because of its expansiveness beyond merely one tribe. Melchizedek is the Son's pattern as one lacking *any and all* genealogy in the Scriptural record, before and after.[135]

---

[129] Cockerill, *Hebrews*, 319. See BDAG, s.v. "ἀνατέλλω."
[130] Johnson, *Hebrews*, 187; Koester, *Hebrews*, 354; Attridge, *Hebrews*, 201.
[131] Cockerill, *Hebrews*, 319 is right that the verb strictly means "arise" rather than "descend" but the combination with the prepositional phrase surely connotes physical descent here.
[132] Koester, *Hebrews*, 348.
[133] This is frequently the direction in which note of the tension moves. See, e.g. Paul, "The Order of Melchizedek (Ps 110:4 and Heb 7:3)," 205–8. Koester, *Hebrews*, 348, on the other hand, maintains the tension.
[134] Paul, "The Order of Melchizedek (Ps 110:4 and Heb 7:3)," 207.
[135] Peeler, *My Son*, 121.

In this way, the tension in Heb 7 in connection with the Son stands, though it is not a tension without some order to it. The Son can be considered from two aspects, in which each of these antinomic genealogical statements can be held true. On the one hand, the Son can be spoken of with respect to his temporal precedence over Melchizedek, the latter patterned after the former. With regard to the literary portrait of the scriptural figure of Melchizedek, the description portrays eternity and unbounded life. On the other hand, the state in which the Son comes, in which he "comes after" Melchizedek in salvation history, can be fittingly portrayed with respect to genealogy. This description involves his sharing in flesh and blood. Thus essentially both "undescended" (7:3) and "descended" (7:13, 14) are, for the Pastor, predicable of the one Son, depending on whether he is considered in his timeless divine existence or in relation to his succession to Melchizedek.[136] When considered as one on whom Melchizedek was patterned, he is by necessity "before" and "without father and mother." Considered as one arising in the order of Melchizedek, he is however also "after" and possessing a line of descent from Judah.

This antinomy can be strengthened by further considering the relation of Jesus not only to one tribe but also to the fountainhead of the tribes himself, Abraham. In speaking of Jesus as ἐξ Ἰούδα, he is by implication one of the sons of Abraham. And yet at the same time, statements like that of 2:16 already form a tension with such a statement, distinguishing him from that seed of Abraham of whom he "takes hold."[137] How otherwise can he bring help to a group to whom he belongs, sharing the same incapacitating nature of slavery to the fear of death (2:14, 15)?

This tension over descent is particularly heightened in connection to Abraham himself, whether the Son is "over" him and unconnected, or descended and "below" in Heb 7. In describing the Son as taking part in the tribe of Judah, Jesus has, in some way, become one "in the loins of [Abraham]" (7:10). He is a descendant along with the other sons of Israel. However, in describing Melchizedek it is clarified that he is not descended "from them" (7:6).[138] This might be thought to refer back to the sons of Levi in v. 5. However, the reference might be taken more broadly to all those who, like Levites, arise from Abraham. This makes more sense when considering the description of Melchizedek; for he is not merely not a Levite, but genealogically unconnected to Abraham (7:3). This broader lack of connection informs the contrast over the issue of tithing. The Levites tax their own brothers and yet, in spite of the familial connection to them, require a legal sanction to do so. By contrast, Melchizedek taxes the patriarch himself and within him all the sons of Abraham (7:9). That the detail of particular tribes is not in mind in 7:6, when speaking of the "them" from whom Melchizedek is not descended, is further reinforced by the tangential nature of the Pastor's remark about the taxation of Levi through Abraham.[139] In regard to the Levites the comparison

---

[136] Cockerill, "Melchizedek Christology," 111, 112.
[137] On this sense of ἐπιλαμβάνομαι, see Attridge, *Hebrews*, 94.
[138] This tension was often felt over the relation of Christ to Abraham's loins particularly in paying tithes or not to Melchizedek (Demarest, *A History of Interpretation of Hebrews 7, 1–10*, 14, 15; Koester, *Hebrews*, 351n227; Johnson, *Hebrews*, 180).
[139] See Cockerill, "Melchizedek without Speculation," 130; Kurianal, *High Priest*, 100. Pace Michel, *Hebräer*, 163. On the tangential nature of the remark, see Johnson, *Hebrews*, 180.

is with brothers, but in regard to Melchizedek it is primarily connected to Abraham, because of the Pastor's strategy of drawing the shape of his discussion from the account of Gen 14.

In effect, these salvation historical distinctions between promise and fulfilment, between the Son as the pattern for Melchizedek and the Son as one arising according to him, suggest that the Pastor has in mind something like a two natures Christology, in which properties proper to divine transcendence and those proper to human historical existence are both predicated of the one person.[140] It is not merely that a natures Christology preserves what the Pastor hints at in a more historical mode, but rather, because both seem equally related to the Christ who comes in history, that there must be a way for the Pastor to speak of both as applying to Christ now.[141]

4.2.6 Tensions over the humanity of Christ

The statement that Jesus shared in a particular tribe is surely enough to locate him in the sphere of humanity in the discourse of Heb 7, and this is only strengthened, as was noted above, through the shared use of μετέχω which connects back to 2:14. There the passage stresses that all that can be predicated of the human sons, both in constitution and experience, may also be predicated of Jesus, the Son, in history.[142] 2:10–18 is significant in connection to Heb 7, not only because of this language of sharing but also because it lays out the connection between this real humanity and priestly ministry of the Son. This connection is picked up again at 5:1, where the Pastor encourages his hearers to evaluate Jesus' identity as priest in relation to the calling of priests under the old covenant.

Heb 5:1–4, as noted above, uses the qualifications of the Levitical system for priesthood, to sketch what the Son must possess to qualify as High Priest. Within these qualifications, it is clear that the raising up of the priests requires, with 2:17, their participation as a human.[143] They are "chosen from amongst people on behalf of people" (5:1). This twofold description contains the same principles seen in Heb 2. In order for the priest to represent the people he must be one of them, taken from among their number by God. Thus the Pastor develops in both 2:10–18 and 5:1–10 the concept that human nature is necessary to mediation on behalf of God's people.

In moving to Heb 7 certain threads, not least the language of Jesus' descent and his relation to a particular tribe, fit well with this relationship of human nature to priestly

---

[140] The point here is not that such diachronic and metaphysical categories line up exactly, nor that the Scriptures speak only in the first vein and not in the second. There is, however, here a rough correlation between the Son considered before his coming and after, and relative stresses on his timeless life and timed descent.

[141] This perception raises questions over the tendency to straighten out perceived antinomies in the Christology of Hebrews. Such a process always involves theological judgements about what is or is not appropriate in moving from the text towards a Christological model, on which see particularly Bruce L. MacCormack, "'With Loud Cries and Tears': The Humanity of the Son in the Epistle to the Hebrews," in *The Epistle to the Hebrews and Christian Theology*, ed. Richard Bauckham et al. (Grand Rapids, MI: Eerdmans, 2009) and the discussion of Chapter 6.

[142] Scholer, *Proleptic Priests*, 89; Mason, *Priest Forever*, 19.

[143] Westcott, *Hebrews*, 120; Spicq, *Hébreux*, 2, 105.

qualification. However, the stress on the clear humanity of the Son makes it all the more striking, when twice in Heb 7 a contrast is made between the Son as Melchizedekian priest and the Levitical priests as ἄνθρωποι.[144] Furthermore, the location of these contrasts clarifies that the point being made extends both to the type of the Son in Melchizedek (7:8) and to the Son himself (7:28).

The first contrast, at 7:8, concerns the greatness of Melchizedek with respect to his Genesis portrait (7:4). The Pastor pursues this greatness of Melchizedek by comparing him with the sons of Levi (7:5) in two μέν/δέ constructions, 7:5, 6 and 7:8a, b.[145] In the second of the constructions the Pastor contrasts the Levites as ἀποθνῄσκοντες ἄνθρωποι with Melchizedek as one μαρτυρούμενος ὅτι ζῇ. Clear here is the contrast of death and life; Melchizedek's ongoing life is derived from the Genesis record, portrayed in the summary of 7:3, and the mortal quality of the Levites may already arise from their multiplicity, which the Pastor notes at 7:23.[146] However, in the contrasting description of the Levites, their designation also includes their designation as ἄνθρωποι.[147] There is no clear counterpart to this element in the description of Melchizedek, and it might be thought to function purely as a noun to which is attached the attributive participle of ἀποθνῄσκω. However, the usage is unnecessarily pleonastic. A substantival use of ἀποθνῄσκω (οἱ ἀποθνῄσκοντες) is entirely possible. Rather, both elements of the twin designation of the Levites as "humans who die" is the point of comparison with the unbounded life of Melchizedek.[148] On such a reading death and humanity are both important in contrasting the Levites to the person of Melchizedek.

This connection of human nature and death is both entirely at home in the theology of Hebrews and connected to a key soteriological problem related to the Epistle's theology of priesthood: the inherent tension between a truly representative priest and a priestly ministry that is salvifically effective in the face of a humanity in the thrall of death.[149] On the former point one may note again the connections of humanity and death developed in 2:14–18. To be human is, by nature, to be enslaved to the fear of death and under its power.[150] This subjection of humanity to death as an enslaving power is probably what the Pastor has in mind when he contrasts the intended purpose of humanity in 2:6–8a and the clear failure of that goal, described as a world in which "not all things are subject to [mankind]" (2:8c).[151] Chief among these un-subjugated

---

[144] Moffitt, *Atonement*, 205 takes these contrasts as suggestions that Melchizedek ought to be seen as an angelic figure. However as noted above, these contrasts apply to both Melchizedek and the Son, and to appeal to an angelic type seems rather difficult, having made such an effort to distinguish Christ from angels in the opening chapters of the Epistle, so Ellingworth, "'Like the Son of God'," 258. Pace Mason, *Priest Forever*, 201.

[145] Lane, *Hebrews 1–8*, 168.

[146] This itself relates to the explicitly generational quality of the Levitical priesthood (Exod 40:15) (Johnson, *Hebrews*, 179).

[147] Owen, *Hebrews*, 5, 578.

[148] Kurianal sees the two elements as mutually "reinforc[ing] one another" (Kurianal, *High Priest*, 103).

[149] Koester, *Hebrews*, 296; Albert Vanhoye, *Old Testament Priests and the New Priest: According to the New Testament*, trans. J. B. Orchard (Petersham: St. Bede's, 1986), 112.

[150] Cockerill, *Hebrews*, 148, 311. On the wider NT connections between death and the power of the devil, see Spicq, *Hébreux*, 2, 43.

[151] This somewhat relies on an anthropological interpretation of this passage, for which see Craig L. Blomberg, "'But We See Jesus': The Relationship between the Son of Man in Hebrews 2.6 and 2.9 and the Implications for English Translations," in *A Cloud of Witnesses: The Theology of Hebrews*

realities are those of the devil and the power of death which he wields, lording it over the human sphere. For the Son, then, to become human is to expose himself purposefully to the sphere of death, through which he may destroy its power and take hold of many sons for God (2:14–16).[152] This however raises the second aspect of the tension noted. In order to have full solidarity with the sons, the priest must be human, thus being subject to death; yet at the same time to dispense an effective priestly ministry, he must somehow lord it over death, drawing on resources which cannot be comprehended by the category of human.

This tension of priestly requirements for both participation and the power of "otherness" becomes the background for a portrayal of Melchizedek which stresses the very opposite of human participation.[153] Unlike the Levites as dying humans, Melchizedek lives, a fact contrasted both with death and the sphere of humanity in which it exercises its power. It might be argued at this point that the nonhuman portrayal of Melchizedek arises from speculation in contemporary Melchizedek traditions over his heavenly identity and that this is what motivates the Pastor's contrast. However, as alluded to above, the nature of the contrast of Melchizedek's persona with the Levitical priests is entirely derived from what is "testified" to, that is, the scriptural testimony of Gen 14.[154] Further, the sketch of Melchizedek drawn from that chapter is neither ad hoc nor unreflective. Rather it is precisely drawn in order to make the move from the typical Melchizedek to the fulfilment in the Son: from a Melchizedek made like the Son (7:3) to a Son arisen in his likeness (7:15).

That this contrast between Melchizedek and human identity is focused ultimately on application to the Son is made even more certain by the second contrast in 7:28.[155] By this point in Heb 7 the discussion has clearly moved to the fulfilment of Ps 110:4 in Christ and the statement of v. 28 acts as a capstone, drawing together the contrast of priesthoods and their authorizations via law or oath. As in 7:8, part of the description of the many Levitical priests includes their designation as ἄνθρωποι. They are ἀνθρώπους ... ἔχοντας ἀσθένειαν, whom the law appoints as priests. Similar to the issues at work in 7:8 a simple substantive expression οἱ ἔχοντες ἀσθένειαν might have sufficed; but instead the participle is attributed to ἀνθρώπους. Unlike 7:8, however, this noun has its own distinct element of comparison in v. 28b. So those who are weak, are inferior and preparatory in relation to the one who is "perfected forever."[156]

---

in Its Ancient Contexts, ed. Richard Bauckham et al., LNTS 387 (London: T&T Clark, 2008). Pace Cockerill, *Hebrews*, 131, the Pastor does not have in mind the, as yet, unsubjected nature of Christ's enemies to him, but rather the fact that humanity has not yet attained its glorious goal, as laid out in Ps 8, and to which Christ brings his people. See further my discussion in Chapter 6.

[152] Spicq, *Hébreux*, 2, 43.

[153] Gräßer, *Hebräer*, 2, 74. Michel, *Hebräer*, 129 notes this twin characterization of Christ's priesthood as both one with humanity and at the same time other but seeks to relate it to Christ's exalted state. Though Christ's present exaltation is certainly a sign of this distinction (7:26), that it remains the goal of all believers, however (2:10), demonstrates that there is a deeper foundation that lies behind it.

[154] On this textual shape, see Attridge, *Hebrews*, 196 and the excursus of the current chapter below.

[155] Cockerill, "Melchizedek Christology," 189; Weiss, *Hebräer*, 426; Gaffin, "The Priesthood of Christ," 66.

[156] On the absence of weakness in Christ's ministry as priest, see Kurianal, *High Priest*, 211–12.

Similarly the many are "humans" but the perfected one, the priest fitting for us, is a "Son."[157] As in the above example it is tempting to rush to straighten out the rather perplexing contrast. Surely the Son is not other than human. Even his description as perfected forever would include his enfleshed life of obedience under testing which is undertaken as human. And yet, the Pastor portrays the climax of contrasts between the Son and the Levites as one of a contrast in humanity. This only makes sense if, at some level, the person of the Son, though in the process of salvation assuming human nature, may, at the same time, also be considered apart from it and even in contrast to it.

4.3 Conclusion

Having demonstrated that a reading focused purely on priesthood as a human category is not able to subsume the thought of Hebrews especially in Heb 7, it might be tempting to seek a purely divine reading. However, though the purely human reading outlined in the introduction to the chapter lacks total explanatory force, the evidence adduced above for the necessity of Christ's humanity is still significant. Noted in parallel is the way Hebrews does frequently speak of, in some sense, Christ's becoming priest, focused in the ascension and session at God's right hand. It demonstrates in effect that neither categories of humanity or divinity are by themselves sufficient to exhaust the nature and significance of Christ's priesthood in Hebrews.

Noting then that categories of humanity and divinity are both important for handling issues of Christ's priesthood, 7:16 provides an interesting and significant example of how these twin natures may function together in understanding the description of Christ. Through this grounding of Christ's priesthood in the possession of an indestructible life, the Pastor activates a category that, unlike others, is reflected both in Christ's humanity and divinity.[158] This indestructible life, read in the context of what we have noted above in Heb 7, can be seen as touching on both the divine boundless life, portrayed in Melchizedek, and the association of immortal bodily life, in the exaltation of Christ, demonstrated in the use of Ps 110:4. John Owen's comments on 7:16 perhaps do the most to bring out this compatibility of attributes and their relation to both Christ's humanity and divinity:

> But Christ is made a priest according to the power of an endless life; that is through the power and efficacy which is in his divine person, both his human nature is preserved always in the discharge of his office, and he is thereby enabled to work out eternal life on the behalf of them for whom he is a priest.[159]

---

[157] Interesting again here is the anarthrous use of υἱόν that calls to mind the opening use in 1:1.
[158] The sense of quite what character this "indestructible life" has must be determined by a wide reading of themes in Hebrews as I have attempted here. It is not recoverable simply by appeal to lexicography or immediate context.
[159] Owen, *Hebrews*, 5, 451, 452.

Owen's comments are suggestive of the harmony that obtains, through the concept of life, between the Son's humanity and divinity, particularly in relation to the ascended Christ.

Such a reading also exposes the weakness of the alternative, of simply relating the indestructible life of 7:16 to the resurrected life of the Son without reference to his divinity. Under that suggestion Christ becomes High Priest on the basis of a resurrected life, through which he is designated High Priest according to Melchizedek. However, under such a view there seems to be no real connection of Christ's installation as High Priest and the person so installed. Why is it, under this reading, that the Son must be priest? Ps 110:4 becomes the prediction of an event but not an actual figure; in this sense it seems an open question why another might not become priest according to Melchizedek.[160] Could anyone raised from the dead fill this role by virtue of an *a parte post* indestructible life?

Rather Owen's comments push towards a method of reading that better reflects the Pastor's thought about the relationship of Christ's sonship to his priesthood, and in particular the life which qualifies him for the latter. The Pastor's thought reflects what might be seen as a fittingness to the relationship of Christ's eternal nature, career and installation as priest. The one who is raised from death, now possessing an eternal risen human existence, is the one on whom Melchizedek's boundless portrait was modelled as the possessor of divine life.[161]

In placing together the eternal life of the Son, patterned in Melchizedek, with the risen life, alluded to in Ps 110:4, we ought not see the indestructability of the Son's life as priest as merely being that, having risen, he no longer dies. Rather, that though, by virtue of incarnation, he became subject to death, his divine eternity meant that his life could not be destroyed by it. Unlike the sons of Levi, though he was at once subject to death, he triumphed over it, guaranteeing the triumph by his resurrection and raising up as High Priest. In this way Christ's indestructible life denotes his divine eternity, but by virtue of the incarnation, through the lens of his risen and exalted state.[162] Thus viewed from the point of eternity the eternal divine life of Christ grounds the resurrected human life of the incarnate Son. Viewed from the event of the resurrection, in part, Christ's exaltation says something about the character of that life which he always possessed.[163] In this way, the movement of Heb 7:16 in contrasting the Levitical priests, as those who became such through a "fleshly commandment of the Law" to the

---

[160] On the contrary, "The Priesthood of Christ derives its eminence from the Sonship of Christ" (D. P. Wallace, "Texts in Tandem: The Coalescent Usage of Psalm 2 and Psalm 110 in Early Christianity" (PhD Diss., Baylor University, 1995), 110).

[161] Westcott, *Hebrews*, 187. "Therefore, ultimately, through Melchizedek as the typical link, it is Christ's divine, eternal nature as the Son of God that shapes his priesthood and gives it its uniqueness. His divine, eternal Sonship makes his priesthood what it is in distinction from every other kind of priesthood" (Gaffin, "The Priesthood of Christ," 65).

[162] Owen develops a similar point via the unity of Christ's Person of Christ and the dependence of the Son's human nature on the divine Person (Owen, *Hebrews*, 5, 451).

[163] Thus to assert, with Koester, *Hebrews*, 355 and Moffitt, *Atonement*, 198, that 7:16 must be about the human life because it makes no sense for a divine living person to die is again to prejudge the issue and mistake that these very tensions are part and parcel of a Chalcedon-like appropriation of Hebrews. See the similar argument of Cockerill, *Hebrews*, 323n351. For similar Tendenz in the Reformation era cf. Calvin *Inst.* II.14.4.

One who became such because of "indestructible life," compares those whose death defeats their priesthood and prevents them from continuing in its ministry (7:23), to One whose life could not be overcome by death, but even though dying has been established in his effective priestly ministry forever (7:24, 25). Thus the category of Christ's priesthood and its relationship to an indestructible life, though not exhausted by divinity, cannot be adequately discussed apart from it. The qualifications for, and exercise of, that ministry are integrally related to the divinity of the one assuming it. This clarifies further two significant points in relation to the priesthood.

First, it suggests that the necessity of divine life to the Melchizedekian priesthood is the reason that it must be the Son that becomes High Priest. Only one in possession of that eternal life on which Melchizedek was patterned may fulfil its promissory reflection in Ps 110:4 and be raised to resurrected human life. In systematic theological terms, this is to recognize that the typological portrayal and its fulfilment sketch in the realm of history the Person who comes from beyond that history and who alone can accomplish it.

The second point closely follows. Namely, that the issue of eternity in relation to soteriology similarly relies on the Son's divinity.[164] He is able to save to the uttermost because of his perpetual priesthood. This perpetual priesthood is founded on that indestructible life which is grounded upon his divine nature. Thus again, as we saw in Chapter 2, the identity of the Son as God is closely related to his saving work: he, unlike the Levitical priests, has established a truly effective priestly ministry, for he brings to that ministry of reconciliation an access to power that lies beyond the world of human priests characterized by weakness, externality, temporality and subjection to the rule of the devil and death. The Son, by contrast, because he lives forever as the bearer of the divine life, now incarnate, and fittingly raised from the dead, may thereby save his people to the uttermost.

Excursus

On the nature of Melchizedek and his relation to the Son in Heb 7

The Pastor's use of the obscure figure of Melchizedek in developing his argument for the superiority of Christ's priesthood over that of Levi has occasioned interpretative disagreement for almost as long as the Epistle has been read.[165] In particular, the text raises the question who or what the Pastor thought the figure of Melchizedek was and how his argument sheds light on his identity. This question was significant enough to spawn its own heretical movement, the Melchizedekians, who saw in Christ's likeness to the OT priest a sign of his inferiority to the latter.[166]

---

[164] Backhaus, "'Licht vom Licht,'" 77–100.
[165] On early church debates see Horton, *The Melchizedek Tradition*, 2, 87–8.
[166] Ibid., 89. Ps-Tertullian relates the heresy in *Adv. Omn. Haer.* VIII. Cf. Hippolytus *Haer.* 7.35, 6; 10.23, 4.

The Son as Bearer of the Divine Life 145

Aside from this unique view, four main positions have held sway in the history of interpretation. These variously identify Melchizedek as a mere man,[167] as a heavenly being or angel,[168] as a pre-incarnate Christophany[169] or as a Scriptural portrait and type.[170] The second view of Melchizedek as an angelic figure has been bolstered in recent times through the discovery of texts at Qumran which suggest interest in a heavenly figure called "Melchizedek" who plays a key eschatological role in the purposes of God.[171]

In the exegesis above I have followed the last of the categories mentioned which sees the Pastor's method of argument as relying not on the historical person of Melchizedek per se but rather on the function of God in shaping Scripture. Through the divine character of Scripture, Melchizedek's portrait bears certain literary contours which the Pastor takes as sketching ahead of time the person of the Son and the resultant shape of his eternal priestly ministry. This view is held by some contemporary interpreters, though it tends to receive short shrift in comparison to the two more common views: that the Pastor sees Melchizedek merely as a man or as a heavenly being. This choice has significant bearing on the question of the nature of Christ portrayed in Melchizedek, particularly whether the eternity related to the latter is predicated of his person or of his office only. Where Melchizedek is identified as human, it is taken as immediately consequent that his function as a type of eternity is only related to his office as High Priest and thereby *a parte post*.[172] His lack of genealogy relates then to his priestly lack of qualification. On the other hand, seeing Melchizedek as angelic or heavenly allows application of eternity in the portrayal of the Son, and thus in relation to his priesthood, in a more open way and results in a description of the Son that is potentially more than human. However this second view suffers from a considerable problem. Where Melchizedek actually possesses the attributes by which he bears the image of the Son, Melchizedek potentially becomes a rival to the Son himself. Under

---

[167] E.g. Justin, Jerome. For a contemporary example see Demarest's own views (Demarest, *A History of Interpretation of Hebrews 7, 1-10*, 133-6).

[168] Mason, *Priest Forever*, 201-3; Marinus De Jonge and Adam S. Van Der Woude, "11QMelchizedek and the New Testament," *NTS* 12 (1966); Moffitt, *Atonement*; Didymus the Blind.

[169] Anthony Tyrrell Hanson, *Jesus Christ in the Old Testament* (London: SPCK, 1965), 65-82.

[170] Westcott, *Hebrews*, 175; Calvin, *Hebrews*, 157.

[171] This includes 11QMelch and 4Q405. For a very positive assessment of 11QMelch's significance for interpretation of Heb 7 see De Jonge and Van Der Woude, "11QMelchizedek and the New Testament," 301-26. That this exalted Qumranic figure probably does little for understanding the argument of Heb 7 may be seen both from the lack of relation to the key Scriptural texts (Ps 110:4; Gen 14:18-20) and of relation to the office of priesthood (Horton, *The Melchizedek Tradition*, 79; Kurianal, *High Priest*, 178; Lane, *Hebrews 1-8*, 161). This is before noting that this heavenly development of a Melchizedek figure is limited to only a few documents at Qumran and not reflected outside of it (Mason, *Priest Forever*, 146, 164-5). For a negative assessment of Qumran's helpfulness in interpreting Melchizedek in Heb 7 see Bauckham, "Divinity of Jesus," 28; Cockerill, "Melchizedek without Speculation," 129. Mason's assessment is more positive (Mason, *Priest Forever*, 193), but he perhaps underplays the differences between Hebrews and other literature. The commonalities he notes (ibid., 197) are frequently the result of the reception of common texts rather than some kind of direct dependence or relation.

[172] Demarest's own reading seems to suffer from this tendency to limit in application to Christ what could be conceivable of the human Melchizedek (Demarest, *A History of Interpretation of Hebrews 7, 1-10*, 133n134).

this view Melchizedek is himself an eternal Melchizedekian priest, and not the Son uniquely.[173]

The Scriptural portrait view avoids these problems, both allowing the predication of eternity of the person, which coheres better with the whole argument of the text, and also prevents the actual historical person of Melchizedek from rising to an ontological status rivalling the Son.[174] It is not Melchizedek himself in his historical personage who is "without mother, without father, without genealogy," but rather the portrait of Melchizedek in Scripture whose shape sketches the pre-incarnate Son in his eternity. This further explains why unlike the Pastor's usual method of argument in relation to OT persons and institutions, he does not employ any element of syncrisis in his argument in Heb 7. Christ is not a greater Melchizedek, because the person Melchizedek himself does not function as a type in the way actual figures and institutions, like the Levitical cult, do elsewhere in Hebrews.[175] Rather Christ is High Priest according to the scriptural portrait of Melchizedek, the shape of which bore witness ahead of time, about one who lives (7:8) and would remain priest forever (7:3, 24, 25).

---

[173] See Cockerill, "Melchizedek without Speculation," 132 and Horton, *The Melchizedek Tradition*, 164. A further problem lies in the fact that even of an angelic figure, predication of "no beginning of life" does not seem consonant with biblical ontology (Cockerill, "Melchizedek without Speculation," 132).

[174] This can be in part seen by Kurianal's rather strange assertions about required discontinuities between Melchizedek and Jesus, something to which the Pastor himself pays no attention (*High Priest*, 207).

[175] The lack of syncrisis also strengthens the sense that saliency of Qumranic ideas is also unlikely; surely otherwise, the Pastor would feel the need to stress Jesus' superiority to Melchizedek (Compton, *Psalm 110*, 80; Hughes, *Hebrews*, 250); Cockerill, "Melchizedek Christology," 188. *Pace* Michel, *Hebräer*, 164.

5

The Son as divine surety

5.0 Introduction

At the high point of Reformed Orthodoxy in the seventeenth century, a particular doctrine sprang up as if from nowhere and was quickly, and enthusiastically, embraced by much of the Reformed movement. This doctrine came to be known as the *pactum salutis*, or covenant of redemption, a title drawn from Zech 6:13.[1] The *pactum salutis* expressed the idea that, behind the historical unfolding of the Covenant of Grace lay a super-temporal covenant between the Father and the Son. In forming this covenant, the Father had called on the Son to act as surety for the fallen people of God. The Son, in turn, agreed to act as Surety and be sent on his incarnate mission, with the promise that he would be rewarded for its successful completion.[2] In developing this doctrinal concept, Reformed theologians of the seventeenth century drew on a wide range of scriptural themes and exegesis of key texts.[3] Not insignificant among the latter were texts drawn from Hebrews, or OT texts which feature significantly in the Epistle.

In demonstrating this concept of a covenant between the persons of the Trinity, the language of oath-swearing and covenants, which surfaces several times in the Epistle, played an important role, in particular the swearing of the Father to the Son in Ps

---

[1] On the historical emergence of the *pactum salutis*, see J. V. Fesko, *The Covenant of Redemption: Origins, Development, and Reception*, Reformed Historical Theology 35 (Göttingen: Vandenhoeck & Ruprecht, 2016); Richard A. Muller, "Toward the *Pactum Salutis*: Locating the Origins of a Concept," *MAJT* 18 (2007): 11–65. For a modern dogmatic survey, see Scott R. Swain, "Covenant of Redemption," in *Christian Dogmatics: Reformed Theology for the Church Catholic*, ed. Michael Allen and Scott R. Swain (Grand Rapids, MI: Baker Academic, 2016), 107–25.

[2] Fesko defines the concept as "the eternal intra-trinitarian covenant to appoint the Son as covenant surety of the elect and to redeem them in the temporal execution of the covenant of grace" (Fesko, *Covenant of Redemption*, 15).

[3] Particularly significant in relation to Hebrews is Excertitation XVIII of Owen's Hebrews commentary entitled "Federal transactions between the Father and the Son" (Owen, *An Exposition of the Epistle to the Hebrews*, 2, 77–8) in which he outlines his understanding of the *pactum salutis* with particular reference to Hebrews. For the use of the concept in handling Christ as surety, see *Hebrews*, 5, 493–512 and Herman Witsius, *Economy of the Covenants between God and Man* (Escondido: Den Dulk Foundation, 1992), II.2.4. Exegetical connection to Hebrews is also clear through the significance of texts from the Psalter which figure importantly in Hebrews (Fesko, *Covenant of Redemption*, 35, 42–5).

110:4.[4] This oath, by which the Son is appointed to the Melchizedekian priesthood, was identified as an act of swearing within the Godhead, often in connection with the act of God's swearing to Abraham "by himself" in Heb 6:13.[5] In this way the developers of the *pactum salutis* moved from certain assumptions about the deity of the Son and the nature of the economy of salvation, towards a demonstration of the existence of a pre-temporal and intra-Trinitarian pact, upon which the historical covenantal economy was founded and by which it was driven forward.

Whether or not this doctrinal argument is judged to be convincing,[6] its exegetical development raises interesting questions about the relationships of certain *loci* of thought in Hebrews. Is there, as the developers of the *pactum salutis* thought, a relationship between Hebrews' concepts of covenant, oaths, the character of God and the deity of Christ?[7] The method of argument of the *pactum salutis* moved from the latter elements towards the former, working from the shared divinity of the Father and the Son towards the relationship of the persons in the pre-temporal covenant. However, if such a connection, or something like it, exists, it might be possible to move in the reverse direction: to inquire whether the nature of the covenant structures at work in Hebrews, alongside statements about God's character in relation to oaths, impacts on the portrayal of Christ's divinity in Hebrews. Indeed, I wish to argue in this chapter that this is the case.

I will argue in this chapter that in portraying the outworking of God's faithfulness in fulfilling the Abrahamic Promises (AP), the Son plays a role in the New Covenant (NC) in which his faithfulness is seen as the unfolding of God's own faithfulness. Though the persons of the Father and the Son remain conceptually distinct, at the same time, the implication for the believer in Hebrews is that faith in the promises of God and trust in the faithful response of the Son to the Father are effectively indistinguishable. Trust in God and trust in the Son are mutually inferring and reinforcing, placing believers in relation to the Son, as the surety and guarantor of God's promises, as to the God of Abraham. I will pursue this argument in four stages: first, through an exploration of God's character in relation to oath-swearing in Heb 6:13–20; second, by

---

[4] On the role of oath-swearing in Hebrews, see in general the comments of David R. Worley, "Fleeing to Two Immutable Things, God's Oath-Taking and Oathwitnessing: The Use of Litigant Oath in Hebrews 6:12–20," *ResQ* 36 (1994): 231; John Dunnill, *Covenant and Sacrifice in the Letter to the Hebrews*, SNTSMS 75 (Cambridge: Cambridge University Press, 1992), 250.

[5] In drawing out arguments in relation to Christ's deity from the act of God's self-binding oath the Reformed Orthodox were, in effect, developing an argument not unlike that of Gregory of Nyssa in his work "On the Divinity of the Son and the Holy Spirit, and on Abraham." The Latin work may be found in Gregory of Nyssa, *Sermones, Volume 2 Pars iii*, Gregorii Nysseni Opera Vol. 12 (Leiden: Brill, 1996), a French translation which may be found in Matthieu Cassin, "Gregorie de Nysse, Sur la divinité du fils et de L'espirt et sur Abraham," *Conférence* 29 (2009): 581–611.

[6] On particular criticisms, most notably Karl Barth's characterization of the concept as "pure mythology," see Fesko, *Covenant of Redemption*, 18. As Fesko notes, however, the degree to which the covenant of redemption was well or poorly received closely matched the varied evaluations of the Protestant scholastic tenor of the period of Reformed Orthodoxy (ibid., 28).

[7] On the peculiar centrality of covenant concepts in Hebrews see Susanne Lehne, *The New Covenant in Hebrews*, SNTSMS 44 (Cambridge: Cambridge University Press, 1990), 11, 12 and Jörg Frey, "Die alte und neue Diathhkh nach dem Hebäerbrief," in *Bund und Tora: zur theologischen Begriffsgeschichte in Alttestamentlicher, frühjüdischer und urchristlicher Tradition*, ed. Friedrich Avemarie and Hermann Lichtenberger (Tübingen: Mohr Siebeck, 1996), 266, 295.

exploring the connection of the NC to the AP in Hebrews; third, through the relation of the work of Christ as an act of obedience to the Father in establishing the NC; fourth, and finally, to demonstrate the mutual implication of faith in God and faith in Christ by the preceding elements. In holding these threads together, I hope to demonstrate that covenant and oath-binding features of Hebrews rely on the divinity of the Son, as the guarantor of God's oath-bound promises and, thus, his equal standing as an object of the believer's faith.

5.1 The character of God and the oath to Abraham in 6:13–20

The description of Abraham and his relation to God in 6:13–18 follow a section in which the Pastor has warned his hearers of their apparent sluggishness (5:11) and appeals to them that "they might not be sluggish, but imitators of those who through faith and endurance inherit the promises" (6:12).[8] These verses leading into 6:13 already establish certain key concepts which the passage that follows develops: the necessity of persevering in faith to the end (6:11); and the correlate in God's character which they must consider in pursuing perseverance (6:10).

The discussion of Abraham, as one whom they must imitate,[9] deals with both of these aspects in relation to the specific promises made by God to him.[10] The Pastor relies on Abraham both as chief exemplar of one who through faith and endurance inherited the promise and also, that in his perseverance he reckoned with the faithfulness of God in relation to his promises. I will return to the nature of Abraham's response as the corollary of God's character later, but here focus on the latter as a key element at work in 6:13–20 and of importance to my argument at this point.

As noted above, that God's character plays a central role here is flagged by the appearance of the theme in the verse just preceding, 6:10, a verse paralleled in 11:11.[11] In 5:10 God is highlighted as just through the use of *litotes*. He will "certainly not forget" the faithful fruit which they have borne, and continue to bear, in their service of the saints (6:10). This appeal to the justice of God in relation to their service both encourages the Pastor's audience to identify themselves as the fruitful ground of 6:7a and also to expect the blessing that follows within the metaphor (6:7b). In the flow of 6:7–12 this expected blessing is described in two complimentary ways: as the salvation which the Pastor expects on their behalf (6:9) and, further, the reception of

---

[8] Though "faith and endurance" may potentially constitute a hendiadys ("enduring faith"), there seems little exegetical significance in whether it is to be taken as such or not. Cf. Dennis Hamm, "Faith in the Epistle to the Hebrews: The Jesus Factor," *CBQ* 52 (1990): 92; Calvin, *Hebrews*, 146.

[9] Markus N. A. Bockmuehl, "Abraham's Faith in Hebrews 11," in *The Epistle to the Hebrews and Christian Theology*, ed. Richard Bauckham, Daniel Driver and Trevor Hart (Grand Rapids, MI: Eerdmans, 2009), 364.

[10] On the significance of promise language in Hebrews, see Christian Rose, "Verheissung und Erfüllung zum Verständnis von Epangelia im Hebräerbrief," *Biblische Zeitschrift* 33 (1989): 60–80, 178–91.

[11] On the connection of oath to God's justice in 6:10, see Koester, *Hebrews*, 331. This intertwining of God's character and the faith of the saints tightly connects 6:13–20 and 11:1–40 (Cockerill, *Hebrews*, 288).

the *bonum* which has been promised by God (6:12).[12] God's own character is central to the connection the Pastor forges, of summoned faithful response and future reward.

If the justice of God grounds this appeal in 6:9–12, the character of God is equally at play in 6:13–20. Here God's faithfulness to his promise, and thus his dependability for the encouragement of believers, is developed through discussion of the shape of God's dealings with Abraham drawn from the Genesis account. The description of God's speech to Abraham as "when God promised" naturally connects to multiple horizons in the Genesis account (Gen 12:1–3, 7; 15:13–16, 18; 17:4–8; 22:15–18). However the immediate focus on the language of oaths, alongside the quotation in Gen 22:17, clarifies that the dominant intertext is Gen 22 and Isaac's binding. The Pastor's appeal to this event reflects both its status in the Abraham narrative as a capstone of the AP,[13] reflected in Second Temple readings,[14] and the concept of oaths which it raises.[15]

As the Pastor's exposition itself shows, the issue of oath-swearing, in which the gods were frequently invoked as a party to human relationships, was well known in Israel's scriptures and in Greek and Roman cultures.[16] Common to each was that the God or the gods were invoked in order to involve them in the potential administration of punishment for broken promises; this divine invocation thus served to strengthen the solemnity of commitments which were undertaken in covenants and pacts.[17] This function of threatened curses is reflected in the common self-maledictory nature of such oaths.[18] In fact, all three of these elements (oath, the invocation of God and

---

[12] The concept of blessing and curse for conduct already relates to the covenant thought that ensues (Lehne, *The New Covenant in Hebrews*, 112). See also Frey, "Die alte und neue Diathhkh nach dem Hebäerbrief," 268 who notes that though the language of covenant appears first at 7:22, it is foreshadowed by earlier themes.

[13] Scott W. Hahn, "Covenant in the Old and New Testaments: Some Current Research (1994–2004)," *CurBS* 3 (2005): 263–92.

[14] E.g. *Jub.* 18:14–16; 4Q225; *L.A.B.* 32:1–4; Josephus, *Ant.* 1.13.4. See also the discussion of the reworking of the Aqedah in Jewish texts in Jon D. Levenson, *The Death and Resurrection of the Beloved Son: The Transformation of Child Sacrifice in Judaism and Christianity* (New Haven, CT: Yale University Press, 1993), 173–99.

[15] The ritual of Gen 15:9–21 engages oath-swearing alongside covenant language (David Noel Freedman and David Miano, "People of the New Covenant," in *The Concept of the Covenant in the Second Temple Period*, ed. Stanley E. Porter and Jacqueline C. R. De Roo, JSJSup 71 (Leiden: Brill, 2003), 7, 8; Scott W. Hahn, "Canon, Cult and Covenant," in *Canon and Biblical Interpretation*, ed. Craig G. Bartholomew et al., *Scripture and Hermeneutics Series* (Grand Rapids, MI: Zondervan, 2006), 78) and is latent in the tautological infinitive of Gen 15:13 LXX.

[16] On Roman oaths and their self-maledictory character see the examples given in Koester, *Hebrews*, 326. Though the principal background to the function of oaths in Hebrews is clearly the Hebrew Bible, familiarity with oaths in the daily life would have been high among those in the Graeco-Roman world (S. M. Baugh, "Oath and Covenant in Hebrews and the Graeco-Roman World," Unpublished paper (2016), 2; Matthew Dillon, "By Gods, Tongues, and Dogs: The Use of Oaths in Aristophanic Comedy," *Greece and Rome (Second Series)* 42 (1995): 135). On the use of oaths in the HB as implying "die Selbstverpflichtung Jahwes," see Hanz-Dieter Neef, "Aspekte alttestamentlicher Bundestheologie," in *Bund und Tora: zur theologischen Begriffsgeschichte in Alttestamentlicher, frühjüdischer und urchristlicher Tradition*, ed. Friedrich Avemarie and Hermann Lichtenberger, WUNT 92 (Tübingen: Mohr Siebeck, 1996), 8, 9.

[17] On the extensive data of covenants in the HB, see "Aspekte alttestamentlicher Bundestheologie," 3, 4.

[18] Though not essential, self-imprecation is a frequent component of oaths (Hahn, "Covenant in the Old and New Testaments," 266; "Canon, Cult and Covenant," 76, 77).

self-imprecation) are reflected in the Gen 22 account itself, which the Pastor cites, with the slight adjustment that there the character swearing is God himself.

The quotation of Gen 22:17 takes the form of a protasis with assumed apodosis, that is, "If I do not surely bless you ... (may curses befall me!)." The Pastor remarks, however, not on this self-maledictory aspect but rather on the strangeness of swearing done by God himself. The recognition that such divine swearing is strange is not however novel but is attested in other contemporary readings of the Pentateuch. Philo, in *Alleg. Interp.* 3.207, discusses the way in which God's swearing seems inappropriate for him, for at least two reasons: first, because it seems to raise questions over God's trustworthiness; second, because God would lack a higher authority to which he might appeal, a prerequisite of oaths.[19]

The Pastor rather deftly deals with both issues in his discussion of the AP. God's use of self-imprecation is taken as evidence that he swore by himself, because, indeed, he does lack one greater by whom to swear. There is no god (or gods) who are his superior. Furthermore, God's addition of an oath to the promise is to be viewed, not in relation to any infidelity in God but rather as an act of condescension to the audience of the promise. It is not about God's nature but about his people's need for reassurance and strengthening in faith. The addition of the oath was "in order to show to the heirs of the promise" that God's purposes were fixed and immovable (6:17, 19). The addition of the second speech act of oath buttresses the word of promise but not via appeal to a different ground: both find their foundation in God's inability to deceive.[20] Thus for Abraham the issue was simply one of waiting until fulfilment came, the oath giving "strong assurance" that it would (6:18). This swearing was, however, not only for Abraham but for all who would inherit the promise (6:17).

In the first instance this might be taken as the patriarchs, but viewed within the breadth of Hebrews it includes both the near horizon of the hall of faith in Heb 11 and in fact all "the seed of Abraham" (2:16), to whom the audience themselves belong. This is clarified by the chain of characters that follow from God's intention: from Abraham (v. 13) to the heirs (v. 15) to "we" (v. 18).[21] That is, the addition of God's oath to his promises to Abraham had in mind not only the sustaining of Abraham's confidence but also the audience of the Pastor.[22] In this way the faith of Abraham is not merely "analogous" to the faith of the Pastor's audience. Rather, that the latter share the patriarchal promises, and were in mind in God's dealings with Abraham, means that their faith is to be seen as "identical" with that of believing Abraham.[23]

Having established the fact that an oath is indeed present in God's dealings with Abraham, 6:17, 18 unfold how it generates this "strong encouragement" for both Abraham and all successive inheritors of the promise. They do so by focusing on how the oath functions as the means by which God's will is shown to be fixed and

---

[19] Koester, *Hebrews*, 325; Attridge, *Hebrews*, 179. Cf. with Philo's similar comments in *Sacrifices* 91–94 on appropriateness, and in relation to the purpose of strengthening faith, *Abraham* 273.
[20] Num 23:19; 1 Sam 15:29; Pss 19:10; 89:35; 119:43, 160. In contemporary Jewish literature, see also Philo, *Drunkeness*, 139; *Moses* 1.283 and the discussion of Koester, *Hebrews*, 328.
[21] Attridge, *Hebrews*, 181.
[22] Weiss, *Hebräer*, 363.
[23] Bockmuehl, "Abraham's Faith," 365, 369, 373; Cockerill, *Hebrews*, 284, 285.

determined. To discuss the Pastor's argument here requires briefly touching on two significant points of exegesis.

First, we must note the unusual language which the Pastor uses in relation to God's use of an oath. The concept is introduced straightforwardly in 6:13, 16 via ὀμνύω and ὅρκος language, later combined in the more abstract ὁρκωμοσία (7:20, 21, 28); in 6:17, however, he uses the rather unusual verb μεσιτεύω. Most translations gloss this unusual lexis as "interpose" or similar, but by doing so they obscure its unusual function.[24] The lexeme is nowhere else used in the LXX or the NT and seldom in extrabiblical literature. Where it is used, its sense relates to the more common noun μεσίτης, which the Pastor will go on to use in due course to describe Christ's role in the NC (8:6; 9:15; 12:24).[25] The verb seems to bear the sense of acting as μεσίτης, where it is used intransitively the object represents the circumstances which are mediated.[26]

Worley's discussion of these issues, in particular the force of μεσιτεύω, highlights its unusual character and has rightly questioned its handling in modern translations.[27] He appeals to the use of μεσιτ- language in connection to God as one making covenants, and his discussion forms a helpful background to its usage in Hebrews. However, his argument goes astray when it concludes from this evidence that the verb μεσιτεύω means "to act as witness."[28] Worley effectively confuses the denotation of the μεσιτ- language "to act as mediator," with the connotation of God as all-seeing witness.

In fact, both texts to which Worley appeals demonstrate this concept of God as a mediator in human relationships.[29] Both examples involve only two parties, or groups, where the commitments undertaken are viewed as unstable. This is particularly clear in *Spec. Leg.* 4.31. Here Philo discusses the exchange of a deposit, where the action is taken privately and thus only giver and receiver know what remains owing. The invocation of God within this arrangement introduces a third party, by which to ensure that the obligation of repayment and its recognition are met. Note here in Philo, though, that, although God is the subject of the verb μεσιτεύω, as in Hebrews, that the verb is used intransitively. In the relationship of deposit between donor and recipient, God "acts as mediator," not in the sense that the gift passes through God, but that God's presence as an invisible, but all-seeing, party secures the relationship and its obligations.[30] The noun μεσίτης, as Worley also notes, is used in respect to God in Josephus *Ant.* 4.133.

---

[24] E.g. Koester, *Hebrews*, 327; Westcott, *Hebrews*, 163.
[25] Attridge, *Hebrews*, 181. Cf. *BDAG* s.v. μεσιτεύω.
[26] Where the accusative compliment is the circumstances in which one acts as mediator. Heb 6:17 has the rather unusual syntax of an intransitive use of μεσιτεύω with an indirect object. This may function, as in some translations, to suggest it is the oath that is interposed. Or it may suggest the meaning that God himself acts as mediator with the concept of the oath as instrumental means. The consequent focus on the "two immutable things" and their concrete value seems to suggest that the former meaning is the one intended. In other words, though the syntax does not technically make the oath that which is placed in a mediating position this seems to be the theological sense.
[27] Worley, "Two Immutable Things," 226–8.
[28] Ibid., 223n222, 227.
[29] Worley draws attention, in particular, to the use of μεσιτ- language in Philo, *Spec. Leg.* 4.31 and Josephus, *Ant.* 4.133.
[30] Thus within the context of Heb 6:13 the sense can well be translated as "guarantee," e.g. Cockerill, *Hebrews*, 287; Spicq, *Hébreux*, 2, 160. See also Weiss, *Hebräer*, 362n316 on the sense in *Ant.* IV.133 of μεσίτης "als 'Garant, Bürge.'"

On this occasion the group of Hebrew men invoke God as μεσίτης in order to secure the commitments they are promising to their intended brides.

Returning to 6:13–20, we may note that though God here is the subject of the verb, the use of the dative ὅρκῳ denotes what God is bringing in as mediator.[31] That is, the two parties involved are God and Abraham in the AP. Yet God seeks to establish the fixedness of this relationship by introducing another party, a μεσίτης. This μεσίτης, however, is metaphorical, as it involves not another person but the word of oath.[32] This is because, as the Pastor points out, the involvement of another party for security could only come about through appeal to a higher authority. When God is already one of the parties involved, however, a separate, personal μεσίτης is an impossibility. This results in the highly metaphorical use of μεσιτεύω with respect to God's own oath, highlighting that, in effect, God plays a double role within his relationship to Abraham, both making and securing the promise to him. As I will explain below, this metaphorical usage is significant for the depiction of Christ as mediator in the NC.

A second, and more debated, point of exegesis concerns the supposed results of this "interposed" μεσίτης-oath. That the immutability of God's plan is established by two unchanged things is clear. But quite what these two things are is debated.[33] Most commentators have opted for some combination of God's promise and God's oath,[34] but differed as to which promise and oath are in view. The most convincing option sees the terms as designating the most immediate referents of each: God's promises to Abraham and the word of oath drawn from Gen 22:17.[35]

Thus the Pastor in effect relates three secure things to the believers' hope, which he believes gives them strong encouragement. The promise and oath reveal the immutability of God's plan to give an inheritance to his people. Behind both, however, is the unchanged character of God. With regard to his person this is termed "faithfulness" (10:23); in relation to his speech it is, by inference, truthfulness because in neither promise nor oath can God lie (6:18). Thus key to the Pastor's discussion here is the way in which, via the language of oaths, the encouraged response of God's people precisely corresponds to the character of God himself.[36] He is just, faithful and truthful; and is so unchangingly. In this way God's unchangeable character grounds his

---

[31] The syntax allows both the concept of God acting as mediator by an oath (instrumental) and bringing in a mediator, namely the oath, with the accusative argument of μεσιτεύω marking the circumstances which are mediated (LSJ, s.v. μεσιτεύω, 2); I assume the latter here due to the concrete role of the oath in the argument. However, even if the former is preferred, the overall argument stands *mutatis mutandis*, for then God's role as μεσίτης in the AP is still mirrored in the Son's role in the NC, and perhaps even more clearly.

[32] On the unique combination of μεσιτεύω and ὅρκος in extant Greek, see Worley, "Two Immutable Things," 226.

[33] Weiss, *Hebräer*, 364.

[34] Koester, *Hebrews*, 328.

[35] Ibid. Though this is the majority view, other options include: the oaths of Gen 22:16 and Ps 110:4 (Attridge, *Hebrews*, 181, 182; DeSilva, *Perseverance*, 250); the words establishing Christ as Son and Priest in Ps 110:4 and Ps 2:7 (Robert Jewett, *Letter to Pilgrims: A Commentary on the Epistle to the Hebrews* (New York: Pilgrim Press, 1981), 104) or the (unspecified) promise to believers and the oath of Ps 110:4 (Gräßer, *Hebräer*, 2, 381).

[36] As Weiss notes, the accent remains upon God's character (*Hebräer*, 358). Though *pace* ibid., this does not remove thought of the nature of Abraham's faith, but rather sees it as a corollary of God's promises.

unerring words, which reveal a secure plan. Through their dependence on the God's immutable words, in promise and oath, the Pastor's audience are to find hope in what is itself fixed and stable.

This discussion of God's stable promises leads to a change of metaphor,[37] in which the hope is pictured as an anchor within the presence of God, the seat of ultimate blessing (6:19). Following the metaphor, in 6:19, 20, the Pastor seems to change tack, returning to the Melchizedekian priesthood which he intended to address in 5:11, but left off because of the audience's sluggishness. However, this sudden return to Melchizedek is not merely a rhetorical *inclusio*, allowing him to return to that initial theme. It signals that the hope of believers, connected through the inner veil into God's presence, and grounded in God's oath to Abraham, is at the same time integrally related to Christ's own entrance into that space as Melchizedekian priest.[38] Christ's entrance is not for himself alone but is as "forerunner on [their] behalf," securing the future entrance of all believers.[39] Thus, in the turn to Melchizedek, the Pastor hints at what I now explore: that Christ's becoming High Priest according to Melchizedek is the filling up of the oath-bound promises of God to Abraham, which believers inherit.

5.2 The NC as the full flowering of the AP

Though I suggested above that the identity of the "two unchangeable things" of 6:18 is made clear by the surrounding discussion, the range of options proposed by commentators raise an interesting question: upon which promises does the Pastor expect his hearers to fix their hope? And through which promises does he wish them to find strong encouragement?[40] Are they the promises to Abraham, strengthened by the oath of Gen 22? Or are they the promises associated with the NC, of which Christ has become μεσίτης, appointed by an act of oath-swearing (7:21)?[41] In fact the range of exegetical suggestions for 6:18 reveal that, though strictly the δύο πραγμάτων (6:18) have an immediate and clear reference, at a theological level the choice between, on the one hand, the AP and, on the other, the promises associated with the inauguration of the NC is a false one.[42] Within the thought of Hebrews, and central to the point the Pastor wishes to make to his hearers, the NC represents the full flowering of the promises made to Abraham.[43]

---

[37] Koester, *Hebrews*, 334.
[38] Rose, "Verheissung und Erfüllung," 70, 71.
[39] On the language of πρόδρομος, see Attridge, *Hebrews*, 185.
[40] Worley, "Two Immutable Things," 234.
[41] The range of options footnoted above in n39 demonstrate this uncertainty in commentators variously opting for either the horizon of Genesis and Abraham or the horizon of the NC and the Epistle's audience.
[42] This can often be seen in equivocation over how the Pastor's audience are themselves inheritors of the promises to Abraham. Cf. Attridge, *Hebrews*, 183. This is frequently occasioned by reducing the AP to the promise of a seed, which is then difficult to see as applicable to Abraham's descendants. Cf. Rose, "Verheissung und Erfüllung," 78, 184; Harris, "The Eternal Inheritance in Hebrews," 197, 198; Weiss, *Hebräer* 360; and Worley, "Two Immutable Things," 235.
[43] See Koester's comment that the AP "establish[es] … the goal of God's design for [his] people" (Koester, *Hebrews*, 110).

This organic relation is hinted at in Hebrews as early as 2:14–18. There the work of the Son in sanctifying believers and releasing them from the powers of Satan is seen as terminating on the "seed of Abraham" (2:16).[44] The phraseology here suggests that those who benefit from the work of Christ, himself the ἔγγυος and μεσίτης of the NC, are those who represent the heirs of the AP.[45]

In fact, the language of inheritance represents one of the strongest connections between the description of the audience of Hebrews as sons and those hoping to receive the promises of Abraham.[46] This language is explicitly developed in relation to the AP in 6:12, 17,[47] and as I outlined above, the relationship between different participants in 6:13–20 strengthens the relation of Abraham to the Epistle's audience.[48] God's oath was given to Abraham specifically (6:13) in the act of promise. However, God's purview in such was to demonstrate something to many inheritors (6:17). This act, however, results in the encouragement of the Pastor's audience (6:18). Reliance on the oath-bound promise to Abraham is somehow the object of their own hope and faith.

Such a connection is further strengthened in 6:19, 20. Here the language shifts to that of the heavenly tabernacle. Their hope goes within the veil where Christ has entered. In other words the encouragement and hope which the audience may have, on the basis of the shape of the oath-bound promise to Abraham, inhabits the same sphere of heavenly ultimacy into which Christ as ἔγγυος and μεσίτης of the NC has entered. The end of the AP and the goal of the work of Christ terminate on the same sphere.

This connection of the AP and the NC becomes even more explicit as the Epistle continues. It is particularly made clear when the hopes of the OT saints are considered in 11:39, 40. Here, following the account of their perseverant faith, the Pastor clarifies what has been implicit before: these saints lived in a manner directed towards the future. They demonstrated faith in that which was "not [yet] seen" (11:1) and did not "gain what was promised" (11:39).[49] This language of "promise" itself harkens back to 6:13–20, and the inclusion of Abraham, Isaac and Jacob in Heb 11 strengthens the association (11:8–22).[50] The patriarch's obtaining of what was promised awaited a time of something "better" (κρείττων 11:19). The use of this lexeme already suggests connection to the inaugurated NC, which is frequently characterized by it (1:4; 6:9; 7:7, 19, 22 and so on). This is only confirmed by 11:20. In the economy of God, the delay OT saints experienced was so that the Pastor's audience might share with those saints

---

[44] Westcott, *Hebrews*, 163; Lehne, *The New Covenant in Hebrews*, 21; Rose, "Verheissung und Erfüllung," 188.
[45] On the connection of 6:13–20 to Christ as NC mediator, see DeSilva, *Perseverance*, 248.
[46] Koester, *Hebrews*, 111, 417. On 6:12–20 in relation to inheritance language see Harris, "The Eternal Inheritance in Hebrews," 194–5.
[47] The language of inheritance is extensive in Hebrews occurring at 1:2, 4, 14; 6:12, 17; 9:15; 11:7, 8; 12:17, variously applied both to Christ and believers, arising from their identity as both the unique Son and the many sons.
[48] Bockmuehl, "Abraham's Faith," 369; Rose, "Verheissung und Erfüllung," 65–72.
[49] On harmonizing the issue of whether Abraham gained the promise, noted at least as early as Chrysostom, cf. Westcott, *Hebrews*, 161 and Lane, *Hebrews 1–8*, 151. The Pastor perhaps has in mind the gaining of Isaac as a real, though partial, reception of the promises' fulfilment and this seems to preserve the apparent antinomy and fit the horizon of 6:13–15. See Koester, *Hebrews*, 326 and Worley, "Two Immutable Things," 228.
[50] Rose, "Verheissung und Erfüllung," 181.

in the same act of fulfilment. This act is termed "be[ing] made perfect" (11:40)[51] and thus further connects this joint reception to the work of Christ to which the lexeme is connected in Hebrews.[52]

This unity is hinted at as early as 3:6. Both parties, the patriarchs of Heb 11 and the Pastor's audience, are ultimately sons in the household of God, over which Christ is the Son and in which Moses served (3:6). Further, just as the heavenly sphere is frequently represented as the true home of believers in Hebrews (1:6; 2:5; 3:1; 4:1; 6:20; 10:19; 12:18–19) and the seat of their hope, so the description of OT saints in their heavenly orientation secures the connection of NC fulfilment to the faith and promises of the patriarchs (11:2, 10, 16).[53] The heavenly city and homeland to which OT saints looked forward in hope is that space into which Christ as NC mediator and priest gives his people perfected access. Thus the connection of Abrahamic promise to NC fulfilment is essential to the unity of the OT saints with the Pastor's audience as the one people of God, itself a corollary of the unity of divine revelation, begun in the prophets and climaxing in the Son, which underpins the whole Epistle (1:1, 2; 4:2).

Understanding the Pastor's view that the AP finds its fulfilment in the NC also further clarifies the metaphorical usage of the language of μεσιτεύω which was mentioned above. By using μεσιτεύω to describe God's oath, the Pastor doubles the lexical connections between the structure of the AP and the NC.[54] Both are related to the swearing of oaths by God (6:13–15; 7:21), an unusual element of the OT record.[55] But by relating this oath language to the language of μεσίτης a further lexical connection is forged from the AP to the NC, in which Jesus' role as priest is also that of covenantal mediator. The concept of a person as μεσίτης is a much more routine usage of the word group and suggests that the Pastor is analysing the nature of the AP through the lens of the structure of the NC and drawing out parallels between them in such a way that leads to the more metaphorically extended sense of μεσιτεύω in 6:17.[56]

One objection that might be made to this reading of the Epistle's theology is via the key language of κρείττων that characterizes the NC.[57] Does not this language "better" imply that the NC is distinct vis-à-vis prior salvific realities? Does it not problematize a connection between what is better (NC) and supposedly what is, by comparison,

---

[51] The *litotes* here stresses the united manner by which they find perfection via the Christ-event, to the end of the same hope, the presence of God.
[52] See 2:10; 5:9; 6:1; 7:11, 19, 25, 28; 8:8; 9:9, 29, etc.
[53] This is similarly exploited in the discussion of the desert generation in 3:7–8 (Rose, "Verheissung und Erfüllung," 63, 64).
[54] On the lexical echo of the "interposing" oath (6:17) and Christ as "mediator" (8:6; 9:15; 12:24) see Attridge, *Hebrews*, 181.
[55] Many commentators note the connection of oath-swearing in both the AP and NC (ibid., 178) and relate it to God's character (Koester, *Hebrews*, 331). However, they fail to relate it to the oneness of God's salvific plan and the congruent unity of God's people across the testaments and their common hope (3:2, 6; 11:39, 40). Further, the nature of an oath as sealing some kind of promise raises the question as to which promise the oath to Christ in Ps 110:4 is sealing.
[56] One might also further note the concept of immutability that is raised in both contexts of 6:13 and the quotation of Ps 110:4 in which God swears he "will not change his mind" (7:21). See Attridge, *Hebrews*, 360.
[57] See verses cited above.

then worse (AP)?[58] However, whatever the complexities of relating the contrast of Old and New in Hebrews, this contrast is only ever deployed with respect to the Mosaic administration and never towards the AP itself.[59]

This becomes clear, for example, at 7:11 in which the orbit of thought is explicitly the legal structures of the Mosaic Law and their inability to bring about perfection (6:11, 19).[60] In comparison to this inefficacy, the NC is better because it effectively achieves the perfection of God's people and of their access to God (6:19). In fact, several linguistic elements suggest that in contrasting the NC with the Mosaic law the Pastor is not distancing the NC from the AP, but in fact taking the AP as paradigmatic for the shape of what must be realized.

This can be seen in the language of promise and oath which span both the AP and NC, as I have noted above. So in explaining the "better" qualities of the NC over the Mosaic λειτουργία he reintroduces the language of promise in 8:6, which is absent from the discussion of the Mosaic structures, but is last used in relation to Abraham in Heb 6. Similarly, the connection between the AP and the NC also makes sense of an otherwise unexplained axiological commitment to oath-swearing at 7:20. There, in arguing for the superiority of the NC, he frames its relation to oath-swearing as a double negative, that it is "not without oath-swearing."[61] This suggests that for the Pastor, the presence of oath-swearing is already established as a criterion of eschatological permanency. But from where has this criterion been derived? It is simplest to see this as established on the basis of the AP and that its shape is defining for the Pastor in terms of what the NC must look like. This final move demonstrates that his reading of the AP–NC relationship is not merely in one direction, reshaping his reading of promise in the light of fulfilment, but equally significantly in the opposite direction. The nature of the structures of promise establishes certain parameters for validating the work of Christ in the NC as the true fulfilment to which the promises were always directed.

It is hardly surprising that the Pastor sees the AP–NC connection in such terms when one considers the foundational role the OT plays for his theological vision. The OT material comes to the Pastor, not as a series of disconnected structures and texts,

---

[58] It is worth noting that in spite of the language of "better," the Pastor never uses the language of "worse" (χείρων). The criticism of the old is not as a mode of revelation but as a salvific reality in itself when not taken as something leading to Christ (e.g. 7:18). As Rose notes, the "betterness" of the NC is principally in relation to its efficacy (Rose, "Verheissung und Erfüllung," 75, 76). See also Calvin's comments on 8:6 and the "better promises" of the NC (*Hebrews*, 185).

[59] Owen, *Hebrews*, 5, 474. The references to the first covenant in Hebrews are always clearly to the covenant under Moses. Westcott, *Hebrews*, 266. 11:39, 40 further clarifies that though there is a degree of opposition between the OC and NC, the former effectively furthers the latter by delaying the fulfilment of promise to the patriarchs. Further, though the OC is removed, its revelatory status is clear as "the NC [is always] presented in language drawn from the old" (Dunnill, *Covenant*, 115). Cf. also Frey, "Die alte und neue Diathhkh nach dem Hebäerbrief," 277.

[60] Bockmuehl, "Abraham's Faith," 367. Sim. I. Howard Marshall, "Soteriology in Hebrews," in *The Epistle to the Hebrews and Christian Theology*, ed. Richard Bauckham, Daniel Driver and Trevor Hart (Grand Rapids, MI: Eerdmans, 2009), 266, 267; Rose, "Verheissung und Erfüllung," 72. As Ribbens notes the contrast between OC and NC is not as absolute as might first appear, but actually trades on a degree of similarity in which the NC effectively provides the answer which the OC raises through its cultic structures (Benjamin J. Ribbens, *Levitical Sacrifice and Heavenly Cult in Hebrews*, BZNW 222 (Berlin: De Gruyter, 2016), 1; Lehne, *The New Covenant in Hebrews*, 98).

[61] On this double negative as *litotes* see Attridge, *Hebrews*, 207n221.

from which he develops a free-floating system. Rather the texts with which the Pastor interacts are already themselves texts in conversation, his intercanonical reading relying on prior embedded intracanonical development.[62]

An example of this can be seen in the Pastor's reflection on the covenant thought of Jer 31. This chapter, which functions so significantly for the Pastor, itself establishes both patterns of discontinuity and fulfilment in its discussion of the New and Old covenants. So the NC in Jeremiah's own language is somehow not like the Sinaitic covenant, perhaps in relation to some perception of violability. However, when Jeremiah declares that the realization of the NC will mean that Israel will be God's people, and he their God (Jer 38:33 LXX), the "newness" of this covenant is strikingly old, reflecting the central *Bundesformular* which stems from the patriarchal promises.[63] Thus for the Pastor to read and receive the testimony of Jeremiah is to see the NC's "newness," that it is efficacious; yet, at the same time, it is also to recall the bond of God and people integral to the AP, which trades on the continuity of promise and fulfilment. Indeed, Jeremiah's connection of the superiority of the NC to the concept of inviolability may also strengthen the Pastor's understanding of the role of oaths.[64] A promise in which God binds himself with an oath is truly inviolable. This seems to both distance the NC from the Mosaic somewhat, with its stress, not on God's entering into covenant with them, but the undertaking of total obedience by the people (Exod 24:3, 8; Heb 9:20), and at the same time draws the connection of the inviolability of the NC via oath-swearing to the AP. That is, the two oaths sworn "Surely I will bless you!" (6:14 // Gen 22:17) and "You are a priest forever!" (7:21 // Ps 110:4) become natural companions for the Pastor, as they both speak the same NC language of God's oath-swearing commitment to eschatological realization.[65]

5.3 The Son's faithful response to the Father as the linchpin of the NC

Before moving to synthesize what is noted above, one final step remains, to develop an essential element of the structure of the NC itself: that the work of Christ in founding the NC, described in cultic and covenantal terms, is an outworking of the mutual

---

[62] Cf. the relative paucity of reflection on the NC in the Jewish world around the Pastor; Koester, *Hebrews*, 113. Cf. Bar 2:30–35; Jub. 1:15–18.
[63] See Gen 17:7; Exod 29:45; Lev 26:45; Jer 24:7; 31:33; 32:38; Ezek 34:24; Zech 8:8 and so on, and see ibid., 391, 490. This is further reflected in the way in which God is spoken of in 11:16 as not being ashamed to be called "their God," a covenantal concept clearly tied to the *Bundesformular*.
[64] Important to the promise of the NC in Jer 38:31–2 LXX is that the NC will be "not according to the covenant which I made with their fathers," that is, not like the Mosaic economy. This seems explained by the phrase "because they did not remain in my covenant" (38:32b). Thus an aspect of the difference between the Old and New Covenants perhaps relates to inviolability, and the related issue of internalization which is important for the NC, i.e. 38:33, 34 LXX.
[65] Westcott comments on 6:17 that there "The oath directly referred to is that to Abraham; but the mention of the oath carries the mind of the reader to the oath by which Christ's priesthood was confirmed." And even more strongly that "The latter oath shows how the first oath was to attain fulfillment" (*Hebrews*, 163).

relationship of the Father and Son. Hebrews' understanding of the NC makes the interaction of God and his people turn on the pivot of the relationship of the Father and his Son. In particular, this is seen in the high priestly career of the Son portrayed as the obediently faithful response to his vocation, a career which established his perfection and thus right relation to God for the sake of many. The key result for the Pastor's understanding of the NC follows that the linchpin of that covenant's salvific efficacy is the faithfulness of the Son to his Father.

This structure can most easily be brought out in Hebrews by noting two related concepts, each important to understanding the relationship of Father and Son and the establishment of the NC:

First, the action of Christ in his self-offering is the key step in the ratification of the NC relationship of believers to God.[66] This thought pervades Heb 7–10 but is particularly clear at several points. In order to understand the nature of this ratification, one must first ascertain what the Pastor thinks is the heart of the NC.[67] Because of the lengthy nature of the citation of Jer 31 in Heb 8 it is not immediately clear quite what aspect(s) the Pastor sees as central to the "better covenant." The fact that the quotation is so long in comparison to other OT quotations in Hebrews suggests either that the whole is uniformly significant or that the points of key significance form the outer limits of the quotation. The latter view best explains the shape of the quotation within the argument.[68] Certainly the starting point of the quotation at Jer 38:31 LXX proves particularly germane to his point, providing both the language of NC and its contrast to the previous Sinaitic one. We might enquire whether the same can be said for the closing boundary. Is the closing concept of forgiveness central to his understanding of the significance of the NC? The quotation in Heb 8 as it stands does not answer this question. However, when the Pastor returns to the Jer 31 quotation in 10:16, the Pastor again restates the forgiveness language.[69] It is the NC's ability to supply this effective "forgiveness of these" (10:18), namely sins and lawless deeds (10:17), that represents its fullness and finality.[70] This has already been signalled in the section that stands between the two Jeremiah quotations, 9:1–10:14, which discusses the change of cultus and covenant.[71] The intervening argument makes clear that the great need which

---

[66] For texts which clearly articulate this point, see 7:20–28; 9:15; 10:12–18 and the discussions of Koester, *Hebrews*, 391; Lehne, *The New Covenant in Hebrews*, 107; Frank Crüsemann, "Der neue Bund im Neuen Testament. Erwägungen zum Verständnis des Christusbundes in der Abendmahlstradition und im Hebräerbrief," in *Mincha. Festgabe für Rolf Rendtorff zum 75 Geburtstag*, ed. E. Blum (Neukirchen-Vluyn: Neukirchener Verlag, 2000), 57.

[67] Especially in relation to the conception of "newness," see Lehne, *The New Covenant in Hebrews*, 13. Lehne notes that the quotation of Jer 31 itself seems to imply at least three significant aspects of promise to be realized in the NC: "Torahverheissung," "Erkenntnisverheissung" and "Vergerbungsverheissung" (ibid., 75).

[68] This is not to suggest that the Pastor does not see significance to other elements of the NC promise of Jeremiah (ibid.) but the shape of his argument concentrates first on the issue of newness and then on the decisiveness of forgiveness, demonstrating that these are foregrounded.

[69] Erich Gräßer, *Der Alte Bund im Neuen: exegetische Studien zur Israelfrage im Neuen Testament*, vol. 35, WUNT (Tübingen: J.C.B. Mohr, 1985), 104.

[70] Westcott, *Hebrews*, 224; Frey, "Die alte und neue Diathhkh nach dem Hebäerbrief," 279, 280. On the related centrality of access to God see Spicq, *Hébreux*, 1, 14.

[71] On the interrelation of cult and covenant in Hebrews, see Susan Haber, "From Priestly Torah to Christ Cultus: The Re-Vision of Covenant and Cult in Hebrews," *JSNT* 28 (2005): 105–24.

the NC meets is for "redemption from these sins committed on the basis of the first covenant" (9:15). The Pastor's point in this extended discussion of 9:1–10:14 is that the effective forgiveness of these sins was not itself internal to the Mosaic economy (10:4). It provided only outward cleansing (9:10, 13) and the continual reminder that sins had not yet been effectively dealt with (10:3, 11). Understanding that this procurement of true and final forgiveness is, for the Pastor, the centre of the NC's establishment highlights the pivotal role of Christ's work to its establishment. In contrast to the Mosaic economy, Christ's once-for-all self-offering fulfilled all that OT sacrifice pointed to and provided the efficacy it lacked. By his death real cleansing was achieved, and by that death the NC was inaugurated.[72]

This connection of the inauguration of the NC and Christ's death is especially clear in 9:15–22.[73] Whatever the precise meaning of the διαθήκη language here (9:15–17), whether covenant or testament, the function of the argument is clear.[74] Ratification of a διαθήκη comes about consequent to death. For the Old Covenant this death was represented by the blood of sacrificial animals sprinkled on the people (9:19–22).[75] Likewise, for the NC, the inauguration of the covenant, and its heavenly cultus, has been brought about by the death of Christ, the better sacrifice that speaks a better word (12:24).[76]

This argument is further supported by the way in which the better covenant language is first introduced via the related concept of the priesthood in Heb 7. The Levitical priesthood was unable to attain the perfection aimed at (7:11), so Jesus has been introduced as a better priest related to the oath-swearing of Ps 110:4 (7:18–22).[77] Remembering that oaths are sworn in connection to the ratifying of covenants, the introduction of Christ into his priesthood by an oath suggests that this priesthood functions in the context of a covenant.[78] Indeed this is what we see in the logic of Hebrews: the oath of Ps 110:4 not only makes Christ priest but also ἔγγυος of a better covenant (7:22).

Second, we may note that the context of this work of Christ, which establishes the NC, is the framework of his identity as Son. The culmination of Christ's career in sacrificial self-offering is conceived as the Son's positive offering of himself to the Father. This offering constitutes a supreme act of faithful obedience of the Son to his Father on behalf of his people.[79] Thus though the offering of himself is "for us," it occurs

---

[72] Koester, *Hebrews*, 337; Lane, *Hebrews 1–8*, 208.
[73] Westcott, *Hebrews*, 264, 265.
[74] On which see the Excursus below.
[75] For the way in which the Pastor's description draws in details from across the Mosaic law to form a "composite covenant ceremony," see Dunnill, *Covenant*, 127.
[76] Haber, "Torah to Cultus," 108–10. This trajectory of thought, in which the NC is inaugurated by the self-offering of Christ, is in fact already alluded to in the Epistle before the more explicit discussion of Heb 8–10. Previously, though, it is articulated not in the language of covenant and cultus but in the language of perfection (2:10; 5:9).
[77] The language of "oath-swearing" acts as an *inclusio* at 7:20, 28 (Attridge, *Hebrews*, 206; Vanhoye, *Structure*, 133; Lane, *Hebrews 1–8*, 178).
[78] This mutual connection via the OT between the concepts of priesthood, law, oath and covenant allows the smooth transition from discussion of the former through the language of the oath to the latter in 7:22.
[79] Unsurprisingly, it is by the supremely filial action of faithful obedience to his Father's command and subjection to his discipline that he leads many sons into the glory of their fulfilled sonship.

within the context of the Son's relation to the Father. It essentially has two horizons in view, the Son in relationship to the people as their substitute and the Son in relation to his Father as his obedient Apostle.[80]

This relationship of Father and Son within Hebrews is notable, not for the pattern per se but for the remarkable way it is explored via interpersonal speech.[81] Frequently the relationship is portrayed through the taking up of OT texts as the speech of Father and Son to each other. Though texts may be spoken by either party, the focus of these quotations is more usually to explicate the nature and mission of the Son.

This portrayal of the Son via direct divine speech is already on view in Heb 1 and 2, including both the address of the Father to the Son (1:5–13) and the response of the Son to the Father (2:13, 14).[82] This phenomenon, of scriptural language taken up as direct divine speech, continues in the Epistle emerging again at 5:5, 6; 7:21 and 10:5 and establishes that, just as with the identity of the Son, so also the career of the Son is carried out with particular reference to the Father, that is, in a peculiarly filial manner and context.[83]

This is particularly clear in 10:5–6.[84] Here the Son speaks, describing the nature and purpose of his incarnation in the language of Ps 40.[85] As we noted before in Chapter 4,[86] the method of citation is interpretative.[87] By removing the second half of the colon of Ps 40:9, the words of the Son explicitly identify the function of his historical coming: he has come to do God's will.[88] Thus, already central to the Psalm quotation here is the fact that the incarnation of the Son is itself an act of obedience.[89]

The b colon of Ps 40:8 // Heb 10:7 expands on what this act of obedience entails. The coming to do God's will is in relationship to the scroll of the book written concerning him. Though discussed previously we need here only note that the context suggests, in the Pastor's development of the Psalm, the written encoding of the will of God in the

---

[80] Noting the way in which the Son's entrance into the world as a faithful and obedient response to the Father's sending of the Son immediately suggests that the twin designation of the Son in 3:1 as Apostle ("sent one") and faithful High Priest is far from arbitrary.

[81] On the significance of interpersonal speech in Hebrews, see Madison N. Pierce, *Divine Discourse in the Epistle to the Hebrews: The Recontextualization of Spoken Quotations in Scripture*, SNTSMS 178 (Cambridge: Cambridge University Press, 2020); ibid.; Knut Backhaus, *Der sprechende Gott: Gesammelte Studien zum Hebräerbrief* (Mohr Siebeck, 2009), 105–8; Harold W. Attridge, "Giving Voice to Jesus: The Use of the Psalms in the New Testament," in *Essays on John and Hebrews*, WUNT 264 (Tübingen: Mohr Siebeck, 2010), 326–30; "God in Hebrews: Urging Children to Heavenly Glory," 313, 314.

[82] Heb 2:12 // Ps 22:22 LXX.

[83] On Ps 40 as the word of the Son to the Father see Lane, *Hebrews 1–8*, 262, 263 and particularly Pierce, *Divine Discourse*, 116–18.

[84] See the discussion in Chapter 4 (Section 4.2.2).

[85] On the connection of 10:5, 10 to previous incarnational passages in 2:14; 5:17, see Otfried Hofius, "Inkarnation und Opfertod Jesu nach Hebr 10, 19f.," in *Der Ruf Jesu und die Antwort der Gemeinde: Exegetische Untersuchungen Joachim Jeremias zum 70. Geburtstag Gewidmet von Seinen Schülern*, ed. Eduard Lohse (Göttingen: Vandenhoeck & Ruprecht, 1970), 139.

[86] Section 4.2.2.

[87] Attridge, *Hebrews*, 274. On the handling of the Ps 40 text see Jobes, "Rhetorical Achievement in the Hebrews 10 'Misquote' of Psalm 40," 387–96.

[88] Westcott, *Hebrews*, 313; Gräßer, *Hebräer*, 2, 217.

[89] That the act of incarnation is itself obedience suggests that the concept of Christ's pre-existence is clearly entailed, *pace Hebräer*, 2, 214. Cf. Lane, *Hebrews 9–13*, 270.

word of God.⁹⁰ God has spoken in Scripture concerning the Son, and included in that speech about the Son is a plan that must be executed by him. His incarnation is both preparatory to and, at the same time, part of undertaking this will. Beginning with this central verse allows, then, a richer understanding of the use of Ps 40:7, 8 in 10:5, 6. The rejection of offering and sacrifices is not the rejection of sacrifice per se.⁹¹ Rather it is the rejection of the offering of something non-equivalent, and hence insufficient, in the worshipper's place.⁹² "It is impossible for the blood of bulls and goats to take away sins" (10:4), because the sons being led to glory are not bulls and goats but bearers of "[human] blood and flesh" (2:14). In the place of the offering of animals the Son has a *human* body prepared for him.

In comparison with the MT text of Ps 40:8 where the text reads "ears you have dug for me,"⁹³ the imagery of the Pastor's source text (the preparation of a body) seems discordant.⁹⁴ However, both focus on the comparison of sacrifice on the one hand (θυσία καὶ προσφορά) and an image of obedience on the other: an ear open to hear God's spoken will; a body prepared to act upon it.⁹⁵ God's preference is for the latter over the former, itself a well-known comparison in the Hebrew Bible.⁹⁶ Obviously the preference for the body imagery of the Pastor's text not only suits the context of incarnation but also demonstrates that this possession is in fact key to the obedience the Son is called to perform. The Son's obedience is whole and entire, the offering of the whole self to God in his once-for-all self-offering in death.⁹⁷ This clarifies why the blood of animals will not do. Though it might be seen as a kind of *pars pro toto* in which the worshipper offers something they have as a symbol of self-offering, the Pastor's view is that atonement can only come through an equitable offering, a whole human worshipper.⁹⁸ The movement of thought does not rely on the criticism of sacrifice per se,⁹⁹ but rather the offering of a true sacrifice, which requires one in which total obedience and sacrifice meet.¹⁰⁰

---

⁹⁰ The reference of the "book" is very likely the Pentateuch, and in particular Deuteronomy within which is detailed the responsibilities of the King (Deut 17:18, 19). Westcott, *Hebrews*, 313. *Pace* Gräßer, *Hebräer*, 2, 215. Note further the connection the language of βιβλίον makes between 9:19 and the responsibilities of the people to the Mosaic Law and the Son's achievement in 10:7 (Koester, *Hebrews*, 419). The concept of Davidic obedience as a key to eschatological restoration is developed in a parallel manner at Qumran (Freedman and Miano, "People of the New Covenant," 19).
⁹¹ Koester, *Hebrews*, 438.
⁹² Dunnill insightfully notes the connection between the personalizing speech of the Son in Hebrews and the replacement, by Christ, of the "sub-personal mediation of 'goats and calves' " (*Covenant*, 262).
⁹³ The MT reads אזנים כרית לי (Ps 40:6). The LXX's translation more closely follows the Hebrew, though its usage of καταρτίζω bridges the LXX and the Pastor's text somewhat.
⁹⁴ On the principal textual differences, see Karen H. Jobes, "The Function of Paranomasia in Hebrews 10:15–17," *TrinJ* 13 (1992): 181, 182. *Pace* ibid., 186, it is difficult to see how deliberate alterations to his source text, in effect enforced discontinuities, could be seen as signalling "dynastic continuity" between David as the original speaker and Christ as re-speaker.
⁹⁵ Koester, *Hebrews*, 432, 433; Westcott, *Hebrews*, 312.
⁹⁶ 1 Sam 15:22; Amos 5:22, 24; Mic 6:6–8. Koester, *Hebrews*, 439.
⁹⁷ Hamm, "Faith in the Epistle to the Hebrews," 284.
⁹⁸ Gräßer, *Hebräer*, 2, 216, 221; Lane, *Hebrews 9–13*, 263.
⁹⁹ *Pace* Alexander J. M. Wedderburn, "Sawing Off the Branches: Theologizing Dangerously Ad Hebraeos," *JTS* 56 (2005): 406; Gräßer, *Hebräer*, 2, 221–3.
¹⁰⁰ Lane, *Hebrews 1–8*, cxxxiii, iv.

Thus the use of Ps 40 here in 10:5–6 brings out the nature of the Son's work within the filial relationship. The Father has a will which involves the sending of the Son. On the Son's part, this plan involves his entire filial obedience in which he lives a human life entirely devoted to that will.[101] Though the speech of Ps 40 is spoken entirely by the Son and from his side of the relationship, what the text actually conveys reveals not only the Son's commitments but also the character of the Father to whom he relates. In this way, the speech of Ps 40, though framed as a response, causes the Son to narrate the call of the Father on him, echoing the language of the patriarchs and prophets in their response to the divine call: "Behold I" (Gen 22:1, 11; Exod 3:4; 1 Sam 3:4, 8, 16; Isa 6:8).[102] The Pastor's comments clarify further that the Son's obedience to the Father, though undertaken within this relationship, is not primarily for the Son's own sake; rather, the plan to which God calls the Son is the will by which the many sons "are sanctified by the offering of [his] body … once for all" (10:10).

That the key linchpin of the NC sits within this relational matrix, involving the faithful obedience of the Son to the Father, is hinted at in the Epistle's opening verses. The quotation of Ps 110:4, spoken by the Father to the Son, comes as the Father's response to the Son because of his accomplishment of the purification of God's people (1:3). This is reinforced by the logic of the catena, and, in particular, the quotation of Ps 45 in 1:8. It is the Son's own obedience to God's will, described as his royal/moral purity, which leads to his enthronement.[103] Not only does the Son's speech testify to his faithful submission, but also in the catena the Father himself testifies to it. God has anointed him as supreme, because of his supreme obedience. Thus his description as faithful to the One who appointed him in 3:1 is no mere empty rhetoric but foreshadows the surrendering of his life to incarnate career and death.

Thus 10:10 explicitly draws together the two key aspects of this section. The once-for-all character of Christ's sacrifice, which inaugurates the covenant under which believers are set apart for God, comes about only via the faithful self-offering of the Son in obedience to God. In this way, the self-offering of the Son, through which a new and living way is opened to God, is fundamentally in Hebrews an act of faithful obedience of the Son to his Father, a submission to the vocation of the Father placed upon him.

5.4 Faith in God, trust in Christ and the Son as the surety of God's promises

Having surveyed the above elements of Hebrews' thought, one may now unite these threads in the argument stated at the outset of the chapter: that the covenantal structures within Hebrews, read alongside the relationship of Father and Son, draw

---

[101] In this sense, as crucial as the taking on of a body is, it is the whole bodily career in Hebrews, including its offering in death, that constitutes the "decisive [salvific] event," rather than the incarnation *simpliciter pace* Hofius, "Inkarnation und Opfertod Jesu nach Hebr 10, 19f.," 139.

[102] Westcott, *Hebrews*, 312.

[103] Note the markedly causal connection (διὰ τοῦτο) linking 1:9a and 9b, which grounds the heavenly exaltation of the Son on his prior moral conduct.

out the reality that, for the believer in Hebrews, faith in God and faith in Christ are effectively indistinguishable, and thus place believers in relation to Christ as to God, because of his status as the surety and mediator of God's self-bound oath.

The concept of faith in God has already been touched upon in dealing with Heb 6. There believers are exhorted to emulate Abraham's faith and endurance. This faith is that by which he responded to the promise of God and sought to gain it.[104] In the promises of God something is offered which believers seek to gain by faith; in this way, the believer pursues God as a rewarder of those who believe (6:7, 10; 11:6).[105]

Indeed this instrumentality of faith is returned to at length in Heb 11. The commending of the saints of the past was because they believed like Abraham. Connecting Abraham's attitude and "those who inherit" in Heb 6 to the hall of faith in Heb 11 is an act of reckoning about God and his character.[106] This connects both to the language of ἡγέομαι and λογίζομαι which occur in 11:11, 19, 26 but also to statements about the character of God. Because the God who promises is faithful and able (6:13; 11:11, 19), the people of God were right to entrust themselves to him and await the fulfilment of his purposes, knowing that they would receive what was promised.[107]

As we noted, this concept of God's identity as one who makes promises, and is bound to fulfil them, is a thread which connects the discourse on the AP in 6:13–20 to the priestly work of Christ in Heb 7–10. This can be seen, not least, in the *inclusio* formed by the language of promise in 6:13 and 10:23. The NC, inaugurated by the self-giving action of Christ, is the fulfilment of those promises made by God. The coming of Christ in time and his opening of a way for God's people represents the gaining of the promise, and thus the faithful keeping of God's promises to his people.[108] This faithfulness is implicitly seen in the way in which the incarnation is the sending of the Son by the Father; though the focus is on filial response, its counterpart is the initiative of the Father in the divine mission of the Son. The NC has only come about because of the Father's will (10:9, 10) and plan (6:17). However, equally, the essential nature of the Son to the establishment of that NC demonstrates that his role is not that of a mere servant or agent. Because of the structure of the NC, the faithfulness of God to his promises absolutely entails the faithful responsive obedience of the Son to the Father.

This would seem to create a serious tension. After all, God has bound himself by his oath and sworn by himself as his own guarantor (6:13). Now, though, in the economy of the promises' fulfilment, an internal structure develops in God's self-binding. God's swearing that the flowering of the AP depends on him alone embraces the work of the

---

[104] Koester, *Hebrews*, 111, 112.
[105] Ibid., 126.
[106] Cockerill, *Hebrews*, 284. As Koester, *Hebrews*, 334 notes the failure to persevere is, in effect, portrayed by the Pastor as a besmirching of God's character.
[107] This plays off the frequent bivalence of the character of ἐπαγγελία in the NT, which can signal both "Verheissungsgut" and "Verheissungswort" (Rose, "Verheissung und Erfüllung," 184). Though Rose's taxonomic distinction is helpful, his attempt to resolve eschatological tension via assigning the latter to the present and the former to fulfilment proper, though neat, is probably too simplistic.
[108] Koester notes this connection of Christ's achievement to God's faithfulness, especially in relation to the resulting Christological nature of faith. *Hebrews*, 127.

Son in an absolute and necessary way.[109] This would raise a problem of certainty for the people of God, which is what the oath is aimed at (6:17), were the agent merely a son or servant among many. But rather, because he is *the Son* of God the link in the chain of God's faithfulness, relative to Christ's faithfulness, is equally secure, for the Son is the obedient and true Son of the Father (1:9; 2:13; 3:1; 10:5-7).[110] Just as the Father is faithful, so also is he faithful.[111] Thus the oath-swearing and promise-keeping nature of Abraham's God, in which his own faithfulness is sole linchpin, does not exclude, but rather includes the divine Son, who shares in the nature of his Father, and whose oneness of nature is expressed in an inseparable salvific economy.

Note then that the Christological enactment of the NC, as the outworking of God's promises to Abraham, comes with entailments for the faith of his readers. To trust in the one who is faithful to his promises entails trusting in the sufficient and effective faithfulness of the Son to the Father in his work.[112] For the believer faith in God entails faith in the Son and vice versa. In this way God and the Son become distinguishable but, equally, inseparable objects of the believers' confidence.[113] This truth, though perhaps not immediately obvious on a first reading of Hebrews, is nevertheless an essential theological reflex of the Epistle's rhetorical strategy. If the pastoral aim of the Letter is to reinvigorate enduring faith in the speaking God on the part of the audience, the homiletical strategy is to do so by exploring the supremely effective work of the Son in his high priestly accomplishments and resultant heavenly standing.[114]

Though the language of faith in Christ is far more implicit than that of faith in God, it is demonstrated in the audience's need to renew their reckoning about Christ himself.[115] They must learn to consider him as faithful, just as they also consider God such (3:2; 10:23; 11:11). This true faith approaches God boldly, because of confidence, that is faith, grounded in the sufficiency of the work of Christ (10:19-23), in which he acts as God's own surety.[116] The whole flow of these verses 10:19-23 bears witness

---

[109] Hamm explains the relation of Christ's work to the issue of the certainty of God's dealings in Heb 6 that "there is even greater reason for confidence in God because of the New Covenant established in the self-offering of his Son." ("Faith in the Epistle to the Hebrews," 276).

[110] On the termination of confidence on both the unchanging trustworthiness of God (13:5b) and the Son (13:8), see ibid.

[111] Note the way the language of faithfulness straddles both the Son (2:17; 3:2) and the Father (10:23; 11:11) in Hebrews.

[112] "After the death and exaltation of Jesus, faith in God is implicitly faith in Jesus" (Hamm, "Faith in the Epistle to the Hebrews," 291).

[113] On the relation of the believer's confidence to Christ in 4:16; 10:19, 36, see Victor Rhee, "Christology and the Concept of Faith in Hebrews 5:11-6:20," *JETS* 43 (2000): 60. It is instructive at this point to compare this entailment of Hebrews' thought with Philo's description in *Abraham*, 263-9 of the fittingness of faith in God alone rather than other objects or hopes, especially when he states that "we may say with all truth that belief in the former things," namely, wealth, fame, beauty, honour or status, "is disbelief in God, and disbelief in them is belief in God." In this way Philo seems to set up God alone as the proper object of faith. Cf. Attridge, *Hebrews*, 313.

[114] Rhee, "Christology," 152; Lane, *Hebrews 1-8*, c. So Lane's description of Hebrews via the phrase "Christology as pastoral response" is most fitting (ibid., cxxxv). This may be seen even in the formal correspondence in our argument between the purpose of God's oath-taking in 6:18 and the description of the whole letter as a λόγος τῆς παρακλήσεως (13:22) (Gräßer, *Hebräer*, 2, 382).

[115] Rhee, "Christology," 168-71. On reckoning with regard to Christ see explicitly the language of 10:29, where the act of negative reckoning of Christ's sacrificial act is warned against in serious terms.

[116] Hamm, "Faith in the Epistle to the Hebrews," 274; Rhee, "Christology," 161, 162.

to these connections, in moving from the completed work of Christ (10:19–21), through the exhortation to confidence in believers (10:22, 23a), to a statement about the faithfulness, and thus trustworthiness, of God himself (10:23b). Thus this mutual implication for the believer of faith in God, and faith in the Son's work, in Hebrews is reflected in the Epistle's most fundamental union: of doctrine about Christ and paraenesis from and towards God.[117]

5.4.1 Objections to the concept of faith in Christ as faith in God

To further buttress this argument and to demonstrate its coherence with the details of the text of Hebrews, one may consider two objections at this point.

The first objection to connecting faith in Christ to faith in God might be to question whether the concept of belief or trust in Christ is actually present in Hebrews at all. As is often remarked, the language of Christ as the object of faith is formally lacking in Hebrews, with the πιστ- language in this sense reserved for trusting God (6:1; 11:3, 6, 11).[118] One might argue from this that trusting in Christ's work as linchpin of the NC is really a concept foreign to the Pastor's theological world.[119] However, though formally the language of faith does terminate exclusively on God, the sense that believers are to place their confidence in the efficacy of Christ's work is present.[120] That is, Christ's work by its nature engenders confidence and boldness in the approach to God, which is in conscious dependence on what Christ, himself the living way, has opened (4:16; 10:19, 20).[121]

This is particularly brought out by the way in which formal faith in God involves judgements which are, in essence, parallel to those believers are to make about the Son. Just as believing saints of old reckoned God faithful (11:11) and able (11:19) to keep his promises, so also the Pastor's hearers are to make correct reckonings about Christ (10:29). They are not to reckon as common his blood, exposing themselves to judgement; rather they are to consider Jesus as faithful (3:1).[122] Similarly, to continue

---

[117] Rhee, "Christology," 152, 155, 156.
[118] The proposed semantic range of πίστις in Hebrews is generally agreed as covering "faithfulness, trustworthiness, …, and confidence in God's promise" (Hamm, "Christology," 252). On denial that Jesus is ever construed as the object of faith in Hebrews see Gräßer, *Hebräer*, 2, 63–66; Attridge, *Hebrews*, 313.
[119] On the diversity of views of πίστις language in Hebrews see Rhee, "Christology," 4–5 and Matthew C. Easter, *Faith and the Faithfulness of Jesus in Hebrews*, SNTSMS 160 (Cambridge: Cambridge University Press, 2014), 11–23.
[120] On Christ as the object of faith in Hebrews, though implicitly see Rhee, "Christology," 84–5.
[121] See at length Hamm, "Faith in the Epistle to the Hebrews." One might further connect this to the concept of God's word in the Epistle. The Pastor's word is profoundly a word about Christ (6:1), the exposition of his person and work. This word is the same living and active word that exposes the human heart as being either rightly "combined with faith" (4:2) or shunned in disobedience (4:6, 11). As Griffiths notes, the word of God in Hebrews is definitively "God's speech 'in the Son' … [which] stand[s] at the heart of Hebrews' soteriology" (Griffiths, *Divine Speech*, 164). In this way, though Easter rejects faith in Hebrews as directed towards Christ as object (Easter, *Faith and the Faithfulness of Jesus in Hebrews*, 194), his statement that Jesus' career "assure[s] the conclusion to faith itself, and in so doing invites others to share in the same faith and the same blessed conclusion" surely amounts to the same thing. To rely on Christ's role as "assur[ing] … the blessed conclusion" is surely nothing other than trusting in Christ. Cf. ibid., 154.
[122] Rhee, "Christology," 90.

as sharers in Christ one must "hold fast the beginning of [one's] confidence firm to the end" (3:14) rather than follow the opposing path of being inwardly hardened in unbelief (3:13, 4:6). This confidence stands on the action of Christ and his present status in heaven. Because he is "forerunner on [their] behalf" believers ought to have confidence to the end, because those "who believe enter that rest" (4:3). Thus the concept of dependence and trust, the theological *locus* of faith in Hebrews, is by no means limited to the lexis of πιστ- words, and in fact in regard to Christ plays little role in shaping the concept. Frequently, those studies which have focused upon the πιστ- group alone have tended to result in a lopsided evaluation, woodenly tracing lexis rather than the full scope of the Pastor's thought.[123]

A second objection might be to question whether trust in Christ really ought to be equated with trust in God as a kind of posture towards Christ in his divinity. In reflection on various other biblical figures, is not a trust and confidence in God's servants a general feature of piety towards God? Indeed, would the Pastor be unaware of the way in which, for example, God deals with Israel for the express purpose of their trust in Moses?[124]

The Pastor's familiarity with the gathering at Sinai (12:18–24) surely suggests that this is the case. As such, it might then be objected that faith in the Son is not unlike the response required of God's people to all through whom God spoke and acted.[125] One might argue that, though the Son proves in Hebrews to be the greatest of agents, there is no more demonstration of the divinity of Christ in this concept of mutually inferred faith than in the relationship of God and his faithful servant Moses (3:2). It is however helpful at this point to return to some of the language which in particular connects 6:13–20 and Heb 8–10, in order to demonstrate that the role of God and the Son in the structure of promise and fulfilment is not one of mere agency but participation of the Son in divine prerogative.

In order to answer this second objection it is worth recalling the unusual role of mediator language which is introduced by the Pastor in discussing the AP. As was noted above, in Heb 6:13–18 the Pastor, drawing on elements of OT texts which were much debated in Second Temple Judaism, forms his own portrait of God in relation to the AP. In making promises to Abraham, God effectively speaks twice (6:18), with both promise and oath, to guarantee the immutable certainty of his plans. The normal process in the act of covenantal oath is to call in a higher authority, through which to swear and secure confirmation (6:16); however, because no higher than God exists, he may only swear by himself. God himself, for the Pastor, is clearly the ultimate and

---

[123] Though Easter distinguishes between the systematic theological concept of faith and the πίστις group in Hebrews he tends to then straightforwardly impute the results of his study of the latter to the former (Easter, *Faith and the Faithfulness of Jesus in Hebrews*, 8, 9). In this he effectively makes an error of domain of discourse, failing to account for the way in which systematic theological loci cannot be mapped onto the particular lexical usage of any one biblical writer. On which, see D. A. Carson, "The Vindication of Imputation: On Fields of Discourse and Semantic Fields," in *Justification: What's at Stake in the Current Debates*, ed. Daniel J. Treier and Mark Husbands (Downers Grove, IL: IVP, 2004), 46–78.

[124] See Exod 19:9 LXX.

[125] On the clear use of other agents in Hebrews, see 1:1, 7, 14; 2:3; 3:2, 5; and the general thread that the words of OT scripture are the words of God (1:5–14; 3:7; 4:3, 4, 7; 8:8–12; 10:5–7; 13:5).

only standard by which his promises are secured and to appeal to a higher guarantor is inappropriate (6:13). This leads into this rather interesting usage of μεσιτεύω as the verb describing his act of adding an oath to his promissory word.[126] As Worley points out there exist examples of both μεσιτεύω and μεσίτης in relationship to God's role as participant being invoked in human relationships.[127] Though Worley argues that these instances reflect the concept of God as witness the context points in a different direction. The μεσιτεύω group here is utilized to guarantee and secure promises being made, as for example in the account of Josephus *Ant.* 4.133 in which God is invoked to act as μεσίτης in order to solemnize human promises and make it clear they are going to be kept. Thus the use of μεσιτεύω in 6:17 is somewhat metaphorical. Because there is no higher party to call into the midst of God's promissory relationship with Abraham, the oath of God is called in, personified as if a further party to the relationship.[128]

To deal, then, with this second objection that the Son is mere agent in God's purposes, one may note how the Pastor's understanding of divine oaths rules this out. His discussion of oaths and their swearing establishes specific criteria for divine prerogative in the relationship of God to his people. The only one who can secure the realization of God's promises is God himself. The responsibility of certainty must be his, both because of his supremacy and also because of the requirement that the securing factor leads to the certainty of believers in him. However, having noted this, we may see that both the lexical elements (μεσίτης, ἔγγυος) and the related concepts of guarantee and certainty, which are so clearly attached to God's prerogative and unique status in Heb 6, are the very elements which then pervade the discussion of Christ's role in the NC. The metaphorical introduction by God of a "mediating" oath in 6:17 leads to Christ's role as a μεσίτης of the NC itself (8:6; 9:15; 12:24). The oath which secures God's plan (6:17, 18) issues in an oath of God to the Son (1:13; 5:6; 7:22).[129] Thus, though in promise-mode, God is spoken of as the sole guarantor, Christ is the guarantor himself of the NC, in its fulfilment.[130] It is not simply that Christ has a role to play in the establishment of God's promises, something perhaps which says little ultimately about his status. But as the one guaranteeing the relationship of God to his people in the terms established by 6:13–18 he must be God with the Father.

---

[126] On the unusual usage of μεσίτ- language see Worley, "Two Immutable Things," 226–7 and Section 5.1.

[127] Westcott notes the standard sense as "that which interposes between conflicting powers or persons" (Westcott, *Hebrews*, 163) as does Attridge, *Hebrews*, 181. However the sense of "guarantee" is often explained as somehow an extension of this sense without much substantiation. Cf. ibid.

[128] Failure to recognize the concrete way in which the oath potentially functions as a μεσίτης, rather than strictly God himself, is a contributing factor to the weakness of Worley's handling of 6:13–14. Cf. Worley, "Two Immutable Things," 227 in which he portrays God in a double role, as swearer and witness. For similar criticism of Worley's position see Baugh, "Oath," 10.

[129] Westcott, *Hebrews*, 161.

[130] Cockerill, *Hebrews*, 329–31. As Cockerill notes on the connection of divinity to Christ's NC role,

> Thus the superiority of the New Covenant is founded on God. It is effective because the Son shares God's eternal life and because he has been established by God's oath as its 'Guarantor'. As eternal Son and Guarantor he gives God's people all the reason they could possibly need to persevere through faith in the availability of God's power and the certainty of his promises. (ibid., 331)

Thus Christ's role as μεσίτης in the NC is not to be interpreted outside of the relationship to the structure of God's oath-bound promises which establish that NC. The Son is not a third party brought in to act as intermediary. To do so would violate the principle that, as regards the AP, God is his own μεσίτης. Rather Christ as μεσίτης is Christ the divine ἔγγυος of the NC.[131] In coming to him, they have come to true knowledge of, and true access to God, not merely through him but also in him; and in reckoning properly the work of his shed blood (10:29), that is, trusting the efficacy of his sacrifice and ministry as HP, undertaken as the covenant surety, they rightly persevere in their faith towards God (10:19–23).[132]

5.5 Conclusion

At the beginning of the chapter I began with a brief outline of the development in seventeenth-century Reformed theology of the *pactum salutis*, noting its intertwining of certain themes in Hebrews: covenants, oaths and their swearing, the character of God and the deity of Christ. Though the argument of the chapter has not been to establish whether or not the *pactum salutis* concept is to be found in Hebrews, it has demonstrated that the themes on which it relies are profoundly interlaced in the Epistle. In fact, they interact in such a way as to demonstrate and depend on the divinity of the Son. The God who made promises to Abraham, wanting to bind himself to his people and give them confidence (6:17, 18), did so with the swearing of an oath (6:13, 14). And yet, because "there was no-one greater by whom he might swear" (6:13), he swore by himself that he would do as he had promised, blessing his people and multiplying the seed of Abraham. The final enactment of this central divine promise, for the Pastor, comes about in the establishment of the NC, in which truly God is the God of his people, and they his (8:10c). Crucial to this enacted covenant is the work of Christ, the perfection and fullness of which is the ground of its finality (7:28). He as the divine Son is the surety (7:22), the one guaranteeing the very realities which God had promised and bound himself to bring about. Thus, the swearing of God to his people (6:13, 14) is intimately related to the swearing of God to his own Son, "You are a priest forever!" (7:21). The pattern of the God who promises, and the Son who keeps those promises, engenders a similar reflexive pattern of faith, in which faith in Christ is the proper embodiment of faith in the promising God (10:19–23).

As I further noted, though the explicit language of trusting in Christ is absent from Hebrews, it can be demonstrated that the concept is present and significant. The certainty and efficacy of Christ's ministry as HP is the foundation of the community's hope that they, together with believing saints of old, will inherit the blessing which God had promised to the patriarchs (10:39, 40). In this way the Pastor develops his

---

[131] This equivalence of ἔγγυος and μεσίτης in Hebrews is frequently hinted at by commentators but largely undeveloped. Cf. Koester, *Hebrews*, 424; Lehne, *The New Covenant in Hebrews*, 102; Lane, *Hebrews 1–8*, 188; Spicq, *Hébreux*, 1, 309.

[132] "Christus selbst ist Gottes eschatologisches Verheissungswort" (Rose, "Verheissung und Erfüllung," 71).

sermon around the necessary theological corollary, that to persevere in trusting the unchangeable plan of God, one must put one's trust both in the immutable nature of God's oath and the obedient response of the Son to the Father that is crucial to its establishment. The oath to Abraham necessitates the obedience of the Son; the obedience of the Son calls forth the oath of God (Ps 110:4; Heb 5:6; 7:22). Thus the high priest of the NC, as a fulfilment of a God-guaranteed promise, may not be any human, but must be the divine Son himself. For only one who is God's equal may act as guarantor (ἔγγυος), both securing the accomplishment of his plan and also the perseverant faith of the people in God. In this way the Pastor warns his audience that to forsake a believing attitude with respect to the work of Christ, that is, to reckon it common (10:29), is to reject God himself and fall into his hands (10:31); but, conversely and positively, to reckon his value rightly as mediator and guarantor of a better covenant is to persevere to the saving of one's life and to approach God with the full confidence of faith (10:19–23).

6

Polyvalent sonship and the divine Son

6.0 Introduction

The description of Jesus as the Son in Hebrews is perhaps the central title for the Christology of the Epistle.[1] This divine sonship entails both his unique relationship to God as his Father and also his redemptive relationship to the many people of God, who he is "not ashamed to call brothers" (2:11) and who are themselves described as many sons (2:10; 12:5, 7).[2]

Though the language of sonship thus spans both Jesus and his many brothers, it clearly terminates on Jesus in a unique way. As Büchsel notes, Jesus' lack of shame in participating in flesh and blood, that is, his willingness to call many "brothers," suggests that he has the right to feel otherwise.[3] Jesus' sonship stands in unique relationship to his person, an identity to which human nature is essentially additive.

In a similar vein, that God spoke through many in the past, but now in "one who is Son" relates not merely to the singular and unique mode of God's latter-day speech but, further, to the unique nature of that One through whom God finally spoke.[4] This may be seen in the way in which the title "Son" appears at rhetorically significant points in the Epistle, where the Pastor exhorts his audience to rely on the Son or, conversely, warns them against the perils of rejecting him.[5] The response to God which the Pastor

---

[1] John P. Meier, "Structure and Theology in Heb 1, 1–14," *Bib* 66 (1985): 170–2; Büchsel, *Die Christologie des Hebräerbriefs*, 177–9; Peeler, *My Son*, 4, 4n11, 10; Hengel, *Christology*, 169; Bauckham, "Divinity of Jesus," 18, 19; Rascher, *Schriftauslegung*, 45; J. Kögel, *Der Sohn und die Söhne: Eine exegetische Studie zu Hebräer 2, 5–18* (Gütersloh: C. Bertelsman, 1904), 116. No distinction seems to hold in Hebrews between the use of Son and Son of God, so Weiss, *Hebräer* 134. The texts which refer to Jesus as the Son are numerous: 1:2, 5, 8; 3:6; 4:14; 5:5, 8; 6:6; 7:3, 28; 10:29, and appear at rhetorically significant moments, so Mason, *Priest Forever*, 12. On the relation of Christ as Son to the content of Christian confession in Hebrews, see Koester, *Hebrews*, 104.

[2] With which one might also compare the language of believers as "inheritors" (1:15; 6:12; 9:15; 11:8) and "firstborn" (12:23). Peeler, *My Son*, 6n14; Weiss, *Hebräer* 141, 142. On the canonical width of "son of God" language, see Carson, *Son of God*, 15.

[3] Büchsel, *Die Christologie des Hebräerbriefs*, 78. Sim. Loader, *Sohn Und Hohepriester*, 80.

[4] See Vanhoye, *Situation*, 60–2; Lane, *Hebrews 1–8*, 11; Webster, "One Who Is Son," 78–80.

[5] For further suggestion of the uniqueness of the Son in relation to God see the discussion of Manzi, "La Fede Degli Uomini e la Singolare Relazione Filiale Di Gesù Con Dio nell'Epistola agli Ebrei," 57–8, who particularly focuses on the asymmetry of faith language in respect to the many sons and Christ.

seeks is fundamentally centred on the Son. The call to trust for the Pastor is peculiarly to "hold fast [the] confession" and "draw near to the throne of grace" (4:14, 16) motivated by the fact that their priest is the Son (4:14) and conversely, the horror of apostasy is to "trample underfoot the Son of God" (10:29).[6]

This unique designation of Jesus as the Son *par excellence* has frequently been seen as suggesting the Son's divinity in Hebrews. The Son is the one who is heir of the whole cosmos and through whom God made all created things (1:2, 4). His involvement in the work of creation, in which he is addressed by the Father as Son, is one with his address as God and Lord (1:8; 1:10–12). His supremacy as the Son in comparison to the angels within the catena turns on the superiority of Creator over his creation: of true Son, over mere servant.[7] Thus in summarizing the implied narrative of Hebrews' Christology, and understanding sonship as deity, it is tempting to summarize Jesus' identity that though he becomes High Priest, he simply is, from eternity, the Son.[8]

However, as is frequently noted the predication of sonship to Jesus in Hebrews is not quite this straightforward. Alongside statements which seem to assume the identity as Son, and tie this identity to eternal and pre-existent categories, stand other statements which seem to suggest that Jesus has become the Son.[9] So almost as soon as we have been introduced to the unique Son we are told, in 1:2, that he has been appointed as heir of all things. Surely if he is Son, he is heir by right and does not require appointment? If the tension only featured in 1:2 it might be seen as anomalous, or resolved by softening the language of appointment. Perhaps this appointment is simply a way of framing his natural rights of inheritance—an eternal appointment.[10] However in 1:5 the thought appears again. The language of Ps 2:7 and 2 Sam 7:14, which speaks of the adoption of a Davidic scion, is applied to Jesus. At some moment, termed "today," God has pronounced Jesus to be his son. Though some early exegetes, notably Augustine, sought to distance this from an appointment in time, suggesting an eternal "today,"[11] the temporal language of the catena ties this appointment directly to the resurrection and ascension.[12] The reception of Jesus' filial address by the Father is subsequent to, and in a real sense dependent on, the completion of his earthly career and its successful accomplishment.

---

[6] Scott D. Mackie, "Confession of the Son of God in Hebrews," *NTS* 53 (2007): 114–29; "Confession of the Son of God in the Exordium of Hebrews," *JSNT* 30 (2008): 437–53.
[7] On quotation of Ps 104:4, see Bauckham, *Jesus and the God of Israel*, 180.
[8] This seems close to the position of Mason when he asserts that "[Jesus] becomes priest ... *because* he is the divine Son" (*Priest Forever*, 38). Similarly, Vanhoye, *Situation*, 71. Bauckham is more careful in noting that divinity and humanity, or "being" and "becoming," cannot be easily lined up with priesthood and sonship in such a fashion ("Divinity of Jesus," 27).
[9] Koester, *Hebrews*, 186. Koester suggests that this tension need not be resolved because they both find harmony in the focus of the Epistle, "not on who the Son *was* ... [but] who the Son *is*" (ibid.). However, though certainly the present position of Christ in his exaltation is a focus of the Epistle, the Pastor knows full well that past events are crucial for the present life of faith. Cf. also Vanhoye, *Situation*, 62.
[10] E.g. Bruce, *Hebrews*, 8; Webster, "One Who Is Son," 82.
[11] See comments of Loader, *Sohn Und Hohepriester*, 12; and on the weaknesses of the position Vanhoye, *Situation*, 139, 140.
[12] Loader, *Sohn Und Hohepriester*, 8, 9.

This perception is strengthened by the way in which the context of Ps 2 resonates with the language of inheritance in 1:2. In Ps 2 the divine appointment of the Son (2:7) leads to the promise of global inheritance (2:8, 9).[13] Thus, as 1:2 hinted, Jesus seems to come to the rights of his inheritance consequent on his accomplishment and appointment as Son. Indeed, related to this inheritance is the name of Son itself, which, in part, constitutes his supremacy over the angels. It is because he is greater than the angels by virtue of his inherited Name that the Father addresses him uniquely. Though the addresses of the catena move beyond the single designation Son, including Lord and God, the catena certainly includes "Son" among its number. Jesus seems then to have come to inherit the designation Son as something consequent on his career and timed, via the *inclusio* of the catena, with the address of High Priest in the language of Ps 110:4 at his ascension.[14]

For some this line of evidence is further strengthened by the shape of the Pastor's argument at 5:5, in which we find the twin addresses of Jesus as Son and High Priest. The address as High Priest is clearly contingent on his priestly death, resurrection and heavenly offering, such that Christ becomes High Priest.[15] So, it is reasoned, the logic concerning appointment to priesthood, dependent on the address of Ps 110:4, is mirrored in the address of Ps 2:7, and thus is not sonship equally something which Christ gains at some point? This allocation of Ps 2:7's address to the ascended Son, consequent on his salvific accomplishment, is further strengthened when one notes the wider use of Ps 2 in early Christian exegesis.[16] For example, in the speech of Paul and Barnabas in Acts 13:33, the quotation of Ps 2:7 is interpreted to be the address of God naming Jesus as "Son" and this event is equated with his resurrection from the dead and enthronement as Sovereign at God's right hand.[17]

This line of argument is surely relevant to understanding Jesus' deity in Hebrews. If sonship is central to the Pastor's Christology and if it is tied to deity, how can he be said to become Son? Surely categories of deity and becoming are severely problematic.[18] Even if the concept of the Son's becoming son is balanced by an appeal to evidence for his eternal status as Son, does not this tension, of "being" and "becoming" Son, threaten the Pastor's Christology with a fatal incoherence, particularly striking at the Son's perceived divinity?[19]

The recognition of this tension of the Son's being and becoming son is not a new one, and the primary solutions suggested in the history of interpretation continued to

---

[13] Bruce, *Hebrews*, 4; Loader, *Sohn Und Hohepriester*, 11.
[14] On this issue of incepted priesthood see the arguments that are often marshalled in Section 4.0.1.
[15] Lane, *Hebrews 1–8*, 118; Attridge, *Hebrews*, 146, 147.
[16] Vanhoye, *Situation*, 142, 143, and at greater length S. Janse, *"You Are My Son": The Reception History of Psalm 2 in Early Judaism and the Early Church*, CBET 51 (Leuven: Peeters, 2009), 77–99, 160–2.
[17] Loader, *Sohn Und Hohepriester*, 7–9.
[18] To assert such is not merely to impose later patristic concepts of divine immutability onto early Christianity. Rather, as is even clear in Hebrews, immutability and eternality are seen as essentially theological correlates of each other, a thought which is found also outside of Hebrews in Josephus, *Ag. Ap.* 2:167–169; Philo, *Deus* 22. For reflection on the overlap of Hebrew's God language with that of Hellenism see Harold W. Attridge, "Hebrews and Historical Interpretation: a Biblical Scholar's Response," in *Christology, Hermeneutics, and Hebrews: Profiles from the History of Interpretation*, ed. Jon C. Laansma and Daniel J. Treier, LNTS 423 (London; New York: Bloomsbury, 2012), 208.
[19] Again, on the perceived tensions see Attridge, *Hebrews*, 25.

play out in contemporary scholarship both explicitly, in discussing the tension, and implicitly, in discussing the nature of sonship in Hebrews.[20] The proposed solutions fall into roughly four categories:[21]

First, the perceived antinomy may be left to stand as it is. This may occur because of fear of overly systematizing the Pastor's thought and imposing a resolution that goes beyond it, or due to the conviction that attempting to resolve the tension invariably softens one aspect of the Pastor's testimony in favour of another.[22] Alongside such a position, some suggest that the tension arises from the amalgamation of various irreconcilable Christological traditions, related to various stages of development in early Christology. So, perhaps, the adoption of Christ as Son represents an early reflection on the application of Ps 2 to Jesus, which in the thought of Hebrews becomes supplemented by later Christologies which include a protological role for Christ and putative pre-existence.[23] The latter coheres with a divine Christology, but in Hebrews cannot be easily reconciled with the more primitive strands. Thus the first position does not seek to resolve the conundrum but sees it as essential, or explains the tension via diachrony.[24]

The second and third options, by contrast, effectively remove one of the poles of tension in favour of the other, and in this way resolve it. So, second, some have attempted a resolution by a softening of the eternal nature of the Son's identity. Historically this can be seen in the arguments of those favouring Arian Christology and is especially evident in the arguments put forward by John Owen's Socinian interlocutors.[25] Statements in Hebrews which portray the Son as coming into possession of either the filial name, or related benefits, clearly demonstrate that Jesus simply becomes the Son in Hebrews.[26] Elements that support the Son's deity, eternal possession of filial status, or even pre-existence, must then be demonstrated as not really suggesting an eternal divine sonship. The most sophisticated example of this line of thought is the previously noted work of Caird,[27] developed by Hurst and Dunn,[28] and most fully

---

[20] It is, according to Loader, "der klassische Problem seiner Christologie" (Loader, *Sohn Und Hohepriester*, 2). See also Attridge, *Hebrews*, 55; "The Psalms in Hebrews," in *The Psalms in the New Testament*, ed. Steve Moyise and M. J. J. Menken, *The New Testament and the Scriptures of Israel* (London: T&T Clark, 2004), 200; Mason, *Priest Forever*, 12n19. On the tension in the NT more widely, see Peppard, *Son of God*, 133–5.

[21] One might compare here the similar taxonomy of MacCormack in Bruce L. MacCormack, "The Identity of the Son: Karl Barth's Exegesis of Hebrews 1.1–4," in *Christology, Hermeneutics, and Hebrews: Profiles from the History of Interpretation*, ed. Jon C. Laansma and Daniel J. Treier, LNTS 423 (London: Bloomsbury, 2012), 160–2.

[22] See, in particular, Loader, *Sohn Und Hohepriester*, 2, 3; Attridge, "Historical Interpretation," 207.

[23] For this view in handling similar tensions in Paul see Wilhelm Bousset, *Kyrios Christos: A History of the Belief in Christ from the Beginnings of Christianity to Irenaeus*, trans. J. Steely (Waco, TX: Baylor University Press, 2013), 337, 338.

[24] Loader, *Sohn Und Hohepriester*, 140, 141. Though Loader does note the overlap of both pre-existence and exaltation in reinforcing the present lordship of Christ (ibid., 251).

[25] E.g. Owen, *Hebrews*, 3, 40, 41; Koester, *Hebrews*, 35.

[26] One of the great weaknesses of this position may be seen in noting the connection of Son language to messianism within the scope of the whole NT (Hengel, *Christology*, 3). The consequence of this connection is that Hengel's well-known argument against the resurrection as a sufficient impetus for the assignment ex nihilo of messianic status to Jesus forms a similar obstacle for the role of exaltation conferring an ex nihilo sonship on Jesus in Hebrews. Ibid., 10–13.

[27] Caird, "Son by Appointment," 18–24.

[28] Hurst, "Christology," 151–64; Dunn, *Christology*, 51–6, 206–9.

articulated by Schenck.²⁹ There the pre-existence motif is seen as a retrojection of the Son's teleological role into the pre-temporal sphere. The pre-existent plan of God which comes to fruition in the temporal work of the Son is the extent of a non-personal pre-existence.³⁰ The Son's identification as Son, before his temporal accomplishment, is merely the proleptic application of what becomes his in the eschatological sphere. Though this thread of argumentation is limited to a small strand of modern Hebrews scholarship the modern preference for history as a meaningful category, over against metaphysics, tends to place a burden of proof on other views.³¹ Similarly the renewed attention in recent Hebrews' studies on the timing of the sacrificial and priestly work of Christ furthers this emphasis.³² Where Jesus' identity is peculiarly centred on what he becomes in his work, sonship as achievement will tend to predominate, though Christological data in Hebrews which does not fit the scheme may receive short shrift.

The third option is essentially the polar opposite of the second. It is notable when little or no attention is given to the Son's becoming, or the fact is even denied. This is at times simply asserted: the Son is Son, and was so eternally, thus in no meaningful way may he become Son.³³ Or an exegete may seek to reinterpret verses used to support the Son's becoming. Bauckham does not clearly fit into the first category, but his reading at times approaches the second.³⁴ Though he helpfully notes that categories of sonship and high priesthood in Hebrew do not facilely align with being and becoming, respectively, his position on the Name which Jesus inherits in 1:4 certainly removes one of the main supports for Son's adoption as Son within the Epistle, and it is unclear what exegetical evidence would then support that idea.³⁵ The direction of Bauckham's exegesis of Heb 1 thus views Sonship in Hebrews largely through the lens of divinity.

Fourth, the position that comes closest to a majority report in modern scholarship on Hebrews, and is also closest to that argued by much of Christian tradition sympathetic to early creeds, seeks to reconcile the two poles of data with each other, or hold them synchronically. Such an approach recognizes both that Christ is the eternal divine Son, and that in some sense he attains certain aspects of sonship in the Epistle. Because both

---

²⁹ Schenck, "Enthroned Son," 469–485.
³⁰ Schenck, "Keeping His Appointment," 91–117; ibid., 105–12; Dunn, *Christology*, 56.
³¹ On the "allergy" to metaphysics in contemporary theology see Sonderegger, *Systematic Theology*, Vol. 1, xxin1 and on its reflection in biblical studies Levering, *Scripture and Metaphysics: Aquinas and the Renewal of Trinitarian Theology*, 1–12.
³² Moffitt, *Atonement*, 219–29; "Jesus' Heavenly Sacrifice in Early Christian Reception of Hebrews: A Survey," *JTS* 68 (2017): 46–71; Michael Kibbe, "Is It Finished? When Did It Start? Hebrews, Priesthood, and Atonement in Biblical, Systematic, and Historical Perspective," *JTS* 65 (2014): 25–61.
³³ E.g. Webster, "One Who Is Son," 82. For Webster the eternal appointment of the Father drives the Son's action in time, but this action is "not the means whereby the Son comes to possess his inheritance or enhance his dignity;" (ibid.) Sim. Peeler, *My Son*, 12n14 and also, Rascher, *Schriftauslegung*, 40. However, at times those stressing that Christ was always son will still introduce a soft two-stage approach, e.g. when Peeler explains the use of Ps 2:7 in connection to the exaltation of Christ as "not [an] establishment of Jesus' status as God's Son, but a restatement of the fact," appealing to 1 Chr 28:6 (Peeler, *My Son*, 44). However, rather tellingly Peeler reads 1:5 as a lens for 1:1–4 and hives it off from discussion of the catena that would push it towards Christ's entrance into a new state in the exaltation (ibid., 51, 52).
³⁴ Cf. Moffitt, *Atonement*, 47n42.
³⁵ Bauckham, *Jesus and the God of Israel*, 239. On the more usual route of taking the inherited name as "Son" see Koester, *Hebrews*, 182; Mackie, "Confession of the Son of God in Hebrews," 116.

are perceived as part of the Pastor's thought they are seen principally as reconcilable. This often results in a two-stage model aimed at handling both aspects of Christ's sonship.[36] Some write of the Son's eternal identity as Son, but also of the Son's historical "becoming" as the manifestation of his filial identity in time through his career.[37] Or, if tied to Chalcedonian Christology, this may be articulated as a difference between the Son's eternal divine person as God, versus what he becomes in his enfleshed career in time.[38] This may also be articulated from within the sonship metaphor itself, relying on the distinction between the birth rights of a son and the coming into possession of them at maturity.[39] However these two stages are articulated, each relies on a common pattern: what is latent in the eternal pre-existent sonship of Christ becomes patent and fulfilled through historical achievement. What is promised within sonship finds fulfilment in his career;[40] what is hidden in eternity becomes manifest in the temporal sphere of creation.

6.1 Evaluation

Though each of the above positions has its own merits and weaknesses, the aim of the chapter that follows is to advance and sharpen a version of the fourth position outlined above. In doing so I hope to demonstrate that the perceived tension around sonship language of Hebrews is not so much a problem to be solved, as rather an integral part of the Pastor's soteriological portrayal of the divine Son in Hebrews.

However, before moving to develop this fourth position more fully, it is necessary briefly to explain why I have not pursued a line of argument based on the first three positions, or forged an altogether different one. First, I would note MacCormack's perceptive point in his own work on Hebrews' sonship language, that judgements on the presence of irreconcilable tensions within the Christology of the Epistle are themselves unavoidably theological ones which precede the movement to diachronic explanation.[41] In essence, theology precedes historical explanation, because the text of Hebrews is a synchronic entity. In this way a burden of proof will always remain on one who posits irreconcilable antinomies in Hebrews, as it requires the complementary assertion that no reasonable theological model may incorporate the data as it stands.

---

[36] Some sort of two-stage model can be seen in George Milligan, *The Theology of the Epistle to the Hebrews: With a Critical Introduction* (Edinburgh: T&T Clark, 1899), 74; Bruce, *Hebrews*, 13; Michel, *Hebräer*; Spicq, *Hébreux*, 2, 16; Mackie, "Confession of the Son of God in Hebrews," 116, 117; Lee, *Preexistent Son*, 276.

[37] This is often worked out in similar fashion in handling of Rom 1:4, so see Hengel, *Christology*, 11 and more recently Michael F. Bird, *Jesus the Eternal Son: Answering Adoptionist Christology* (Grand Rapids, MI: Eerdmans, 2017), 11–33.

[38] Frances M. Young, "Christological Ideas in the Greek Commentaries on the Epistle to the Hebrews," in *Christology, Hermeneutics, and Hebrews: Profiles from the History of Interpretation*, ed. Jon C. Laansma and Daniel J. Treier, LNTS 423 (Bloomsbury, 2012), 34, 35; Koester, *Hebrews*, 105n120. Such a view was common among patristic and mediaeval theologians, Keating, "Thomas Aquinas and the Epistle to the Hebrews: 'The Excellence of Christ'," 86, 89.

[39] Peeler, *My Son*, 44–6; Vanhoye, *Situation*, 61.

[40] Cockerill, *Hebrews*, 92.

[41] MacCormack, "Identity of the Son," 38.

This posture of assuming a coherent reading of Hebrews is one that has found most resonance with those receiving Hebrews as Christian scripture, the coherence of the text functioning as a corollary to the consonance of God's own voice. Though this may seem to anachronistically bring back the nature of the later reception of Hebrews among Christians into the original horizon of the Epistle, it is simply to argue that this consonant reading in the history of the Church would likely have been the experience of the Epistle's earliest readers, unless pressing evidence suggests otherwise.[42]

With respect to the second and third approaches, in effect they demonstrate a mutual insufficiency, the arguments of each showing that Christ's being Son and becoming Son are equally well supported, and that rather than try to dismiss a significant strand of data, one should seek a way to harmonize the arguments.[43]

It is perhaps then unsurprising that the fourth position is the most common. Here, both kinds of statements about the Son are taken as integral to the Pastor's Christology and an attempt at reconciling them is made. The predominant question for this position, as for all systematization, is whether the synthesis proffered actually arises from the structures of the Pastor's own theology or is an imposition on it.

One example of this weakness can be seen in another article by MacCormack, in which he brings Barth's theology to bear on the Exordium.[44] He suggests that Barth's view of the *logos asarkos* acts as a helpful resource in reading Hebrews, in particular, that tensions between Christ's eternal being and historical achievement are dissolved when one adopts a view in which God's identity is bound up, not with a *logos asarkos* divorced from history but with the man, Jesus Christ, to whom the various predications of Heb 1:1–4 apply.[45] Though the solution itself might seem plausible, as Attridge rightly notes, the interpreter must take care to avoid anachronism: the application of concepts developed much later to an earlier problem.[46] If one is simply sharpening conceptual resources which would have been available to the original author, it is unproblematic. However, there remains a question whether the ontology essential

---

[42] One might here appeal to the witness of textual variants as occasions of theological pressure among early Christians, in which texts were potentially harmonized away from expressions which might offend other commitments derived from other texts or beliefs; see Bart D. Ehrman, *The Orthodox Corruption of Scripture: The Effect of Early Christological Controversies on the Text of the New Testament* (Oxford: Oxford University Press, 1996). However, there seems to be an absence of any scribal emendation touching on the sonship of Christ in Hebrews. In fact, the argument that emendation is at times theologically driven points in the other direction, suggesting that early scribes, as early Christian readers, were themselves systematic and theological in their thought, seeking at times, even misguidedly, to emend the text of scripture in such a way as to render it more easily comprehensible within a particular framework.

[43] Particularly in connection to the concept of the Son's becoming Son, if there is any note of messianism implied in the title, it is difficult to see how the concept of attainment of messianic status does not itself raise the question of origin. As Novenson notes, the question of the Messiah's descent was a live one in Second Temple Judaism, if not always ubiquitous, and is reflected in the New Testament itself (*Grammar*, 65, 82–84, 92, 93). This is clearly reinforced by questions around Christ's descent or lack thereof in relation to the anointed office of priest in Heb 7. In fact, as Novenson notes, the ideal Messiah is one who can qualify for the ascription both by descent and personal merit—to be David's son by lineage and David's son by likeness (ibid., 110).

[44] MacCormack, "'With Loud Cries,'" 55–86.

[45] "Identity of the Son," 163.

[46] Attridge, "Historical Interpretation," 207.

to MacCormack's solution would have been in the least intelligible within Hebrews thought world.[47] Despite the failure of McCormack's solution on these grounds, his suggestion in both his articles[48] that the handling of the seemingly conflicting data in Hebrews is a theological one, and that the perceived reconcilability or not of such data turns on the ability of any Christological model to integrate it is surely right. With Attridge's question in mind, we might then also add the *desideratum* that such a model be understandable from within the Pastor's own thought world and, moreover, that it connect to other aspects of his Christology, suggesting that it is not merely a synthesis that floats above the text but arises from it.[49]

In this chapter then, I articulate a model of Christ's sonship which, I argue, integrates both Christ's eternal sonship and his temporal assumption of sonship via his career. Central to this model is the terminology which initially seems to bring into question Christ's uniqueness: the status of humanity as sons in Hebrews. I hope in working out this model to demonstrate more fully what it is that is attained in the two-step Christological solutions, namely, that Hebrews' conception of sonship turns on a three-fold valency: eternal, created and messianic sonships. These three come together in the unique Son enfleshed, who as the eternal Son in history fulfils the destiny of the temporal sons via fulfilment of the Davidic sonship trajectory laid down by "prophets [speaking] of old" (1:1). I hope that such a solution may prove to be both theologically self-aware, as McCormack requests, and function within the metaphors of Hebrews' own Christology in such a way that it might be seen as both arising from the text of Hebrews and demonstrating the coherence of the Pastor's thought about the identity of Christ.[50] In this way I hope to sharpen previous examples of the fourth kind of handling, which, though essentially correct in what they affirm, fail at several points. In particular, they fail to articulate quite what it is that Christ attains in completing his career. In this way they seem to operate at a conceptual distance from the text of Hebrews. In other words, the suggestion may represent an admissible theological solution and one consonant with a creedal Christology generally, but is it actually that of the Pastor's and how are we to know? The solution I propose argues that a point of integration may be found in the role of David in the Christology of the Epistle.[51] The Son as Messiah acts as a middle term drawing together the Son's unique eternal status with the frustrated and fulfilled temporal sonship of the redeemed.

My argument here turns on understanding how Davidic sonship and its typology involve the soteriological intertwining of two other sonships on display in Hebrews. Integral to grasping this is to see that this soteriological intertwining acts upon prior existing types of sonship, both created and uncreated, relative to, on the one hand, humanity as sons and, on the other, the eternal Son of God.

---

[47] Ibid.
[48] MacCormack, "'With Loud Cries,'" 55–86; "Identity of the Son," 155–72.
[49] As MacCormack notes, the danger in any theological synthesis is that "a theological possibility [may be proffered] … for which no foundation can be found in the text currently under examination" to which MacCormack denies the term "exegesis" ("Identity of the Son," 158).
[50] Ibid., 18.
[51] For a similar criticism of, in particular, Bauckham's lack of attention to Davidic typology in the catena, see the comments of Carson, *Son of God*, 60n13.

Before moving to trace this deployment of sonship language in Hebrews, it is first necessary to note that the language of sonship is often attended by certain other concepts in early Christian thought. We have already seen this in relation to the concept of inheritance, a further image however, deployed widely in the NT, is that of image.[52] This connection of sonship and imaging is one that finds its roots in the earliest chapters of the Hebrew Bible,[53] but also, as we have noted earlier in Chapter 3, relies on a first-century understanding that a son reflects his father.[54] Though the technical language of imaging may seem slim within Hebrews, restricted to the language of Christ as the χαρακτήρ of God (1:3), the concept is far more widespread in the Epistle. It can be seen both in humanity's creational destiny to be "like" God and, further, in the Son's obedient career in which he reveals God. That God has at last spoken ἐν υἱῷ (1:2) means within Hebrews that God has revealed himself visibly—in image form. For the Son is marked first and foremost not by what he says but by his visible work.[55]

I suggest then that to explore how the sonship language functions in connection to the divinity of Christ, one must also pay attention to the concept of imaging God in connection both to the unique Son and the many sons.

6.2 The eternal image in the Son

It is usually well recognized that the Christology of the Epistle to the Hebrews relies on the eternal filial identity of the Son of God, that he is both Son and eternally Son.[56] However for the sake of clear argument, and partly in order to demonstrate the inadequacy of the second solution above, in which eternal personal sonship is removed, it is helpful to consider the evidence of Hebrews for it. Pertinent here is the Son's pre-existence which has already been encountered several times thus far.[57] However the task at hand concerns not merely his personal pre-existence but his eternal existence in Hebrews *as Son*.[58] In support of this we may note the following:

First, that within the space of the opening verses, Jesus is already identified as the Son in relation to God's latter-day speech (1:1).[59] Here, as is often noted, the comparison with prior prophetic revelation is a qualitative one.[60] God's latter-day word is "in one who is Son."[61] Its uniqueness and finality is bound up with the nature of the Son's own

---

[52] Vanhoye, *Situation*, 71, 72.
[53] On the OT background in Gen 1 see A. Jónsson Gunnlaugur, *The Image of God: Genesis 1:26–28 in a Century of Old Testament Research*, ConBOT 26 (Stockholm, Sweden: Almqvist & Wiksell, 1988); W. Randall Garr, *In His Own Image and Likeness: Humanity, Divinity, and Monotheism*, Culture and History of the Ancient Near East (Leiden: Brill, 2003).
[54] Carson, *Son of God*, 17–18.
[55] Michel, *Hebräer*, 95.
[56] See, e.g. Attridge, *Hebrews*, 38–42; Vanhoye, *Situation*, 51.
[57] See, in particular, Section 4.2.2.
[58] Milligan, *Theology of Hebrews*, 73–4.
[59] Koester, *Hebrews*, 177, 180.
[60] Vanhoye, *Situation*, 61.
[61] Webster, "One Who Is Son," 78.

sonship.⁶² In itself this does not establish his sonship in eternality past. However what it does is tie Jesus' filial status to revelation in a way that spans the entirety of his career. All that Jesus said and did, his entire person and work, is constitutive of this revelation.⁶³ It cannot be merely limited to a post-ascension mode of existence. This is especially clear when considering the express statement of 2:3, in which the Son's role in revelation is connected to speech during his earthly career. The fact that this represents the only spoken ministry of Jesus is a thin objection to this line of evidence. All descriptions of Jesus' life in Hebrews which precede his death, resurrection and ascension are equal parts of this revelatory career and are seen as pastorally necessary for the Pastor's audience.

Second, and related to the above, the concrete description of Jesus in his earthly career as Son is no mere proleptic application of the title.⁶⁴ His testing and suffering as Son is essential to the nature of God's revelation through him. His earthly career is, for the Pastor, is as Son and because he is Son. Indeed it is difficult to parse the logic of 5:8 without the concept of Jesus' prior identity as Son. Though the participial phrase of 5:8, "although he was [a] son" is rightly seen as concessive, its strangeness becomes apparent in the light of 12:5–11. To be a son is to expect the unpleasant, but necessary, exercise of paternal discipline.⁶⁵ However, the peculiarity of Jesus' sonship and suffering is on account of the kind of son he is—the peculiar and eternal Son. The force of 5:8 thus brings to bear that, even though Jesus was the Son *par excellence*, he still suffered as a son.⁶⁶ Thus within the context of Heb 5, the train of thought is not career and then sonship, but rather the Son undertaking his work as Son, resulting in sonship perfected (5:10).

Third, though the language of sonship is not present, the description of the Son as ἀπαύγασμα καὶ χαρακτήρ in 1:3 is deeply relevant to the concept, connected to the Son's imaging of God.⁶⁷ As others have noted, the polyvalent nature of the lexemes

---

⁶² Peeler, *My Son*, 12; Mackie, "Confession," 438n435; Daniel J. Ebert, "Wisdom in New Testament Christology: With Special Reference to Hebrews 1:1–4" (PhD Diss., Trinity Evangelical Divinity School, 1998), 170; Meier, "Symmetry and Theology in the Old Testament Citations of Heb 1, 5–14," 522.

⁶³ In comparison to the prophets the Son is both the focus of final revelation and final redemptive action, so Vanhoye, *Situation*, 51.

⁶⁴ As below, this would essentially be to make him less Son than the many sons who are so by virtue not merely of salvation but creation. *Pace* Käsemann, *The Wandering People of God: An Investigation of the Letter to the Hebrews*, 98; Loader, *Sohn Und Hohepriester*, 14.

⁶⁵ Peeler, *My Son*, 151–63.

⁶⁶ As will be noted below, to place Jesus' sonship squarely and completely after his suffering would be at this point not only to make him less than the created sons but in fact to remove the ground of pastoral analogy here. The Pastor's audience are suffering in the midst of their sonship; but they are to understand the filial framework for such an experience, one of receiving discipline from the hand of a wise Father—just as was the case supremely and foundationally for Christ the Son.

⁶⁷ On potential connotation of parent–son relation to this language and imaging, see Stephen Muir, "The Anti-Imperial Rhetoric of Hebrews 1.3: Χαρακτηρ as a 'Double-Edged Sword,'" in *The Epistle to the Hebrews and Christian Theology*, ed. Richard Bauckham et al. (Grand Rapids, MI: Eerdmans, 2009), 174, 175, in particular evident in concepts of moral formation of children in 4 Macc 15:4. Also Koester, *Hebrews*, 180; Weiss, *Hebräer* 145. The phrase has usually been compared to Wis 7:26 and a good deal made of the verse as an instance of Wisdom Christology (e.g. Dunn, Christology, 166, 167) or the effects of wisdom traditions (e.g. Attridge, Hebrews, 43, 44). However, neither of the key words in 1:3b occur in the text of Wis 7:26 and the concept of Wisdom seems to contribute little

can make it difficult to render the Christological value of the statement, and this may in part explain Mackie's observation that too little has been done to integrate this description of the Son into reading the Epistle as a whole.⁶⁸ Because of this issue of semantics commentators often are tempted to debate the denotation of the terms without fully developing their significance, which is considerable.

In considering their significance it is helpful, because of the polyvalence of ἀπαύγασμα, to begin by exploring the second term in the phrase.⁶⁹ It has rarely, if ever, been remarked quite how odd the combination of χαρακτήρ and ὑπόστασις is. With most commentators I take ὑπόστασις and its parallel noun, δόξα, to refer obliquely to God, the Father, himself.⁷⁰ Thus the modification of these two nouns (δόξα/ὑπόστασις) via the head nouns (ἀπαύγασμα/χαρακτήρ) is one of relating the Son to God. ὑπόστασις here denotes the essence or nature of a thing,⁷¹ and in our construction what God is: his being. Thus, the phrase most closely approaches a metaphysical description of God, his quiddity.⁷² At the same time, the combination of "substance" with χαρακτήρ suggests the idea of representation. Were the phraseology χαρακτήρ θεοῦ, it would be rather unremarkable. However, that the writer combines here the language of derivation with language related to the very being of God is remarkable.⁷³

---

to the concerns of Hebrews itself, so Michel, Hebräer, 37; Ellingworth, Hebrews, 99; Ebert, "Wisdom in NT Christology," 5–7, 74.

⁶⁸ Mackie terms the phrase as "multivalent and cryptic [in its] terminology" (Mackie, "Confession," 438, 441); Koester, Hebrews, 180–1. The relative paucity of attention to this verse in recent scholarship is in contrast to the importance afforded to it in early Christological patristic debate. See Young, "Christological Ideas in the Greek Commentaries on the Epistle to the Hebrews," 34.

⁶⁹ The issue has been normally seen to lie between the active sense ("radiance" or "effulgence") or the passive sense ("reflection"). See Mackie, "Confession," 441. And this ambiguity is similarly reflected in usage elsewhere in Philo, Creation, 146; Plant., 50 and similarly in Wis 7:26a. With Ebert, the fact that an active sense for the term thus makes it slightly additive to the meaning of v. 3b, rather than tautologically identical to it, slightly pushes towards an active interpretation, one which was favoured by the early Fathers (Ebert, "Wisdom in NT Christology," 78; Young, "Christological Ideas in the Greek Commentaries on the Epistle to the Hebrews," 34–6).

⁷⁰ Or as descriptions of the divine nature, principally focused on the Father, Michel, Hebräer, 39. On the compatibility of this language see Weiss, Hebräer 145.

⁷¹ LSJ: 1895. See Koester, Hebrews, 180; Vanhoye, Situation, 75 and cf. Philo, Dreams, 1.188; Aet., 88, 92. Mackie notes that the usage of ὑπόστασις could often extend to the world of inner constitution (Mackie, "Confession," 445). The fact that these statements approach most closely metaphysical statements about divinity perhaps explains the polyvalence and difficulty of them. As Hibbert writes on the connection of human words to divine realities, "they must have the possibility of being open, being able to point beyond themselves, beyond the sphere and context of their own immediate origin; or in other words by way of analogical predication they must have the possibility of metaphysical realization" (Giles Hibbert, "Mystery and Metaphysics in the Trinitarian Theology of Saint Thomas," ITQ 31 (1964): 187, 188 quoted in Levering, Scripture and Metaphysics: Aquinas and the Renewal of Trinitarian Theology, 5).

⁷² Vanhoye, Situation, 75 notes the concrete substance meaning in Aristotle, De Mundo, 4.

⁷³ The presence of language pertaining to God's being and the present participle ὤν suggest that the horizon of 1:3 is not to be limited to Christ's exalted state, pace Koester, Hebrews, 176, 178. Even if one wished to argue that the description of Christ is focused on his present seat at God's right hand, his imaging of the Father reaches back to his participation in the founding of the ages. As Michel, Hebräer, 40, notes, "die partizipialen Aussagen ... nicht nur vom erhöhten oder vom präexistenten, geschweige denn nur vom irdischen Christus redden, sondern daß hier eine Einheit des Denkens erreicht ist." And in comparison to the surrounding array of verbs, "[ὤν] stands out like a metaphysical diamond against the black crepe of narrative" (Meier, "Structure and Theology in Heb 1, 1–14," 180).

The Son in the description is both related to, and distinct from, the very being of God the Father.[74] In this way it is not to overread the phraseology to see the Son as both sharing in the properties of the Father (his eternality, power, aseity) and also being distinguished from him.[75] Understanding the latter phrase χαρακτήρ τῆς ὑποστάσεως αὐτοῦ (1:3a) in such a way suggests a resolution to the language of the prior phrase. The Son is the "radiance" of the glory of God.[76] Again glory represents here the closest approximation to a description of what God is and what attends his presence.[77] The concept of Jesus as the ἀπαύγασμα represents then the concept of both derivation, he shines forth as one with that light, and yet also of real distinction from the light of the Father.[78] Underlying both phrases is a concept of derivation and visual imaging that is not only consonant with the concept of Christ as Son but also an extension of it. Sons, in antiquity, image their fathers.[79] Thus the expectation in Hebrews it that the Son will image God, radiating and displaying God the Father.[80]

This is clear immediately in 1:2. Here the Son is described as the one through whom the ages were created. Similarly the Son is the subject, not the object, of the powers of creation and providence, distinguishing him from the created sphere. This instrumental agency is to be seen in the context of the Son as image. He participates with his Father in works which are properly God's. The work of the Son in creating is his work as God and part of his address as Son (1:10–12).

This line of thought however is not restricted to the work of creation and providence in the Exordium,[81] but is present more widely in depiction of the Son's character. Frequently what the Son is, he is as the Father is. The Son is faithful (2:17; 3:2), eternal (1:8, 10–12; 7:3; 13:8), powerful (1:3; 2:18; 7:25) and present (4:14–16; 13:8), just as the

---

[74] Loader's point that this cannot be taken to ascribe deity because the Pastor has not thought of the ontological implications seems to run afoul of the highly ontological nature of the language at work in 1:3 (Loader, *Sohn Und Hohepriester*, 73). Cf. Rascher, *Schriftauslegung*, 80; Cockerill, *Hebrews*, 94.

[75] This is further strengthened by the way in which χαρακτήρ can refer to personal "characteristics" (Herodotus *Hist.* 1.116; Plato *Phaedr.* 263b; Jos *Ant.* 13.12.1) and see Peeler, *My Son*, 17. As Mackie puts it, the phrase conjures up "the mutuality and reciprocitative relationship shared between the Father and Son in this salvific and regnal drama" ("Confession," 445).

[76] That is, the active sense better portrays the combination of distinction and identification with what God is (Cockerill, *Hebrews*, 94).

[77] Vanhoye, *Situation*, 73 notes glory as God's distinct possession, e.g. in Isa 42:8; 48:11.

[78] Koester, *Hebrews*, 189; Hughes, *Hebrews*, 42. And see Athanasius, *Ep. Aeg. Lib.*, 2.4.

[79] In this sense though Vanhoye, *Situation*, 71 is certainly correct that, with regard to the Son, "Seul son rapport avec Dieu définit l'être du Fils," it is more accurate to say that 1:3 speaks of the nature of the Son in relation, not merely to the person of the Father but to *God's own nature*: a slight, but significant, qualification which drives the Pastor's point home even more forcefully.

[80] For similarity of the language of 1:3 to that of the more common language of Christ as the εἰκών of God (2 Cor 4:4; Col 1:15), see Koester, *Hebrews*, 187; Muir, "The Anti-Imperial Rhetoric of Hebrews 1.3: Χαρακτηρ as a 'Double-Edged Sword,'" 177; Loader, *Sohn Und Hohepriester*, 69; Bruce, *Hebrews*, 6. Thus the description is often seen as pertaining to revelation (Ebert, "Wisdom in NT Christology," 67, 68) but at times insufficiently connected to how the Son reveals the Father in his works, and tends to pursue a false choice between revelatory functions or essential categories. Cf. Rascher, *Schriftauslegung*, 82.

[81] Though creation and providence are most obvious in the overlap of the Father and Son in the Exordium, one might at the same time recognize that the concept of the Son's imaging of the Father also works in the reverse direction. This is in effect the corollary of the basic tenor of Peeler's thesis (Peeler, *My Son*, 3–8). That the Son is portrayed in a redemptive capacity reminds the reader that the roots of this salvation are found not only in the Son but also in the Father.

Father is also each of these (2:4, 10; 3:12; 4:13; 10:23; 11:11). He is thus the very image of the Father. And as this uncreated image, the Son has always been that filial image, just as there can be no glory without its radiance.

In these ways the sonship of Jesus in Hebrews functions in inextricable relation to the Father, and in clear connection to his divinity.[82] It cannot be limited to a function he plays or a later state which he enters consequent on his incarnate career.[83] However, as was noted above, it is then striking that though the Son is portrayed as uniquely Son, qualitatively distinct from the created order, the language of sonship also extends to describe the created people of God in an analogical way which also includes imaging.

6.3 The analogical image in the many created sons

As has already been remarked, it is an aspect of the genius of Hebrews that its central language of sonship spans both the articulation of the unique Son of God and is integral to exploring the sharing of human things by the Son in order to redeem many sons for God.[84] The strongly soteriological cast of this sonship language in Hebrews in relation to humanity ought not obscure that, though its use is primarily occasioned by issues of redemption, the sonship of the many does not begin with redemption.[85] The many do not become sons in Hebrews, but rather are sons whose sonship must be fulfilled by the work of Christ, having been frustrated in its *telos* by sin.[86] Human sonship does not begin with redemption in Hebrews, rather it finds its roots in the created nature of humanity as divine sons.[87]

This may be seen rather straightforwardly in the language of redemption as the "bringing [of] many sons to glory" (2:10) rather than the concept of adoption which would entail the "becoming" of sons de novo. However, the concept of creational sonship is more pervasively recognized when one sees the entailments of resemblance in connection to sonship. In at least two ways the argument of Hebrews reveals that humanity had an original creational *telos*, which was one clearly related to the character

---

[82] Though their comments are in relation to John's Gospel, Swain and Köstenberger's discussion of the relation of the Son's deity to the Father is remarkably consonant with the thought of Hebrews at this point, see chapter 7 of Andreas J. Köstenberger and Scott R. Swain, *Father, Son, and Spirit: The Trinity and John's Gospel*, NSBT (Nottingham, England: IVP, 2008), 111–34.

[83] Pace Peppard, *Son of God*, 4, 30, 56, 94, 105, 150; though the concept of sonship could function solely in relation to issues of inheritance via adoption, it is hard to see how this entirely serves to sever the language of sonship from questions of origin, that the underlying biology of parent–child language raises, not least with regard to issues around legitimate and illegitimate children, on which see Sara Elise Phang, *The Marriage of Roman Soldiers (13 BC–AD 235): Law and Family in the Imperial Army*, Columbia Studies in the Classical Tradition 24 (Leiden: Brill, 2001), 296–324). And for a more balanced discussion of Messiahs as "born and made" see chapter 3 of Novenson, *Grammar*.

[84] On the use of son of God language for Israel see Exod 4:22, 23; Deut 1:31; Jer 31:9, 20; Wis 2:10, 13–20 and discussion of Adela Yarbro Collins, "Mark and His Readers: The Son of God among Jews," HTR 92 (1999): 396.

[85] *Pace*, among others, Attridge, *Hebrews*, 91.

[86] Cockerill, *Hebrews*, 137.

[87] On the interface of protology and eschatology in Hebrews, Laansma, "*I Will Give You Rest*," 291, 292 notes 1:2, 7:3; 9:26; 11:1–2. 9:26, though difficult, is particularly significant in tying together cosmic beginnings and ends (ἀπὸ καταβολῆς κόσμου … ἐπὶ συντελείᾳ τῶν αἰώνων).

of God himself and participation in such.⁸⁸ These two categories in which humanity clearly reflects God in Hebrews, at least in its design, are those of rule and rest, being respectively developed in the handling of two strongly creational OT texts: Ps 8 in 2:5–9 and Gen 2:2 in 4:4.⁸⁹

6.3.1 The imaging of God in the intended regency of the created sons

Though the Pastor applies his discussion of the supremacy of the Son in 2:1–4, he effectively returns to where he left off in 1:14 at 2:6–7.⁹⁰ In 1:14 he spoke of the way in which not only has the Son assumed a position above angels but that they are subject even to mankind in their inheritance of salvation. Already this language of inheritance clarifies that the effect of the Son's work is to bestow the full right of sons on the redeemed people. Returning to this topic "about which [he is] speaking,"⁹¹ he describes the relative position of the angels in relation to the "world to come" (2:5). He begins with the negative conclusion, "For it was not to angels he subjected," raising a significant question: does he have in mind the submission of the coming world, not to angels, but to the Son, or, not to angels, but to the sons?⁹² This question relates, *in nuce*, to the well-worn disagreement over the interpretation of Ps 8 in Heb 2:6–9.⁹³ In moving to his quotation of the son of man to whom all is submitted does he principally have in mind an anthropological reading of Ps 8, in which the many sons are in mind, or a Christological one, in which the phraseology "Son of man" takes on a peculiar significance?⁹⁴

As has been noted by others the choice is probably a false one.⁹⁵ The flow of the argument relates the use of Ps 8, both to humanity broadly and to Christ as representative human, concepts which are clearly at play in the Pastor's subsequent exegesis of the Psalm.⁹⁶ This is particularly clear in the Pastor's movement from 2:8 to

---

⁸⁸ On this concept of human destiny in Hebrews see also in general Craig R. Koester, "Hebrews, Rhetoric, and the Future of Humanity," *CBQ* 64 (2002). One need not agree with Koester's understanding of Hebrews' structure to agree with his central theological point that "The question of God's purposes for humanity undergirds the speech" (ibid., 111), and especially the apologetic role this plays in relation to human suffering and the frustration of God's promises, so ibid., 112, 123.

⁸⁹ Thus in general one may see here the cosmological reflection of the Christology of the Exordium in which "Das Ende und der Anfang sollen einander entsprechen" (Michel, *Hebräer*, 37 apparently quoting Franz Deliztsch).

⁹⁰ Cockerill, *Hebrews*, 126.

⁹¹ This resumption suggests that ἡ οἰκουμένη ἡ μέλλουσα (2:5) and the "salvation [to be] inherit[ed]" (1:14) are equivalent realities, an equation further strengthened by the "Stichwortverknüpfung" via the Pastor's use of μέλλω in both phrases (Gräßer, *Hebräer*, 2, 112).

⁹² Moffitt, "Resurrection and High Priestly Christology," 120.

⁹³ See the discussions of Blomberg, "But We See Jesus," 89, 90; Moffitt, "Resurrection and High Priestly Christology," 121–2.

⁹⁴ On the terms of the debate see Blomberg, "But We See Jesus," 89–92.

⁹⁵ Peeler, *My Son*, 12n14; Bruce, *Hebrews*, 37; Rascher, *Schriftauslegung*, 55.

⁹⁶ That the position of humanity and the people of God as rulers over the age to come was an issue at play in contemporary Judaism further strengthens that the original horizon of Ps 8 would have been almost impossible to extinguish in the mind of readers. See, e.g. 1QS 3:17–20; 3 En. 5:10; 2 Esd 6:53, 54 and discussion of George H. Guthrie and Russell D. Quinn, "A Discourse Analysis of the Use of Psalm 8:4–6 in Hebrews 2:5–9," *JETS* 49 (2006): 236, 237 and the extensive discussion of Moffitt, *Atonement*, 118–42.

2:9. Ps 8:7 speaks of all things being subjected to humanity in the created intention of God.[97] However, due to the results of the entrance of the power of sin, death and the devil into the world, "we do not yet see all things subjected to him."[98] In the face of this failure of human regency, evident in the ruling power of Satan over fallen humanity (2:14, 15), Christ has been exalted as incarnate one, fulfilling humanity's intended goal.[99] This explains well the opposition of 2:8, 9 between what "we do not yet see," the subjection of all to mankind broadly, and what we now see, Jesus ascended on high.[100] Thus the Pastor reads Ps 8 in its application both to humanity, revealing what it was intended to be and failed to do, and in application to Christ, demonstrating what he has accomplished via his incarnate career.[101]

In understanding the Pastor's use of Ps 8 reveals a clear creational *telos* to the Pastor's conception of humanity.[102] Humans were made, in the Pastor's understanding, to rule over all things, to which Ps 8 bears witness. This rule is pictured in royal terms and is reflected in the immediate context in various ways. In Heb 2 it is signalled in both the language of sonship itself, in its connection to Israelite kingship, and also through the language of glory, crowning and subjection. Further, the context of Ps 8 itself depicts the royal standing of humanity in relation to God's supreme status as King. As the Creator YHWH is, by divine right, creation's ruler. Yet, the surprise of Ps 8 is that, though God is king by rights, he has subjected his world to humanity.[103] Thus, humanity in Ps 8 is a viceregent to God and an image of him in his own rule.

---

[97] On the interpretation of Ps 8 in contemporary Judaism see Guthrie and Quinn, "Discourse Analysis," 237.

[98] On the ambiguity of the αὐτῷ in 2:8, see Bruce, *Hebrews*, 37n35.

[99] Ibid., 36; Rascher, *Schriftauslegung*, 62, 63. In essence then Christ's enthronement in the language of Ps 110 is connected to his fulfilment of Ps 8, a connection which seems to have been at work more broadly in early Christianity; see Hengel, *Christology*, 165.

[100] Guthrie and Quinn, "Discourse Analysis," 242. Kevin B. McCruden, "Christ's Perfection in Hebrews: Divine Beneficence as an Exegetical Key to Hebrews 2: 10," *BibRes* 47 (2002): 43, notes the way in which Ἰησοῦν is displaced late in the syntax, and sees this as evidence for the presentation of Jesus as the solution to the human problem of not reigning.

[101] To see the οὔπω ὁρῶμεν αὐτῷ τὰ πάντα ὑποτεταγμένα in v. 8 as connected to Christ not yet having all things subjected to him, e.g. Spicq, *Hébreux*, 2, 32; Weiss, *Hebräer* 195, both demolishes any sense of the original Psalm's meaning with respect to humankind in general and, even more problematically, struggles with the past tense of the Psalm text itself. How was he already crowned with glory and honour, having all things submitted to him, both of which Ps 8 characterizes as past action, if the Pastor then temporally distinguishes these in relation to Christ. The tense here, however, makes complete sense when Ps 8 is seen as a description of humanity's created purpose which was thwarted by sin and is restored via Christ's career.

[102] Cockerill objects to this anthropological reading of the text as "a foreign body" (Cockerill, *Hebrews*, 130n130). Indeed, his objection that the Pastor shows no interest in humanity in general, but only in regard to the perseverance of the people of God is well made. However, it does seem that this is reconcilable by seeing the purposes of God for humanity fulfilled in the "seed of Abraham," who are by nature human. That is, at the theological level, Cockerill's reading seems to require that either salvation entirely mirrors creation or is of no relation to it. Rather the Pastor's soteriology holds out the renewal of all things, and thus the destiny of new creation is the goal of God's perseverant people.

[103] On the interplay of "doxology" and "dominion," see Walter Brueggemann, *The Message of the Psalms: A Theological Commentary*, Augsburg Old Testament Studies (Minneapolis, MN: Augsburg Pub. House, 1984), 36, 37.

More broadly one may consider other foundational creation texts in the LXX, similar to Ps 8, in particular Gen 1:26, 27. This verse integrates both the intended purpose of humanity not only to "rule over" the created order but also that this ruling goal is itself tightly related to the status of humans as images of the invisible God.[104] In this way Hebrew's portrayal of humanity as God's sons demonstrates that part of their intended goal in imaging God was to be established as vice-regents over the world he made, reflecting his royal status as sovereign Creator.

6.3.2 The image of God in the intended rest of the created sons

Though the use of Ps 8 in Heb 2 is perhaps the most obvious of references to creational order, a similar concern arises in the Pastor's argument concerning God's rest in 3:7–4:13.[105] This concept of divine rest is quickly traced to the initial horizon of creation and Gen 2:2, from which the Pastor quotes.[106] In drawing in the horizon of God's own creational rest, the Pastor also uncovers certain assumptions about the intended goal of humanity in resting with God, which forms a second aspect of imaging in humanity's design.[107] In order to demonstrate this point we must attend to the broad direction of the Pastor's argument at this juncture in Hebrews.

The principal focus of the Pastor's argument in 3:7–4:13 is to convince his audience of the point he twice makes in 4:1 and 4:9, that the rest of God is both open to be entered and that the offer to enter it remains open to his audience.[108] This is directed to the same rhetorical appeal of 4:1 and 4:11, that his audience should both "fear" and "exert every effort" to ensure entry into that rest. In this way the focused temporal horizon in 3:7–4:13 is the future possibility of entrance and the present need for the audience to respond rightly to that offer of rest in the word of God and its warnings.[109] However, though the present and future horizons of the "today" of God's appeal are primary,[110] the Pastor's argument depends on various past moments of God's dealing with his people. So the Pastor draws in Joshua's day (4:8), the time of the desert

---

[104] In Gen 1:26, 27 the ruling over the world stands in apposition to the formation of humanity as κατ' εἰκόνα ἡμετέραν καὶ καθ' ὁμοίωσιν.
[105] Cockerill, *Hebrews*, 206, 207; Koester, *Hebrews*, 279 notes the potential connections of the Sabbath as a general concept to the glory of humanity in Ps 8, a tie which would further connect these aspects of ruling and resting, and this seems further supported by patterns of worship at Qumran, so Crispin H. T. Fletcher-Louis, *All the Glory of Adam: Liturgical Anthropology in the Dead Sea Scrolls*, STDJ 42 (Leiden: Brill, 2002), 252–3. This connection is independent of the specifics of Fletcher-Louis's argument, as, even if the horizon of earthly and heavenly worship are distinct, the focus of the former is on the latter.
[106] Bruce, *Hebrews*, 73; Laansma argues that the combination of the Genesis and Psalm text "is the assumed idea behind the whole of 4:1–11" (Laansma, "*I Will Give You Rest*," 261).
[107] On the role of cosmology at work in the argument, see Ibid., "*I Will Give You Rest*," 284.
[108] Ibid., 260; that is, he is focused on the "appeal for diligence" in 4:11 and, similarly, Lane, *Hebrews 1–8*, 96.
[109] This is particularly revealed in the ongoing speaking of Ps 95 to the Pastor's hearers, and which in their midst acts as the living word of God, exposing their inward attitudes and response, just as the unbelieving generation of Israel's response was eventually exposed through its falling in the desert.
[110] σήμερον appears both through quotation and the Pastor's own use at 3:7, 13, 15 and 4:7.

wandering (3:16–19; 4:6), the time of the Davidic kingship (4:7) and even the initial horizon of creation itself (4:3, 4).[111]

This final horizon comes via appeal to Gen 2:2 and the original rest of God, entered subsequent to the work of creation. It is this creational text and temporal horizon that is of prime interest here, as it again reveals certain theological assumptions about the created nature and *telos* of humanity. The Pastor notes the warning of Ps 95:11 which characterizes the rest, into which the wilderness generation were invited, as "my rest," that is, God's own, rather than one simply tailored for his people.[112] He thus appeals to the initial scriptural text that speaks of God entering his own state of rest, not at the borders of Canaan, nor in the land, but at the beginning of the world. God's rest cannot be dated to Canaan for "his works were performed at the foundation of the world" (3:3). So Gen 2:2 establishes that the rest on offer both in the past and in the audience's day is God's own creational rest.

However, this is not the sole point of the Gen 2:2 quotation. The shape of the Pastor's argument reveals that he sees it as establishing, not simply that the gospel invitation is to share the creational rest with God (4:3, 4), and not merely that his promise still stands (4:6), but that this invitation has stood since the beginning of the world. The moment of the creational rest, and the beginning of invitation to God's people to share in it, are temporally the same. This is a subtle but important distinction, for it reveals that part of humanity's created *telos* in the Pastor's thinking was from the beginning to enter God's own rest and rest with him.

This infrequently recognized point is revealed in the flow of thought from 4:3–4:7.[113] The principal point, that the rest on offer is not to be equated with Canaan,

---

[111] On the importance of these historical horizons to the Pastor's argument see Sargent, *David Being a Prophet: The Contingency of Scripture Upon History in the New Testament*, 11–17.

[112] *Pace* Lane, *Hebrews 1–8*, 100; Cf. Richard B. Gaffin, "A Sabbath Rest Still Awaits the People of God," in *Pressing toward the Mark: Essays Commemorating Fifty Years of the Orthodox Presbyterian Church*, ed. Charles G. Dennison and Richard C. Gamble (Philadelphia, PA: Committee for the Historian of the OPC, 1986), 40.

[113] Cockerill, *Hebrews*, 207, 208 traces the logic rather perspicuously:

> The modern reader must grasps the Pastor's underlying assumption: if God established his eternal rest at the culmination of creation and invited the wilderness generation into it, then he must have intended his people to join him in his "rest." Since God's purposes will not be frustrated, the failure of the wilderness generation to enter is certain evidence that others will.

Even closer to my point here is Gaffin when he remarks that

> the writer knows of only one rest, "my rest," entered by God at creation and by believers at the consummation. Further, it appears that in Gen 2:2b ... he finds not only a reference to the existence of God's rest, but the *design* and *mandate* that others should enter and share it; Gen 2:2 is prescriptive as well as descriptive. If this were not the case the first premise in v 6 ... would be without foundation. (Gaffin, "A Sabbath Rest Still Awaits the People of God," 39, 40)

On the difficulty of these verses, especially the juxtaposition of 4:3, 4 see Laansma, "*I Will Give You Rest*," 283, 288. Cf. Koester, *Hebrews*, 278. As I hope to demonstrate below, the reason this concept of protological invitation is so often missed in 4:3, 4 is because the Pastor's argument is dense and requires the reconstruction of two assumptions he makes by inference. Because of this terseness his point about Canaan and Joshua's ministry in 4:8, 9 is frequently read back into vv. 4:4–6 and seen as a total explanation of his logic on the enduring offer of rest.

and thus still remains as something to be entered, is usually recognized as key to the Pastor's argument. This is particularly clear in the reference to Joshua in 4:8, and the way in which David's warning in Ps 95 postdates Israel's entry into the Land. If the Land equalled that promised rest, they would already be in it; thus the Psalm's warning to obtain what one already has would be meaningless. Though this is certainly the point the Pastor is making, he in fact feels it is already established prior to 4:8, the Joshua argument representing a supplementary proof to one already given. This can be seen by the fact that he concludes with a *quod est demonstrandum* at 4:6, namely, "since then it remains for some to go into it," and this precedes the appeal to Joshua at 4:8. This conclusion reveals that the Pastor believes the collocation of Gen 2:2 and Ps 95:11 already makes his point for him, not only about the identity of the rest into which God's people are invited but also the very fact of invitation in the first place.[114]

The only way to reconstruct such an argument is to see that Ps 95:11 makes explicit what is already implicit in Gen 2:2: that God in fact inaugurated a state of rest which by its very nature was invitational, calling humanity to join him in that Rest, an invitation still open to his audience. The only alternative explanation of the logic is to claim that the initial invitation to enter the rest was issued to Israel and remains open from that time, namely the wilderness period, until the time of the Pastor's hearers. On such a reading the argument would be essentially: God invited Israel into his own rest, equated with his creational rest, at the time of their exodus from Egypt and, since they failed to enter that offered Rest, such an offer still stands today for others to take up. However this construal stumbles over the order of statements in 4:4–6;[115] 4:6 does not narrate the failure of the people to go into the Land from the desert which results in the promise remaining for others.[116] Rather he articulates two reasons: *since* (1) the promise to enter God's own rest remains *and* (2) (since) those who were formerly evangelized failed to believe and enter, *therefore* the possibility of entrance by others remains open. So for the Pastor the offer of 95:11 is one that has existed for as long as God's own rest has, ever since creation itself.[117]

This makes clear that important for Pastor's anthropology is a sabbath state into which God had always intended to bring humanity.[118] Just as God rested (4:4 // Gen 2:2), he intended humanity as part of their protological goal to rest with him, entering his own rest and thus "resting from his own works just as God did from his" (4:10). It suffices to note here that, not only is humanity's goal one of rest and communion with

---

[114] Laansma, "*I Will Give You Rest*," 284 notes similarly that there is more than the argument via Joshua at work in the flow of these verses.

[115] As ibid. notes, "neither 4,1 nor 4,6 argue that an entrance remains *because* of the failure of the 'fathers' to enter; … it remains *in spite of* [it] … . The order of the clauses in v.6a, b tells against all such [other] proposals."

[116] *Pace* Koester, *Hebrews*, 278; Otfried Hofius, *Katapausis: die Vorstellung vom endzeitlichen Ruheort im Hebräerbrief* (Tübingen: Mohr Siebeck, 1970), 178n329.

[117] Laansma, though not quite explicitly defending this, comes very close when he reads 4:3a as suggesting "that [this rest of Gen 2.2] will not remain unattained" ("*I Will Give You Rest*," 290). However, his tendency to see the eschatological goal in Hebrews as the repristination of the original order, rather than its surpassing, somewhat hinders his synthesis. That is, Laansma is right to see the offer of entering God's rest is as old as "salvation" itself, but is indeed older, reaching back to the moment of Gen 2:2 (ibid., 294).

[118] Ibid., 290.

God in his own rest, it is by nature an imaging destiny. Humanity were intended to rest just as God did (ὥσπερ ... ὁ θεός), to enter into a state of imitation of God as depicted in Gen 2:2. In this way, for the Pastor, the collocation of his two principal OT texts in this section not only witnesses to his understanding of the goal of humanity as resting with God but also to the equally fundamental anthropological conviction that in this rest humanity will fill up their identity as sons, by resting in the same way that God, whose image they bear, has done ever since the completion of his creation work.

As was noted at the start of this section, creational states and their goals are not strictly speaking the rhetorical focus of the Pastor's argument so much as salvation and the necessity of "making every effort" (4:11) to share in it. However, to the extent that salvation in Hebrews is understood as the realization of creational *teloi*, to which humanity are ordered as God's sons—his images—then the demonstration of the Pastor's soteriology will often uncover his understanding of creational order. Put otherwise, because the Pastor's eschatology involves the state of creation fulfilled, though the emphasis lies on fulfilment, the process of argument reveals something about creation.

The next step in my argument examines the nature of Christ's work as the filling up of the divine image in humanity, outlined above. However, before doing so, it is first worth noting that in understanding the shape of the eternal Son as the image bearer *par excellence*, and the created sons as analogical image bearers, we have potentially already shed some light on the issue of the coherence of sonship Christology in Hebrews. This is particularly the case in relation to the Pastor's anthropology. For on the basis of it we may see that even in the case of humanity, the concept of a hard inception of sonship, in which one who is simply not son becomes son, is absent from the Epistle. To describe Christ's career as if he were one who was not Son but simply became son would in fact be to make him less than any human being. In effect then already a certain plausibility is leant to the fourth kind of solution mentioned above, in which Christ's becoming son represents the developing of a prior filial identity through some kind of temporal and soteriological attainment. It is the shape of this attainment to which Sections 6.4 and 6.5 attend.

6.4 The Son's work as fulfilling the sonship of the many

As we have noted above, the concept of redemption in Hebrews is tied to the realization of initial creational goals, not least in the way that the Son's career fills up the filial *telos* of the many sons.

In pursuing this concept further, it is first of all worth noting the representative nature of soteriology of Hebrews. The Pastor's exposition of the career of Christ—his enfleshment, obedience, death, ascension and heavenly session—is all of supreme relevance to his audience because they are described consistently as "for us."[119] All that the Son undergoes in Hebrews is for the sake of his many brothers, but also guarantees

---

[119] This solidarity of Christ with the many children of God especially emerges in 2:5–6. See Attridge, *Hebrews*, 88, 90; Lane, *Hebrews 1–8*, 53, 58, 59.

that what is Christ's by right and accomplishment will be shared with them.[120] Just as he became a sharer in blood and flesh (2:14), "their things," so they have become sharers in Christ and in what is his (3:14). This may be seen not only in the repeated use of the preposition ὑπέρ (2:9; 6:20; 7:25; 9:24) but also in two further ways. First, in the use of titles that speak of Christ as going before believers. This is true of the titles ἀρχηγός (2:10; 12:2), πρόδρομος (6:20) and πρωτότοκος (1:6). Each evokes the idea that Christ has accomplished something on behalf of his people. In the case of ἀρχηγός it is the tasting of death so as to deliver his people from its power (2:9). In the case of the latter two, it is representative entrance into the heavenly tabernacle. This entrance is most explicit in the concept of Christ as πρόδρομος in 6:20, where the believers' hope is explicitly connected to Christ's present heavenly location. However, it equally applies to Christ as πρωτότοκος. As firstborn he has entered the heavenly οἰκουμένη (1:6) on behalf of his many brethren (2:5). Though each title stresses representation, the latter two also contain a promissory note in respect of Christ's location. He is not merely in the divine presence on the behalf of believers, as significant as that is within Hebrews for believers' present access to God and his help (2:18; 4:16), but also his heavenly entrance as πρόδρομος and πρωτότοκος guarantees that where he, as firstborn, has gone, they soon will follow.[121] The access of the πρωτότοκος, Christ, holds out the guarantee of the assembly of the πρωτότοκοι (12:23).[122]

Second, the strongly representative nature of Christ's work is also encoded in its cultic description. As the Pastor himself notes, priests are appointed on behalf of others (5:1), to represent them in divine matters. Again, this priestly conception moves beyond OT metaphor in not merely granting representative access—the people vicariously present through their priest—but also that just as Christ has passed through the inner veil as their priestly representative, so soon shall they.

This representative cast within Hebrews is important for understanding its soteriology as the filling up of humanity's creational *telos*. Soteriology is not merely creation regained in Hebrews, but the creational goal reached. Thus the Son's role in taking on flesh is to fill up the sonship of the many sons, a goal unattainable by their own powers because of the incapacitating and defiling effects of sin (2:14, 15; 7:23, 28; 9:14). Thus the concept of "leading many sons to glory" is an effective strapline to the soteriology of Hebrews; not the gaining of sonship de novo but the fulfilment of sonship glorified.[123] This glory, when understood via representation, can be seen in the

---

[120] Weiss, *Hebräer*, 210–11. Cf. also the way in which Christ's "sharing" in 2:14 is connected to the "sharing" in heavenly vocation of the many in 3:1, as Attridge, *Hebrews*, 92.

[121] Mason, *Priest Forever*, 10, 11.

[122] This can similarly be seen in the concept of inheritance in relation to the Son and the sons, as Weiss notes, "Was für ihn, den 'Sohn,' jetzt schon gilt, das wird dereinst auch für die Christen (als die 'Söhne') gelten" (Weiss, *Hebräer* 142).

[123] This is further reflected in language parallel to that of sonship, that of inheritance language, which equally spans both the destiny of the Son and the sons. Though it is implicit in this language, it is at least intimated in the way that inheritance language surrounds the catena of Heb 1. The Son's appointment to an inheritance is paralleled by his supremacy over angels. It is to him that the world to come belongs, both as its maker and as its ascended King. However, the pay out of his enthroned position is not only his inheritance but also that of the many sons with him. Attridge, *Hebrews*, 40; Peeler, *My Son*, 10–29; Harris, "The Eternal Inheritance in Hebrews," 256–66.

way in which Christ's own career is itself the completion of the created *teloi* outlined in the section above—in rule and rest.[124]

So first, in his incarnate career Christ is established in reigning glory in such a way that guarantees the reign of his many brothers. So in 1:3, "having accomplished purification for sins he sat down." He both has completed his priestly activity and also is enthroned at God's right hand.[125] This enthronement has a promissory aspect for the sons. Though, as 2:8 explains, we may not now see all the created world under humanity's rule, this failure is not merely recounted as "not subjected" but as "not *yet* seeing all things ... subjected." Christ's reign guarantees that humanity, in general, will reign over the world as was its original goal. This is similarly reflected in the language of glory. That Christ's role establishes the many sons as glorious suggests equally it will establish them as crowned in the manner Ps 8:5 envisions (2:7). Because the Son reigns as enfleshed One, he will ensure the future reign of the many human sons over the world to come (2:5).

This pattern is similarly observed in the Son's filling up of the sons' *telos* of rest. The connection can be most tightly observed in the movement from 3:7–4:13 to 4:14–16. The prior section centres on holding out the continuing offer of entrance into God's own rest, while also warning the audience to make every effort to enter it. The move to 4:14–16 introduces Christ's work in priestly terms and stresses the access that hearers have to heavenly help because of Christ's already having "passed through the heavens" (4:14). Their hope for persevering in their confession, of combining the word of the gospel with faith (4:2), of not hardening their heart (3:12) and so entering the promised rest (4:1, 3), is the high priestly ministry of Christ. Though the focus is on the successful completion of the journey by Christ's enablement, this certainly includes the final entrance into the promised rest itself. Because Christ has entered that rest as their πρόδρομος, they themselves, having held fast to their confession through the heavenly help of the Son-Priest, will soon enter that same rest as well.

In this way Christ's own career fills up the sonship of the many. His work, which results in the reward of heavenly ascension and enthronement, is also a representative and promissory action on their behalf. What he accomplishes he has done "on our behalf" (6:20; 9:24) and for "each" (2:9).[126]

This action, however, in filling up the sonship of the many also makes clear that the Son himself has a course to run, a mission to be fulfilled. It is not merely that the Son fills up the sonship of the many, but that this action is itself a filling up of his own Sonship. This key concept may be seen in at least two parallel ways:

---

[124] Thus the comparison of the glorification of the Son to the glory expected of humanity in Jewish literature (1QS 4:22, 23; 1QM 1.8,9; 4Q504 frag. 8 and the discussion of Fletcher-Louis, *Glory of Adam*, 91–97), while helpful, must be understood within the matrix of the Son's dual identity as God and man, rather than simply being reduced to the Son as representative human. In this sense Rascher's analysis of the function of the Son's glory as driving force, enabling the representative salvific work, ought to be combined with the thought of Moffitt on the glorification of humanity in the Son (Rascher, *Schriftauslegung*, 62, 63; Moffitt, *Atonement*, 84).

[125] Already alluding to the mixing of kingship and priesthood in the exposition of Christ's person and work.

[126] Mackie, "Confession of the Son of God in Hebrews," 121.

First, it is visible in the way already noted in the previous chapter, that the accomplishment of the redemption of the sons is carried out within the matrix of the Son's relationship to the Father.[127] The use of Ps 40 in 10:5–6 is, again, the *locus classicus* for such reflection. The Psalm quotation integrates both themes of the Son's obedience to the Father and the goal of human existence as obedience to God in general.

With respect to the latter, the application of Ps 40 to the incarnation of the Son reveals a further aspect, in addition to rule and rest, as the *telos* of human life: to be in a body is for the sake of obedience to God. The raison d'être of human embodiment is one of response to God: "Behold, I have come … I desire, O my God, to do your will";[128] it is the sacrifice of total and unqualified obedience. At the same time the location of Ps 40 here within the matrix of speech between the Father and the Son makes clear that total human obedience, which is entailed for all sons by virtue of possessing a body, has a peculiar significance for the Son of God. The timed confession of the Psalm, as the Son comes into the world (10:5), pushes the act of obedience back before the assumption of flesh in a way that could be said of no other.[129] The assumption of flesh is, uniquely for Christ, itself an act of obedience in response to the sending of the Father.[130] As noted in the previous chapter, the responsive character of the Son's word reveals that the obedient assumption of flesh is in response to the divine will.[131] Thus the performance of the Son in his career has, in effect, a double significance. It represents narrowly both the filling up of what is required of humanity generally and also the filling up of what is required of the Son in his salvific mission.[132] In this way, the Son's filling up of his own peculiar filial obedience and mission is one with, and coextensive with, the filling up of the obedience for which human nature—the σῶμα—was originally intended.[133]

Second, this is encoded in the language of perfection, over which so much ink has been spilled.[134] The basic denotation of the language represents the reaching of a goal.[135] Debate over a sense more specific than this has tended to want to illegitimately

---

[127] The note of obedience is especially strong in 10:1–2, so Attridge, *Hebrews*, 269.
[128] τοῦ ποιῆσαι τὸ θέλημά σου, ὁ θεός μου, ἐβουλήθην καὶ τὸν νόμον σου ἐν μέσῳ τῆς κοιλίας μου. Ps 39:9 LXX Cf. Heb 10:7.
[129] Attridge, *Hebrews*, 273; Lane, *Hebrews 9–13*, 262.
[130] Bruce, *Hebrews*, 234.
[131] This understanding of the reception of the body and the will of God as being congruent is often recognized (e.g. Peeler, *My Son*, 135); however, it is rarely noted that, by reflex, Christology at this point also unveils theological anthropology in stressing that the body is thus a vehicle for obedience.
[132] As commented before, this double meaning is itself the reflex of the way the Pastor uses the language of θέλημα to bridge between the horizon of the Psalm text and his own argument. The will of God, which the Psalm envisions, is entire obedience to what is written in the scroll of the book; this obedience though for the eternal Son enfleshed operates at a higher level, where his law obedience is drawn up into the salvific θέλημα of God, his will to save a people, setting them apart for himself (10:10).
[133] By "eradicat[ing] the disparity between sacrifice and obedience … Christ's self-sacrifice fulfilled the human vocation enunciated in Psalm [40]" (Lane, *Hebrews 1–8*, 266).
[134] See ibid., 57–8; Attridge, *Hebrews*, 273; David Peterson, *Hebrews and Perfection: An Examination of the Concept of Perfection in the "Epistle to the Hebrews,"* SNTSMS 47 (Cambridge: Cambridge University Press, 2005), 1–19 and for a more recent overview of the debate, McCruden, *Solidarity*, 5–24.
[135] Koester, *Hebrews*, 122, 123; in this sense it is not entirely clear that the language ought, in the first lexical analysis, be narrowed to the clearly factitive meaning "to complete [something]." At times it seems more to bear the sense "come to a state of maturity," for example, when in relation to

transfer into the semantic range of the lexeme the theological connotations of this goal within the thought of Hebrews. As mistaken as this is within the realm of lexical semantics, it reveals that Christ's priesthood touches on many of the theological aspects of human destiny in the Epistle. To "reach one's goal" within Hebrews involves both cultic elements of purification and access (7:19; 9:9; 10:1, 14), filial discipline (2:10) and moral maturity (2:10; 7:28). The latter does not involve movement from sinfulness to sinlessness, which would preclude relation to Christ (4:15), but rather the movement from enfleshment to full-matured obedience, humanity's created *telos*, even when sin is not in view.[136] So the perfection language reflects the double filling up and completion that is represented in the Son. He is completing his own unique career as redeemer and priest, and by its completion is "perfected," reaching the goal of performing the will of the Father (2:10; 5:9; 7:28). At the same time this completes not only his unique sonship and role, but because of his representative participation in human flesh, it represents the perfection of the many sons (11:40).

Understanding this concept of double fulfilment in the one career of Christ is then crucial for grasping the significance of the sonship theme in Hebrews. The same obedience, suffering and perfected work of Christ has a double significance: the obedience of the unique, eternal Son to the mission of his Father, resulting in his specific reward as divine Son; and the filling up of human destiny with the consequence for his people of access to, and enthronement in, the divine rest. By virtue of the divine mission, and because of the enfleshment of the eternal Son, these two filial paths effectively become two distinguishable, but inseparable, aspects of the one identity of the Son.

6.5 The dual sonship foreshadowed in the Davidic son

A final crucial strand in understanding Christ's identity as Son in the Epistle is in relation to Davidic sonship. Obviously the concept of the Davidic king as son of God is a significant theme in the Pastor's Scriptures. Though the figure of David himself is scarcely discussed in Hebrews (4:7; 11:32), the concept of Davidic typology and Christ as fulfilment of that typology is deeply significant for the Pastor.[137] This can be seen

---

the maturation of children, see, e.g. Plato, *Sym*. 192. Though the passive forms seem to connote factivity by virtue of the implied transitivity of passives, i.e. "be completed, perfected" it is again not always the case, e.g. Plato, *Resp*. 466. Cf. McCruden, *Solidarity*, 5.

[136] This false equation of maturation with sinlessness is the root behind the unnecessary exclusion of ethical overtones from the perfection concept in Hebrews. See, e.g. Loader, *Sohn Und Hohepriester*, 39; McCruden, *Solidarity*, 19, 20; Peeler, *My Son*, 79. Koester's appeal to the passivity of the language is a much stronger argument (Koester, *Hebrews*, 124), but the fact that it probably focuses on divine agency does not thereby remove the language from the sphere of moral performance or development which is alongside it. For those advancing an ethical view see Hughes, *Hebrews*, 187; Westcott, *Hebrews*, 39.

[137] Peeler, *My Son*, 41, 119; Cortez, "Anchor." In this way the Pastor mirrors general NT concern for the fulfilment of promises to David and Davidic expectation in Jewish literature, e.g. Pss. Sol. 17:37; 4QpIsa and the discussions of Collins, "Son of God," 398; Collins, *Scepter and Star*, 57, 58 and Novenson, *Grammar*, 52–64. *Pace* Laansma, '*I Will Give You Rest*', 290; Ellingworth, *Hebrews*, 114–16.

in the prevalence of quotations and allusions of key LXX texts connected to David.[138] These include Ps 2:7 (1:5; 5:5); Ps 39:6–8 (10:5–7); Ps 44:6, 7 (1:8, 9); Ps 94:8–12 (3:7–11); Ps 109:1, 4 (1:13; 5:6; 7:17); Ps 22:22 (2:12); 2 Sam 7:14 // 1 Chron 7:14 (1:5). It also extends to lexical stock related to Davidic kingship: the description of the Son as inheriting all things (1:2; Ps 2:8), or as firstborn (1:6; Ps 89:27), or the association of Jesus with the language of Christ (3:6, 14; 5:5 and so on) and shepherd (13:20).[139]

A simple account of the data, however, fails to demonstrate the way in which this Davidic typological strand plays in the Christology of Hebrews. So, for example, the fact that Ps 110:1 is associated with the Davidic King, along with its centrality to the whole argument of the Epistle, draws the shadow of David into a central position with respect to the main themes of Hebrews. It is not explicitly developed in the section of the Epistle most concerned with Christ as Melchizedekian priest, but it may still appear, as if from nowhere, in such a discussion. In commenting that Christ was not descended from a priestly tribe (7:13), it is hard to believe that Jesus' obviously well-known descent from Judah, a point which can be alluded to as common knowledge (πρόδηλον 7:14), would be seen as unconnected to a messianic and kingly status, especially when it is mentioned in connection to the language of ἀνατέλλω, with its relation to the oracle of Num 24:17.[140]

However, the cluster of texts in which Davidic allusion is most significant is surely Heb 1. The Exordium contains both the language of sonship and allusions to Pss 110 and 2, in the space of four verses. The subsequent catena substantiates these opening statements with a significant weight of Davidic texts: Ps 2:7; 2 Sam 7:14; Ps 89:27; Ps 45:7, 8 and perhaps Ps 97:7. Of the seven texts quoted in the relation to the description of the Son in the catena, fully four are Davidic in provenance.[141]

Noting the degree to which David functions as a key OT character in relation to the identity of the Son in Heb 1 is especially significant in understanding the role of the catena in explicating the Son's identity.[142] The Pastor's point is surely that the ascension of the Son and his establishment at the right hand of God (1:3) represent the fulfilment of the promises and the covenant made with David. Jesus is the true seed promised, who has God as Father and is God's recognized son; in fact, the combination of Davidic texts and allusions, especially in relation to Ps 2 and Ps 89, makes clear that in OT terms the Son David was promised was not fulfilled within the history of Israel itself.[143]

---

[138] I classify here Davidic texts as those which explicitly mention David or connect to him, e.g. via LXX superscription of Psalm texts.

[139] On David as anointed see 3:4; 13:20; 2 Sam 22:51; 23:1; 2 Chr 6:42; Pss 2:2; 20:6; 28:8; 89:38, 51 and so on. On David as shepherd see 1 Sam 16:11; 2 Sam 5:2; Ezra 34:24; 37:24 and Ps 2:9. On messianic readings of Ps 2 in contemporary Jewish and Christian literature see Koester, *Hebrews*, 191 and Janse, "*You Are My Son.*"

[140] Pace Gräßer, *Hebräer*, 2, 41. On the "influential" role in messianic thought of Num 24:15–19, see Collins, *Scepter and Star*, 26, 27; Chester, *Messiah and Exaltation*, 337, 338 and the quotation of the Numbers text in 1QM 11.4–7 and 4Q175.

[141] As Cockerill, *Hebrews*, 105 notes, then, 1:5, 6 both highlight the fulfilling of Davidic promise as the assumption of messianic status (Ps 2:7) and the elevation of the firstborn above all rule (Ps 89:27). And on the conceptual connection of firstborn and supreme rule see Michel, *Hebräer*, 52, 53. If 1:6 intends to allude to Ps 97:7, and Davidic superscription is included, this increases to six out of seven texts.

[142] See the extensive discussion of Cortez, "Anchor," 212–73.

[143] This is similarly reflected in Pss. Sol. 17:21–32, 18:5–9. As Trafton remarks,

The Pastor's point within the catena is to demonstrate that the enthronement of the Son via his ascension is, itself, his enthronement as Davidic king.

Recognizing this brings into view that the Davidic strand of sonship in Hebrews does contribute something rather different to the creational and eternal aspects of understanding that identity. The Davidic typology, though it certainly includes the idea of descent as a right to kingship, is particularly concerned with the concept of one descendant becoming king, and thus Son, in a decisive way.[144] Though issues of descent are certainly necessary and prerequisite for the enthronement, descent is not a sufficient cause itself. Rather the Davidic enthronement envisioned in the catena emphasizes qualification for enthronement via achievement.[145] It is because of the Son's moral achievement and constitution that he ascends to the throne; he is anointed in recognition of his supremacy in ethical terms, and in reflection of YHWH himself, in comparison with the wider throng of companions (1:8, 9).[146] Thus the enthronement represents a real adoptive process. The pronouncement of sonship, in the narrowly Davidic sense, is no mere recognition—it is a real becoming, a constitution as true and ultimate Davidide.

However, it is equally important to recognize that the Davidic note does not stand alone within the context of Heb 1, but is connected to the identity of the Son as God.[147] This again is particularly on view in the catena. There, in essence, we find a combined description of the Son as both Davidic Son and LORD God himself. It may seem tempting at this point to compress the ascription of divine texts into a Davidic mould that would seem to merely connote human vice-regency. This is the direction of Compton's argument as we have noted before.[148] However, as we have seen above,

> For the psalmist, then, the expectation of a Davidic king is ... a central component in the psalmist's response to the complex web of calamities that have befallen the Jewish people and that stand behind the writing and collection of the Psalms of Solomon. Among many of their other failures ... the Hasmoneans established a kingship *from the wrong family*. But God has promised to "raise up" ... the son of David .... When he comes, as Ps. Sol. 17 makes clear and as Ps. Sol. 18, which stands as a brief epilogue to the entire collection, confirms, everything will be made right. (Joseph L. Trafton, "What Would David Do? Messianic Expectation and Surprise in Ps. Sol. 17," in *The Psalms of Solomon: Language, History, Theology*, ed. Eberhard Bons and Patrick Pouchelle, SBLEJL 40 (Atlanta: SBL Press, 2015), 163)

[144] This may be tied to the question of the unconditionality and conditionality of the Davidic promises which was alluded to in Chapter 3 of the present work (Section 3.4.2). YHWH promises to keep his covenant with David, itself a source of both hope and consternation in Israel's scriptures, though the scion upon whom this fulfilment turns must himself represent a faithful son of David, in being "like David" (1 Kgs 9:4). Thus to proclaim Jesus as Son within the frame of Davidic texts is to find in him the fitting character upon and through whom the Davidic covenant and its promised blessing may reach their zenith. That is, it is not only a statement of office but also one of identity in respect to moral character and achievement: "because you have loved righteousness and hated wickedness *therefore* God, your God" (1:9).

[145] As noted above this may be related both to the session following the act of purification (1:3) and to the anointing in relation to moral superiority (1:9).

[146] On the identity of the many μετόχοι in 1:9, see the arguments of Moffitt, *Atonement*, 51, 51n58. The messianic orbit strengthens the sense that his exaltation is from among the people on account of his moral and royal superiority, rather than in respect of the angels as "untergeordnete Diener" (Eduard Riggenbach, *Der Brief an die Hebräer*, KNT 14 (Leipzig: Deichert, 1922), 24).

[147] Bruce, *Hebrews*, 20.

[148] Compton, *Psalm 110*, 27–36.

the Son's eternality as Son resists such a straightforward move. Rather the catena bears witness to the concept that the filling up of the Davidic typology, in which one becomes the Davidic son, is (and must be) in the person of the divine Son.[149] This is not merely the synthesis of the Pastor, but according to the Pastor's method of scriptural hermeneutics, latent in the Davidic typology itself. This latter point may be seen in the manner in which divine and Davidic elements come together in the enthronement address of Ps 45:6, 7. There the king himself is addressed as God by name.[150] Some have sought to soften the effect of this on the Son's divinity in Hebrews, arguing that the description of Davidic monarchs in divine terms limits the Son's status to that horizon.[151] However, this is to misunderstand the nature of the Pastor's typology in which fulfilment represents not only "correspondence" but also "heightening" and "otherness."[152] Just as the Davidic kingship texts find their unique and final terminus in the Son, so the address of the enthroned Davidide finds in the Son one who may fittingly be addressed as Lord and God, without either appeal to hyperbole or concepts of representation.[153]

This Davidic element of the sonship portrayal of Hebrews is thus particularly significant for understanding issues of the Son's being and becoming as Son in the Epistle. The concept of Davidic enthronement contains within itself the nomenclature of one who becomes Son, that is, the true and ultimate Davidic monarch. At the same time, the integration of this Davidic theme in the catena and the letter as a whole demonstrates that the one who comes to fill up the Davidic Christology is one whose sonship does not begin with it. The reason that the Davidic kingship languished in seemingly broken promises was that it awaited God's final speech in the Son. It was this unique Son of God who was capable of coming to fulfil the Davidic strand in the Pastor's scriptures, rescuing God's people and being enthroned as messianic Son.[154]

---

[149] "In a fuller sense than was possible for David or any of his successors in ancient days, this Messiah can be addressed not mere as God's Son (verse 5) but actually as God, for He is both the Messiah of David's line and also the effulgence of God's glory and the very image of his substance" (Bruce, *Hebrews*, 20).

[150] That the title ὁ θεὸς (Ps 44:7 LXX) was able to be read as a vocative addressing the kingly figure can be clearly seen from the rendering of Aquila and Theodotion, who explicitly render the noun in vocative form. As Cockerill, *Hebrews*, 109, 110 notes, the only other viable syntax results in a translation, "God is your throne," which although potentially highlighting the enduring rule, seems both to make God oddly subservient and would ill fit in Hebrews with the position of Christ ἐν δεξιᾷ τοῦ θεοῦ (10:12). *Pace* Westcott, *Hebrews*, 95, 96. See also Murray J. Harris, "The Translation and Significance of Ὁ Θεος in Hebrews 1:8–9," *TynBul* 36 (1985): 138–9.

[151] Hurst, "Christology," 161; Compton, *Psalm 110*, 24n23.

[152] Schierse, *Verheissung und Heilsvollendung*, 59 originally applies this threefold phrase to the relation of the earthly to the heavenly tabernacle, but it serves a general explanatory function of almost all typological events, characters and institutions in Hebrews.

[153] On the way in which 1:8 functions pivotally in the catena then, Harris, "The Translation and Significance of Ὁ Θεος in Hebrews 1:8–9," 141 writes, "If it contains an address to the Son as 'God', v. 8 may be described as pivotal, since in that case it applies to Jesus the divine title implied in v. 3a and it is the first of three terms of address (in vv. 8, 10, 13) in which the Father speaks to the Son." In this way Koester's comment that "the Son's divinity could be seen as an extension of his messiahship" is not strong enough (Koester, *Hebrews*, 199). The Pastor's reading of Davidic texts demonstrates for him a clear trajectory: the Messiah must be the divine Son.

[154] On the import of the Davidic thought in Hebrews, Cortez writes,

6.6 Conclusion

The nature of the above argument suggests that it is not perhaps surprising that the concept of sonship in Hebrews has been controverted, especially in relation to the Son's being and becoming son. This is in part due to the fact that this sonship is polyvalent, corresponding to at least three lines of thought which come together in the soteriology, anthropology and Christology of the Pastor. This is not merely the disparate and unfortunate terminology of humanity as sons, the eternal Son as son and the Davidic king as son of God. Rather the intertwining of terms reflects that the three strands are integrally related in the Pastor's soteriology and Christology in particular, both at the theological level and in relation to his understanding of OT texts.

In order to fulfil the image-bearing humanity of the many, the eternal radiance of God took on the fleshly image, in order to lead the many to glory, their intended end. This coming in time was foreshadowed in the promise of a Davidic scion who would both act as representative Saviour and also be more than any mere human descendant. In this way the three sonships come together: as the eternal divine Son enters history, redeeming many sons by becoming the true Davidic Son and being enthroned as such.[155]

In this way we may see, with the fourth solution outlined in 6.1, that it is appropriate to see the story of the Son's enthronement in Hebrews as both legitimately a becoming of what he was not before and a demonstration of what and who he has always been and is. The enthronement of the Son at God's right hand represents his attainment of Davidic sonship, the fulfilment of the Davidic promise and the promissory enthronement of humanity above the created order in rule and rest—there is real attainment. At the same time it also is a demonstration that the only one who could bring about such was no ordinary human being, but "one who is Son." That is, his achievement of what humanity was unable in itself to do, and what had languished in the form of the Davidic promise, demonstrates his identity as the true, eternal and divine Son who was before the ages, came into the world and to whom ultimately the created ages and their worship belong (1:2, 6; 10:5). In this way then the assumed narrative of Hebrews itself might be related as a story of sonship: of the one and only Son, who became David's son, in order to lead many sons to glory. So within Hebrews

---

> Hebrews' purpose ... is not to prove that Jesus' exaltation fulfills the expectations for an eschatological Davidic ruler; instead, it assumes that the readers know this and establishes this notion as the foundation for his exhortation to the readers to hold on to their faith. In other words, these Davidic traditions function as an essential subtext of the Letter that provide the necessary force to its hortatory argument. Thus, the author of Hebrews argues that Jesus' exaltation in heaven as the eschatological Davidic king and faithful high priest— which the readers have witnessed through the Scriptures (pp. 432–55)—demands their allegiance to him. (Cortez, "Anchor," 460)

Also see Carson, *Son of God*, 41, 59.

[155] In this sense, as Vanhoye, *Situation*, 139 notes, within the canon of the OT the promise of the Davidic scion of Ps 2:7 is also a son, who is a gift, given to the people (Isa 9:15), for their redemption and consolation.

the recognition that the one described as Son, also becomes son, is not a threat to his portrayal and understanding as the divine and eternal Son of God. Rather it is the depiction of the way in which the Eternal Divine Son alone could bring about the salvation, which was promised in the prophets, and is being held out in the last days by the Pastor to his audience.

7

Conclusion

7.1 Summary

In this book, I have sought to demonstrate that the divinity of the Son in Hebrews is present, pervasive and salient to the Epistle and deserves more attention than has been afforded it in recent scholarship. This is principally because the Pastor both at times argues explicitly for the Son's divinity and, even more frequently, argues *from* such a concept, assuming the equal divine nature of the Son with his Father, as an essential element in the shape of his theology and discourse.

The work went about demonstrating this from Hebrews in Chapters 2 through 6. In Chapter 2, I focused on two texts, 1:6 and 1:10–12, both drawn from the catena of Hebrews' opening chapter, and both of which employ the same hermeneutical trope of applying to the Son texts that, in their original horizon, are directed to Israel's covenant God. I argued that, not only does the Pastor's application of these texts to Christ demonstrate his belief in the Son's divinity, but that, equally, his hermeneutic reveals basic convictions about the shape of his divine Christology. The action of the Son in these last days, especially centred on his exaltation and enthronement as royal Son, is the fulfilment of God's promises to come to the rescue of his people, bringing the resources of the One Creator God to bear on the salvific predicament of his people. Thus the Son's central role in fulfilling these promises of final salvific action reveals him as the God of whom Moses and the psalmist spoke.

In Chapter 3, I continued to develop this concept, of eschatological divine prerogative, in relation to Heb 3:3, 4 and the building of God's house. Historically these verses have often been seen as an argument relying on the Son's divinity and I argued that, with some modification, this ought to be maintained. Indeed, Heb 3:3, 4 assigned to the Son the divine glory and honour which, properly speaking, belong only to the Creator of all things. I demonstrated that this is applied to the Son as the one who built God's eschatological house, his household of redeemed people, and suggested that the concept of this eschatological house-building as divine right could be seen, both in relation to the melding of roles in comparison to the Nathan Oracle and, further, by understanding Hebrews' underlying commitment to the establishment of eschatological states as something only achievable by divine power.

In Chapter 4, I pursued an argument which, though similar to the two previous chapters in dealing with a single point of exegesis, draws in a wider array of connections between the Son's divinity and his qualification for priestly ministry in Hebrews. I discussed, in particular, the role of Heb 7:16 and the nature there of the Son's "indestructible life" in relation to his divinity. Though scholarship on Hebrews has tended to focus on one pole of divinity or humanity in relation to this life of the Son, I argued that both were in view, however with a certain taxis: the divine eternal life of the Son grounds his qualification for High Priesthood in the order of Melchizedek, because it pertains to his person, which though indeed human is also properly divine. I buttressed this by demonstrating that the portrait of the unbounded life of Melchizedek sustains far more than simply an unending priestly office, and that the Son described in Heb 7, with respect to his priesthood, succeeds where the Levitical order failed, because he cannot be exhaustively described by appeal to human nature. Thus his qualification via an indestructible life, though certainly consonant with his enfleshed resurrection from death, is grounded in the Son as bearer of divine, and eternal, life.

In Chapters 5 and 6, I sought to demonstrate connections in Hebrews between the Son's divinity and other more synthetic categories, namely, covenant and sonship. In Chapter 5 this involved demonstrating that, within the structure of the Abrahamic Promises, as read by the Pastor, the function of divine oath was such as to bind God to be himself the guarantor of his own promises, a conviction encoded in the metaphorical use of mediator language in 6:13–18. In the fulfilment of the Abrahamic Promises which comes about in the establishment of the New Covenant, however, the Son's work takes on an absolutely central and necessary role. Thus the Son assumes, in the plan of God, the role of guaranteeing and assuring the final efficacy and fulfilment of God's promises and becomes a fitting object of the trust and confidence of God's people. In this way, trust in Christ and trust in the God of the covenant promises and their keeping in his Son become mutually inferring and reinforcing postures for the Pastor's audience and result in the clear depiction of the Son's divinity in his role as divine surety.

Chapter 6, finally, tackled the controverted language of sonship in the Epistle, arguing that though the polyvalence of the term "son" may be initially seen as problematic, it, in fact, encodes the assumed salvific narrative of Hebrews. The eternal and uncreated One, who was always Son, came at the sending of the Father to fulfil a filial mission, in which he filled up the sonship of those who were created in the divine image. This mission was previously spoken about and foreshadowed in the prophets through the person and promises concerning David and his seed, a seed who would be final King, descended from his line, and yet far more than a mere human descendant, one properly addressed as "God" (1:8). I argued this by setting forth the three predominant strands of sonship in Hebrews: the sonship of Christ as the eternal image of God; the destiny of the many sons as created images; and the fulfilment of this sonship encoded in the scriptural person of David. In this way I demonstrated that the polyvalent sonship language of Hebrews captures the person and work of the Son, as the divine eternal Son sent to bring many sons to glory (2:10; 10:5–10).

The structure and scope of the chapters demonstrate that not only is the divinity of the Son present in Hebrews, it is also pervasive. It ranges far beyond Heb 1, even if a heightened explicitness is recognized in the earlier chapters, and is present throughout the Epistle. This pervasiveness is further seen in the interaction of the concept of the Son's divinity with both discrete arguments distributed through different sections of the Epistle and also its connection to broader themes, especially those which relate to the central twin motifs of Priesthood (Chapter 4) and Sonship (Chapter 6).

Perhaps what is most striking, however, is the aspect of theological salience, raised in the introduction. One might imagine a concept in Hebrews which, though present and even pervasive, acts as either something disconnected from the thought of the Epistle or as a theological addendum which is poorly integrated with its fundamental concepts. The divinity of the Son, however, occupies a position which is as far from this as is possible. In fact, its salience consistently emerges in the above chapters, in ways which demonstrate its importance—the divine person of the Son in Hebrews is the necessary presupposition of his eschatological work in its finality and efficacy. The work the Son has been sent into the world to do, is his, as God alone, to do and requires the divine resources he alone can bring. In him are kept the promises of God himself coming to save his people (Chapters 2 and 5); his is the divine glory proper to the redemptive building of God's household (Chapter 3); his is the divine role as the keeper of God's self-committing promises (Chapter 5); he alone is the one who can be both like God's people in representing them as priest, and yet at the same time bring power to their situation which is outside of the nature he shares with them (Chapters 2 and 4). Hebrews exploits both that the promise of the final One is of a divine figure (Chapters 2 and 6), and that the execution of this work requires a divine person to achieve it (Chapter 3 through 5). Thus, though at times Hebrews argues *for* the Son's divinity, frequently the salience of the Son's divinity is more easily seen in his argument *from* it: the Son can only be the fully effective Saviour and Priest he is, because he is himself true God, and thus brings to his people resources beyond their own, those of God himself.

7.2 Reflections

It remains to briefly reflect on the results of the above chapters in light of several areas upon which it touches that are related to wider fields of NT study. Though, no doubt, much more could be said in this regard, I would suggest the following two reflections.

7.2.1 Divine Christology in Hebrews and its status in NT studies

I remarked in the introduction that, considering the abundance of scholarship surrounding high Christology in the NT, both for and against, it is surprising that more research has not been done in relation to the Epistle to the Hebrews. This may arise from suggestions of a late date for Hebrews and the desire for evidence of early Christology; however, the fact that even a late date for Hebrews is not far removed from the writing of the Synoptic Gospels, and certainly not the Fourth Gospel, along with the uncertainty concerning the dating of Hebrews generally, suggests that this neglect of Hebrews in relation to divine Christology is not well-founded. In fact, read alongside the scholarship on Early High Christology, the Epistle to the Hebrews has several things to offer, both of which were raised in Section 1.2 of the introduction. So, the way in which the Son's divinity is articulated in Hebrews and the parallel criteria for adjudicating divine Christology are evidently very broad. They certainly include questions around what constitutes proper divine actions, and yet frequently in ways that are connected not to generic description but to concrete threads of promise in the OT Scripture of the Pastor—divine action is frequently pursued alongside the lines of scriptural, promised action. Other aspects move beyond divine action however. Generally, I have noted ways in which the Son's general imaging of his Father, their shared general character, may impact divine portrayal; this may also more specifically be evidenced not only in language on divine attributes, for example, the divine life of 7:16, but also at the level of assumptions about salvific power. Perhaps most pointedly, as I noted in the introduction, certain aspects of the divine portrait of the Son only take on their full Christological value when viewed from within the Pastor's own system of thought. For example, to debate in relation to literature outside of Hebrews, whether the phrase "Son of God" or the language or concepts of mediators, sureties, covenants and oath-swearing entail divinity in the abstract would probably result in a negative judgement. Yet, relative to their use in Hebrews and within the Pastor's system of thought, they play key roles in articulating the divinity of the Son. This suggests, as I noted before, that matching predications across systems can only get one so far, and that though this methodology is not useless, it will effectively act as a Procrustean bed in handling the data of the Christology of the NT authors.

A further point in relation to divine Christology in Hebrews might be also helpfully noted in relation to the development of early Christology. Though the reconstruction of Christological development is always a somewhat speculative and tentative endeavour, a question alongside that of the status of Christ's divinity in the NT writings has also been posed, that of how its articulation came about. One line of thought suggests that Christians began with convictions about the exaltation of Jesus in relation to the divine throne, and moved backward from this climactic stage in Christ's career and its relation to divinity, towards beliefs about Christ's role in relation to creation. That is, Christological development involved a movement backward in time, from eschatological manifestation and enthronement towards involvement in creation as *Schöpfungsmittler*. The Epistle to the Hebrews, and the reading of various divine passages I have explored above, raises a rather straightforward connection, through which early Christians may have made this movement. Namely, that the Son's divinity is frequently connected to his eschatological and salvific role, where this eschatological role is conceived of in ways parallel to the work of creation. Where early Christians understood the eschatological work of Christ as both a divine work and a work of renewing the creation, or making creation anew, it would have been very natural to connect this eschatological work, in Christological terms, backwards to protology. In other words, where the conviction that the work of redemption via the Son is a re-creational work, the inauguration of final things in a new world, it is a natural process to see this divine pattern of the Father working through the Son, not only at work in redemption but also in the creation of the world at the beginning itself.

7.2.2 Divine Christology in Hebrews and other *loci* of thought

In pursuing the Pastor's argument for, and argument from, the divinity of the Son in Hebrews, I have noted the numerous ways in which his divine Christology does not stand alone, but rather is deeply interwoven with his understanding of redemption (soteriology) and his understanding of human nature and its goals (anthropology). With this in mind, it is again worth noting that, if these connections hold, to discuss and understand what Hebrews has to say about these other *loci* of thought, without sufficiently taking into account the relationship to the Son's divinity, will be artificially truncated and perhaps even quite mistaken. For example, one may take the topic of soteriology in Hebrews. Relatively little has been written explicitly under this locus, though a good deal has been written on concepts integrally related to it in the Epistle, for example, perfection, faith and faithfulness, atonement, priesthood and the role of warnings. A proper focus on the divinity of the Son in Hebrews will raise questions in general with regard to the Son's divine role in redemption. The predominant themes noted in the chapters above often reveal a connection between the Son's divinity, soteriology and the state of the people of God. That is, the Son's divinity is construed in relation to this unique salvific power and prerogative, the obverse of which is formed by the sorry state of humanity and human agency, one constantly marked by disempowerment, sin, the effects of sin, the threat of divine judgement and the controlling rule of evil powers (3:19; 5:2, 11; 6:1, 8; 7:27; 8:8; 9:9, 14; 10:22; 26–31). To pursue an understanding and exposition of soteriology, or the themes connected to it in Hebrews, without the concept of the Son's divinity firmly in mind will tend to downplay these obverse elements, and this seems to be borne out in the literature, at least in some measure. This is particularly evident where Christological exemplarism dominates discussion of the Epistle's soteriology. While Christ as example is certainly a dominant and rhetorically salient aspect of the Letter, it must be understood alongside the shape of divine Christology and its concomitants, which stress other aspects of thought: the vicarious work of the Son, which uniquely arises from his divine person, achieving for his people what they could not do for themselves. Thus, it seems to me, this understanding of Christ's unique vicarious work, which is so connected to his divine person, must play a due and weighty role in shaping a balanced understanding of salvation in Hebrews, both in its achievement and its application.

In conclusion, the portrait of the Son in Hebrews is one in which his divinity is a central and necessary component. Its presence, in the thought of the Pastor, not only pervades the whole, but is salient to its most obvious features. To hear, then, the Pastor aright is to hear his word about God's final speech in his Son, and thereby to understand and encounter the final work of God in his Son, a work integrally related to his divine Person. And to hear and heed the Pastor's word is not only to understand that the Son is true God, but to begin to understand why, in fact, this must be the case.

Bibliography

Aalen, Sverre. "'Reign' and 'House' in the Kingdom of God in the Gospels." *NTS* 8 (1962): 215–40.
Adams, Edward. "The Cosmology of Hebrews." Pages 122–39 in *A Cloud of Witnesses: The Theology of Hebrews in Its Ancient Contexts*. Edited by Richard Bauckham, Daniel Driver, Trevor Hart and Nathan MacDonald. LNTS 387. London: T&T Clark, 2008.
Adams, Edward. *The Stars Will Fall from Heaven: Cosmic Catastrophe in the New Testament and Its World*. LNTS 347. London: T&T Clark, 2007.
Albani, Matthias. "'Wo sollte ein Haus sein, das Ihr mir bauen könntet?' (Jes 66,1): Schöpfung als Tempel Jhwhs?" Pages 37–56 in *Gemeinde ohne Tempel = Community without Temple: zur Substituierung und Transformation des Jerusalemer Tempels und seines Kults im Alten Testament, antiken Judentum und frühen Christentum*. Edited by Beate Ego, Armin Lange, Peter Pilhofer and Kathrin Ehlers. Tübingen: Mohr Siebeck, 1999.
Allen, David M. *Deuteronomy and Exhortation in Hebrews: A Study in Narrative Re-Presentation*. WUNT 2/238. Tübingen: Mohr Siebeck, 2008.
Allen, David M. "Who, What and Why? The Worship of the Firstborn in Hebrews 1:6." Pages 159–75 in *Mark, Manuscripts, and Monotheism: Essays in Honor of Larry Hurtado*. Edited by Chris Keith and Dieter T. Roth. LNTS 528. London: T&T Clark, 2015.
Allen, Leslie C. *Psalms 101–150*. WBC 21. Waco, TX: Word Books, 1983.
Andriessen, P. C. B. "La Teneur Judéo-Chrétienne de He 1:6 et 2:14b–3:2." *NovT* 18 (1976): 293–313.
Argyle, A. W. "The Causal Use of the Relative Pronouns in the Greek New Testament." *BT* 6 (1955): 165–9.
Attridge, Harold W. *The Epistle to the Hebrews: A Commentary on the Epistle to the Hebrews*. Hermeneia. Philadelphia, PA: Fortress Press, 1989.
Attridge, Harold W. "Giving Voice to Jesus: The Use of the Psalms in the New Testament." Pages 320–30 in *Essays on John and Hebrews*. WUNT 264. Tübingen: Mohr Siebeck, 2010.
Attridge, Harold W. "God in Hebrews." Pages 95–102 in *The Epistle to the Hebrews and Christian Theology*. Edited by Richard Bauckham, Daniel Driver and Trevor Hart. Grand Rapids, MI: Eerdmans, 2009.
Attridge, Harold W. "God in Hebrews: Urging Children to Heavenly Glory." Pages 308–19 in *Essays on John and Hebrews*. WUNT 264. Tübingen: Mohr Siebeck, 2010.
Attridge, Harold W. "Hebrews and Historical Interpretation: A Biblical Scholar's Response." Pages 202–12 in *Christology, Hermeneutics, and Hebrews: Profiles from the History of Interpretation*. Edited by Jon C. Laansma and Daniel J. Treier. LNTS 423. London: Bloomsbury, 2012.
Attridge, Harold W. "The Psalms in Hebrews." Pages 197–212 in *The Psalms in the New Testament*. Edited by Steve Moyise and M. J. J. Menken. The New Testament and the Scriptures of Israel. London: T&T Clark, 2004.

Ayres, Lewis. *Nicaea and Its Legacy: An Approach to Fourth-Century Trinitarian Theology.* Oxford: Oxford University Press, 2004.
Ayres, Lewis. "On Not Three People: The Fundamental Themes of Gregory of Nyssa's Trinitarian Theology as Seen In: To Ablabius: On Not Three Gods." Pages 15–44 in *Re-Thinking Gregory of Nyssa: Introduction—Gender, Trinitarian Analogies, and the Pedagogy of the Song.* Edited by Sarah Coakley. London: Wiley-Blackwell, 2002.
Backhaus, Knut. *Der Hebräerbrief: Übersetzt und erklärt von Knut Backhaus.* RNT 38. Regensburg: Friedrich Pustet, 2009.
Backhaus, Knut. *Der sprechende Gott: Gesammelte Studien zum Hebräerbrief.* WUNT 240. Tübingen: Mohr Siebeck, 2009.
Backhaus, Knut. "'Licht vom Licht': Die Präexistenz Christi im Hebräerbrief." Pages 77–100 in *Der sprechende Gott: Gesammelte Studien zum Hebräerbrief.* WUNT 240. Tübingen: Mohr Siebeck, 2009.
Bacon, Benjamin Wisner. "Heb I, 10—12 and the Septuagint Rendering of Ps 102, 23." *ZNW* 3 (1902): 280–5.
Barnes, Michel R. *The Power of God: Dunamis in Gregory of Nyssa's Trinitarian Theology.* Washington, DC: CUA Press, 2001.
Barrett, C. K. "The Christology of Hebrews." Pages 110–27 in *Who Do You Say That I Am?: Essays on Christology.* Edited by Mark Allan Powell, David R. Bauer and Jack Dean Kingsbury. Louisville, KY: W/JKP, 1999.
Barton, John. "*Déjà Lu*: Intertextuality, Method or Theory?" Pages 1–16 in *Reading Job Intertextually.* Edited by Katharine J. Dell and William L. Kynes. New York: Bloomsbury, 2013.
Bateman, Herbert W. *Early Jewish Hermeneutics and Hebrews 1:5-13: The Impact of Early Jewish Exegesis on the Interpretation of a Significant New Testament Passage.* American University Studies, 7. Theology and Religion. New York: Peter Lang, 1997.
Bates, Matthew W. *The Birth of the Trinity: Jesus, God, and Spirit in New Testament and Early Christian Interpretations of the Old Testament.* Oxford: Oxford University Press, 2015.
Bauckham, Richard. "The Divinity of Jesus Christ in the Epistle to the Hebrews." Pages 15–36 in *The Epistle to the Hebrews and Christian Theology.* Edited by Richard Bauckham, Daniel Driver and Trevor Hart. Grand Rapids, MI: Eerdmans, 2009.
Bauckham, Richard. *God Crucified: Monotheism and Christology in the New Testament.* Didsbury Lectures. Grand Rapids, MI: Eerdmans, 1999.
Bauckham, Richard. *Jesus and the God of Israel: God Crucified and Other Studies on the New Testament's Christology of Divine Identity.* Grand Rapids, MI: Eerdmans, 2009.
Bauckham, Richard. "Monotheism and Christology in Hebrews 1." Pages 167–85 in *Early Jewish and Christian Monotheism.* Edited by Loren T. Stuckenbruck and Wendy E. S. North. London: T&T Clark, 2004.
Bauckham, Richard "The 'Most High God' and the Nature of Early Jewish Monotheism." Pages 107–26 in *Israel's God and Rebecca's Children: Christology and Community in Early Judaism and Christianity: Essays in Honor of Larry W. Hurtado and Alan F. Segal.* Edited by David B. Capes, Larry W. Hurtado and Alan F. Segal. Waco, TX: Baylor University Press, 2007.
Bauckham, Richard. "The Throne of God and the Worship of Jesus." Pages 43–69 in *The Jewish Roots of Christological Monotheism: Papers from the St. Andrews Conference on the Historical Origins of the Worship of Jesus.* Edited by Carey C. Newman, James R. Davila and Gladys S. Lewis. JSJSup 63. Leiden: Brill, 1999.

Baugh, S. M., "Oath and Covenant in Hebrews and the Graeco-Roman World." Unpublished paper (2016).
Bird, Michael F. *Are You the One Who Is to Come?: The Historical Jesus and the Messianic Question.* Grand Rapids, MI: Baker Academic, 2009.
Bird, Michael F., ed. *How God Became Jesus: The Real Origins of Belief in Jesus' Divine Nature—A Response to Bart Ehrman.* Grand Rapids, MI: Zondervan, 2014.
Bird, Michael F. *Jesus the Eternal Son: Answering Adoptionist Christology.* Grand Rapids, MI: Eerdmans, 2017.
Bisping, Augustus. *Erklärung des Briefes an die Hebräer.* Münster: Aschendorff, 1854.
Blomberg, Craig L. " 'But We See Jesus': The Relationship between the Son of Man in Hebrews 2.6 and 2.9 and the Implications for English Translations." Pages 88–99 in *A Cloud of Witnesses: The Theology of Hebrews in Its Ancient Contexts.* Edited by Richard Bauckham, Daniel Driver, Trevor Hart and Nathan MacDonald. LNTS 387. London: T&T Clark, 2008.
Bockmuehl, Markus N. A. "Abraham's Faith in Hebrews 11." Pages 353–63 in *The Epistle to the Hebrews and Christian Theology.* Edited by Richard Bauckham, Daniel Driver and Trevor Hart. Grand Rapids, MI: Eerdmans, 2009.
Bousset, Wilhelm. *Kyrios Christos: A History of the Belief in Christ from the Beginnings of Christianity to Irenaeus.* Translated by J. Steely. Waco, TX: Baylor University Press, 2013. Originally Published 1903.
Braun, Johannes. *Commentarius in Epistolam Ad Hebraeos.* Amsterdam: H. & T. Boom, 1705.
Bruce, F. F. *The Book of the Acts.* NICNT. Rev. ed. Grand Rapids, MI: Eerdmans, 1988.
Bruce, F. F. *The Epistle to the Hebrews.* NICNT. Rev. ed. Grand Rapids, MI: Eerdmans, 1990.
Bruce, F. F. *This Is That.* Carlisle: Paternoster, 1968.
Brueggemann, Walter. *The Message of the Psalms: A Theological Commentary.* Augsburg Old Testament Studies. Minneapolis, MN: Augsburg Pub. House, 1984.
Buchanan, George Wesley. *To the Hebrews.* AB 36. Garden City, NY: Doubleday, 1972.
Büchsel, D. Friedrich. *Die Christologie des Hebräerbriefs.* Gütersloh: C. Berterlsmann, 1922.
Bunta, Silviu N. "The Convergence of Adamic and Merkabah Traditions in the Christology of Hebrews." Pages 277–96 in *Searching the Scriptures: Studies in Context and Intertextuality.* Edited by Craig A. Evans and Jeremiah J. Johnston. LSNT 543. London: Bloomsbury, 2015.
Caird, George Bradford. "The Exegetical Method of the Epistle to the Hebrews." *CJT* 5 (1959): 44–51.
Caird, George Bradford. "Son by Appointment." Pages 18–24 in *The New Testament Age.* Edited by William C. Weinrich. Macon, GA: Mercer University Press, 1984.
Calaway, Jared. *The Sabbath and the Sanctuary: Access to God in the Letter to the Hebrews and Its Priestly Context.* WUNT 349. Tübingen: Mohr Siebeck, 2013.
Calvin, Jean. *Commentaries on the Epistle of Paul the Apostle to the Hebrews.* Edinburgh: Calvin Translation Society, 1853.
Caneday, Ardel B. "The Eschatological World Already Subjected to the Son: The Oikumenh of Hebrews 1.6 and the Son's Enthronement." Pages 28–39 in *A Cloud of Witnesses: The Theology of Hebrews in Its Ancient Contexts.* Edited by Richard Bauckham, Daniel Driver, Trevor Hart and Nathan MacDonald. LNTS 387. London: T&T Clark, 2008.

Capes, David B. *Old Testament Yahweh Texts in Paul's Christology*. WUNT 2/47. Tübingen: J.C.B. Mohr, 1992.
Carr, G. Lloyd. *The Song of Solomon: An Introduction and Commentary*. TOTC. Leicester: Inter-Varsity Press, 1984.
Carson, D. A. *Jesus the Son of God: A Christological Title Often Overlooked, Sometimes Misunderstood, and Currently Disputed*. Wheaton, IL: Crossway, 2012.
Carson, D. A. "The Vindication of Imputation: On Fields of Discourse and Semantic Fields." Pages 46–78 in *Justification: What's at Stake in the Current Debates*. Edited by Daniel J. Treier and Mark Husbands. Downers Grove, IL: IVP, 2004.
Cassin, Matthieu. "Gregorie de Nysse, Sur la divinité du fils et de L'Esprit et sur Abraham." *Conférence* 29 (2009): 581–611.
Chan, Alan Kam-Yau. *Melchizedek Passages in the Bible: a Case Study for Inner-Biblical and Inter-Biblical Interpretation*. Warsaw: De Gruyter Open, 2016.
Chester, Andrew. *Messiah and Exaltation: Jewish Messianic and Visionary Traditions and New Testament Christology*. WUNT 207. Tübingen: Mohr Siebeck, 2007.
Chester, Andrew. "The Sibyl and the Temple." Pages 37–69 in *Templum Amicitiae: Essays on the Second Temple Presented to Ernst Bammel*. Edited by William Horbury. LNTS 48. Sheffield: Sheffield Academic Press, 1991.
Cockerill, Gareth Lee. *The Epistle to the Hebrews* NICNT. Grand Rapids, MI: Eerdmans, 2012.
Cockerill, Gareth Lee. "Hebrews 1:6: Source and Significance." *BBR* 9 (1999): 51–64.
Cockerill, Gareth Lee. "The Melchizedek Christology in Heb. 7: 1–28." PhD Diss., Union Theological Seminary, 1976.
Cockerill, Gareth Lee. "Melchizedek without Speculation: Hebrews 7.1–25 and Genesis 14.17–24." Pages 128–44 in *A Cloud of Witnesses: The Theology of Hebrews in Its Ancient Contexts*. Edited by Richard Bauckham, Daniel Driver, Trevor Hart and Nathan MacDonald. LNTS 387. London: T&T Clark, 2008.
Collins, Adela Yarbro. "Mark and His Readers: The Son of God among Jews." *HTR* 92 (1999): 393–408.
Collins, John J. *The Scepter and the Star: Messianism in Light of the Dead Sea Scrolls*. 2nd ed. Grand Rapids, MI: Eerdmans, 2010.
Compton, Jared. *Psalm 110 and the Logic of Hebrews*. LNTS 537. New York: Bloomsbury T&T Clark, 2015.
Conway-Jones, Ann. *Gregory of Nyssa's Tabernacle Imagery in Its Jewish and Christian Contexts*. OECS. Oxford: Oxford University Press, 2014.
Cook, John A. *Time and the Biblical Hebrew Verb: The Expression of Tense, Aspect, and Modality in Biblical Hebrew*. Linguistic Studies in Ancient West Semitic. Winona Lake, IN: Eisenbrauns, 2012.
Cortez, Felix H. "'The Anchor of the Soul That Enters within the Veil': The Ascension of the "Son" in the Letter to the Hebrews." PhD Diss., Andrews University, 2008.
Crüsemann, Frank. "Der neue Bund im Neuen Testament. Erwägungen zum Verständnis des Christusbundes in der Abendmahlstradition und im Hebräerbrief." Pages 47–60 in *Mincha. Festgabe für Rolf Rendtorff zum 75 Geburtstag*. Edited by E. Blum. Neukirchen-Vluyn: Neukirchener Verlag, 2000.
Cullmann, Oscar. *The Christology of the New Testament*. Philadelphia, PA: Westminster Press, 1959.
Culy, Martin M. "Double Case Constructions in Koine Greek." *JGRChJ* 6 (2009): 82–106.
D'Angelo, Mary Rose. *Moses in the Letter to the Hebrews*. SBLDS 42. Missoula, MT: Scholars Press, 1979.

Dahl, Nils A. "The Neglected Factor in New Testament Theology." *Reflections* 73 (1975): 5–8.
Dahl, Nils A. "Sources of Christological Language." Pages 113–36 in *Jesus the Christ: The Historical Origins of Christological Doctrine*. Edited by Donald Juel. Minneapolis, MN: Fortress Press, 1991.
Dan, Robert, and Antal Pirnat, eds. *Antitrinitarianism in the Second Half of the Sixteenth Century*. Budpest: Akademiái Kiadó, 1982.
De Jonge, Marinus, and Adam S. Van Der Woude. "11QMelchizedek and the New Testament." *NTS* 12 (1966): 301–26.
Delitzsch, Franz. *Biblical Commentary on the Psalms*. Vol 5. Grand Rapids,: Eerdmans, 2011.
Delitzsch, Franz. *Commentary on the Epistle to the Hebrews*. 2 vols. T&T Clark, 1874.
Delitzsch, Franz. "Must We Follow the New Testament Interpretation of Old Testament Texts?" *Old Testament Student* 6 (1886): 77–8.
Demarest, Bruce A. *A History of Interpretation of Hebrews 7, 1–10 from the Reformation to the Present*. BGBE 19. Tübingen: Mohr Siebeck, 1976.
DeSilva, David Arthur. *Perseverance in Gratitude: A Socio-Rhetorical Commentary on the Epistle "to the Hebrews."* Grand Rapids, MI: Eerdmans, 2000.
Dey, Lala Kalyan Kumar. *The Intermediary World and Patterns of Perfection in Philo and Hebrews*. SBLDS 35. Missoula: SBL Press, 1975.
Dillon, Matthew. "By Gods, Tongues, and Dogs: The Use of Oaths in Aristophanic Comedy." *Greece and Rome (Second Series)* 42 (1995): 135–51.
Dines, Jennifer M., and Michael A. Knibb. *The Septuagint*. London: T&T Clark, 2004.
Docherty, Susan E. *The Use of the Old Testament in Hebrews: a Case Study in Early Jewish Bible Interpretation*. WUNT 2/260. Tübingen: Mohr Siebeck, 2009.
Dogniez, C., and M. Harl. *Le Deutéronome*. La Bible D'Alexandrie vol. 5. Paris: Cerf, 1992.
Driver, S. R. *A Treatise on the Use of the Tenses in Hebrew and Some Other Syntactical Questions*. The Biblical Resource Series. Grand Rapids, MI: Eerdmans, 1998.
Dunn, James D. G. *Christology in the Making: a New Testament Inquiry into the Origins of the Doctrine of the Incarnation*. 2nd ed. Philadelphia, PA: Westminster Press, 1989.
Dunn, James D. G. *The Partings of the Ways: Between Christianity and Judaism and Their Significance for the Character of Christianity*. London: SCM Press, 2006.
Dunnill, John. *Covenant and Sacrifice in the Letter to the Hebrews*. SNTSMS 75. Cambridge: Cambridge University Press, 1992.
Dyer, Bryan R. "The Epistle to the Hebrews in Recent Research: Studies on the Author's Identity, His Use of the Old Testament, and Theology." *JGRChJ* 9 (2013): 104–31.
Easter, Matthew C. *Faith and the Faithfulness of Jesus in Hebrews*. SNTSMS 160. Cambridge: Cambridge University Press, 2014.
Ebert, Daniel J. "Wisdom in New Testament Christology: With Special Reference to Hebrews 1:1–4." PhD Diss., Trinity Evangelical Divinity School, 1998.
Edmondson, Stephen. *Calvin's Christology*. Cambridge: Cambridge University Press, 2004.
Ehrman, Bart D. *The Orthodox Corruption of Scripture: The Effect of Early Christological Controversies on the Text of the New Testament*. Oxford: Oxford University Press, 1996.
Ellingworth, Paul. *The Epistle to the Hebrews: a Commentary on the Greek Text*. NIGTC. Grand Rapids, MI: Eerdmans, 1993.
Ellingworth, Paul. " 'Like the Son of God': Form and Content in Hebrews 7, 1–10." *Bib* 64 (1983): 255–62.
England, Emma, and William John Lyons, eds. *Reception History and Biblical Studies: Theory and Practice*, OTS 615. New York: Bloomsbury T&T Clark, 2015.

Eslinger, Lyle M. *House of God or House of David: The Rhetoric of 2 Samuel 7*. JSOTSup 164. Sheffield: JSOT Press, 1994.

Evans, Robert. *Reception History, Tradition and Biblical Interpretation*. LNTS 510. London: Bloomsbury, 2014.

Fee, Gordon D. *Pauline Christology: An Exegetical-Theological Study*. Peabody, MA: Hendrickson, 2007.

Fesko, J. V. *The Covenant of Redemption: Origins, Development, and Reception*. Reformed Historical Theology 35. Göttingen: Vandenhoeck & Ruprecht, 2016.

Fitzmyer, Joseph A. "'Now This Melchizedek …' (Heb. 7:1)." Pages 221–43 in *Essays on the Semitic Background of the New Testament*. Grand Rapids, MI: Eerdmans, 1997.

Fitzmyer, Joseph A. "Melchizedek in the MT, LXX, and the NT." *Bib* 81 (2000): 63–69.

Fitzmyer, Joseph A. *The One Who Is to Come*. Grand Rapids, MI: Eerdmans, 2007.

Fletcher-Louis, Crispin H. T. *All the Glory of Adam: Liturgical Anthropology in the Dead Sea Scrolls*. STDJ 42. Leiden: Brill, 2002.

Fletcher-Louis, Crispin H. T. *Jesus Monotheism: Volume 1: Christological Origins: The Emerging Consensus and Beyond*. Eugene, OR: Wipf & Stock, 2015.

France, R. T. "The Writer of Hebrews as a Biblical Expositor." *TynBul* 47 (1996): 245–76.

Freedman, David Noel. "The Chronicler's Purpose." *CBQ* 23 (1961): 436–42.

Freedman, David Noel. "Temple without Hands." Pages 21–30 in *Temples and High Places in Biblical Times*. Jerusalem: Hebrew Union College, 1981.

Freedman, David Noel, and David Miano. "People of the New Covenant." Pages 7–13 in *The Concept of the Covenant in the Second Temple Period*. Edited by Stanley E. Porter and Jacqueline C. R. De Roo. JSJSup 71. Leiden: Brill, 2003.

Frey, Jörg. "Die alte und neue διαθήκη nach dem Hebäerbrief." Pages 263–310 in *Bund und Tora: zur theologischen Begriffsgeschichte in Alttestamentlicher, frühjüdischer und urchristlicher Tradition*. Edited by Friedrich Avemarie and Hermann Lichtenberger. Tübingen: Mohr Siebeck, 1996.

Gadamer, Hans-Georg. *Truth and Method*. 1st Englisg ed. London: Sheed & Ward, 1975.

Gaffin, Richard B. "The Priesthood of Christ." Pages 49–68 in *The Perfect Saviour*. Edited by Jonathan I. Griffiths. Nottingham: IVP, 2012.

Gaffin, Richard B. "A Sabbath Rest Still Awaits the People of God." Pages 33–51 in *Pressing toward the Mark: Essays Commemorating Fifty Years of the Orthodox Presbyterian Church*. Edited by Charles G. Dennison and Richard C. Gamble. Philadelphia, PA: Committee for the Historian of the OPC, 1986.

Garr, W. Randall. *In His Own Image and Likeness: Humanity, Divinity, and Monotheism*. Culture and History of the Ancient Near East 15. Leiden: Brill, 2003.

Gärtner, Bertil E. *The Temple and the Community in Qumran and the New Testament: a Comparative Study in the Temple Symbolism of the Qumran Texts and the New Testament*. SNTSMS 1. New York: Cambridge University Press, 1965.

Gaston, Lloyd. *No Stone on Another: Studies in the Significance of the Fall of Jerusalem in the Synoptic Gospels*. NovTSup 23. Leiden: Brill, 1970.

Gathercole, Simon J. *The Preexistent Son: Recovering the Christologies of Matthew, Mark, and Luke*. Grand Rapids, MI: Eerdmans, 2006.

Gheorghita, Radu. *The Role of the Septuagint in Hebrews: An Investigation of Its Influence with Special Consideration to the Use of Hab 2:3–4 in Heb 10:37–38*. WUNT 2/160. Tübingen: Mohr Siebeck, 2003.

Glasson, T. F. "'Plurality of Divine Persons' and the Quotations in Hebrews I. 6ff." *NTS* 12 (1966): 270–2.
Gräßer, Erich. "Mose und Jesus: Zur Auslegung von Hebr 3:1–6." *ZNW* 75 (1984): 2–23.
Gräßer, Erich. *Der Alte Bund im Neuen: exegetische Studien zur Israelfrage im Neuen Testament*. WUNT 35. Tübingen: J.C.B. Mohr, 1985.
Gräßer, Erich. *An die Hebräer*. 3 vols. Zürich: Neukirchener Verlag, 1990.
Greer, Rowan A. *The Captain of Our Salvation: a Study in the Patristic Exegesis of Hebrews*. BBET 15. Tübingen: Mohr Siebeck, 1973.
Greer, Rowan A. "The Jesus of Hebrews and the Christ of Chalcedon." Pages 231–50 in *Reading the Epistle to the Hebrews: a Resource for Students*. Edited by Eric Farrel Mason and Kevin B. McCruden. Atlanta, GA: SBL Press, 2011.
Griffiths, Jonathan I. *Hebrews and Divine Speech*. LNTS 507. London: Bloomsbury, 2015.
Gunnlaugur, A. Jánsson. *The Image of God: Genesis 1:26–28 in a Century of Old Testament Research*. ConBOT 26. Stockholm, Sweden: Almqvist & Wiksell, 1988.
Guthrie, George H. "Hebrews in Its First Century Contexts: Recent Research." Pages 414–43 in *The Face of New Testament Studies: a Survey of Recent Research*. Edited by Scot McKnight and Grant R. Osborne. Grand Rapids, MI: Baker Academic, 2004.
Guthrie, George H. *Hebrews*. NIVAC. Grand Rapids, MI: Zondervan, 1998.
Guthrie, George H. "Hebrews." Pages 952–95 in *Commentary on the New Testament Use of the Old Testament*. Edited by G. K. Beale and D. A. Carson. Grand Rapids, MI: Baker Academic, 2007.
Guthrie, George H. "Hebrews' Use of the Old Testament: Recent Trends in Research." *CurBS* 1 (2003): 271–94.
Guthrie, George H., and Russell D. Quinn. "A Discourse Analysis of the Use of Psalm 8:4–6 in Hebrews 2:5–9." *JETS* 49 (2006): 235–46.
Haber, Susan. "From Priestly Torah to Christ Cultus: The Re-Vision of Covenant and Cult in Hebrews." *JSNT* 28 (2005): 105–24.
Hahn, Scott W. "A Broken Covenant and the Curse of Death: A Study of Hebrews 9: 15–22." *CBQ* 66 (2004): 416–36.
Hahn, Scott W. "Canon, Cult and Covenant." Pages 207–29 in *Canon and Biblical Interpretation*. Edited by Craig G. Bartholomew, Scott Hahn, Robin Parry, Christopher Seitz and Al Wolters. Scripture and Hermeneutics Series. Grand Rapids, MI: Zondervan, 2006.
Hahn, Scott W. "Covenant in the Old and New Testaments: Some Current Research (1994–2004)." *CurBS* 3 (2005): 263–92.
Hamm, Dennis. "Faith in the Epistle to the Hebrews: The Jesus Factor." *CBQ* 52 (1990): 270–91.
Hanson, Anthony Tyrrell. *Jesus Christ in the Old Testament*. London: SPCK, 1965.
Hardy, Edward Rochie. *Christology of the Later Fathers*. Philadelphia, PA: Westminster John Knox Press, 1954.
Harris, Dana M. "The Eternal Inheritance in Hebrews: The Appropriation of the Old Testament Inheritance Motif by the Author of Hebrews." PhD Diss., Trinity Evangelical Divinity School, 2009.
Harris, Murray J. *Colossians & Philemon*. Exegetical Guide to the Greek New Testament. Grand Rapids, MI: Eerdmans, 1991.
Harris, Murray J. *Jesus as God: The New Testament Use of Theos in Reference to Jesus*. Grand Rapids, MI: Baker, 1992.

Harris, Murray J. "The Translation and Significance of Ὁ Θεος in Hebrews 1:8–9." *TynBul* 36 (1985): 129–62.
Hart, Trevor A. *Making Good: Creation, Creativity, and Artistry*. Waco, TX: Baylor University Press, 2014.
Hatina, Thomas R. "Intertextuality and Historical Criticism in New Testament Studies: Is There a Relationship?" *BibInt* 7 (1999): 28–43.
Hay, David M. *Glory at the Right Hand: Psalm 110 in Early Christianity*. SBLMS 18. Nashville, TN: Abingdon Press, 1973.
Hays, Richard B. *Echoes of Scripture in the Letters of Paul*. New Haven, CT: Yale University Press, 1989.
Hengel, Martin. "Psalm 110 und die Erhöhung des Auferstandenen zur Rechten Gottes." Pages 43–76 in *Anfänge der Christologie: Festschrift für Ferdinand Hahn zum 65. Geburtstag*. Edited by Cilliers Breytenbach and Henning Paulsen. Göttingen: Vanderhoeck & Ruprecht, 1991.
Hengel, Martin. *Studies in Early Christology*. London: T&T Clark, 2004.
Henrichs-Tarasenkova, Nina. *Luke's Christology of Divine Identity*. LNTS 542. London: Bloomsbury, 2015.
Hibbert, Giles. "Mystery and Metaphysics in the Trinitarian Theology of Saint Thomas." *ITQ* 31 (1964): 187–213.
Hill, Wesley. *Paul and the Trinity: Persons, Relations, and the Pauline Letters*. Grand Rapids, MI: Eerdmans, 2015.
Hofius, Otfried. "Inkarnation und Opfertod Jesu nach Hebr 10, 19f." Pages 132–41 in *Der Ruf Jesu und die Antwort der Gemeinde: Exegetische Untersuchungen Joachim Jeremias zum 70. Geburtstag Gewidmet von Seinen Schülern*. Edited by Eduard Lohse. Göttingen: Vandenhoeck & Ruprecht, 1970.
Hofius, Otfried. *Katapausis: die Vorstellung vom endzeitlichen Ruheort im Hebräerbrief*. Tübingen: Mohr Siebeck, 1970.
Hofmann, Johann C. K. *Der Schriftbeweis: ein theologischer Versuch*. vol. 2. CH Beck, 1860.
Holmes, Stephen R. *The Quest for the Trinity: The Doctrine of God in Scripture, History and Modernity*. Downers Grove, IL: IVP, 2012.
Horbury, William. "Herod's Temple and 'Herod's Days.'" Pages 107–49 in *Templum Amicitiae: Essays on the Second Temple Presented to Ernst Bammel*. Edited by William Horbury. LNTS 48. Sheffield: Sheffield Academic Press, 1991.
Horbury, William. *Jewish Messianism and the Cult of Christ*. London: SCM Press, 1998.
Horbury, William. *Messianism among Jews and Christians: Twelve Biblical and Historical Studies*. London: T&T Clark, 2003.
Horbury, William, Markus N. A. Bockmuehl and James Carleton Paget. *Redemption and Resistance: The Messianic Hopes of Jews and Christians in Antiquity*. London: T&T Clark, 2007.
Horton, Fred L. *The Melchizedek Tradition: a Critical Examination of the Sources to the Fifth Century A.D. and in the Epistle to the Hebrews*. SNTSMS 30. Cambridge: Cambridge University Press, 1976.
Hughes, Philip Edgcumbe. *A Commentary on the Epistle to the Hebrews*. NICNT. Grand Rapids, MI: Eerdmans, 1977.
Hurst, L. D. "The Christology of Hebrews 1 and 2." Pages 151–64 in *The Glory of Christ in the New Testament: In Memory of George Bradford Caird*. Edited by L. D. Hurst and N. T. Wright. Oxford: Oxford University Press, 1987.

Hurst, L. D. *The Epistle to the Hebrews: Its Background of Thought*. SNTSMS 65. Cambridge: Cambridge University Press, 1990.
Hurtado, Larry W. *Ancient Jewish Monotheism and Early Christian Jesus-Devotion: The Context and Character of Christological Faith*. Waco, TX: Baylor University Press, 2017.
Hurtado, Larry W. "The Binitarian Shape of Early Christian Worship." Pages 189–213 in *The Jewish Roots of Christological Monotheism: Papers from the St. Andrews Conference on the Historical Origins of the Worship of Jesus4*. Edited by Carey C. Newman, James R. Davila and Gladys S. Lewis. JSJSup 63. Leiden: Brill, 1999.
Hurtado, Larry W. *How on Earth Did Jesus Become a God?: Historical Questions About Earliest Devotion to Jesus*. Grand Rapids, MI: Eerdmans, 2005.
Hurtado, Larry W. *Lord Jesus Christ: Devotion to Jesus in Earliest Christianity*. Grand Rapids, MI: Eerdmans, 2003.
Hurtado, Larry W. *One God, One Lord: Early Christian Devotion and Ancient Jewish*. London: T&T Clark, 1988.
Hurtado, Larry W. *What Do We Mean by First Century Jewish Monotheism?* SBLSP 32. Atlanta, GA: SBL Press, 1993.
Isaacs, Marie. *Sacred Space: An Approach to the Theology of the Epistle to the Hebrews*. Edinburgh: T&T Clark, 1992.
Janse, S. *"You Are My Son": The Reception History of Psalm 2 in Early Judaism and the Early Church*. CBET 51. Leuven: Peeters, 2009.
Jenson, Robert W. *Systematic Theology*. 2 Vols. New York: Oxford University Press, 1997.
Jewett, Robert. *Letter to Pilgrims: A Commentary on the Epistle to the Hebrews*. New York: Pilgrim Press, 1981.
Jipp, Joshua W. "The Son's Entrance into the Heavenly World: The Soteriological Necessity of the Scriptural Catena in Hebrews 1.5–14." *NTS* 56 (2010): 557–75.
Jobes, Karen H. "The Function of Paranomasia in Hebrews 10:15–17." *TrinJ* 13 (1992): 181–91.
Jobes, Karen H. "Rhetorical Achievement in the Hebrews 10 'Misquote' of Psalm 40." *Bib* 72 (1991): 387–96.
Johnson, Luke Timothy. *Hebrews: A Commentary*. NTL. Louisville, KY: W/JKP, 2006.
Joosten, Jan. *The Verbal System of Biblical Hebrew: A New Synthesis Elaborated on the Basis of Classical Prose*. Jerusalem: Simor, 2012.
Juel, Donald. *Messiah and Temple: The Trial of Jesus in the Gospel of Mark*. SBLDS 31. Missoula, MT: Scholars Press, 1977.
Karfikovà, Lenka, Scot Douglass, Johannes Zachhuber, Stuart George Hall and Gregory, eds. *Gregory of Nyssa, Contra Eunomium II: An English Version with Supporting Studies: Proceedings of the 10th International Colloquium on Gregory of Nyssa*, Supplements to Vigiliae Christianae, vol. 82. Leiden: Brill, 2007.
Käsemann, Ernst. *Das wandernde Gottesvolk: eine Untersuchung zum Hebräerbrief*. Göttingen: Vandenhoeck & Ruprecht, 1961.
Käsemann, Ernst. *The Wandering People of God: An Investigation of the Letter to the Hebrews*. Minneapolis, MN: Augsburg Pub. House, 1984.
Keating, Daniel. "Thomas Aquinas and the Epistle to the Hebrews: 'The Excellence of Christ.'" Pages 85–99 in *Christology, Hermeneutics, and Hebrews: Profiles from the History of Interpretation*. Edited by Jon C. Laansma and Daniel J. Treier. LNTS 423. London: Bloomsbury, 2012.
Kerr, Alan. *The Temple of Jesus' Body: The Temple Theme in the Gospel of John*. LNTS 220. London: Bloomsbury, 2002.

Kibbe, Michael. "Is It Finished? When Did It Start? Hebrews, Priesthood, and Atonement in Biblical, Systematic, and Historical Perspective." *JTS* 65 (2014): 25–61.

Kilby, Karen. "Perichoresis and Projection: Problems with Social Doctrines of the Trinity." *New Blackfriars* 81 (2000): 432–45.

Kilgallen, John J. "The Function of Stephen's Speech (Acts 7, 2–53)." *Bib* 70 (1989): 173–93.

Kim, Ju-Won. "Old Testament Quotations within the Context of Stephen's Speech in Acts." PhD Diss., Pretoria University, 2007.

Kirk, J. R. Daniel. *A Man Attested by God: The Human Jesus of the Synoptic Gospels*. Grand Rapids, MI: Eerdmans, 2016.

Kirk, J. R. Daniel. *Unlocking Romans: Resurrection and the Justification of God*. Grand Rapids, MI: Eerdmans, 2008.

Kistemaker, Simon. "The Psalm Citations in the Epistle to the Hebrews." Proefschrift, Vrije Universiteit, 1961.

Klijn, A. F. J. "Stephen's Speech–Acts VII. 2–53." *NTS* 4 (1957): 25–31.

Knowles, Michael P. "Scripture, History, Messiah: Scriptural Fulfilment and the Fullness of Time in Matthew's Gospel." Pages 59–82 in *Hearing the Old Testament in the New Testament*. Edited by Stanley E. Porter. Grand Rapids, MI: Eerdmans, 2006.

Knox, John. *The Humanity and Divinity of Christ: A Study of Pattern in Christology*. Cambridge: Cambridge University Press, 1967.

Koester, Craig R. *The Dwelling of God: The Tabernacle in the Old Testament, Intertestamental Jewish Literature, and the Old Testament*. CBQMS 22. Washington, DC: Catholic Biblical Association of America, 1989.

Koester, Craig R. "Hebrews, Rhetoric, and the Future of Humanity." *CBQ* 64 (2002): 103–23.

Koester, Craig R. *Hebrews: A New Translation with Introduction and Commentary*. AB 36. New York: Doubleday, 2001.

Kögel, J. "Der Begriff *Teleioun* im Hebraerbrief im Zussamenhang mit dem neutestamentlichen Sprachgebrauch." Pages 37–68 in *Theologische Studien Fur M. Kahler*. Leipzig: Deichert, 1905.

Kögel, J. *Der Sohn und die Söhne: Eine exegetische Studie zu Hebräer 2, 5–18*. Gütersloh: C. Bertelsman, 1904.

Köstenberger, Andreas J., and Scott R. Swain. *Father, Son, and Spirit: The Trinity and John's Gospel*. NSBT. Nottingham: IVP, 2008.

Kraus, Hans-Joachim. *Psalms 60–150: a Commentary*. Minneapolis, MN: Fortress Press, 1993.

Kurianal, James. *Jesus Our High Priest: Ps. 110,4 as the Substructure of Heb 5,1–7,28*. Europäische Hochschulschriften Reihe XXIII, Theologie. Frankfurt am Main: Peter Lang, 2000.

Laansma, Jon. "The Cosmology of Hebrews." Pages 125–43 in *Cosmology and New Testament Theology*. Edited by Jonathan T. Pennington and Sean M. McDonough. London: T&T Clark, 2008.

Laansma, Jon. "Hidden Stories in Hebrews: Cosmology and Theology." Pages 28–39 in *A Cloud of Witnesses: The Theology of Hebrews in Its Ancient Contexts*. Edited by Richard Bauckham, Daniel Driver, Trevor Hart and Nathan MacDonald. LNTS 387. London: T&T Clark, 2008.

Laansma, Jon. *"I Will Give You Rest": The "Rest" Motif in the New Testament with Specal Reference to Mt 11 and Heb 3–4*. WUNT 98. Tübingen: Mohr Siebeck, 1997.

Laato, Antti. *A Star Is Rising: The Historical Development of the Old Testament Royal Ideology and the Rise of the Jewish Messianic Expectations*. University of South Florida

International Studies in Formative Christianity and Judaism. Atlanta, GA: Scholars Press, 1997.
Lane, William L. *Hebrews 1–8*. WBC 47a. Nashville, TN: Thomas Nelson, 1991.
Lane, William L. *Hebrews 9–13*. WBC 47b. Nashville, TN: Thomas Nelson, 1991.
Larson, Richard K. "On the Double Object Construction." *Linguistic Inquiry* (1988): 335–91.
Layton, Scott C. "Christ over His House (Hebrews 3.6) and Hebrew." *NTS* 37 (1991): 473–7.
Lee, Aquila H. I. *From Messiah to Preexistent Son*. WUNT 2/192. Tübingen: Mohr Siebeck, 2005.
Leemans, Johan, ed. *Gregory of Nyssa: Contra Eunomium III: An English Translation with Commentary and Supporting Studies: Proceedings of the 12th International Colloquium on Gregory of Nyssa (Leuven, 14–17 September 2010)*, Supplements to Vigiliae Christianae, vol. 124. Leiden: Brill, 2014.
Lehne, Susanne. *The New Covenant in Hebrews*. SNTSMS 44. Cambridge: Cambridge University Press, 1990.
Levenson, Jon D. "The Davidic Covenant and Its Modern Interpreters." *CBQ* 41 (1979): 205–19.
Levenson, Jon D. *The Death and Resurrection of the Beloved Son: The Transformation of Child Sacrifice in Judaism and Christianity*. New Haven, CT: Yale University Press, 1993.
Levering, Matthew. "God and Greek Philosophy in Contemporary Biblical Scholarship." *JTI* 4 (2010): 169–85.
Levering, Matthew. *Scripture and Metaphysics: Aquinas and the Renewal of Trinitarian Theology*. Challenges in Contemporary Theology. Malden, MA: Blackwell, 2004.
Lim, Timothy H. "Deuteronomy in the Judaism of the Second Temple Period." Pages 6–26 in *Deuteronomy in the New Testament: The New Testament and the Scriptures of Israel*. London: T&T Clark, 2007.
Lincicum, David. *Paul and the Early Jewish Encounter with Deuteronomy*. WUNT 284. Tübingen: Mohr Siebeck, 2010.
Lincoln, Andrew T. *Hebrews: a Guide*. London: T&T Clark, 2006.
Lindars, Barnabas. *The Theology of the Letter to the Hebrews*. Cambridge: Cambridge University Press, 1991.
Lindbeck, George A. *The Nature of Doctrine: Religion and Theology in a Postliberal Age*. 25th anniversary ed. Louisville, KY: W/JKP, 2009.
Loader, William R. G. *Sohn und Hoherpriester: eine traditionsgeschichtliche Untersuchung zur Christologie des Hebräerbriefes*. WMANT 53. Neukirchen-Vluyn: Neukirchener Verlag, 1981.
Long, D. Stephen. *Hebrews*. Belief: a Theological Commentary on the Bible. Louisville, KY: W/JKP, 2011.
Lundbom, Jack R. *Deuteronomy: a Commentary*. Grand Rapids, MI: Eerdmans, 2013.
Lunn, Nicholas P. *Word-Order Variation in Biblical Hebrew Poetry: Differentiating Pragmatics and Poetics*. Carlisle: Paternoster Press, 2006.
Luz, Ulrich. *Das Evangelium nach Matthäus*. EKK. 3 Vol Neukirchen-Vluyn: Neukirchener Verlag, 2002.
Luz, Ulrich. *Matthew 1–7: A Commentary*. Hermeneia. Rev. ed. Minneapolis, MN: Fortress Press, 2007.

MacCormack, Bruce L. "The Identity of the Son: Karl Barth's Exegesis of Hebrews 1.1–4." Pages 155–72 in *Christology, Hermeneutics, and Hebrews: Profiles from the History of Interpretation*. Edited by Jon C. Laansma and Daniel J. Treier. LNTS 423. London: Bloomsbury, 2012.

MacCormack, Bruce L. "'With Loud Cries and Tears': The Humanity of the Son in the Epistle to the Hebrews." Pages 55–86 in *The Epistle to the Hebrews and Christian Theology*. Edited by Richard Bauckham, Daniel Driver, Trevor Hart and Nathan MacDonald. Grand Rapids, MI: Eerdmans, 2009.

Mackie, Scott D. "Confession of the Son of God in Hebrews." *NTS* 53 (2007): 114–29.

Mackie, Scott D. "Confession of the Son of God in the Exordium of Hebrews." *JSNT* 30 (2008): 437–53.

Manson, Thomas W. *The Epistle to the Hebrews: An Historical and Theological Reconsideration; the Baird Lecture, 1949*. London: Hodder & Stoughton, 1951.

Manzi, Franco. "La fede degli uomini e la singolare relazione filiale di gesù con Dio nell'Epistola agli Ebrei." *Bib* 81 (2000): 32–62.

Manzi, Franco. *Melchisedek e l'Angelologia nell'Epistola agli Ebrei e a Qumran*. AnBib 136. Roma: Pontificio Istituto Biblico, 1997.

Marshall, I. Howard. "Soteriology in Hebrews." Pages 252–77 in *The Epistle to the Hebrews and Christian Theology*. Edited by Richard Bauckham, Daniel Driver and Trevor Hart. Grand Rapids, MI: Eerdmans, 2009.

Martyr, Justin. *The Fathers of the Church*. Translated by Thomas B. Falls. Vol. 6. Christian Heritage, 1949.

Mason, Eric Farrel. *"You Are a Priest Forever": Second Temple Jewish Messianism and the Priestly Christology of the Epistle to the Hebrews*. STDJ 74. Leiden: Brill, 2008.

Mason, Eric Farrel, and Kevin B. McCruden. *Reading the Epistle to the Hebrews: a Resource for Students*. SBLRBS. Atlanta, GA: SBL Press, 2011.

Maspero, Giulio. *Trinity and Man: Gregory of Nyssa's Ad Ablabium*. Leiden: Brill, 2007.

Mateo Seco, Lucas F., and Giulio Maspero. *The Brill Dictionary of Gregory of Nyssa*. Supplements to Vigiliae Christianae, vol. 99. Leiden: Brill, 2010.

Mays, James Luther. *Psalms*. Interpretation, a Bible Commentary for Teaching and Preaching. Louisville, KY: John Knox Press, 1994.

McCarter, P. Kyle. *II Samuel: A New Translation with Introduction, Notes, and Commentary*. AB 9. Garden City, NY: Doubleday, 1984.

McConville, J. G. *Deuteronomy*. Apollos Old Testament Commentary 5. Leicester: Apollos, 2002.

McCruden, Kevin B. "Christ's Perfection in Hebrews: Divine Beneficence as an Exegetical Key to Hebrews 2: 10." *BibRes* 47 (2002): 40–62.

McCruden, Kevin B. *Solidarity Perfected: Beneficent Christology in the Epistle to the Hebrews*. BZNW 159. Berlin: Walter de Gruyter, 2008.

Meier, John P. "Structure and Theology in Heb 1, 1–14." *Bib* 66 (1985): 168–89.

Meier, John P. "Symmetry and Theology in the Old Testament Citations of Heb 1, 5–14." *Bib* 66 (1985): 504–33.

Meyer, Ben F. *The Aims of Jesus*. London: SCM, 1979.

Michel, Otto. *Der Brief an die Hebräer*. KEK 13. Göttingen: Vandenhoeck & Ruprecht, 1966.

Milik, J. T. "Milki-Sedeq et Milki-Reša dans Les Anciens Éscrits Juifs et Chrétiens." *JJS* 23 (1972): 130–7.

Miller, Cynthia L. *The Representation of Speech in Biblical Hebrew Narrative: a Linguistic Analysis*. Harvard Semitic Museum Publications. Atlanta, GA: Scholars Press, 1996.

Milligan, George. *The Theology of the Epistle to the Hebrews: With a Critical Introduction*. Edinburgh: T&T Clark, 1899.

Moffatt, James. *A Critical and Exegetical Commentary on the Epistle to the Hebrews*. New York: Scribners, 1924.

Moffitt, David M. *Atonement and the Logic of Resurrection in the Epistle to the Hebrews*. NovTSup 141. Leiden: Brill, 2011.

Moffitt, David M. "'If Another Priest Arises': Jesus' Resurrection and the High Priestly Christology of Hebrews." Pages 68–79 in *A Cloud of Witnesses: The Theology of Hebrews in Its Ancient Contexts*. Edited by Richard Bauckham, Daniel Driver, Trevor Hart and Nathan MacDonald. LNTS 387. London: T&T Clark, 2008.

Moffitt, David M. "Jesus' Heavenly Sacrifice in Early Christian Reception of Hebrews: A Survey." *JTS* 68 (2017): 46–71.

Montefiore, Hugh. *A Commentary on the Epistle to the Hebrews*. HNTC. New York: Harper & Row, 1964.

Motyer, Stephen. "The Psalm Quotations of Hebrews 1: A Hermeneutic-Free Zone?." *TynBul* 50 (1999): 3–22.

Moule, C. F. D. *The Birth of the New Testament*. BNTC (Companion Volume). 2nd ed. London: Black, 1966.

Moule, C. F. D. *The Origin of Christology*. Cambridge: Cambridge University Press, 1977.

Moule, C. F. D. "Sanctuary and Sacrifice in the Church of the New Testament." *JTS* 1 (1950): 29–41.

Moyise, Steve. "Intertextuality and Biblical Studies: a Review." *Verbum et Ecclesia* 23 (2002): 418–31.

Moyise, Steve. "Intertextuality and Historical Approaches to the Use of Scripture in the New Testament." Pages 23–32 in *Reading the Bible Intertextually*. Edited by Richard B. Hays, Stefan Alkier and Leroy Andrew Huizenga. Waco, TX: Baylor University Press, 2009.

Moyise, Steve. "Intertextuality and the Study of the Old Testament in the New Testament." Pages 14–41 in *The Old Testament in the New Testament: Essays in Honour of J. L. North*. Edited by Steve Moyise and J. L. North. JSNTSup 189. Sheffield: Sheffield Academic Press, 2000.

Muir, Stephen. "The Anti-Imperial Rhetoric of Hebrews 1.3: Χαρακτηρ as a 'Double-Edged Sword.'" Pages 170–86 in *The Epistle to the Hebrews and Christian Theology*. Edited by Richard Bauckham, Daniel Driver, Trevor Hart and Nathan MacDonald. Grand Rapids, MI: Eerdmans, 2009.

Muller, Richard A. "Divine Covenants, Absolute and Conditional: John Cameron and the Early Orthodox Development of Reformed Covenant Theology." *MAJT* 17 (2006): 11–56.

Muller, Richard A. "Toward the *Pactum Salutis*: Locaing the Origins of a Concept." *MAJT* 18 (2007): 11–65.

Murphy, Francesca Aran. *God Is Not a Story: Realism Revisited*. Oxford: Oxford University Press, 2007.

Neef, Hanz-Dieter. "Aspekte altestamentlicher Bundestheologie." Pages 1–24 in *Bund und Tora: zur theologischen Begriffsgeschichte in alttestamentlicher, frühjüdischer und urchristlicher Tradition*. Edited by Friedrich Avemarie and Hermann Lichtenberger. WUNT 92. Tübingen: Mohr Siebeck, 1996.

Neyrey, Jerome H. "'Without Beginning of Days or End of Life' (Hebrews 7:3): Topos for a True Deity." *CBQ* 53 (1991): 439–55.
Novenson, Matthew V. *The Grammar of Messianism: An Ancient Jewish Political Idiom and Its Users*. New York: Oxford University Press, 2016.
Nyssa, Gregory of. *Sermones, Volume 2 Pars iii*. Gregorii Nysseni Opera Vol. 12. Leiden: Brill, 1996.
O'Brien, Peter Thomas. *The Letter to the Hebrews*. Pillar New Testament Commentary. Grand Rapids, MI: Eerdmans, 2010.
O'Connor, Michael Patrick. *Hebrew Verse Structure*. Winona Lake, IN: Eisenbrauns, 1997.
Olofsson, Staffan. *As a Deer Longs for Flowing Streams: A Study of the Septuagint Version of Psalm 42-43 in Its Relation to the Hebrew Text*. DSI 1. Göttingen: Vandenhoeck & Ruprecht, 2011.
Olofsson, Staffan. "Studying the Word Order of the Septuagint. Questions and Possibilities." *SJOT* 10 (1996): 217–37.
Owen, John. *An Exposition of the Epistle to the Hebrews*. 8 vols. Grand Rapids, MI: Baker Books, 1980.
Paul, M. J. "The Order of Melchizedek (Ps 110:4 and Heb 7:3)." *WTJ* 49 (1987): 195–211.
Peeler, Amy L. B. *You Are My Son: The Family of God in the Epistle to the Hebrews*. LNTS 486. London: Bloomsbury, 2014.
Peppard, Michael. *The Son of God in the Roman World: Divine Sonship in Its Social and Political Context*. Oxford: Oxford University Press, 2011.
Perrin, Nicholas. *Jesus the Temple*. London: SPCK, 2011.
Peterson, David. *Hebrews and Perfection: An Examination of the Concept of Perfection in the "Epistle to the Hebrews."* SNTSMS 47. Cambridge: Cambridge University Press, 1982.
Phang, Sara Elise. *The Marriage of Roman Soldiers (13 BC-AD 235): Law and Family in the Imperial Army*. Columbia Studies in the Classical Tradition 24. Leiden: Brill, 2001.
Pierce, Madison N. "Divine Discourse in the Epistle to the Hebrews." PhD Diss., University of Durham, 2017.
Pomykala, Kenneth. *The Davidic Dynasty Tradition in Early Judaism: Its History and Significance for Messianism*. Early Judaism and Its Literature. Atlanta, GA: Scholars Press, 1995.
Porter, Stanley E. "The Use of the Old Testament in the New Testament: a Brief Comment on Method and Terminology." Pages 79–97 in *Early Christian Interpretation of the Scriptures of Israel: Investigations and Proposals*. Edited by Craig A. Evans and James A. Sanders. JSNTSup 148. Sheffield: Sheffield Academic Press, 1997.
Rahlfs, A., ed. *Psalmi Cum Odis*. Vol. X, Septuagina: Societatis Scientiarum Gottingensis, vol. X. Göttingen: Vanderhoeck and Ruprecht, 1931.
Rainbow, Paul. "Melchizedek as a Messiah at Qumran." *BBR* 7 (1997): 179–94.
Rascher, Angela. *Schriftauslegung und Christologie im Hebräerbrief*. BZNW 153. Berlin: Walter de Gruyter, 2007.
Reicke, Bo. *Glaube und Leben der Urgemeinde: Bemerkungen zu Apg. 1–7*. Zürich: Zwingli-Verlag, 1957.
Rhee, Victor. "Christology and the Concept of Faith in Hebrews 5:11–6:20." *JETS* 43 (2000): 83–96.
Rhee, Victor. *Faith in Hebrews: Analysis within the Context of Christology, Eschatology, and Ethics*. Studies in Biblical Literature 19. New York: Peter Lang, 2001.

Ribbens, Benjamin J. *Levitical Sacrifice and Heavenly Cult in Hebrews*. BZNW 222. Berlin: De Gruyter, 2016.
Richardson, Christopher A. *Pioneer and Perfecter of Faith: Jesus' Faith as the Climax of Israel's History in the Epistle to the Hebrews*. WUNT 338. Tübingen: Mohr Siebeck, 2012.
Riggenbach, Eduard. *Der Brief an die Hebräer*. KNT 14. Leipzig: Deichert, 1922.
Robinson, Robert. *A Plea for the Divinity of Our Lord Jesus Christ*. Cambridge: Fletcher & Hodson, 1776.
Rogland, M. F. *Alleged Non-Past Uses of Qatal in Classical Hebrew*. Leiden: Van Gorcum, 2001.
Rose, Christian. "Verheissung und Erfüllung zum Verständnis von Epangelia im Hebräerbrief." *Biblische Zeitschrift* 33 (1989): 60–80, 178–91.
Rowe, C. Kavin. "Biblical Pressure and Trinitarian Hermeneutics." *Pro Ecclesia* 11 (2002): 295–312.
Rowe, C. Kavin. "The Trinity in the Letters of St. Paul and Hebrews." Pages 41–53 in *The Oxford Handbook of the Trinity*. Edited by Gilles Emery and Matthew Levering. Oxford: Oxford University Press, 2011.
Rowland, C. C. "The Second Temple: Focus of Ideological Struggle?." Pages 175–98 in *Templum Amicitiae: Essays on the Second Temple Presented to Ernst Bammel*. Edited by William Horbury. LNTS 48. Sheffield: Sheffield Academic Press, 1991.
Runge, Steven E. *Discourse Grammar of the Greek New Testament: a Practical Introduction for Teaching and Exegesis*. Lexham Bible Reference Series. Peabody, MA: Hendrickson, 2010.
Sanders, E. P. *Jesus and Judaism*. Philadelphia, PA: Fortress Press, 1985.
Sargent, Benjamin. *David Being a Prophet: The Contingency of Scripture Upon History in the New Testament*. BZNW 207. Berlin: Walter de Gruyter 207, 2014.
Schenck, Kenneth L. "A Celebration of the Enthroned Son: The Catena of Hebrews 1." *JBL* 120 (2001): 469–85.
Schenck, Kenneth L. *Cosmology and Eschatology in Hebrews: The Setting of the Sacrifice*. SNTSMS 143. Cambridge: Cambridge University Press, 2007.
Schenck, Kenneth L. "'God Has Spoken': Hebrews' Theology of the Scriptures." Pages 321–54 in *The Epistle to the Hebrews and Christian Theology*. Edited by Richard Bauckham, Daniel Driver and Trevor Hart. Grand Rapids, MI: Eerdmans, 2009.
Schenck, Kenneth L. "Keeping His Appointment: Creation and Enthronement in Hebrews." *JSNT* 66 (1997): 91–117.
Schenck, Kenneth L. "The Worship of Jesus among Early Christians: The Evidence of Hebrews." Pages 114–24 in *Jesus and Paul*. Edited by B. J. Oropeza, C. K. Robertson and Douglas C. Mohrmann. LNTS 514. London: T&T Clark, 2009.
Schierse, Franz Joseph. *Verheissung und Heilsvollendung: zur theologischen Grundfrage des Hebräerbriefes*. Munich: Karl Zink Verlag, 1955.
Schniedewind, William M. *Society and the Promise to David: The Reception History of 2 Samuel 7:1–17*. New York: Oxford University Press, 1999.
Scholer, John. *Proleptic Priests: Priesthood in the Epistle to the Hebrews*. LNTS 49. Sheffield: JSOT Press, 1991.
Schramm, Brooks. *The Opponents of Third Isaiah: Reconstructing the Cultic History of the Restoration*. JSOT 193. Sheffield: Sheffield Academic Press, 1995.
Schweitzer, Albert. *Paul and His Interpreters: a Critical History*. London: A. and C. Black, 1912.

Schwöbel, Christoph. "The Renaissance of Trinitarian Theology: Reasons, Problems and Tasks." Pages 1–30 in *Trinitarian Theology Today: Essays on Divine Being and Act*. Edited by Christoph Schwöbel. Edinburgh: T&T Clark, 1995.
Silvas, Anna M. *Gregory of Nyssa: The Letters: Introduction, Translation and Commentary*. Leiden: Brill, 2006.
Simon, Marcel. "Saint Stephen and the Jerusalem Temple." *JEH* 2 (1951): 127–42.
Skehan, Patrick W. "The Structure of the Song of Moses in Deuteronomy (32:1–43)." Pages 156–68 in *A Song of Power and the Power of Song: Essays on the Book of Deuteronomy*. Edited by Duane L. Christensen. Winona Lake, IN: Eisenbrauns, 1993.
Smillie, Gene R. "Contrast or Continuity in Hebrews 1.1–2?." *NTS* 51 (2005): 543–60.
Smillie, Gene R. "Living and Active: The Word of God in the Book of Hebrews." PhD Diss., Trinity Evangelical Divinity School, 2000.
Sonderegger, Katherine. *Systematic Theology*. vol. 1. Minneapolis, MN: Fortress Press, 2015.
Spicq, Ceslas. *L'Épître aux Hébreux*. 2 vols. Paris: Gabalda, 1953.
Stebler, A. "Beweistelle für die Gottheit Jesu Christi: Zu Hebr 3.1–6." *ThPQ* 76 (1923): 461–8.
Stec, David M. *The Targum of Psalms*. The Aramaic Bible. Collegeville, MN: Liturgical Press, 2004.
Steyn, Gert J. "Deuteronomy in Hebrews." Pages 152–68 in *Deuteronomy in the New Testament: The New Testament and the Scriptures of Israel*. NTSI. London: T&T Clark, 2007.
Steyn, Gert J. "Moses as Therapwn in Heb 3: 5–6: Portrait of a Cultic Prophet-Priest in Egypt?" *JNSL* 40 (2014): 113–25.
Steyn, Gert J. *A Quest for the Assumed LXX Vorlage of the Explicit Quotations in Hebrews*. FRLANT 235. Göttingen: Vandenhoeck & Ruprecht, 2011.
Steyn, Gert J. "A Quest for the Vorlage of the 'Song of Moses' (Deut 32) Quotations in Hebrews." *Neot* 34 (2000): 263–72.
Stolz, Lukas. "Das Einführen des Erstgeborenen in die Oikumene (Hebr 1,6a)." *Bib* 95 (2014): 405–23.
Stuart, Moses. *A Commentary on the Epistle to the Hebrews*. New York: Flagg, Gould, and Newman, 1833.
Stuckenbruck, Loren T., and Wendy E. S. North. *Early Jewish and Christian Monotheism*. JSNTSup 263. London: T&T Clark, 2004.
Swain, Scott R. "The Bible and the Trinity in Recent Thought: Review, Analysis and Constructive Proposal." *JETS* 60 (2017): 35–48.
Swain, Scott R. "Covenant of Redemption." Pages 107–25 in *Christian Dogmatics: Reformed Theology for the Church Catholic*. Edited by Michael Allen and Scott R. Swain. Grand Rapids, MI: Baker Academic, 2016.
Sweeney, James P. "Stephen's Speech (Acts 7: 2–53): Is It as 'Anti-Temple' as Is Frequently Alleged?" *TrinJ* 23 (2002): 185.
Sweet, J. P. M. "A House Not Made with Hands." Pages 368–90 in *Templum Amicitiae: Essays on the Second Temple Presented to Ernst Bammel*. Edited by William Horbury. LNTS 48. Sheffield: Sheffield Academic Press, 1991.
Swetnam, James. "'The Greater and More Perfect Tent': A Contribution to the Discussion of Hebrews 9, 11." *Bib* 47 (1966): 91–106.
Thiselton, Anthony C. *Thiselton on Hermeneutics: The Collected Works and New Essays of Anthony Thiselton*. Grand Rapids, MI: Eerdmans, 2006.

Thompson, James W. "Structure and Purpose of the Catena in Heb 1:5–13." *CBQ* 38 (1976): 352–63.
Tilling, Chris. *Paul's Divine Christology*. WUNT 2/323. Tübingen: Mohr Siebeck, 2012.
Trafton, Joseph L. "What Would David Do? Messianic Expectation and Surprise in Ps. Sol. 17." Pages 155–74 in *The Psalms of Solomon: Language, History, Theology*. Edited by Eberhard Bons and Patrick Pouchelle. SBLEJL 40. Atlanta, GA: SBL Press, 2015.
Tylenda, Joseph. "Christ the Mediator: Calvin Versus Stancaro." *CTJ* 8 (1973): 1–16.
Tylenda, Joseph. "The Controversy on Christ the Mediator: Calvin's Second Reply to Stancaro." *CTJ* 8 (1973): 131–57.
Ulrich, Eugene, ed. *Qumran Cave 4: Genesis to Numbers*. Vol. VII, DJD. Oxford: Clarendon Press, 1994.
van der Ploeg, J. S. "L'Exégèse de l'Ancien Testament dans l'Epitre aux Hébreux." *RB* 54 (1947): 200–3.
Van Ruiten, J. T. A. G. M. "Visions of the Temple in the Book of Jubilees." Pages 215–27 in *Gemeinde ohne Tempel = Community without Temple: zur Substituierung und Transformation des Jerusalemer Tempels und seines Kults im Alten Testament, antiken Judentum und frühen Christentum*. Edited by Beate Ego, Armin Lange, Peter Pilhofer and Kathrin Ehlers. Tübingen: Mohr Siebeck, 1999.
Vanhoye, Albert. "L'Oracle de Natan dans l'Épître aux Hébreux." Pages 146–52 in *Gesù Apostolo e Sommo Sacerdote: Studi Biblici in Memoria Di P. Teodorico Ballarini*. Edited by E. Vallauri, A.-S. DiMarco and I. Volpi. Rome: Marietti, 1984.
Vanhoye, Albert. "L'Oikoumene dans l'Épître aux Hébreux." *Bib* 45 (1964): 248–53.
Vanhoye, Albert. *La Structure Littéraire de l'Épître aux Hébreux*. 2nd ed. Paris: Desclée De Brouwer, 1976.
Vanhoye, Albert. *The Letter to the Hebrews: a New Commentary*. New York: Paulist Press, 2015.
Vanhoye, Albert. *Old Testament Priests and the New Priest: According to the New Testament*. Translated by J. B. Orchard. Petersham: St. Bede's, 1986.
Vanhoye, Albert. *Situation du Christ: Hébreux 1–2*. Paris: Cerf, 1969.
von Rad, Gerhard. *Deuteronomy: a Commentary*. OTL. Philadelphia, PA: Westminster Press, 1966.
Walker, Peter. "Jerusalem in Hebrews 13: 9–14 and the Dating of the Epistle." *TynBul* 45 (1994): 39–71.
Wallace, D. P. "Texts in Tandem: The Coalescent Usage of Psalm 2 and Psalm 110 in Early Christianity." PhD Diss., Baylor University, 1995.
Wallace, Daniel B. "The Semantics and Exegetical Significance of the Object-Complement Construction in the New Testament." *Grace Theological Journal* 6 (1985): 113–60.
Watson, Francis. "The Triune Divine Identity: Reflections on Pauline God-Language, in Disagreement with JDG Dunn." *JSNT* 23 (2001): 99–124.
Webster, John. "One Who Is Son: Theological Reflections on the Exordium to the Epistle to the Hebrews." Pages 87–112 in *The Epistle to the Hebrews and Christian Theology*. Edited by Richard Bauckham, Daniel Driver and Trevor Hart. Grand Rapids, MI: Eerdmans, 2009.
Webster, John. "Theologies of Retrieval." Pages 583–99 in *The Oxford Handbook of Systematic Theology*. Edited by John Webster, Kathryn Tanner and Iain R. Torrance. Oxford: Oxford University Press, 2009.
Wedderburn, Alexander J. M. "Sawing Off the Branches: Theologizing Dangerously Ad Hebraeos." *JTS* 56 (2005): 393–414.

Weinfeld, Moshe. *Deuteronomy 1–11: a New Translation with Introduction and Commentary.* AB 5. New York: Doubleday, 1991.
Weiss, Hans-Friedrich. *Der Brief an die Hebräer.* KEK. Gottingen: Vandenhoeck & Ruprecht, 1991.
Westcott, Brooke Foss. *The Epistle to the Hebrews: The Greek Text with Notes and Essays.* 3rd ed. London: Macmillan, 1906.
Westfall, Cynthia Long. *A Discourse Analysis of the Letter to the Hebrews: The Relationship between Form and Meaning.* LNTS 297. London: T&T Clark, 2005.
Westfall, Cynthia Long. "Moses and Hebrews 3.1–6: Approach or Avoidance?." Pages 175–201 in *Christian-Jewish Relations through the Centuries.* Edited by Stanley E. Porter and Brook W. Pearson. London: A&C Black, 2000.
White, Thomas Joseph. *The Incarnate Lord: A Thomistic Study in Christology.* Thomistic Ressourcement Series. Washington, DC: Catholic University of America Press, 2015.
Whitlark, Jason A. *Enabling Fidelity to God: Perseverance in Hebrews in Light of the Reciprocity Systems of the Ancient Mediterranean World.* Carlisle: Authentic Media, 2008.
Wider, David. *Theozentrik und Bekenntnis: Untersuchungen zur Theologie des Redens Gottes im Hebräerbrief.* BZNW 87. Berlin: Walter de Gruyter, 1997.
Williamson, H. G. M. "The Temple in the Book of Chronicles." Pages 15–31 in *Templum Amicitiae: Essays on the Second Temple Presented to Ernst Bammel.* Edited by William Horbury. LNTS 48: Sheffield: Sheffield Academic Press, 1991.
Windisch, Hans. *Der Hebraerbrief.* HNT 14. Tübingen: Mohr Siebeck, 1913.
Wisse, Maarten. *Trinitarian Theology beyond Participation: Augustine's De Trinitate and Contemporary Theology.* T&T Clark Studies in Systematic Theology 11. London: T&T Clark, 2011.
Witsius, Herman. *Economy of the Covenants between God and Man.* Escondido: Den Dulk Foundation, 1992.
Worley, David R. "Fleeing to Two Immutable Things, God's Oath-Taking and Oathwitnessing: The Use of Litigant Oath in Hebrews 6:12–20." *ResQ* 36 (1994): 223–36.
Wright, N. T. *The New Testament and the People of God.* Christian Origins and the Question of God. vol. 1. Minneapolis, MN: Fortress Press, 1992.
Wright, N. T. *Jesus and the Victory of God.* Christian Origins and the Question of God. vol. 2. London: SPCK, 2012.
Wright, N. T. *Paul and the Faithfulness of God.* Christian Origins and the Question of God. vol. 4. parts III & IV. Minneapolis, MN: Fortress Press, 2016.
Young, Frances M. "Christological Ideas in the Greek Commentaries on the Epistle to the Hebrews." Pages 33–47 in *Christology, Hermeneutics, and Hebrews: Profiles from the History of Interpretation.* Edited by Jon C. Laansma and Daniel J. Treier. LNTS 423. London: T&T Clark, 2012.

Index of References

Hebrew Bible/Old Testament

Genesis
1:26, 27	186
1:26–28	179
2:2	93, 103, 108, 109, 186, 188, 189
2:5	137
3:18	137
5:1–32	130
5:6–31	130
11:10–32	130
12:1–3	150
12:7	150
14	129, 130, 132, 139
14:18–20	128, 129, 145
15:9–21	150
15:13–16	150
15:18	150
17:4–8	150
17:7	158
22:1	163
22:11	163
22:15–18	150, 154
22:17	151, 153, 158
32:31	137

Exodus
3:2	59
3:4	163
4:22, 23	183
6:9	130
15:13–18	97
15:17	97, 98, 101, 109
25:40	98
29:45	158
32–34	76
34:6	58
35:30–35	98, 105

Leviticus
6:10	130
19:16–18	59
26:1	94
26:30	94
26:45	158

Numbers
9:8–27	130
12	76
12:6–8	76
12:7	75, 79, 83, 87, 88
23:19	151
24:17	137
24:15–19	194

Deuteronomy
1:26–46	48
1:30	53
1:31	183
4:21–24	48
5:10	134
6:16	48
9:6–29	48
8:7–9	49
9:3	53
10:1–32	130
11:10–12	49
12:9	108
12:29	53
17:18, 19	162
17:18–20	133
20:4	53
29:3 LXX	48
29:23	137
31:6 LXX	53
32	35, 48, 51, 52, 69, 71
32:1–4	49
32:5	70
32:5, 6	49

32:8, 9	51, 52	7:14	172
32:10–14	49	7:14	194
32:11	50	7:4–17	89
32:15	49	18, 19	90
32:15–18	49	22:51	194
32:19–22	49	23:24	137
32:26	70	23:1, 2	194
32:26, 27	49		
32:28–32	49	*1 Kings*	
32:31	51	3:2	65
32:34–42	49, 51	5:3	65
32:39	51	5:5	65
32:43	18, 31, 34–8, 47, 50, 53, 54, 65–9	8:17, 20	65
		9:4	195
32:37, 38	69		
32:38, 39	54	*2 Kings*	
32:40–42	49	19:14	134
32:43 42–5		19:16	134
		19:29	137
Joshua			
3:16	134	*1 Chronicles*	
		7:10	91
Judges		13:17	19
9:33	137	17	86
		17:4	88
1 Samuel		17:7	86
2:35	86	17:10	88
3:4	163	17:14	87–9
3:8	163	17:14	88
3:16	163	28	96
15:22	162		
15:29	151	*2 Chronicles*	
17:26	134	6:42	194
17:36	134		
		Psalms	
2 Samuel		2	6, 90, 174
7	86	2:2	194
7	91	2:7	19, 36, 46, 51, 153, 172, 173, 194, 197
7:1, 2	89		
7:3	92	2:8	194
7:5–7	92	8	13, 184, 186
7:8, 9	92	8:5	191
7:13	90	8:7	185
7:13	91	19:10	151
7:14	19	20:6	194
7:14	36	23:22	161, 194
7:14	46	28:8	194
7:14	51	31:23	112
7:14	88	40	132, 133, 163, 192

40:6	162, 194	119:43	151
40:8	161, 194	119:160	151
40:9	192	145	24
45	19, 61, 163	146	24
45:6, 7	60–2, 194, 196		
47:6	112	*Isaiah*	
82:1	21	2:18	94
89:27	88, 194	6:8	163
89	93	9:15	197
89:28	36	10:11	94
89:35	151	16:12	94
89:38	194	37:4, 17	134
89:51	194	66:1, 2	95–7
95	40, 108		
95:8–12	194	*Jeremiah*	
95:11	93, 103, 187, 188	24:7	158
97:7	194	31	158
101:14	58	31:9	183
102	25, 31, 36, 38, 39, 55,	31:20	183
	61, 64–6, 134	31:23	98
102:2, 3	55	31:33	158
102:4	55, 57	32:38	158
102:6	70	38:31	159
102:7	70	38:31–34	158
102:10	70	38:33	158
102:12	55, 69		
102:13	56, 57, 69	*Ezekiel*	
102:14	65	34:24	158
102:14–24a	56		
102:14	58	*Daniel*	
102:16, 17	65	6:20	134
102:21	57, 67, 70	6:26, 27	134
102:24	36, 37, 59, 60	7:10	59
102:24b–29	56		
102:26, 27	18, 37, 41, 58, 62, 60,	*Amos*	
	64–9, 132	5:22	162
102:28	57	5:24	162
104:4	58, 60		
104:22	137	*Micah*	
110	18, 41, 64, 128, 129	6:6–8	162
110:1	41, 46, 194		
110:4	41, 116, 119, 121, 124,	*Haggai*	
	128, 129, 131, 132,	2:6	111
	136, 137, 141, 142,		
	144, 145, 148, 153,	*Zechariah*	
	156, 158, 160, 163,	6:12	99, 137
	170, 173, 185	6:13	99, 147
115:2	112	8:8	158

Index of References

New Testament

Matthew
2:11	125
4:24	125
5:9	85
5:45	85
17:16	125
26:61	100

Mark
10:13	125
14:48	100
14:58	94
15:61	100

John
5:19	85

Acts
6:13	95
7	94
7	97
7:2–53	96
7:44	95
7:46	95, 96
7:48	94, 95
7:52	97
8:18	125
13:10	85
13:33	173

Romans
1:4	176
8:14	85

1 Corinthians
8:5	65

2 Corinthians
3:12–18	76
4:4	182
5:1	94
5:1–10	101

Ephesians
2:11	94
2:11	101
2:18–22	93

Colossians
1:15	182
2:11	94, 101

1 Thessalonians
5:5	85

Hebrews
1	3, 11, 16, 17, 18, 19, 50, 53, 200
1:1	15, 29, 124, 137, 142, 178
1:1, 2	156
1:1–4	13, 29, 30, 175, 177
1:2	14, 25, 63, 81, 84, 92, 109, 112, 171, 172, 173, 179, 182, 183, 194, 197
1:2, 3	6, 7, 12
1:3	8, 16, 27, 46, 71, 84, 112, 119, 132, 133, 163, 179, 180, 181, 182, 191
1:4	8, 15, 155, 172, 175, 194
1:5	29, 36, 61, 66, 171, 175, 194
1:5, 6	30
1:5–14	7, 9, 13, 68, 161
1:6	8, 10, 18, 26, 30, 31, 47, 48, 50, 63, 88, 156, 194, 194, 197, 199
1:6b	44–6
1:7	60, 71
1:7–12	62
1:8	8, 12, 18, 27, 61, 63, 163, 171, 172, 182, 196, 200
1:8, 9	194, 195
1:8–12	60, 63, 66
1:9	62, 165, 195
1:10	63, 112
1:10–12	18, 26, 30, 31, 36, 39, 61, 63, 64, 66, 67, 71, 71, 84, 92, 132, 133, 172, 182, 199
1:11, 12	107
1:12	61, 112
1:13	46, 168, 194

1:13, 14	62	3:13	15, 108, 167, 186
1:14	47, 59, 108, 111, 184	3:14	74, 89, 167, 190, 194
1:15	171	3:15	186
2	18	3:16	108
2:1–4	74, 184	3:16–19	108, 187
2:4	183	3:19	203
2:5	45, 47, 47, 102, 108, 156, 184, 190, 191	4:1	108, 156, 186, 191
		4:1–6	109
2:5–9	13, 40, 63, 85, 140, 173, 184, 185, 189	4:2	156, 166, 191
		4:3	60, 108, 167, 191
2:7	191	4:3, 4	92, 103, 106, 187
2:8	39, 102, 111, 191	4:4	93, 188
2:9	46, 185, 190, 191	4:5	108
2:10	14, 86, 92, 93, 109, 112, 156, 160, 171, 183, 193, 200	4:6	167, 187, 188
		4:7	39, 40, 186, 187, 193
		4:8	103, 108, 186, 188
2:10–18	74, 92, 139	4:9	186
2:11	171	4:10	108, 188
2:12	161, 194	4:11	108, 186, 189
2:13	165	4:13	183
2:13, 14	161	4:14	171, 172
2:14	67, 119, 133, 137, 139, 161, 162, 190	4:14–16	126, 182, 191
		4:15	67, 193
2:14–16	138, 140, 141, 155, 185, 190	4:16	6, 47, 123, 165, 166, 172, 190
2:16	93, 133, 138, 151	5:1–3	125, 126
2:17	74, 119, 133, 165, 182	5:1–10	119, 125, 126, 139, 190
2:18	119, 123, 182, 190	5:2	203
2:27	119	5:3	125
3	90, 92, 99, 112	5:4	125, 126
3:1	47, 73, 156, 163, 165, 166	5:5	89, 119, 171, 194, 194
		5:5, 6	116, 126, 161
3:1–6	63, 73, 80–8, 91, 92, 110, 112, 113	5:6	119, 168, 170, 194
		5:7	125
3:2	75, 81, 86, 87, 88, 89, 90, 165, 165, 167, 182	5:7–10	126
		5:8	127, 171, 180
3:3	75, 109, 187	5:9	120, 156, 160, 193
3:3, 4	12, 26, 71, 73, 77–9, 80–4, 86, 90, 91, 93, 110, 112, 199	5:10	119, 149, 180
		5:11	154, 203
		5:17	161
3:4	92	6:1	89, 166, 203
3:5	14, 90	6:2	66, 156
3:6	74, 89, 90, 171, 194	6:6	171
3:7	73, 75, 186	6:7	164
3:7–11	194	6:8	203
3:7–4:11	47, 52, 93, 109, 186, 191	6:9	155
		6:10	149, 164
3:11	108	6:11	157
3:12	74, 107, 134, 183, 191	6:12	149, 150, 155, 171

6:13	148, 152, 168	7:25	123, 146, 156, 182, 190
6:13, 14	108, 169	7:26–28	125
6:13–20	132, 148–50, 153, 155, 164, 167, 168, 200	7:27	119, 125, 203
6:14	158	7:28	129, 140, 141, 152, 156, 169, 171, 190, 193
6:16	152, 167	7:29	156
6:17	152, 155, 164, 165, 168	8	112
6:17–19	151, 169	8:1, 2	116
6:18	153–5, 165	8:2	93, 104, 105, 110
6:19	154, 157	8:3	119, 125
6:20	120, 123, 154, 156, 190, 191	8:4	58, 102, 105, 125
		8:5	98, 131
7	118, 120, 121, 123, 128, 137, 177	8:6	58, 152, 157, 168
		8:7–10	39
7:1–4	129–31	8:8	203
7:1–10	120, 132 136	8:13	40
7:3	6, 116, 120, 129, 130, 131, 132, 135, 138, 141, 146, 171, 182, 183	9	112
		9:1–10:14	159, 160
		9:1–4	103, 105
7:4	124, 130, 140	9:4	105
7:5	58, 123, 124, 140	9:7	125
7:6	58, 120, 130, 138, 140	9:7, 8	105
7:7	155	9:9	103, 105, 125, 156, 193, 203
7:8	58, 121, 132, 140, 141, 146		
		9:10	124
7:9	138	9:11	89, 93, 104, 105, 110
7:10	138	9:11, 12	125
7:11	40, 129, 132, 157, 160	9:12	119
7:12	40, 104	9:13	124
7:13	40, 194	9:14	89, 107, 125, 134, 190, 203,
7:13, 14	137, 138		
7:14	10, 129	9:15	108, 152, 159, 160, 168, 171
7:15	129, 141		
7:16	7, 12, 66, 116, 117, 118, 121, 122, 124, 142, 200, 201	9:15–22	160
		9:23	58, 125
		9:24	89, 93, 102, 104, 105, 107, 110, 119, 190, 191
7:17	194		
7:18	77, 157	9:25	125
7:18–22	58, 160	9:26	183
7:19	40, 155, 193	9:26–28	119
7:20	152, 157	9:29	156
7:20–28	159	10:1	105, 193
7:21	129, 152, 154, 156, 158, 161, 169	10:1, 2	125
		10:4	162
7:22	125, 150, 155, 156, 168, 169, 170	10:5	12, 67, 161, 197
		10:5, 6	162, 163, 192
7:23	129, 140, 144, 190, 123, 156, 182, 190	10:5–7	165, 194
		10:5–10	125, 132, 133, 200
7:24	71, 144, 146	10:7	127, 133, 161, 192

10:8–11	10	12:4, 5	127
10:9, 10	164	12:5	171
10:10	67, 89, 161, 163	12:5–11	180
10:11	125	12:7	171
10:11, 12	58	12:12	70
10:12	196	12:14	111
10:12–18	159	12:18	19, 112, 156
10:13	125, 193	12:18–24	167
10:16	159	12:22	93, 107
10:17	159	12:22, 23	106
10:18	159	12:23	92, 112, 190
10:19	156, 165	12:24	152, 160, 168
10:19–23	123, 166, 169, 170	12:26	103
10:19, 20	166	12:26–28	47, 110–12
10:20	104	12:27	105
10:21	92	12:28	111
10:22	47, 203	13:5	53, 135, 165
10:22, 23	166	13:6	135
10:23	153, 164, 165, 183	13:7	66
10:26–31	203	13:8	66, 89, 134, 135, 165, 182
10:29	166, 170, 171, 172		
10:31	107, 134, 170	13:10–14	106
10:32–39	106	13:13	106
10:34	93, 106	13:14	93, 102, 106, 107
10:35	106	13:20	194
10:36	165	13:21	89
10:39, 40	169	13:22	165
11	106		
11:1	155	*1 Peter*	
11:1, 2	183	2:4, 5	93
11:1–40	149		
11:2	156	**Apocrypha and Septuagint**	
11:3	14, 23, 166		
11:4, 5	82	*2 Esdras*	
11:6	164, 166	6:53, 54	184
11:7	83		
11:8	106, 108, 171	*Tobit*	
11:8–22	155	14:5	99
11:9, 10	106		
11:10	93, 106, 107, 108, 156	*Judith*	
11:11	149, 164, 165, 166, 183	8:18	94
11:16	93, 108, 156, 158		
11:19	164, 166	*Sirach*	
11:25	26	17:17	52
11:26	89, 164		
11:32	193	*Wisdom of Solomon*	
11:39	40	2:10	183
11:40	106, 108, 112, 156	2:13–20	183
12:2	47, 127	7:26	180

7:26	181	*4 Maccabees*	
13:1	107	4:27	136
14:8	94	10:11	124

Baruch
2:30–35 158

Bell and the Dragon
1:419 98
6:438 128

Old Testament Pseudepigrapha

Apocalpyse of Abraham
135, 136

2 Baruch
4:1–4 109
21:9–11 136

1 Enoch
12:4 136
14:8–23 98
15:13 136
25:3 136
25:5 136
25:7 136
27:4 136
46:7 98
53:6 99
90:28, 29 99

2 Enoch
10:6 98
22:2 98
33:4 98

3 Enoch
5:10 184

4 Ezra
8:21 59
8:52 108

3 Maccabees
6:28 136

Odes
2:43 42–5

Joseph and Aseneth
8:6, 7 136
11:10 136

Jubilees
1:15 99
1:15–18 158
18:14–16 150
21:4 136

Liber Antiquitatum Biblicarum.
32:1–4 150

Psalms of Solomon
17:18 90
17:21–24 99
17:21–32 194
17:25 109
17:37 193
18:5–9 194

Sibylline Oracles
1:39 136
1:50 136
1:120 136
2:160 136
2:187 136
2:214 136
2:281 136
3:10 136
3:11–12 135
3:13 98
3:15 136
3:628 136
3:715 136
3:762, 3 136
4:6 98
4:11 98
4:28 98
5:414 100
5:423 99

Dead Sea Scrolls

1QapGen
128

1QM
| 1.8, 9 | 191 |
| 11.4–7 | 194 |

1QH
| 1.10b, 11 | 59 |
| 7.15 | 101 |

1QS
| 3.17–20 | 184 |
| 4.22, 23 | 191 |

1QSa
| 2.12 | 89 |

4Q175
194

4Q225
150

4Q405
145

4Q504
191

4QDeut[q]
36, 44

4QFlor
100

4QpIsa
193

11QMelch
21
128
145

11QTemple
| 29.8–10 | 99 |

Midrash

Exodus Rabbah
| 25.86a | 59 |

Philo

Abr.
| 235 | 128 |
| 273 | 151 |

Alleg. Interp.
| 3.101 | 135 |
| 3.207 | 151 |

Congr.
| 99 | 128 |

Decal.
| 60, 64 | 135 |

Drunkeness
| 139 | 151 |

Moses
1.283	151
2.88	98
2.165	98
2.168	98

Sacrifices
| 91–94 | 151 |

Spec. Laws
| 4.31 | 152 |

Josephus

Against Apion
| 2:167–169 | 135, 173 |

Jewish Antiquities
1.181	128
1.10.2	128
1.13.4	150
4.133	152
4.133	168
4.55	98
10.143	90

Classical and Ancient Christian Writings

Aristotle

De Mundo
181

Augustine

De Trinitate
22

Plato

Resp.
466　　　　193

Sym.
192, 193

Gregory of Nyssa

Ad. Ablab.
23

Ad. Eust.
22, 23

Contr. Eun.
III　　　　23

De Beat.
23

De. Div.
148

Hippolytus

Adv. Omn. Haer.
144

Index of Authors

Aalen, S. 86, 87, 91
Adams, E. 47, 107, 111, 112
Albani, M. 97
Allen, D. M. 39, 41–4, 49, 50, 51, 54
Allen, L. C. 55, 57, 58
Andriessen, P. C. B. 34–6, 45, 50
Argyle, A. W. 107
Attridge, H. W. 3, 29, 30, 32, 33, 36, 37, 45–7, 53, 59, 61, 73, 75, 80, 82, 84, 87, 102–8, 111, 117, 121, 123, 132, 133, 137, 141, 151–4, 156, 157, 160, 161, 165, 166, 168, 173, 174, 177, 179, 180, 183, 189, 190, 192
Ayres, L. 9, 23, 24

Backhaus, K. 29, 46, 58, 65, 76, 77, 80, 81, 83, 115, 130, 132, 133, 144, 161
Bacon, B. W. 37, 54, 65
Barnes, M. R. 22
Barrett, C. K. 1
Barth, K. 148, 174, 177
Barton, J. 68, 69
Bateman, H. W. 32, 45, 50, 59
Bates, M. W. 2
Bauckham, R. 1, 2, 4–7, 10, 11, 16, 20–4, 32, 46, 52, 62, 64, 116, 118, 134, 135, 145, 171, 172, 175, 178
Baugh, S. M. 150, 168
Bird, M. F. 89, 176
Bisping, A. 79
Blomberg, C. L. 140, 184
Bockmuehl, M. N. A. 149, 151, 155, 157
Bousset, W. F. 174
Braun, J. 77, 78
Bruce, F. F. 5, 34, 36, 37, 45, 46, 50, 54, 65, 74, 76, 79, 81, 82, 86, 94, 103, 121, 172, 173, 176, 184–6, 192, 195, 196
Brueggemann, W. 185
Buchanan, G. W. 74, 126
Buchsel, F. 3, 171
Bunta, S. N. 3

Caird, G. B. 4, 13, 31–3, 35, 39, 40, 41, 63, 174
Calaway, J. 102, 103
Calvin, J. 43, 60, 121, 126, 127, 143, 145, 149, 157
Caneday, A. B. 45, 47,
Carr, G. L. 37
Carson, D. A. 85, 167, 171, 178, 179, 197
Chan, A. K.-Y. 122, 125, 126, 128–30, 132
Chester, A. 89, 99, 100, 194
Cockerill, G. 1, 5, 30, 32, 33, 39, 40, 42–5, 51–3, 58–62, 64, 74, 75, 82–4, 86–90, 102–4, 106–9, 112, 117, 118, 122, 124, 127, 129–31, 134–8, 141, 143, 145, 146, 146, 149, 151, 164, 168, 176, 182–7, 194
Collins, A. Y. 183
Collins, J. J. 89, 193, 194
Compton, J. 4, 18, 19, 30, 41, 119, 120, 124, 125, 126, 130, 146, 195, 196
Conway-Jones, A. 96–9
Cook, J. A. 56
Cortez, F. H. 90, 193, 194, 196, 197
Crusemann, F. 159
Cullmann, O. 1
Culy, M. M. 60

D'Angelo, M. R. 80, 86, 87, 88
Dahl, N. A. 11, 22
Dan, R. 2
De Jonge, M. 145
Delitzsch, F. 33, 35, 38, 39, 41, 45, 58, 65, 66, 184
Demarest, B. A. 115, 117, 118, 129, 138, 145
DeSilva, D. A. 32, 60, 66, 153, 155,
Dey, L. K. 80
Dillon, M. 150
Dines, J. M. 42
Docherty, S. E. 42–4, 46, 57, 65
Driver, S. R. 56

Dunn, J. D. G. 4, 11–13, 15, 22, 32, 90, 95, 98
Dunnill, J. 148, 157, 160, 162, 174, 175, 180
Dyer, B. R. 2

Easter, M. C. 166, 167
Ebert, D. J. 180–2
Edmondson, S. 117
Ehrman, B. D. 177
Ellingworth, P. 3, 33, 44–6, 59–61, 65, 73–5, 80, 82, 83, 86, 88, 117, 125, 126, 129, 130, 131, 140, 181, 193
England, E. 26
Eslinger, L. M. 89, 90, 92
Evans, R. 26

Fesko, J. V. 147, 148
Fitzmeyer, J. A. 88–90, 117, 128, 131
Fletcher-Louis, C. 2, 10, 186, 191
France, R. T. 39, 40
Freedman, D. N. 89, 98, 150, 162
Frey, J. 148, 150, 157

Gadamer, H.-G. 25
Gaffin, R. B. 115, 125, 127, 141, 143, 187
Garr, W. R. 179
Gartner, B. E. 90
Gaston, L. 94, 95, 99, 100
Gathercole, S. J. 2
Gheorghita, R. 37, 43–5, 54, 57
Glasson, T. F. 34, 35, 37, 67
Gräßer, E. 46, 47, 59, 60–2, 74–76, 80, 82, 86, 87, 90, 102–5, 108, 111, 117, 121, 125, 130, 141, 153, 159, 161, 162, 165, 166, 184, 194
Greer, R. A. 1, 115
Griffiths, J. I. 29, 166
Gunnlaugur, A. J. 179
Guthrie, G. H. 2, 32, 33, 40, 43, 88, 184, 185

Haber, S. 159, 160
Hahn, S. W. 150
Hamm, D. 149, 162, 165, 166
Hanson, A. T. 145
Harris, M. J. 61, 94
Harris, D. M. 85, 154, 155, 190, 196
Hart, T. A. 95, 96
Hatina, T. R. 68

Hay, D. M. 115, 119, 120, 121, 123
Hays, R. M. 41
Hengel, M. 2, 119, 171, 174, 176, 185
Henrichs-Taresenkova, N. 20
Hill, W. 10
Hofius, O. 161, 163, 188
Hofmann, J. C. K. 33
Holmes, S. R. 2, 11
Horbury, W. 89, 99
Horton, F. L. 115, 120, 131, 144–6
Hughes, P. E. 59, 62, 66, 76, 86, 91, 129, 146, 182, 193
Hurst, L. D. 4, 35, 39, 103, 174, 196
Hurtado, L. W. 2, 20, 22, 51

Isaacs, M. 75, 76, 86

Janse, S. 173, 194
Jenson, R. W. 23
Jewett, R. 153
Jipp, J. W. 30, 45, 71
Jobes, K. H. 133, 161, 162
Johnson, L. T. 1, 30, 74, 77, 81, 83, 118, 124, 126, 129, 137, 138, 140
Joosten, J. 56
Juel, D. 97, 100, 101

Kasemann, E. 14, 180
Keating, D. 1, 176
Kerr, A. 101
Kibbe, M. 175
Kilby, K. 11
Kilgallen, J. J. 95
Kim, J.-W. 95
Kirk, J. R. D. 10, 22, 24
Klijn, A. F. J. 90
Knowles, M. P. 40
Knox, J. 3
Koester, C. R. 5, 19, 44, 45, 58, 62–4, 66, 74–7, 80, 82–4, 95, 96, 103, 105, 107, 111, 112, 117, 121, 126, 130, 132, 134, 137, 138, 140, 143, 149, 151–6, 158–60, 162, 164, 169, 171, 172, 175, 176, 179, 180–2, 184, 186–8, 192–4, 196
Kögel, J. 171
Kostenberger, A. J. 183
Kraus, H.-J. 55, 58
Kurianal, J. 122, 125, 126, 129–31, 138, 140, 141, 146

Laansma, J. 77, 103, 108, 109, 111, 112, 183, 186, 187, 188, 193
Laato, A. 89
Lane, W. L. 1, 36, 58, 59, 61, 62, 65, 73, 74, 77, 80, 81, 86, 102, 104, 107, 112, 117, 123–6, 126, 128, 130, 131, 134, 140, 155, 160, 161, 162, 165, 171, 173, 186, 187, 189, 192
Larson, R. K. 60
Layton, S. C. 83
Lee, A. H. I. 132, 176
Lehne, S. 148, 150, 155, 157, 159, 169
Levenson, J. D. 89, 150
Levering, M. 22–4, 175, 181
Lim, T. H. 35, 49
Lincicum, D. 48
Lincoln, A. T. 29
Lindars, B. 29
Lindbeck, G. A. 21
Loader, W. R. G. 2, 119, 171–4, 180, 182, 193
Long, D. S. 1
Lundbom, J. R. 48, 49
Lunn, N. P. 35
Luz, U. 25, 26
Lyons, W. J. 26

MacCormack, B. L. 139, 174, 176–8
Mackie, S. D. 172, 175, 176, 181, 182, 191
Manson, T. W. 96
Manzi, F. 75, 128, 171
Marshall, I. H. 157
Mason, E. F. 2, 4, 115, 118, 119, 125, 128, 130–2, 140, 145, 171, 172, 190
Maspero, G. 23
Mays, J. L. 55, 56, 58, 67
McCarter, P. K. 88, 92
McConville, J. G. 49
McCruden, K. B. 106, 185, 192, 193
Meier, J. P. 60, 62, 171, 180, 181
Menken, M. J. J. 174
Meyer, B. F. 101
Miano, D. 150, 162
Michel, O. 79, 85, 88, 119, 120, 124, 129, 138, 141, 146, 176, 179, 181, 184, 194
Milik, J. T. 128
Miller, C. L. 46
Milligan, G. 176, 179

Moffitt, D. M. 3, 4, 15–18, 31, 32, 34, 43, 45, 50, 59, 62, 63, 65, 116, 119–21, 123, 127, 131, 140, 143, 145, 175, 184, 191
Moffatt, J. 80, 81, 112
Montefiore, H. 33, 83, 117
Motyer, S. 30, 32, 36, 37, 39, 41, 43
Moule, C. F. D. 30, 37, 39, 40, 41, 54, 66, 94, 100, 101
Moyise, S. 54, 68, 174
Muir, S. 180, 182
Muller, R. A. 147
Murphy, F. A. 24

Neef, H.-D. 150
Neyrey, J. H. 7, 116, 135
Novenson, M V. 21, 85, 177, 183, 193

O'Brien, P. T. 43, 53, 66, 85
O'Connor, M. P. 35
Olofsson, S. 35
Owen, J. 1, 33, 43, 58, 63, 76–81, 86, 91, 110, 117, 118, 121, 128, 142, 143, 147, 157, 174

Paul, M. J. 117, 137
Peeler, A. L. B. 1, 2, 4, 7, 8, 10, 11, 32, 53, 61, 63, 64, 88, 91, 92, 122, 124, 127, 128, 130, 132, 137, 171, 175, 176, 180, 182, 184, 190, 192, 193
Peppard, M. 85, 174, 183
Perrin, N. 101
Peterson, D. 192
Phang, S. E. 183
Pierce, M. N. 161
Pirnat, A. 2
Pomykala, K. 87–91
Porter, S. E. 41, 68

Rainbow, P. 128
Rascher, A. 8–11, 33, 39, 51, 53, 54, 61, 66, 171, 175, 182, 184, 185, 191
Reicke, B. 95
Rhee, V. 165, 166
Ribbens, B. J. 157
Richardson, C. A. 76, 83, 86, 87
Riggenbach, E. 195
Robinson, R. 1
Rogland, M. F. 56
Rose, C. 149, 154–7, 164, 169

Rowe, C. K. 1, 3, 9–11
Rowland, C. C. 100
Runge, S. E. 46

Sanders, E. P. 98, 99
Sargent, B. 39, 187
Schenck, K. L. 4, 13–15, 19, 25, 30–2, 37, 46, 51, 53, 63–6, 102–4, 106, 107, 111, 112, 133, 175
Schierse, F. J. 34, 74, 77, 91, 110, 196
Schniedewind, W. M. 87–91
Scholer, J. 106, 115, 125, 126, 139
Schramm, B. 97
Schweitzer, A. 20
Schwobel, C. 11
Silvas, A. M. 22
Simon, M. 95
Skehan, P. W. 44, 49, 52
Smillie, G. R. 29
Sonderegger, K. 4, 22, 175
Spicq, C. 30, 33, 39, 46, 59, 61, 65, 74, 75–7, 79, 80, 81, 83, 85, 104, 105, 107, 126, 129, 130, 140, 141, 152, 176, 185
Stebler, A. 74, 77, 81, 83
Stec, D. M. 59
Steyn, G. J. 43, 44, 47, 51, 53, 76
Stolz, L. 45, 46
Swain, S. R. 10, 23, 147, 183
Sweeney, J. P. 96
Sweet, J. P. M. 97, 100, 101
Swetnam, J. 80, 104

Thiselton, A. 26
Tilling, C. 10, 20
Trafton, J. L. 194, 195
Tylenda, J. 117

Ulrich, E. 44

van der Ploeg, J. S. 36
von Rad, G. 48, 49, 52
Van Der Woude, A. S. 145
Van Ruiten, J. T. A. G. M. 99
Vanhoye, A. 30, 33, 35, 38, 40, 45, 47, 50, 53, 58, 59, 60, 62, 66, 80, 86, 103, 140, 160, 171–3, 176, 179, 180–2, 197

Walker, P. 102
Wallace, D. B. 59
Wallace, D. P. 143
Watson, F. W. 21, 22
Webster, J. 4, 26, 171, 172, 175, 179
Wedderburn, A. J. M. 162
Weinfeld, M. 48, 49, 52
Weiss, H.-F. 30, 36, 43, 45, 61, 119, 134, 141, 151–4, 171, 180, 181, 185, 190
Westcott, B. F. 30, 38, 39, 41, 45, 46, 52, 59, 61, 62, 65–7, 123, 126, 132, 133, 139, 143, 145, 152, 155, 157–63, 168, 193, 196
Westfall, C. L. 73–5, 81, 83, 84
White, T. J. 23
Whitlark, J. A. 75
Wider, D. 29
Williamson, H. G. M. 96
Windisch, H. 112
Wisse, M. 22
Witsius, H. 147
Worley, D. R. 148, 152–5, 168
Wright, N. T. 4, 21, 31

Young, F. M. 176, 181

www.ingramcontent.com/pod-product-compliance
Lightning Source LLC
Chambersburg PA
CBHW062139300426
44115CB00012BA/1989